MASTERPLOTS
FIFTEEN-VOLUME
COMBINED EDITION

Volume Four
Deat-Essa

MASTERPLOTS

15-Volume Combined Edition
FIFTEEN HUNDRED AND TEN
Plot-Stories and Essay-Reviews
from the
WORLD'S FINE LITERATURE

Edited by
FRANK N. MAGILL

Story Editor
DAYTON KOHLER

VOLUME FOUR—DEAT-ESSA

SALEM PRESS
INCORPORATED
NEW YORK

This work also appears under the title of
MASTERPIECES OF WORLD LITERATURE IN DIGEST FORM

DEATH IN VENICE

Type of work: Novelette
Author: Thomas Mann (1875–1955)
Type of plot: Symbolic realism
Time of plot: Early twentieth century
Locale: Italy
First published: 1912

Principal characters:
GUSTAVE VON ASCHENBACH, a middle-aged German writer
TADZIO, a young Polish boy

Critique:

Death in Venice is a short novel of great psychological intensity and tragic power. To read it simply as the story of a middle-aged artist whose character deteriorates because of his hopeless passion for a young Polish boy and whose death is the final irony of his emotional upheaval is to miss almost all of the writer's intention in this fable. Here Mann brings together most of the conflicting themes which have occupied him in his longer works of fiction: being and death, youth and age, sickness and health, beauty and decay, love and suffering, art and life, the German North and the classic lands of the Mediterranean. The symbols are complex and numerous. One effective device is the reappearance of the same character on different crucial occasions in the narrative. As the stranger in the cemetery, for example, he is a summoner sent to lure Aschenbach from the discipline and devotion which are the standards of the writer's craft, but later, as the mysterious gondolier, he is Charon ferrying a lost soul on his last journey. In this work Mann examines understandingly and critically the solitary position of the artist in modern society, and he uses the theme of Aschenbach's infatuation to dramatize in symbolic fashion the narcissism which can be one of the fatal qualities of art.

The Story:

Gustave von Aschenbach was a distinguished German writer whose work had brought him world fame and a patent of nobility from a grateful government. His career had been honorable and dignified. A man of ambitious nature, unmarried, he had lived a life of personal discipline and dedication to his art, and in his portrayal of heroes who combined the forcefulness of a Frederick the Great with the selfless striving of a Saint Sebastian he believed that he had spoken for his race as well as for the deathless spirit of man. At the same time his devotion to the ideals of duty and achievement had brought him close to physical collapse.

One day, after a morning spent at his desk, he left his house in Munich and went for a walk. His stroll took him as far as a cemetery on the outskirts of the city. While he waited for a streetcar which would carry him back to town, he suddenly became aware of a man who stood watching him from the doorway of the mortuary chapel. The stranger, who had a rucksack on his back and a walking staff in his hand, was evidently a traveler. Although no word passed between the watcher and the watched, Aschenbach felt a sudden desire to take a trip, to leave the cold, wet German spring for the warmer climate of the Mediterranean lands. His impulse was strengthened by a problem of technique which he had been unable to solve in his writing. At last, reluctantly, he decided to take a holiday and leave his work for a time in order to find relaxation for mind and body in Italy.

He went first to an island resort in the Adriatic, but before long he became bored with his surroundings and booked passage for Venice. On the ship he encountered a party of lively young clerks from Pola. With them was an old man whose dyed hair and rouged cheeks made him a ridiculous but sinister caricature of youth. In his disgust Aschenbach failed to notice that the raddled old man bore a vague resemblance to the traveler he had seen at the cemetery in Munich.

Aschenbach's destination was the Lido. At the dock in Venice he transferred to a gondola which took him by the water route to his Lido hotel. The gondolier spoke and acted so strangely that Aschenbach became disturbed, and because of his agitation he never noticed that the man looked something like the drunk old scarecrow on the ship and the silent stranger at the cemetery. After taking his passenger to the landing stage, the gondolier, without waiting for his money, hastily rowed away. Other boatmen suggested that he might have been afraid of the law because he had no license.

Aschenbach stayed at the Hotel des Bains. That night, shortly before dinner, his attention was drawn to a Polish family, a beautiful mother, three daughters, and a handsome boy of about fourteen. Aschenbach was unaccountably attracted to the youngster, so much so that he continued to watch the family all through his meal. The next morning he saw the boy playing with some companions on the beach. His name, as Aschenbach learned while watching their games, was Tadzio.

Disturbed by the appeal the boy had for him, the writer announced his intention of returning home, but on his arrival at the railroad station in Venice he discovered that his trunks had been misdirected to Como. Since there was nothing for him to do but to wait for his missing luggage to turn up, he went back to the hotel. Even though he despised himself for his vacillation, he realized that his true desire was to be near Tadzio. For Aschenbach there began a period of happiness and anguish, happiness in watching the boy, anguish in that they must remain strangers. One day he almost summoned up enough courage to speak to the youngster. A moment later he became panic-stricken lest Tadzio be alarmed by the older man's interest. The time Aschenbach had set for his holiday passed, but the writer had almost forgotten his home and his work. One evening Tadzio smiled at him as they passed one another. Aschenbach trembled with pleasure.

Guests began to leave the hotel; there were rumors that a plague had broken out in nearby cities. Aschenbach, going one day to loiter on the Piazza, detected the sweetish odor of disinfectant in the air, for the authorities were beginning to take precautions against an outbreak of the plague in Venice. Aschenbach stubbornly decided to stay on in spite of the dangers of infection.

A band of entertainers came to the hotel to serenade the guests. In the troupe was an impudent, disreputable-looking street singer whose antics and ballads were insulting and obscene. As he passed among the guests to collect money for the performance, Aschenbach detected on his clothing the almost overpowering smell of disinfectant, an odor suggesting the sweetly corruptive taints of lust and death. The ribald comedian also had a strange similarity to the gondolier, the rouged old rake, and the silent traveler whose disturbing presence had given Aschenbach the idea for his holiday. Aschenbach was torn between fear and desire. The next day he went to a tourist agency where a young clerk told him that people were dying of the plague in Venice. Even that confirmation of his fears failed to speed Aschenbach's departure from the city. That night he dreamed that in a fetid jungle, surrounded by naked orgiasts, he was taking part in horrible, Priapean rites.

By that time his deterioration was almost complete. At last he allowed a barber to dye his hair and tint his cheeks, but he still refused to see the likeness between himself and the raddled old fop whose appearance had disgusted him on shipboard. His behavior became more reckless. One afternoon he followed the Polish family into Venice and trailed them through the city streets. Hungry and thirsty after his exercise, he bought some overripe strawberries at an open stall and ate them. The odor of disinfectant was strong on the sultry breeze.

Several days later Aschenbach went down to the beach where Tadzio was playing with three or four other boys.

They began to fight and one of the boys threw Tadzio to the ground and pressed his face into the sand. As Aschenbach was about to interfere, the other boy released his victim. Humiliated and hurt, Tadzio walked down to the water. He stood facing seaward for a time, as remote and isolated as a young Saint Sebastian, and then he turned and looked with somber, secret gaze at Aschenbach, who was watching from his beach chair. To the writer it seemed as though the boy were summoning him. He started to rise but became so giddy that he fell back into his chair. Attendants carried him to his room. That night the world learned that the great Gustave von Aschenbach had died suddenly of the plague in Venice.

DEATH OF A HERO

Type of work: Novel
Author: Richard Aldington (1892-1962)
Type of plot: Social criticism
Time of plot: World War I
Locale: England
First published: 1929

Principal characters:
GEORGE WINTERBOURNE, killed in the war
MR. GEORGE WINTERBOURNE, his father
MRS. GEORGE WINTERBOURNE, his mother
ELIZABETH, his wife
FANNY WELFORD, his mistress

Critique:

With cynicism that is almost morbid in its brutality, Richard Aldington here tells the story of a soldier killed in World War I. It was the author's belief that the hero had deliberately allowed himself to be killed, so confused and miserable was the life which he had attempted to divide between his wife and mistress. The author, attempting to show that the shabby childhood through which the hero lived was responsible for his troubles, purports to tell only the truth. But the truth as he sees it is so bitter that in the telling Aldington condemns not only a generation but a whole society.

The Story:

When word was received that George Winterbourne had been killed in the war, his friend tried to reconstruct the life of the dead man in order to see what forces had caused his death. The friend had served with George at various times during the war, and it was his belief that George had deliberately exposed himself to German fire because he no longer wanted to live.

George Winterbourne's father had been a sentimental fool and his mother a depraved wanton. The elder Winterbourne had married primarily to spite his dominating mother, and his bride had married him under the mistaken notion that he was rich. They gave themselves up to mutual hatred, the mother showering her thwarted love on young George. She imagined herself young and desirable and was proud of her twenty-two lovers. Her husband conveniently went to a hotel when she was entertaining, but he prayed for her soul. All in all, they were the most depressing parents to whom a child could be exposed and undoubtedly they caused young George to hate them both. Soon after receiving word of their son's death, the elder Winterbourne was killed in an accident. Mrs. Winterbourne married her twenty-second lover and moved to Australia, but not before she had thoroughly enjoyed being a bereft mother and widow.

When he reached young manhood, George mingled with all sorts of queer people. He dabbled in writing and painting—the modern variety. Sexual freedom was his goal, even though he had experienced little of it. At an affair given by his pseudo-intellectual friends he first met Elizabeth. They were immediately compatible; both hated their parents and both sought freedom. At first Elizabeth was shocked by George's attacks on Christianity, morals, the class system, and all other established institutions, but she soon recognized him as a truly "free" man. In fact, it was not long before she adopted his ideas and went him one better. Free love was the only thing she could talk or think about. Thinking themselves extremely sensible, they saw no reason to marry in order to experience love as long as they were careful not to have a baby. Babies complicated matters, for the ignorant middle classes still frowned on such children. Unknowingly, George and Elizabeth were about as middle class as it was possible to be.

The two lovers planned carefully to have no sordidness cloud their affair. They did not talk of love, only sex. They were to take all the other lovers they pleased. That was freedom in an intelligent way. Elizabeth was even more insistent than George upon such freedom.

Finally, Elizabeth mistakenly thought that she was pregnant. Gone were the new freedoms, the enlightened woman; George must marry her at once, for female honor was at stake. All the old clichés were dragged out for poor old George. They were married, much to the horror of their families. When the mistake was discovered, supplemented by the doctor's statement that Elizabeth could not possibly have a child without an operation, back came freedom, stronger than ever. She became an evangelist, even though she detested the word, for sex. Marriage made no difference in their lives. They continued to live separately, meeting as lovers.

When Elizabeth had to make a trip home, George became the lover of her best friend, Fanny Welford, another enlightened woman. He was sure that Elizabeth would not mind, for she had become the mistress of Fanny's lover. Thus he was quite stunned when Elizabeth kicked up a row about Fanny. However, the girls remained surface friends, each one too free to admit horror at the other's duplicity.

War had been approaching fast while these friends had been practicing their enlightened living. George was drafted and sent quickly to France. The war poisoned George. Killing horrified him, and he began to imagine his own death. He was brave, but not from any desire to be a hero; it was just that the monot-ony of his existence seemed to demand that he keep going even though he was ready to drop from fatigue. The knowledge of the ill-concealed dislike between Fanny and Elizabeth began to prey on his mind. There seemed to be only two solutions: to drift along and accept whatever happened or to get himself killed in the war. It seemed to make little difference to him or anyone else which course he chose. His letters to his two women depressed each of them. Had he known their feelings he could have been spared his worry about them. Each took other lovers and gave little thought to George.

His own depression increased. He felt that he was degenerating mentally as well as physically, that he was wasting what should have been his best years. He knew that he would be terribly handicapped if he did live through the war, that those not serving would have passed him by.

George was made an officer and sent back to England for training. There he lived again with Elizabeth, but she left him frequently to go out with other men. Fanny, too, seemed to care little whether she saw him or not. Talk of the war and his experiences obviously bored them, and they made only a small pretense of being interested. He spent his last night in England with Fanny, Elizabeth being off with someone else. Fanny did not bother to get up with him the morning he left. In fact, she awoke lazily, then went to sleep again before he even left the flat.

Back at the front, George found that he was ill-suited to command a company. Although he did his best, he was constantly censured by his colonel, who blamed George for all the faults of his untrained and cowardly troops. George himself could think of little but death. During a particularly heavy German shelling he simply stood upright and let the bullets smash into his chest. Who knows whether his death was an act of heroism or one of complete and utter futility?

DEATH OF A SALESMAN

Type of work: Drama
Author: Arthur Miller (1915-   )
Type of plot: Social criticism
Time of plot: Mid-twentieth century
Locale: New York
First presented: 1949

Principal characters:
WILLY LOMAN, a salesman
LINDA, his wife
BIFF, and
HAPPY, his sons
CHARLEY, his friend
BERNARD, Charley's son
UNCLE BEN, Willy's brother
THE WOMAN

Critique:

Death of a Salesman represents a successful attempt to blend the themes of social and personal tragedy within the same dramatic framework. For the story of Willy Loman is also the story of false values sustained by almost every agency of publicity and advertisement in our national life. Willy Loman accepts at face value the over-publicized ideals of material success and blatant optimism, and therein lies his tragedy. His downfall and final defeat illustrate not only the failure of a man but also the failure of a way of life. The playwright's ability to project the story of his tragic, lower middle-class hero into the common experience of so many Americans who sustain themselves with illusions and ignore realities makes this play one of the most significant in the American theater in recent years.

The Story:

When Willy Loman came home on the same day he had left on a trip through his New England territory, his wife Linda knew that he was near the breaking point. Lately he had begun to talk to himself about things out of the past. That day he had run off the road two or three times without knowing what he was doing, and he had come home in

fear. Willy, sixty-three, had given all his life to the company. He told himself they would just have to make a place for him in the New York home office. Traveling all week and driving futile miles had become too much for him.

Willy had had such hopes before Biff came home from his last job. Biff had always been the favorite, though Happy was the more settled and successful son. Biff was thirty-four now and still had to find himself, but Willy knew he would settle down when the time came. The boy had been the greatest football player his school had ever known. In a game at Ebbets Field he had been a hero. Three colleges offered him scholarships. Biff had not gone to college, had not done anything but bum around the West, never making more than twenty-eight dollars a week. It was hard to understand him.

During the next two days, Willy's whole life unrolled before him, today's reality intermingled with yesterday's half-forgotten episodes. Broken as it was, the pictures told the story of Willy Loman, salesman.

Perhaps the first mistake was in not following his brother Ben to Alaska—or was it Africa? Ben had wanted Willy to join him, but Willy was a salesman. Some weeks he averaged two hundred dollars. No, that was not quite true; it was nearer seventy. But he would make the grade, he told Ben, and so he stayed in New York. Ben went into the jungle a pauper; four years later he came back from the diamond mines a rich man.

Willy's boys were both well liked; that was important. Bernard, Charley's son, was liked, but not well liked. Bernard had begged to carry Biff's shoulder pads that day at Ebbets Field. Sometimes Willy had worried a little about the boys. Biff stole a football from school, and a whole case of them from the sporting goods store where he worked. He did not mean any harm, Willy knew. Willy even laughed when the boys stole a little lumber from a construction job nearby; no one would miss it. Willy and the boys used it to make the front stoop.

But that day at Ebbets Field seemed to be the last great day in Biff's life. Willy had left for Boston after the game, but surely that little Boston affair had not made the difference in the boy. Willy was with a woman when Biff burst in on him. Biff had failed math and could not take one of the scholarships unless Willy talked to the teacher and got him to change the grade. Willy was ready to leave for New York at once, but when Biff saw the woman in Willy's room, he left. Things were never the same afterward.

There was also Happy, who used to stand in Biff's shadow. Happy was a magnificent specimen, just like Biff, and there was not a woman in the world he could not have. An assistant merchandising manager, he would be manager someday, a big man. So would Biff. Biff needed only to find himself.

On the day Willy Loman turned back home he dreamed his biggest dreams. Biff would go back to that sporting goods store and get a loan from the owner to set himself and Happy up in business. That man had always loved Biff. And Willy would go to young Howard Wagner, his boss's son, and demand to be given a place in the New York office. They would celebrate that night at dinner. Biff and Happy would give Willy a night on the town to celebrate their mutual success.

But Biff failed to get the loan. That man who had loved Biff did not even recognize him. To get even, Biff stole a fountain pen and ran down eleven flights with it. And when Howard heard Willy's story, he told him to turn in his samples and take a rest. Willy realized he was through. He went to Charley for more money, for he had been borrowing from Charley since he had been put on straight commission months ago. Bernard was in Charley's office. He was on his way to plead a case before the Supreme Court. Willy could not understand it. Charley had never given his life for his boy as Willy had for his. Charley offered Willy a job, but Willy said he was a salesman. They loved him in New England; he would show them yet.

Willy stumbled in to the dinner they had planned, a failure himself but hoping for good news about Biff. Hearing of Biff's failure, he was completely broken. Happy picked up two girls, and he and Biff left Willy alone.

When Biff and Happy finally came home, Linda ordered them out of the house by morning. She was afraid because Willy had tried to kill himself once before. Giving vent to his anger and sense of defeat, Biff cursed Willy for a fool and a dreamer. He forced himself and Willy to acknowledge that Biff had been only a clerk in that store, not a salesman; that Biff had been jailed in Kansas City for stealing; that Happy was not an assistant manager but a clerk and a philandering, woman-chasing bum; and that Willy had never been a success and never would be. When Biff began to weep, Willy realized for the first time that his son loved him.

Willy, left alone after the others went upstairs, began to see Ben again, to tell him his plan. Willy had twenty thousand in insurance. Biff would be magnificent with twenty thousand. Willy ran out to his car and drove crazily away.

At the funeral, attended only by Linda and the boys and Charley, Charley tried to tell Biff about his father. He said that a salesman had to dream, that without dreams he was nothing. When the dreams were gone, a salesman was finished. Sobbing quietly, Linda stooped and put flowers on the grave of Willy Loman, salesman.

THE DEATH OF IVAN ILYICH

Type of work: Novella
Author: Count Leo Tolstoy (1828-1910)
Type of plot: Psychological realism
Time of plot: 1880's
Locale: St. Petersburg and nearby provinces
First published: 1884

Principal characters:
IVAN ILYICH GOLOVIN, a prominent Russian judge
PRASKOVYA FEDOROVNA GOLOVINA, his wife
PETER IVANOVITCH, his colleague
GERASIM, his servant boy

Critique:

The Death of Ivan Ilyich, a masterpiece of Tolstoy's later period, was written after he had published his most famous novels. Its theme is related to his own struggle against an obsessive fear of death and the conclusion that he had wasted his life, a struggle which culminated for him in a spiritual rebirth. The story itself is a supreme imaginative creation, however deep its roots in the author's own experience. Tolstoy presents, with frankness, simplicity, and kindness, an ordinary man confronted by the irrevocable fact of death. Here is one of the finest examples in literature of the portrayal of the particular—in this case the life and death of Ivan Ilyich—with such realistic understanding that it acquires universal significance.

The Story:

During a break in a hearing, a group of lawyers gathered informally. One, Peter Ivanovitch, interrupted the good-natured arguing of the others with the news that Ivan Ilyich, a colleague they greatly respected, was dead. Unwittingly, each thought first of what this death meant to his own chances of promotion, and each could not help feeling relief that Ivan Ilyich and not himself had died.

That afternoon Peter Ivanovitch visited the dead man's home, where the funeral was to be held. Although he met a playful colleague, Schwartz, he attempted to behave as correctly as possible under such sorrowful circumstances, as if observing the proper protocol would enable him to have the proper feelings. He respectfully looked at the corpse; he talked with Ivan's widow, Praskovya Fedorovna. But he was continually distracted during his talk by an unruly spring in the hassock on which he sat. As he struggled to keep his decorum, Praskovya spoke only of her own exhaustion and suffering. Peter, suddenly terrified by their mutual hypocrisy, longed to leave, and the widow, having gathered from him information about her pension, was glad to end the conversation. At the funeral Peter also saw Ivan's daughter and her fiancé, who were angrily glum, and Ivan's little son, who was tear-stained but naughty. Only the servant boy, Gerasim, spoke cheerfully, for only he could accept death as natural. Leaving, Peter hurried to his nightly card game.

Ivan Ilyich had been the second and most successful of the three sons of a superfluous bureaucrat. An intelligent and popular boy, he seemed able to mold his life into a perfect pattern. As secretary to a provincial governor after completing law school, and later as an examining magistrate, he was the very model of conscientiousness mingled with good humor. He managed the decorum of his official position as well as the ease of his social one. Only marriage, although socially correct, did not conform to his ideas of decorum; his wife, not content to fulfill the role he had chosen for her, became demanding and quarrelsome. As a result, he increasingly shut himself off from his family (for he now had two children), finding the order and peace he needed in his judiciary affairs.

In 1880, however, he was shattered by the loss of two promotions. In desperation he went to St. Petersburg, where a chance meeting led to his obtaining a miraculously good appointment. In the city he found precisely the house he had always wanted and he worked to furnish it just to his taste. Even a fall and a resulting bruise on his side did not dampen his enthusiasm. He and his wife were delighted with their new home, which they felt to be aristocratic, although it looked like all homes of those who wished to appear well-bred. To Ivan, life was at last as it should be: smooth, pleasant, and ordered according to an unwavering routine. His life was properly divided into the official and the personal, and the two halves were always kept dextrously apart.

Then Ivan began to notice an increasing discomfort in his left side. At last he consulted a specialist, but the examination left him frightened and helpless, for although he understood the doctor's objective attitude as akin to his own official one, he felt that it had given his pain an awesome significance. For a time he fancied he grew better from following prescriptions and learning all he could about his illness, but renewed attacks terrified him. Gradually Ivan found all his life colored by the pain. Card games became trivial; friends seemed only to speculate on how long he would live. When Ivan's brother-in-law came for a visit, his shocked look told Ivan how much illness had changed him, and he suddenly realized that he faced not illness but death itself. Through deepening terror and despair, Ivan shrank from this truth. Other men died, not he. Desperately he erected screens against the pain and the knowledge of death it brought, but it lurked behind court duties or quarrels with his family. The knowledge that it had begun with the bruise on his side only made his condition harder to bear.

As Ivan grew steadily worse, drugs failed to help him. But the clean strength and honesty of a peasant boy, Gerasim, nourished him, for he felt that his family were hypocrites who chose to pretend that he was not dying. Death to them was not part of that same decorum he too had once revered and was therefore hidden as unpleasant and shameful. Only Gerasim could understand his pain because only he admitted that death was real and natural.

Ivan retreated increasingly into his private anguish. He hated his knowing doctors, his plump, chiding wife, his daughter and her new fiancé. Lamenting, he longed to have his old, happy life again. But only memories of childhood revealed true happiness. Unwillingly he returned again and again to this knowledge as he continued questioning the reasons for his torment. If he had always lived correctly, why was this happening to him? What if he had been wrong? Suddenly he knew that the faint urges he had consciously stilled in order to do as people thought proper had been the true urges. And since he had not known the truth about life, he also had not known the truth about death. His anguish increased as he thought of the irrevocable choice he had made.

His wife brought the priest, whose sacrament eased him until her presence reminded him of the deception his life had been. He screamed to her to leave him, and he continued screaming as he struggled against death, unable to relinquish the illusion that his life had been good. Then the struggle ceased, and he knew that although his life had not been right, it no longer mattered. Opening his eyes, he saw his wife and son weeping by his bedside. Aware of them for the first time, he felt sorry for them. As he tried to ask their forgiveness, everything became clear to him. He must not hurt them; he must set them free and free himself from his sufferings. The pain and fear of death were no longer there. Instead there was only light and joy.

THE DEATH OF THE GODS

Type of work: Novel
Author: Dmitri Merejkowski (1865-1941)
Type of plot: Historical romance
Time of plot: Fourth century
Locale: Ancient Rome
First published: 1896

Principal characters:
    CAESAR CONSTANTIUS, the Roman Emperor
    JULIAN FLAVIUS, Caesar's cousin
    GALLUS FLAVIUS, Julian's brother
    ARSINOË, Julian's beloved

Critique:

Merejkowski, one of the most successful of modern Russian novelists of the old régime, saw European civilization as a result of the meeting of Hellenism and Christianity. In this novel he attempted to show how that meeting was carried on in the reign of Julian the Apostate, a Roman emperor of the fourth century. The novelist's success in re-creating what is distant, both in point of time and place, is almost unparalleled in any national literature. Little street urchins of Constantinople, common soldiers in the Roman legions, innkeepers of Asia Minor, and fawning courtiers of Caesar's court, all take on flesh and life as they pass through the story, all of them reflecting in greater or lesser degree the struggle between the two great philosophies, paganism and Christianity.

The Story:

The Roman Emperor Constantius had risen to power by a series of assassinations. Two of his cousins, Julian and Gallus, were still alive, prisoners in Cappadocia. No one knew why they were permitted to live, for they were the last people who could challenge the right of the emperor to his position. Julian was the greater of the two, a young man steeped in the teachings of the philosophers. His brother was younger and more girlish in his habits. Both knew that they could expect death momentarily.

When Julian was twenty years old, Constantius gave him permission to travel in Asia Minor, where the lad affected the dress of a monk and passed as a Christian. His younger brother, Gallus, was given high honors as co-regent with Constantius and named Caesar. The affection which Constantius seemed to bestow on Gallus was shortlived, however, for soon the young man was recalled to Milan and on his journey homeward he was beheaded by order of the emperor. When word of his brother's death reached Julian, he wondered how much longer he himself had to live.

While Julian wandered about Asia Minor, he met many philosophers, and was initiated into the mysteries of Mithra, the sun god. Julian felt more power in the religion of the pagans than he did in the Christ which his grandfather had declared the official religion of the Roman Empire. Knowing the danger of his beliefs, Julian kept them secret.

One day, Publius Porphyrius took Julian to an ancient wrestling arena where they watched a young woman playing at the ancient Grecian games. She was Arsinoë, who, like Julian, found more joy in paganism than in Christianity. One night she told him that he must believe in himself rather than in

THE DEATH OF THE GODS by Dmitri Merejkowski. Translated by Herbert Trench. By permission of the publishers, G. P. Putnam's Sons. Copyright, 1901, by Herbert Trench. Renewed, 1929, by Desmond Patrick Trench.

any gods, and he replied to her that such was his aim.

Before long Julian had an opportunity to strike at Constantius. Raised to a position of honor at court and given the purple robe of a Caesar, he was trained as a warrior and sent to Gaul to tame the barbarians. Contrary to Constantius' hopes that the young man would be killed, he was highly successful in Gaul. When Constantius sent an emissary to recall several of Julian's legions, the soldiers revolted and hailed Julian as the emperor and made him accept the crown. Meanwhile Julian's anger against all Christians had risen; his wife refused to share his bed because she had decided to become a nun. He felt no pity when she fell ill and died. He thought her actions had disgraced him.

With his loyal legions Julian began a march of conquest through the empire. While he was crossing Macedonia, he received word that Constantius had died in Constantinople.

As soon as word spread among Julian's legions that he was now the rightful emperor, he gathered his men together for a ceremony at which he denied Christianity and affixed the statue of Apollo in place of the Cross on his standards. That act was only the beginning of changes in the empire. On his arrival in Constantinople he reinstated the pagan gods and returned to their temples the treasure which had been taken from them by the Christian monks.

The Christians were outraged at his practices, and his popularity waned. Few visited the reopened pagan temples. Soon Julian began to wonder if he would be successful in restoring a golden age of Hellenism to his empire. He discovered that even his beloved Arsinoë had become a Christian nun in his absence. When he went to visit her, she agreed to see him; but she refused to marry him and become the empress. Julian began to wonder to what end he was headed.

At the end of the first year of his reign as emperor of the Eastern Roman Empire, Julian found that he had become the laughing-stock of his people, despite his power as a ruler. His appearance and his scholarly activities earned him the disrespect of all his subjects, who were accustomed to a Caesar of martial power. When the Christians began to ridicule him and openly defy his edicts, Julian decided to adopt a different course. He hit upon the idea of a campaign against Persia. He hoped that after he had conquered that country and returned as a victor, his people would respect both him and his anti-Christian views.

Julian's army assembled at Antioch, but before it was ready to march Julian had a demonstration of the feeling he had evoked by championing the Olympian deities against Christianity. When he ordered a Christian chapel removed from the temple of Apollo at Antioch, the Christians burned the temple and destroyed the idol in the presence of the emperor and his legions.

In the spring Julian and his armies left Antioch and started toward the Persian frontier. They marched along the Euphrates until they came to the canal which the Persians had built to connect that river with the Tigris. The Persians had flooded the area to halt the invaders, and Julian's army marched in water up to their knees until they were far down the Tigris. After days of marching under a burning sun, they reached Perizibar, a Persian fortress. The fort was gallantly defended, but the Romans finally battered down the walls.

After resting his army for two days, Julian pushed on to Maogamalki. By brilliant strategy and some luck, he carried the second of the Persian defense posts and then pushed onward to Ctesiphon, the Persian capital.

Arriving at a point across the river from the city, Julian consulted his pagan priests. When they failed to foretell a successful attack on the city, Julian became as enraged at Apollo and the other pagan gods as he had been at Christianity. In a frenzy he overturned the altars, said that he trusted no god but himself, and added that he meant to attack the city immediately.

By a ruse, Julian and his army crossed the Tigris in boats at night. The next morning a single Persian came to their camp and persuaded Julian to burn his boats so that his men would not lose heart and retreat from the assault. He promised also to lead the Romans into the city by a secret way. Too late, his boats destroyed, Julian realized he had been tricked. Unable to take the city, he ordered a retreat. After the Romans had been weakened by forced marches under burning desert suns, the Persians attacked.

In the battle, the Romans won a victory against heavy odds; but it was a victory for the Romans, not for their emperor. In the battle Julian, dressed in his purple robes, refused to wear any armor. He was mortally wounded by a javelin while giving chase to a band of Persians. When he was carried to his tent, Arsinoë, who was still a nun, came to him and attempted to make him see that Christ was a god of beauty and mercy. Julian would not listen to her. As he died, he lifted himself up and cried out to his attendants that the Galilean had defeated him.

THE DEATH OF THE HEART

Type of work: Novel
Author: Elizabeth Bowen (1899-   )
Type of plot: Psychological realism
Time of plot: After World War I
Locale: London and Seale, England
First published: 1938

Principal characters:
THOMAS QUAYNE, of Quayne and Merrett, an advertising agency
ANNA QUAYNE, his wife
PORTIA QUAYNE, his sixteen-year-old half-sister
ST. QUENTIN MILLER, an author and a friend of the Quaynes
EDDIE, an employee of Quayne and Merrett
MAJOR BRUTT, a retired officer
MRS. HECCOMB, Anna's ex-governess

Critique:

The travail of adolescence and its painful emergence into maturity are recorded with keenness and sympathy in Elizabeth Bowen's *The Death of the Heart*. Maturity's gain in awareness, she implies, is offset by childhood's loss in idealism and simplicity; adulthood involves compromises with one's heart and thoughts which the young find intolerable, at least at first. And so the arrival of Portia, with her innocent longings and candid curiosity, provides a kind of catalyst for an upper middle-class English household where compromise and boredom have long held sway. Portia's loneliness and her search for love and understanding are characteristic of her age, sex, and particular situation; but Miss Bowen never allows the individual to be submerged in the typical. Although the ending of the story is no more conclusive than life itself, it crystallizes some truths that are often elusive.

The Story:

Anna Quayne's pique demanded an outlet—she could no longer contain it all within herself. Therefore, while St. Quentin Miller shivered with cold, she marched him around the frozen park, delivering herself of her discontent. The trouble, of course, had started with Portia, for the Quayne household had not been the same since the arrival of Tom's sixteen-year-old half-sister. Not that Portia was all to blame; the business had begun with a deathbed wish. Who could expect dying old Mr. Quayne to ask Tom to take a stepsister he hardly knew, keep her for at least a year, and give her a graceful start in life? Anna herself, she went on to St. Quentin, hardly knew how to cope with the arrangement, though she had tried to accept it with outward tranquillity. Now she had stumbled across the girl's diary, glimpsed her own name, and been tempted to read. It was obvious that Portia was rather less than happy, that she was scanning the atmosphere of her brother's house with an unflattering eye.

While Anna was thus unburdening herself, the subject of her discussion returned home quietly from Miss Paullie's lessons. She was vaguely disturbed to learn from Matchett, the housekeeper, that Anna had commented upon the clutter in Portia's bedroom. Later she shared tea with Anna and St. Quentin when they came in tingling with cold; but the atmosphere seemed a bit stiff, and Portia readily acquiesced in Anna's suggestion that she join her brother in his study. Portia felt more at ease with Tom, even though he obviously found conversation with her awkward.

Portia knew, by now, that there was no one in whom she could readily confide. At 2 Windsor Terrace, Matchett offered a certain possessive friendship; at school, only the inquisitive Lilian took notice of her. Major Brutt was better than either of these; his eyes, in her presence, showed a fatherly gleam, and she liked the picture puzzle he had sent. Anna tolerated the major—he was her only link with an old friend, Pidgeon—but Major Brutt seldom ventured to call, and Portia saw him mostly in the company of others.

Another of Anna's friends whom Portia sometimes saw was Eddie. But Eddie was Anna's property and seemingly beyond the range of Portia's clumsy probing for companionship. Too, he was twenty-three and brightly self-assured. Anna found it amusing to have him around, though she often rebuked his conceit and presumption; she went so far as to find him a job with Quayne and Merrett. One day Portia handed Eddie his hat as he took leave of Anna; the next day he wrote to her. Before long they were meeting regularly and secretly.

Eddie, having no wish to alienate Anna, cautioned Portia not to mention him in her diary. But he reveled in Portia's uncritical adoration. They went to the zoo, to tea, ultimately to his apartment. Matchett, who found Eddie's letter under Portia's pillow, soon became coldly jealous of his influence. Even Anna and Tom became slightly restive, as they began to realize the situation. Meanwhile Portia was falling deeper and deeper in love. When Eddie lightly declared that it was a pity they were too young to marry, Portia innocently took his remarks as a tentative proposal. Though he carefully refrained from real love making, Portia felt sure he returned her love.

With the approach of spring, Anna and Tom revealed their intention of spending a few weeks in Capri. Since Matchett would houseclean while they were gone, they decided to send Portia to Mrs. Heccomb, Anna's old governess, who lived in a seaside house at Seale. Portia, dismayed by the prospect of separation from Eddie, was only partially consoled by his promise to write.

Eddie did write, promptly; so did Major Brutt, with the promise of another picture puzzle. And Seale, happily, turned out better than expected. Having none of Anna's remoteness, Mrs. Heccomb deluged her guest with carefree chatter. Her two grown-up stepchildren reacted somewhat more cautiously, since they were prepared to find Portia a highbrow. Finding her only shy, they quickly relaxed; the radio blared while they vigorously shouted over it about roller-skating, hockey games, and Saturday night parties. Portia gradually withdrew from her shell of loneliness. Within a few days she felt enough at home to ask Daphne Heccomb if Eddie might spend a weekend at Seale. Daphne consented to relay the request to her mother, whereupon Mrs. Heccomb affably approved.

Eddie's visit was not a success. His efforts to be the life of the party soon had Mrs. Heccomb wondering about the wisdom of her invitation. At the cinema his good fellowship extended to holding hands enthusiastically with Daphne. When Portia, distressed, uttered mild reproaches, he intimated that she was a naïve child. Walking together in the woods, on their final afternoon, Portia learned that Eddie had no use for her love unless it could remain uncritical and undemanding. Her vision of an idyllic reunion shattered into bits as she began to see his instability. Two weeks later her stay at Seale ended. Back in London, Matchett triumphantly informed her that Eddie had left word that he would be out of town a few days.

Walking home from school not long afterward, Portia encountered St. Quentin, who inadvertently revealed Anna's perusal of the diary. Upset, she sought comfort from Eddie once more. No longer gratified by her devotion, he made her feel even more unwanted; and the sight of a letter from Anna, lying on Eddie's table, convinced her that they were allied against her. As she left his apartment it seemed unthinkable that she could ever return to Windsor Terrace; her only possible refuge now was Major Brutt. To the Karachi Hotel, therefore, she went, surprising the worthy major as he finished his dinner. Surprise changed to alarm as she pleaded her case: would he take her away, would he marry her? She could relieve his loneliness, she could care for him, she could polish his shoes. Polishing shoes, the major affirmed, with as much serenity as he could muster, was a job women had little success with; with a little time and patience, her position would soon appear less desperate. He wished very much to call the Quaynes, for it was getting late and they would be worried. Portia felt that she had been defeated, but she could still choose ground on which to make a final stand. Very well, she finally agreed, he might call them, but he was not to tell them she was coming. That would depend, she finished enigmatically but firmly, on whether they chose to do the right thing.

The major had been right; the Quaynes were worried. After the telephone rang, their momentary relief was succeeded by real confusion. What, after all, would Portia consider the right thing for them to do? It would have to be simple, without fuss or feathers. With help from St. Quentin, they finally decided, and Matchett was sent in a taxi to fetch her.

THE DEATH OF VIRGIL

Type of work: Novel
Author: Hermann Broch (1886-1951)
Type of plot: Poetic mysticism
Time of plot: 19 B.C.
Locale: Brundisium (Brindisi, Italy)
First published: 1945

Principal characters:
> PUBLIUS VIRGILIUS MARO, chief poet of Rome
> AUGUSTUS CAESAR, Emperor of Rome
> PLOTIA HIERIA, a woman Virgil had once loved
> LYSANIAS, a young boy
> A SLAVE

Critique:

In some respects ·this difficult yet extraordinarily beautiful novel may better be called a poem, for although it is written mostly in prose, its means of presentation and its effect are wholly poetic. There are three different levels of interest: the vivid imagery and uncanny presentation of both the real world and the fever-ridden, hallucinated, yet visionary world of the dying Virgil; the beauty of language and of the rhythmic sentences; the depth of the writer's attempts to explore metaphysical truth. Using a simple plot as a basis, Broch presents a symphony in four movements. Although the mood of the whole is meditative and elegiac, the style of each movement establishes its tempo, from the pages-long sentences of the second movement to the antiphonal bursts of conversation in the third. In each movement, symbols, incidents, and phrases are reëchoed and transformed, so that the meaning of the novel becomes clear to the reader only as the mystic knowledge which approaching death brings becomes clear to the poet.

The Story:

The imperial fleet returned from Greece to Brundisium, bearing with it the Emperor Augustus and his poet, Virgil, who lay dying. Augustus had sought Virgil and brought him back from the peace and calm philosophy in Athens to the shouting Roman throngs — to the mob with its frightening latent capacity for brutality, its fickle adoration of its leaders. Yet these were the Romans whom Virgil had glorified; the nobles he had seen on shipboard greedily eating and gaming were their leaders; dapper, sham-majestic Augustus was their emperor.

Fever-ridden, the poet heard a boy's song as the ship entered the harbor. Later, as he was carried from the ship, a beautiful boy appeared from nowhere to lead his litter away from the tumult surrounding the emperor, through narrow streets crowded with garbage ripening into decay, streets full of the miseries of the flesh where women jeered at him for being rich and weak. The women's insults made him aware of his own sham-divinity and of the futility of his life. Dying, he at last saw clearly what hypocrisy his life had been, like the shining, hollow emperor whom he served.

At the palace he was taken to his chambers. The boy, Lysanias, remained with him as night fell. In the depths of a violent attack Virgil recognized his own lack of love. As he lay, conscious of his dying body and the infested night, he knew that, like the Augustus-worshiping masses, he had followed the wrong gods; that in his devotion to poetry he had from the beginning given up the service of life for that of death; that it was too late for him to be fulfilled, for even the

Aeneid lay unperfected. Some recurrence of vigor drove him to the window. Looking into the night, he knew that not his poem alone remained to be fulfilled; some knowledge still lay ahead for him to achieve. For the necessity of the soul is to discover itself, since through self-discovery it finds the universe: the landscape of the soul is that of all creation. One must learn, not through the stars, but through man.

Interrupting his thoughts, two men and a woman came through the streets quarreling and shouting good-natured obscenities, guffawing their bawdiness with that male laughter whose matter-of-factness annihilates rather than derides. This laughter, juxtaposed against the beautiful night, revealed something of the nature of beauty itself. Beauty is the opponent of knowledge; because it is remote, infinite, and therefore seemingly eternal, it is pursued wrongly for its own sake. The same nonhuman laughter is hidden in it. The artist who pursues beauty plunges into loneliness and self-idolatry; because he chooses beauty rather than life, his work becomes adornment rather than revelation. This path Virgil had chosen: beauty's cold egotism instead of love's warm life which is true creativity. Thus he had died long before, even before his renunciation of the lovely Plotia, whom he now remembered.

The need for contrition because of his refusal of love, a refusal of the pledge given to each man with his life, overwhelmed him. The fever rose within him, bringing strangely prophetic visions of Rome in ruins with wolves howling, of giant birds droning. As reality returned, he knew that for his own salvation he had to do one thing: burn the *Aeneid*.

Lysanias read to him as he drifted into a calm dream, shining with a knowledge of all past earthly happenings and a vision of something to come. Not yet, but soon would come one in whom creation, love, immortality would be united; one who would bear salvation like a single star, whose voice he seemed to hear bidding him open his eyes to love, for he was called to enter the Creation. As the fever left him and dawn broke, he momentarily doubted the voice. Then came the vision of an angel and, at last, undisturbed sleep.

Virgil awoke to find two old friends come to cheer him. Their bluff reassurances changed to incredulity when they heard he planned to burn the *Aeneid*. Their arguments against his own conviction that his book lacked reality because he himself lacked love were blurred by his fevered perception. Lysanias, whose existence seemed questionable to his friends, appeared with a Near Eastern slave to reaffirm that Virgil was the guide, although not the savior. Plotia came and called him on to an exchange of mutual love and the destruction of his work, the renunciation of beauty for love. Suddenly he and Plotia were exposed and power thundered around him.

Augustus had come to ask Virgil not to burn the *Aeneid*. In the ensuing interview, Virgil's rising delirium made him not only supernaturally aware of truth but also confused as to reality: the invisible Plotia guarded the manuscript; the invisible Lysanias lurked nearby; the room sometimes became a landscape. Augustus insisted that the poem was the property of the Romans, for whom it had been written. Virgil tried to explain that poetry is the knowledge of death, for only through death can one understand life; that unlike Aeschylus, whose knowledge had forced him to poetry, he, Virgil, had sought knowledge through writing poetry and had therefore found nothing.

Then Augustus and the slave seemed to be talking, and Augustus was the symbol of the state he had created, which was order and sobriety and humanity's supreme eternal reality. The slave, awaiting the birth of the supreme ancestor's son, was steadfastness and the freedom of community. The truth of the state must be united to the metaphysical by an individual act of truth, must be made human to realize perfection. Such a savior will come, whose sacrificial death will be the supreme symbol of humility and charity. Still Virgil insisted that he must sacrifice his work because he had not sacrificed his life, that destroying a thing which lacked perception redeemed both himself and the Romans.

Augustus, growing angry, accused Virgil of envy, and in a moment of love Virgil gave him the poem, agreeing not to destroy it. He asked, however, that his slaves might go free after his death. As he talked of his will to his friends, renewed attacks of fever brought him more and more strange hallucinations. He called for help and found he could at last say the word for his own salvation.

After he had finished dictating his will, it seemed to him that he was once more on a boat, one smaller than that which had brought him into the harbor the day before, rowed by his friend Plotius and guided by Lysanias. About him were many people he knew. Gradually all disappeared as he floated into the night; the boy became first a seraph whose ring glowed like a star, then Plotia, who led him into the day again. Reaching shore, they entered a garden where, somehow, he knew that she had become the boy and the slave and that he had become all of them; then he was also the animals and plants, then the mountains, and finally the universe, contained in a small white core of unity—and nothing. Then he was commanded to turn around, and the nothing became everything again, created by the word in the circle of time. Finally he was received into the word itself.

DEBIT AND CREDIT

Type of work: Novel
Author: Gustav Freytag (1816-1895)
Type of plot: Social realism
Time of plot: Early nineteenth century
Locale: Eastern Germany and Poland
First published: 1855

Principal characters:
ANTON WOHLFART, an intelligent, industrious middle-class German
T. O. SCHRÖTER, Anton Wohlfart's employer
SABINE SCHRÖTER, T. O. Schröter's young sister
FRITZ VON FINK, an Americanized German, Wohlfart's friend
BARON VON ROTHSATTEL, a German nobleman
LENORE VON ROTHSATTEL, the baron's beautiful daughter
HIRSCH EHRENTHAL, a Jewish usurer
VEITEL ITZIG, a rascally former schoolmate of Anton Wohlfart

Critique:

While Gustav Freytag's novels exhibit certain aspects of romanticism, they also contain a greater, more influential element of realism. The combination has sometimes been compared to the work of Freytag's distinguished British contemporary, Charles Dickens. Freytag, a great champion of the German middle class, believed that Germans as a whole were better, more honorable, more stable people than other Europeans and that in the sober, industrious middle class lay the future greatness of his country. With the nobility Freytag had little patience, portraying them, as he did in *Debit and Credit*, as a group with little talent, little common sense, and an empty sense of honor. Of all Freytag's work, both in drama and fiction, *Debit and Credit* has received the highest praise as an example of the combination of the romance and the realistic social novel.

The Story:

Upon the death of his father, an accountant, Anton Wohlfart, a very young man, traveled to the capital of his province in eastern Germany. In the city he found employment in the mercantile establishment of T. O. Schröter, an industrious and honorable German businessman. During his journey, Wohlfart encountered two people who were later to play an important part in his life. He wandered accidentally onto the estate of Baron von Rothsattel, whose beautiful daughter Lenore made a lasting impression on the boy. He also met Veitel Itzig, a young Jew who had been a former schoolmate, making his way to the city to seek his fortune.

Being an industrious and intelligent young man, as well as personable, Anton Wohlfart soon made a place for himself among his fellow workers and in the esteem of his employer. Among the other clerks in the firm was Fritz von Fink, a young Americanized German whose sense of industry and honor had been warped by a stay in New York City. Von Fink became a close friend of Wohlfart's despite the differences in their social standing and the escapades into which von Fink led Wohlfart, sometimes to the latter's embarrassment and chagrin.

In the meantime Baron von Rothsattel, who had little talent for managing his estates or business, was led to accept the advice of Hirsch Ehrenthal, an unscrupulous Jewish usurer and businessman who plotted the baron's financial ruin so that he might buy up his estates at a fraction of their value. Ehrenthal, who had persuaded the baron to mortgage his estates in order to purchase lands in Poland and to build a factory to extract sugar from beets, depended on the baron's lack of business acumen to ruin him, with a little help from Ehrenthal on the way. Ehrenthal did not realize at the time that Itzig, whom he had taken into his employ, was also plotting to acquire the baron's estates by a dishonest manipulation of documents and the knowledge he had of Ehrenthal's affairs. Itzig was coached in his scheme by a drunken lawyer who also hoped to make some profit from the nobleman's ruin.

Fritz von Fink finally decided to return to America to take over the affairs of a wealthy uncle who had recently died. Before he left, he proposed marriage to Sabine Schröter, Wohlfart's employer's sister, but the young woman refused the nobleman's offer. Shortly after his departure, revolt broke out in the nearby provinces of Poland. In order to prevent business losses and reëstablish his affairs there, Schröter bravely entered Poland, accompanied by Wohlfart. During their stay Wohlfart saved his employer's life, winning his and his sister's gratitude. Because of his employer's trust, Wohlfart was left in Poland for many months as the firm's agent, to reorganize the business of the company. He returned to Germany to be honored by his employer and given a position of considerable responsibility. During his stay in Poland he had met Eugene von Rothsattel, the baron's son, who proved to be a gallant but impractical young man. Because of his admiration for the young nobleman and his romantic regard for Lenore von Rothsattel, Wohlfart had lent a large sum of money to Eugene.

As time passed the financial affairs of Baron von Rothsattel became worse and worse; falling deeper into debt, the nobleman gave personal notes and mortgages to Ehrenthal and the other usurers who were his accomplices. When the baron thought himself on the edge of ruin, a ray of hope appeared in the person of Ehrenthal's son, an upright and noble-hearted young man who tried to persuade his father to give up dishonest gains and let the baron keep his family estates. The young man was ill, however, and he died

before he was able to influence his father's actions. On the night of his death a casket filled with important documents was stolen from Ehrenthal's office by Itzig's accomplice.

The baron, desperate, attempted suicide. He failed in this, but the blast of the pistol blinded him. In desperation, Lenore von Rothsattel appealed to Wohlfart to become her father's agent. After much soul-searching, the young man agreed, although his departure from Schröter's firm made his employer angry and opened a breach between the two men. Schröter felt that the nobility, who constantly proved their inability to manage their affairs, should be allowed to ruin themselves and so lose their place of influence in German culture.

Wohlfart journeyed again to Poland, this time to try to salvage the estate which the baron had acquired in that country. He found the estate in run-down condition and the Poles decidedly incompetent and unfriendly. With the help of loyal German settlers in the area, Wohlfart managed to bring some order to the farms of the estate, to which the baron, his wife, and his daughter moved, knowing that the family estates in Germany were lost. After many months Wohlfart managed to put the baron's affairs in order; however, his efforts were lost on the baron, who had a misplaced sense of rank. Only Wohlfart's regard for Lenore kept him in the position of responsibility after he had been repeatedly insulted.

When the revolutions of 1848 broke out, the troubles spread to the Polish provinces in which the von Rothsattel estate was located. Fortunately, Fritz von Fink appeared and under his leadership the estate was defended from the rebel depredations until help from a military force arrived on the scene. During this period von Fink and Lenore discovered their love for each other. When danger was past, the baron's resentment against Wohlfart exploded, and the young man was dismissed. The baroness, who realized what the young man had sacrificed for her family, spoke to him of her gratitude and asked him to try to straighten out their affairs with the usurers.

Returning to his home city, Wohlfart found a cordial welcome from his former employer's sister, but a rather cool one from Schröter himself. Schröter feared that living with the nobility had spoiled the young man, and he still resented the fact that Wohlfart had left his firm. Through his own efforts and those of a detective, Wohlfart began to trace down the plots which had ruined Baron von Rothsattel. He was informed that Ehrenthal was not the real villain, and soon it appeared that Itzig had been the true culprit in the affair. When the broken-down lawyer who had been Itzig's mentor learned of the investigations, he went to Itzig for money and a chance to leave Germany; he was the one who had stolen the baron's documents and he feared arrest. Itzig, driven by panic, drowned his accomplice. Just at the hour he was to marry Ehrenthal's daughter, a beautiful woman and the usurer's only heir, Itzig was told that the authorities were ready to arrest him. In his attempt to escape, Itzig himself was drowned at the place where he had murdered his accomplice. The documents were recovered, however, and the fortune and honor of Baron von Rothsattel were redeemed.

Having recovered the fortune of the baron's family and overcome his sentimental regard for Lenore, Wohlfart decided to leave the city, for he believed that he had no future in the firm of T. O. Schröter. Before he left, however, he went to see Sabine Schröter, his employer's sister, and the two young people confessed to each other that they were in love. The girl took the young man to her brother, who amazed Wohlfart by his warmth. Sabine revealed to Wohlfart that he was to marry her and become a partner in the firm, if that was his wish.

THE DECAMERON

(SELECTIONS)

Type of work: Tales
Author: Giovanni Boccaccio (1313-1375)
Types of plots: Romantic tragedy, farce, folk tradition
Times of plots: Graeco-Roman times and the Middle Ages
Locale: Italy
First transcribed: 1353

Principal characters:
THE THREE TEDALDO SONS, gentlemen of Florence
ALESSANDRO, their nephew
THE DAUGHTER OF THE KING OF ENGLAND
TANCRED, Prince of Salerno
GHISMONDA, his daughter
GUISCARDO, her lover
ISABETTA, of Messina
LORENZO, her lover
HER THREE BROTHERS
GALESO, of Cyprus, known as Cimone
EFIGENIA, his love
LISIMACO, of Rhodes
FEDERIGO DEGLI ALBERIGHI, of Florence
MONNA GIOVANNA, his love
PERONELLA, a wool carder of Naples
HER HUSBAND
STRIGNARIO, her lover
NATHAN, a rich man of Cathay
MITRIDANES, envious of Nathan
SALADIN, Sultan of Babylon
MESSER TORELLO, of Pavia
GUALTIERI, son of the Marquess of Saluzzo
GRISELDA, his wife

Critique:

Boccaccio, Dante, and Petrarch were the leading lights in a century that is considered the beginning of the Italian Renaissance. Dante died while Boccaccio was a child, but Petrarch was the friend of his middle and later life. Dante's work was essentially of the spirit; Petrarch's was that of the literary man; Boccaccio's broke free of all tradition and created a living literature about ordinary people. His *Decameron* is his most famous work. This collection of one hundred tales is set in a framework much like that in the *Arabian Nights' Tales,* or in Chaucer's *Canterbury Tales,* written later in the same century. A terrible plague was ravaging Florence. To flee from it, a group of seven girls and three young men, who had met by chance in a church, decided to go to a villa out of town. There they set up a working arrangement whereby each would be king or queen for a day. During the ten days they stayed in the country, each told a story following certain stipulations laid down by the daily ruler. The stories range from romance to farce, from comedy to tragedy. They are all told with a wit that carries them above the range of the licentious, a term sometimes used unjustly about the tales. It may be true that none of the plots was original with Boccaccio, but he wrote one hundred excellent stories, and many are the authors since his day who have borrowed from him.

PAMPINEA'S TALE ABOUT THE THREE TEDALDO YOUNG MEN

When Messer Tedaldo died, he left all his goods and chattels to his three sons. With no thought for the future, they lived so extravagantly that they soon had little left. The oldest son suggested that they sell what they could, leave Florence, and go to London, where they were unknown.

In London they lent money at a high rate of interest, and in a few years they had a small fortune. Then they returned to Florence. There they married and began to live extravagantly again, while depending on the monies still coming to them from England.

A nephew named Alessandro took care of their business in England. At that time there were such differences between the king and a son that Alessandro's business was ruined. He stayed in England, however, in hopes that peace would come and his business would recover. Finally he returned to Italy with a group of monks who were taking their young abbot to the pope to get a dispensation for him and a confirmation of the youthful cleric's election.

On the way Alessandro discovered that the abbot was a girl, and he married her in the sight of God. In Rome the girl had an audience with the pope. Her father, the King of England, wished the pope's blessing on her marriage to the old King of Scotland, but she asked the pope's blessing on her marriage to Alessandro instead.

After the wedding Alessandro and his bride went to Florence, where she paid his uncles' debts. Two knights preceded the couple to England and urged the king to forgive his daughter. After the king had knighted Alessandro, the new knight reconciled the king and his rebellious son.

FIAMMETTA'S TALE OF TANCRED AND THE GOLDEN CUP

Tancred, Prince of Salerno, loved his daughter Ghismonda so much that when she was widowed soon after her marriage he did not think to provide her with a second husband, and she was too modest to ask him to do so. Being a lively girl, however, she decided to have as her lover the most valiant man in her father's court. His name was Guiscardo. His only fault was that he was of humble birth.

Ghismonda noticed that Guiscardo returned her interest and they met secretly in a cave, one entrance to which was through a door in the young widow's bedroom. Soon she was taking her lover into her bedroom, where they enjoyed each other frequently.

Tancred was in the habit of visiting his daughter's room at odd times. One day, when he went to visit, she was not there and so he sat down to wait in a place where he was by accident hidden by the bed curtains from his daughter and her lover, who soon came in to use the bed.

Tancred remained hidden, but that night he had Guiscardo arrested. When he berated his daughter for picking so humble a lover, she defied him for letting so brave a man remain poor in his court. She begged nothing from Tancred except that he kill her and her lover with the same stroke.

The prince did not believe Ghismonda would be as resolute as she sounded. When her lover was killed, Tancred had his heart cut from his body and sent to her in a golden cup. Ghismonda thanked her father for his noble gift. After repeatedly kissing the heart, she poured poison into the cup and drank it. Then she lay down upon her bed with Guiscardo's heart upon her own. Tancred's own heart was touched when he saw her cold in death, and he obeyed her last request that she and Guiscardo be buried together.

FILOMENO'S TALE OF THE POT OF BASIL

Isabetta lived in Messina with her three merchant brothers and a young man named Lorenzo, who looked after all their business. Isabetta and Lorenzo fell in love One night, as she went to Lorenzo's room, her oldest brother saw her. He said nothing until the next morning, when the three brothers conferred to see how they could settle the matter so that no shame should fall upon them or upon Isabetta.

Not long afterward the three brothers, setting out with Lorenzo, said that they were going part way with him on a journey. Secretly they killed and buried the young man.

After their return home the brothers answered none of Isabetta's questions about Lorenzo. She wept and refused to be consoled in her grief. One night Lorenzo came to her in a dream and told her what had happened and where he was buried. Without telling her brothers, she went to the spot indicated in her dream and there found her lover's body. She cut off his head and wrapped it in a cloth to take home. She buried the head in dirt in a large flower pot and planted basil over it. The basil flourished, watered by her tears.

She wept so much over the plant that her brothers took away the pot of basil and hid it. Because she asked about it often, the brothers grew curious. At last they investigated and found Lorenzo's head. Abashed, they left the city. Isabetta died of a broken heart.

PAMFILO'S TALE OF CIMONE, WHO BECAME CIVILIZED THROUGH LOVE

Galeso was the tallest and handsomest of Aristippo's children, but he was so stupid that the people of Cyprus called him Cimone, which means Brute. Cimone's stupidity embarrassed his father until the old man sent the boy to the country to live. There Cimone was contented until one day he came upon a sleeping girl, Efigenia, whose beauty completely changed him.

He told his father he intended to live in town. The news worried his father for a while, but Cimone bought fine clothes and associated only with worthy young

men. In four years he was the most accomplished and virtuous young man on the island.

Although he knew she was promised to Pasimunda of Rhodes, Cimone asked Efigenia's father for her hand in marriage. He was refused. When Pasimunda sent for his bride, Cimone and his friends pursued the ship and took Efigenia off the vessel, after which they let the ship's crew go free to return to Rhodes. In the night a storm arose and blew Cimone's ship to the very harbor in Rhodes where Efigenia was supposed to go. Cimone and his men were arrested.

Pasimunda had a brother who had been promised a wife, but this girl was loved by Lisimaco, a youth of Rhodes, as Efigenia was loved by Cimone. The brothers planned a double wedding.

Lisimaco made plans with Cimone. At the double wedding feast, Lisimaco and Cimone with many of their friends snatched the brides away from their prospective husbands. The young men carried their loved ones to Crete, where they lived happily in exile for a time until their fathers interceded for them. Then Cimone took Efigenia home to Cyprus, and Lisimaco took his wife back to Rhodes.

FIAMMETTA'S TALE OF FEDERIGO AND HIS FALCON

Federigo degli Alberighi was famed in Florence for his courtesy and his prowess in arms. He fell in love with Monna Giovanna, a woman who cared nothing for him, though he spent his fortune trying to please her. Finally he was so poor that he went to the country to live on his farm. There he entertained himself only by flying his falcon, which was considered the best in the world.

Monna's husband died, leaving her to enjoy his vast estates with one young son. The son struck up an acquaintance with Federigo and particularly admired the falcon. When the boy became sick, he thought he might get well if he could own Federigo's bird.

Monna, as a last resort, swallowed her pride and called upon Federigo. She told him she would stay for supper, but Federigo, desperately poor as he was, had nothing to serve his love except the falcon, which he promptly killed and roasted for her.

After the meal, with many apologies, Monna told her host that her son, thinking he would get well if he had the falcon, desired Federigo's bird. Federigo wept to think that Monna had asked for the one thing he could not give her.

The boy died soon after and Monna was bereft. When her brothers urged her to remarry, she finally agreed to do so. But she would marry no one but the generous Federigo, who had killed his pet falcon to do her honor. So Federigo married into great riches.

FILOSTRATO'S TALE OF PERONELLA, WHO HID HER LOVER IN A BUTT

Peronella was a Neapolitan woolcomber married to a poor bricklayer. Together they made enough to live comfortably. Peronella had a lover named Strignario, who came to the house each day after the husband went to work.

One day, when the husband returned unexpectedly, Peronella hid Strignario in a butt. Her husband had brought home a man to buy the butt for five florins. Thinking quickly, Peronella told her husband that she already had a buyer who had offered seven florins for the butt, and that he was at that moment inside the butt inspecting it.

Strignario came out, complaining that the butt was dirty. The husband offered to clean it. While the husband was inside scraping, Strignario cuckolded him again, paid for the butt, and went away.

FILOSTRATO'S TALE OF NATHAN'S GENEROSITY

There was once in Cathay a very rich and generous old man named Nathan. He had a splendid palace and many servants, and he entertained lavishly any-one who came his way.

In a country nearby lived Mitridanes who was not nearly so old as Nathan but just as rich. Since he was jealous of Nathan's fame, he built a palace and entertained handsomely everyone who came by. One day a woman came thirteen times asking alms. Furious when Mitridanes called her to task, she told him that she had once asked alms of Nathan forty-two times in one day without reproof. Mitridanes decided that he would have to kill Nathan before his own fame would grow.

Riding near Nathan's palace, Mitridanes came upon Nathan walking alone. When he asked to be directed secretly to Nathan's palace, Nathan cheerfully took him there and established him in a fine apartment. Still not realizing who Nathan was, Mitridanes revealed his plan to kill his rival. Nathan arranged matters so that Mitridanes came upon him alone in the woods.

Mitridanes, curious to see Nathan, caught hold of him before piercing him with a sword. When he discovered that Nathan was the old man who had first directed him to the palace, made him comfortable, and then arranged the meeting in the woods, Mitridanes realized that he could never match Nathan's generosity, and he was greatly ashamed.

Nathan offered to go to Mitridanes' home and become known as Mitridanes, while Mitridanes would remain to be known as Nathan. But by that time Mitridanes thought his own actions would tarnish Nathan's fame. He went home humbled.

PAMFILO'S TALE OF SALADIN AND MESSER TORELLO

In the time of Emperor Frederick the First, all Christendom united in a crusade for the recovery of the Holy Land. To see how the Christians were preparing themselves and to learn to protect himself against them, Saladin, the Sultan of Babylon, took two of his best knights and made a tour through Italy to Paris. The travelers were disguised as merchants.

Outside the little town of Pavia they came upon Messer Torello, who was on his way to his country estate. When they asked him how far they were from Pavia, he told them quickly that the town was too far to be reached that night and sent his servants with them to an inn. Having sensed that the three men were foreign gentlemen and wanting to honor them, he had the servants take them by a roundabout way to his own estate. Meanwhile he rode directly home. The travelers were surprised when they saw him in his own place, but, realizing that he meant only to honor them, they graciously consented to spend the night.

The next day Messer Torello sent word to his wife in town to prepare a banquet. The preparations being made, both Torellos honored the merchants that day. Before they left, the wife gave them handsome suits of clothes like those her husband wore.

When Messer Torello became one of the crusaders, he asked his wife to wait a year and a month before remarrying if she heard nothing from him. She gave him a ring to remember her by. Soon afterward a great plague broke out among the Christians at Acre and killed many men. Most of the survivors were imprisoned by the sultan. Messer Torello was taken to Alexandria, where he trained hawks for Saladin and was called Saladin's Christian. Neither man recognized the other for a long time, until at last Saladin recognized a facial gesture in Torello and made himself known as one of the traveling merchants. Freed, Torello lived happily as Saladin's guest and expected daily to hear from his wife, to whom he had sent word of his adventures. His messenger had been shipwrecked, however, and the day closely approached when his wife would be free to remarry.

At last Torello told Saladin of the arrangement he and his wife had made. The sultan, taking pity on him, had Torello put to sleep on a couch heaped with jewels and gold. Then the couch, whisked off to Italy by magic, was set down in the church of which his uncle was abbot. Torello and the abbot went to the marriage feast prepared for Torello's wife and her new husband. No one recognized Torello because of his strange beard and oriental raiment until he displayed the ring his wife had given him. Then with great rejoicing they were reunited, a reward for their early generosity.

DINEO'S TALE OF THE PATIENT GRISELDA

Gualtieri, eldest son of the Marquess of Saluzzo, was a bachelor whose subjects begged him to marry. Though he was not anxious to take a wife, he decided to wed poor Griselda, who lived in a nearby hamlet. When he went with his friends to bring Griselda home, he asked her if she would always be obedient and try to please him and never be angry. Upon her word that she would do so, Gualtieri had her stripped of her poor gown and dressed in finery becoming her new station.

With her new clothes Griselda changed so much in appearance that she seemed to be a true noblewoman, and Gualtieri's subjects were pleased. She bore him a daughter and a son, both of whom Gualtieri took from her. In order to test her devotion, he pretended to have the children put to death, but Griselda sent them off cheerfully since that was her husband's wish.

When their daughter was in her early teens, Gualtieri sent Griselda home, clad only in a shift, after telling her that he intended to take a new wife. His subjects were sad, but Griselda herself remained composed. A short time later he called Griselda back to his house and ordered her to prepare it for his wedding, saying

851

that no one else knew so well how to arrange it. In her ragged dress she prepared everything for the wedding feast. Welcoming the guests, she was particularly thoughtful of the new bride.

By that time Gualtieri thought he had tested Griselda in every possible way. He introduced the supposed bride as her daughter and the little boy who had accompanied the girl as her son. Then he had Griselda dressed in her best clothes and everyone rejoiced.

DECLINE AND FALL

Type of work: Novel
Author: Evelyn Waugh (1903-   )
Type of plot: Social satire
Time of plot: Twentieth century
Locale: England and Wales
First published: 1928

Principal characters:

> PAUL PENNYFEATHER, a serious-minded young Oxonian
> SIR ALASTAIR DIGBY-VAINE-TRUMPINGTON, a young aristocrat
> ARTHUR POTTS, a noble-minded young man
> DR. AUGUSTUS FAGAN, head of Llanabba Castle School
> FLOSSIE, and
> DIANA, his daughters
> MR. PRENDERGAST, an ex-clergyman
> CAPTAIN GRIMES, a public-school man
> PETER BESTE-CHETWYNDE, one of Paul's pupils
> MARGOT BESTE-CHETWYNDE, his mother
> SOLOMON PHILBRICK, a confidence man
> SIR HUMPHREY MALTRAVERS, later Lord Metroland, a British politician

Critique:

Decline and Fall mingles farce with grim tragedy. Episodic in form, with many of its scenes no more than a page or so in length, it is a penetrating yet hilarious study of disordered English society in the period between wars. Mr. Waugh insists that his books are not intended as satires, since the satirical spirit presupposes a stable and homogeneous society against which to project its critical exposure of folly and vice. For all that, the writer demonstrates in this novel, his first, a tremendous talent for comic satire. Paul Pennyfeather's misadventures reflect one phase of the contemporary mood of disillusionment. On the other hand, Grimes, a bounder and a cad, is timeless, a figure who would have been as much at home in the days of the Caesars as he was in the reign of King George V. Waugh's distortions and exaggerations have also the quality of fantasy, for in his pages the impossible and the believable exist on the same plane at the same time.

The Story:

At Scone College, Oxford, the annual dinner of the Bollinger Club ended with the breaking of glass. Reeling out of Sir Alastair Digby-Vaine-Trumpington's rooms, the drunken aristocrats ran to earth Paul Pennyfeather, an inoffensive divinity student, and forcibly left him trouserless before they went roaring off into the night.

Bollinger members could be fined, but the college authorities felt that Paul deserved severer punishment for running across the quadrangle in his shorts, and he was sent down for indecent behavior. His unsympathetic guardian, after informing him that under his father's will his legacy could be withheld for unsatisfactory behavior, virtuously announced his intention to cut off Paul's allowance.

Through a shoddy firm of scholastic agents Paul became a junior assistant master at Llanabba Castle, Wales. Llanabba was not a good school. Its head was Dr. Augustus Fagan, whose lectures on service were intended to cover up the inadequacies of his institution. He had two daughters, Flossie, a vulgar young woman of matrimonial ambitions, and Diana, who economized on sugar and soap. One of the masters was Mr. Prendergast, a former clergyman who suffered from doubts. The other was Captain Grimes, who wore a false leg and was, as he frankly admitted, periodically in the soup. A bounder and a scoundrel, he put his faith in the public-school system, which may kick a man out but never lets him down. Grimes thought he had been put on his feet more often than any public-school man alive. His reluctant engagement to Flossie was his protection against the next time he found himself in trouble.

Paul was in charge of the fifth form. When he met his class for the first time, most of the boys claimed that their name was Tangent. An uproar arising between would-be Tangents and a few non-Tangents, Paul announced that the writer of the longest essay would receive half a crown. Mr. Prendergast wondered why Paul's classes were always so quiet. His own students behaved outrageously and made fun of his wig. Paul found young Peter Beste-Chetwynde the most interesting of his pupils.

Arthur Potts, one of the few men Paul had known at Scone, wrote that Alastair Trumpington, regretting Paul's dismissal, wanted to send him twenty pounds. Grimes, hearing of the offer, wired for the money in Paul's name.

Some parents planned to visit Llanabba Castle. Dr. Fagan decided to honor their visit with the annual field sports meet. Philbrick, the butler, objected to his extra duties. To Paul he confided that he was a crook who had taken the post in order to kidnap little Lord Tangent, but that he had reformed after falling in love with Diana. He told Mr. Prendergast that he was really Sir Solomon Philbrick, a millionaire shipowner, and he left Grimes under the impression that he was a novelist collecting material for a book.

The sports meet was not a gala occasion. Lady Circumference, Lord Tangent's mother, was rude to everyone in distributing the prizes. The Llanabba Silver Band played. Margot Beste-Chetwynde created a social flurry when she arrived with a Negro. Mr. Prendergast, the starter, accidentally shot Lord Tangent in the heel. Later he became abusively drunk. But Paul, without intending to, fell in love at first sight with Peter Beste-Chetwynde's beautiful widowed mother.

The term dragged to a close. Lord Tangent's foot became infected and he died. Grimes, landing in the soup once more, announced his engagement to Flossie, but the marriage turned out as badly as he had expected. Detectives arrived to arrest Philbrick on charges of false pretense, but their man had already flown. A few days later Grimes' clothing and a suicide note were discovered on the beach.

Paul, engaged to tutor Peter during the vacation, went to Margot's country house, King's Thursday. When she bought the place from her impoverished bachelor brother-in-law, Lord Pastmaster, it had been the finest example of Tudor domestic architecture in England. Bored with it, however, she had commissioned Otto Silenus, an eccentric designer, to build a modernistic house in its place. Silenus built a structure of concrete, glass, and aluminum, a house for dynamos, not people, but people went there anyway for endless house parties.

When Paul finally found enough courage to propose to Margot, she accepted him because Peter thought the young Oxonian would make a better stepfather than a rival suitor, Sir Humphrey Maltravers, Minister of Transport. During preparations for the wedding Paul learned that Margot still carried on her father's business, a syndicate vaguely connected with amusement enterprises in South America. Grimes turned up mysteriously in her employ. Potts, now working for the League of Nations, also took an unexplained interest in Margot's business affairs.

A few days before the wedding Margot asked Paul to fly to Marseilles and arrange for the passage of several cabaret entertainers to Rio de Janeiro. He did so without realizing that he was bribing the officials he interviewed. On his wedding morning Paul was having a final drink with Alastair Trumpington when a Scotland Yard inspector appeared and arrested him on charges of engaging in an international white-slave traffic.

Margot fled to her villa at Corfu and did not appear at the trial. Potts, a special investigator for the League of Nations, was the chief witness for the prosecution. Convicted of Margot's crimes, Paul was sentenced to seven years' penal servitude. The first part of his sentence he served at Blackstone Gaol, where he found Philbrick a trusty and Mr. Prendergast the chaplain. Shortly after Prendergast was killed by a crazed inmate, Paul was removed to Egdon Heath Penal Settlement. Grimes was one of his fellow prisoners, but not for long. One day, while serving on a work gang, he walked off into the fog. Everyone supposed that he perished later in a swamp, but Paul believed otherwise. Grimes, whose roguery was timeless, could never die. Margot came to visit Paul. She announced her intention to marry Maltravers, now Lord Metroland and the Home Secretary.

Paul's escape from Egdon Heath was carefully contrived. On orders from the Home Secretary he was removed for an appendicitis operation in a nursing home owned by Dr. Fagan, who had forsaken education for medicine. After a drunken doctor had signed a death certificate stating that Paul had died under the anesthetic, Alastair Trumpington, who had become Margot's young man, put him on a yacht which carried him to Margot's villa at Corfu. Officially dead, Paul enjoyed the rest he thought he deserved. Some months later, wearing a heavy mustache, he returned to Scone to continue his reading for the church. When the chaplain mentioned another Pennyfeather, a wild undergraduate sent down for misconduct, Paul said that the young man was a distant cousin.

At Scone the annual dinner of the Bollinger Club ended with the breaking of glass. Paul was reading in his room when Peter Beste-Chetwynde, Lord Pastmaster since his uncle's death, came in, very drunk. Paul's great mistake, Peter said, was that he had ever become involved with people like Margot and himself. After his departure Paul settled down to read another chapter in a book on early church heresies.

DEEPHAVEN

Type of work: Tales
Author: Sarah Orne Jewett (1849-1909)
Type of plot: Regional romance
Time of plot: Nineteenth century
Locale: Maine seacoast
First published: 1877

Principal characters:
HELEN DENIS, the narrator
KATE LANCASTER, her friend
THE CAREWS, and
THE LORIMERS, Deephaven's society
MRS. KEW, wife of the lighthouse keeper
CAPTAIN LANT,
CAPTAIN SANDS, and
DANNY, Maine seamen
MRS. BONNY, an elderly eccentric
MISS CHAUNCEY, an elegant woman

Critique:

Deephaven, Miss Jewett's first collection of tales and sketches, contains those characteristics of nature study and character drawing which the author used throughout her later work. This book, although unified in background, and theme, is too diffuse in its effects to be called a novel; it is a series of sketches describing an idyllic summer in an almost forgotten town on the New England coast. It illustrates also Miss Jewett's belief that a writer must know the village well before he can know the world. Willa Cather, in her reminiscences of Sarah Orne Jewett, revealed that the older woman set her on the path to literary achievement by telling her to write about people and places that she knew best. When Miss Cather followed Miss Jewett's advice, books like O Pioneers! and My Ántonia were the result. While Miss Jewett may not have reached Willa Cather's heights as a writer, she wrote pleasantly and nostalgically of familiar things; and Miss Cather never failed to pay her literary debt to her preceptor.

The Story:

Kate Lancaster's great-aunt, Katherine Brandon, had died, leaving to Kate's mother a charming old house and the family estate, including wharf rights, at Deephaven, a quaint sea town that had known better days. Since Kate's family was scattering for the summer, she asked Helen Denis, a friend, to spend the season with her in the old house on the Maine coast. They took with them two maids who came from that part of New England, and they left Boston without regret.

Riding with them in the stagecoach from the railway station was a large, weather-beaten, but good-natured woman who turned out to be Mrs. Kew, the wife of the lighthouse keeper. She was a keenly observant person but so warmhearted that the girls knew that she meant her invitation to visit the Light, and by the end of the summer they knew that wherever she was there was always a home and a heart for them.

Great-aunt Brandon's house was a sedate and imposing one full of furnishings brought home by generations of seagoing ancestors. Its closets were filled with china and its walls were covered by family portraits. The girls rummaged the place from cellar to attic until they felt that they knew Katherine Brandon as well as if she were still alive. Then they started to learn their way around the shore, out to the lighthouse, through the town, and out into the country.

People who had known Katherine Brandon and Kate's mother felt themselves the girls' friends by inheritance and the girls were never lonely. Those people had held Katherine Brandon in great respect but with fond admiration. The girls tried to do nothing to hurt the Brandon name. Through Widow Jim Patton they realized that Kate's aunt had been a thoughtful, generous soul who remembered in her will her less fortunate neighbors.

To the girls it seemed as though the clocks had stopped long ago in Deephaven and that the people went on repeating whatever they had been doing at that time in the past. Even their faces looked like those of colonial times. The people attached a great deal of importance to the tone of their society, handed down from the fabulous times of Governor Chantrey, a rich shipowner and an East India merchant. Now there were few descendants of the old families left; these were treated almost with reverence by the others. Even the simple fishermen felt an unreasoning pride in living in Deephaven. There were no foreigners, and there were no industries to draw people from out of town.

The Carews and the Lorimers, old friends of Katherine Brandon, became friends of Kate and Helen. Mr. Dick Carew had been an East India merchant. Mr. Lorimer was the minister. The ladies were of the old order, inordinately proud of their mementos of the old days and always happy to tell reminiscences of earlier times.

Naturally, in a seacoast town, there were also old sailors, all of whom were called captain by the time they reached a certain age. When attacks of rheumatism did not keep them home, they gathered on the wharves. Huddled close together, for many had grown deaf, they told over and over again the tales of their distant voyages. The girls noticed that silence fell when anyone approached the group, but on one occasion they hid close by to hear the yarns the old men told.

Singly the old mariners were pleased to have a new audience, and before long Kate and Helen were friendly with many of the old men. While some of them told stories of marine superstitions and adventures, others told supernatural tales they swore were true. Captain Lent related the story of Peletiah Daw, to whom he had been bound out in his youth. Old Peletiah put more store by his wild nephew Ben than he did by his own sons. One night, when Peletiah was old and feeble, he cried out and begged his sons to cut down Ben, whom he had seen hanging from a yardarm. The sons thought their father was delirious, but a short time later a sailor came to tell them that Ben had died of a fever. Peletiah called the man a liar, but the sailor held to his story before the women. Outside, he told the sons that Ben had been hanged from the yardarm, just as the old man had said, and on the day Peletiah had cried out.

Kate and Helen came to know Danny, a silent, weather-beaten fisherman who spent most of his time cleaning fish but who told them shyly about a pet cat he owned. Another good friend was Captain Sands, who kept in a warehouse all the souvenirs of his sea voyages that his wife refused to have cluttering her house.

When they took Mrs. Kew with them to a circus in nearby Denby, they all had a hilarious time, although the circus turned out to be a droopy and dispirited performance. Their high spirits were dampened for a while when Mrs. Kew recognized the fat lady as a girl who had once been her neighbor in Vermont.

The girls learned to know people all over the countryside as far as their horses would carry them. The person they liked best was Mrs. Bonny, who they thought looked so wild and unconventional that they always felt they were talking to a good-natured Indian.

One family along the coast was so forlorn that the thought of them preyed on the girls' minds all summer. Neither the father nor the mother had health, and there were several little children with whom they had made friends. Early in the fall Kate and Helen went back along the coast to see them. Receiving no answer, they were standing undecided at the door when some neighbors came up to say that the mother had died a short time before. The father, after drinking heavily, was now lying dead, and the children had been parceled out as best they could be. Not daring to go to the funeral, the girls watched it from a distance. They felt that their everyday world was very close to the boundary of death.

Still closer to that boundary was Miss Chauncey of East Parish, a town even smaller and more forgotten than Deephaven. She was a splendid-looking, aristocratic old lady who had been mildly insane but harmless for years. Hers had been a rich and happy childhood until her father lost his fortune during the embargo early in the century. It was said that a sailor to whom he had broken a promise cursed her father and his family. One brother killed himself; another died insane. Miss Chauncey herself had been so ill that her guardian sold all her household goods to pay her hospital bills. Suddenly she became well, her mind unclouded. No one had told her that her house furnishings had been sold. Her shock at seeing the bare house unbalanced her mind again, but she remained harmless. She refused to leave the house and she never seemed to realize that it was bleak and empty. She was still an elegant woman, possessed of unusual worldly advantages; she lived, however, without seeing the poverty of her surroundings. Although she had no idea of time, she always knew when Sunday came. She read the Bible beautifully. Faith sustained her.

By fall Kate and Helen had become so attached to their friends in Deephaven that they postponed their return to Boston as long as possible. Helen thought that, though they might never return, they would always remember their completely happy summer in that old-fashioned village.

THE DEERSLAYER

Type of work: Novel
Author: James Fenimore Cooper (1789-1851)
Type of plot: Historical romance
Time of plot: 1740
Locale: Northern New York State
First published: 1841

Principal characters:
NATTY BUMPPO, called Deerslayer by the Delawares
HURRY HARRY, a frontier scout
CHINGACHGOOK, Deerslayer's Indian friend
THOMAS HUTTER, owner of the lake
JUDITH HUTTER, a girl Thomas Hutter claims as his daughter
HETTY HUTTER, Judith's sister
WAH-TA!-WAH, Chingachgook's beloved

Critique:

There is no question that the savages and the woodsman, Natty Bumppo, come off best in this first of the Leatherstocking Tales. Deerslayer and the Indians, good and bad, are depicted as having codes of honor and morality. Tom Hutter and Hurry Harry are motivated by greed and viciousness in their efforts to obtain Iroquois scalps and in their murder of an innocent Indian girl. The simpleminded Hetty Hutter and Judith, her vain sister, are but two-dimensional characters, however, in this novel of atmosphere and exciting action.

The Story:

Natty Bumppo, a young woodsman known as Deerslayer, and Hurry Harry traveled to the shores of Lake Glimmerglass together. It was a dangerous journey, for the French and their Iroquois allies were on the warpath. Deerslayer was planning to meet his friend Chingachgook, the young Delaware chief, so that they might go against the Iroquois. Hurry Harry was on his way to the lake to warn Thomas Hutter and his daughters that hostile Indians were raiding along the frontier. Harry was accustomed to hunt and trap with Hutter during the summer, and he was an admirer of Hutter's elder daughter, the spirited Judith.

Hutter and his daughters lived in a cabin built on piles in the middle of the lake. Hutter had also built a great, scow-like vessel, known among frontiersmen as the ark, on which he traveled from one shore of the lake to the other on his hunting and trapping expeditions. On their arrival at the lake the two found a hidden canoe. Having paddled out to the cabin and found it deserted, they proceeded down the lake and came upon the ark anchored in a secluded outlet. Hutter had already learned of the Indian raiders. The party decided to take refuge in the cabin, where they could be attacked only over the water. The men managed to maneuver the ark out of the narrow outlet and sail it to the cabin. They had one narrow escape. As the ark was clearing the outlet, six Indians tried to board the boat by dropping from overhanging limbs of a tree. Each missed and fell into the water.

Under cover of darkness, Hutter, Deerslayer, and Hurry Harry took the canoe and paddled to shore to get Hutter's two remaining canoes hidden there. They found the canoes and, on their way back to the ark, sighted a party of Indians camped under some trees. While Deerslayer waited in a canoe offshore, the other two men attacked the Iroquois camp in an attempt to obtain scalps, for which they could obtain bounties. They were captured. Deerslayer, knowing that he was powerless to help them, lay down to sleep in the canoe until morning.

When Deerslayer awoke, he saw that one of the canoes had drifted close to shore. To rescue it, he was forced to shoot an Indian, the first man he had ever killed.

Returning to the fort with his prizes, Deerslayer told the girls of their father's fate. It was agreed that they should delay any attempt at rescue until the arrival of Chingachgook, whom Deerslayer was to meet that night.

Under cover of darkness, the party went in the ark and met Chingachgook at the spot where the river joined the lake. Back in the cabin, Deerslayer explained that the Delaware had come to the lake to rescue his sweetheart, Wah-ta!-Wah, who had been stolen by the Iroquois. Suddenly they discovered that Hetty Hutter had disappeared. The girl, who was somewhat feeble-minded, had cast off in one of the canoes with the intention of going to the Indian camp to rescue her father and Hurry Harry.

The next morning Wah-ta!-Wah came upon Hetty wandering in the forest. She took the white girl to the Iroquois camp. Because the Indians believed deranged persons were protected by the Great Spirit, she suffered no harm.

It was Deerslayer's idea to ransom the prisoners with some rich brocades and carved ivory he and Judith found in Tom Hutter's chest. Its contents had been known only to Hutter and the simple-minded Hetty, but in this emergency, Judith did not hesitate to open the coffer. Meanwhile a young Iroquois had rowed Hetty back to the cabin on a raft. Deerslayer told him that the party in the cabin would give two ivory chessmen for the release of the captives. He was unable to drive quite the bargain he had planned. In the end, four chessmen were exchanged for the men, who were returned that night.

Hetty brought a message from Wah-ta!-Wah. Chingachgook was to meet the Indian girl at a particular place on the shore when the evening star rose above the hemlocks that night. Hurry Harry and Tom Hutter were still determined to obtain scalps, and when night closed in they and Chingachgook reconnoitered

the camp. To their disappointment, they found it deserted and the Indians camped on the beach, at the spot where Wah-ta!-Wah was to wait for Chingachgook.

While Hutter and Harry slept, the Delaware and Deerslayer attempted to keep the rendezvous. Unfortunately, the girl was under such close watch that it was impossible for her to leave the camp. The two men entered the camp and boldly rescued her from her captors. Deerslayer, who remained at their rear to cover their escape, was taken prisoner.

When Judith heard from Chingachgook of Deerslayer's capture, she rowed Hetty ashore to learn what had become of the woodsman. Once more Hetty walked unharmed among the superstitious savages. Deerslayer assured her there was nothing she could do to help, that he must await the Iroquois' pleasure. She left to return to Judith.

As the girls paddled about, trying to find the ark in the darkness, they heard the report of a gun. Torches on shore showed them that an Indian girl had been mortally wounded by a shot from the ark. Soon the lights went out. Paddling to the center of the lake, they tried to get what rest they might before morning came.

When daylight returned, Hutter headed the ark toward the cabin once more. Missing his daughters, he had concluded the cabin would be the most likely meeting place. Hutter and Harry were the first to leave the ark to go into the cabin. There the Iroquois, who had come aboard in rafts under cover of darkness, were waiting in ambush. Harry managed to escape into the water, where he was saved by Chingachgook. Judith and Hetty came to the ark in their canoe. After the savages had gone ashore, those on the ark went to the cabin. They found Hutter lying dead. That evening he was buried in the lake. Hurry Harry took advantage of the occasion to propose to Judith, but she refused him.

Shortly afterward they were surprised to see Deerslayer paddling toward the ark. He had been given temporary liberty in order to bargain with the fugitives. The Iroquois sent word that Chingachgook would be allowed to return to his own people if Wah-ta!-Wah and Judith became brides of Iroquois warriers. Hetty, they promised, would go unharmed because of her mental condition. Although Deerslayer's life was to be the penalty for refusal, these terms were declined.

Deerslayer did not have to return to his captors until the next day, and that evening he and Judith examined carefully the contents of her father's chest. To the girl's wonder, she found letters indicating that Hutter had not been her real father, but a former buccaneer whom her mother had married when her first husband deserted her. Saddened by this knowledge, Judith no longer wished to live at the lake. She intimated slyly to Deerslayer that she loved him, only to find he considered her above him in education and intelligence.

When Deerslayer returned to the Iroquois the next day, he was put to torture with hatchets. Hetty, Judith, and Wah-ta!-Wah came to the camp and attempted to intercede for him, but to no avail. Suddenly Chingachgook bounded in, and cut his friend's bonds. Deerslayer's release was the signal for the regiment from the nearest fort to attack, for Hurry Harry had gone to summon help during the night.

The Iroquois were routed. Hetty was mortally wounded during the battle. The next day she was buried in the lake beside her parents. Judith joined the soldiers returning to the fort. Deerslayer departed for the Delaware camp with Chingachgook and his bride.

Fifteen years later, Deerslayer, Chingachgook, and the latter's young son, Uncas, revisited the lake. Wah-ta!-Wah was long since dead, and, though the hunter inquired at the fort about Judith Hutter, he could find no one who knew her. Rumor was that a former member of the garrison, then living in England on his paternal estates, was influenced by a woman of rare beauty who was not his wife. The ark and the cabin in the lake were falling into decay.

A DEFENSE OF THE CONSTITUTIONS OF GOVERNMENT OF THE UNITED STATES OF AMERICA

Type of work: Political treatise
Author: John Adams (1735-1826)
First published: 1787-1788

This sprawling work consists of John Adams' selections from writings on republican governments ranging from ancient Greece to America of the 1780's, material interspersed with his own maxims and observations on historical characters and events. He excused his faulty arrangement and style on the grounds of "hasty," fourteen-month compilation, prompted by news of Shays' Rebellion in Massachusetts and moves toward revising the constitution of the American union. Some regard the work as possibly the most complete examination into the philosophy and institutions of republicanism by any American.

Adams' purposes were several: to rebut the French *philosophe* Turgot's charge that Americans showed themselves slavish followers of England in their state constitutions, most of which, like that of Adams for Massachusetts, provided for constitutional checks and balances; to show such governments superior to "simple" ones which centralized authority in an omnipotent, unicameral legislature, like those advocated by Turgot and instituted in Pennsylvania by Benjamin Franklin; and to prove by comparing historic forms of republics that their ruin proceeded from improper division of power.

Adams was convinced that, regardless of all differences, governments "move by unalterable rules." He declared his repugnance for absolutism, whether monarchial or egalitarian, basing his argument on the practical grounds that neither gave "full scope to all the faculties of man," enlisted the talents of all citizens, or checked administrative abuses. Instead, he saw absolutisms sowing furtive suspicion which pitted against one another family and family, rich and poor, edu-

cated and ignorant, the gifted and the dull. He espoused a "mixture" of the advantages of democracy, aristocracy, and monarchy. Although his statement of the favorable aspects of aristocracies and monarchies was turned against him by political rivals later on, the *Defense* contains as many strictures against these two forms of government as against democracy. Alleging that "there can be no free government without a democratical branch in the constitution," Adams even said America would be better off to risk civil war arising from improper balance of power in a democratic republic than to establish an absolute monarchy.

Sure that sovereignty was derived from a majority of the mass of people and that a representative branch of the legislature should be organized on democratic principles, Adams feared to trust without restraint all power to the masses. As a check on the representative house, he advocated a senate in terms which have seldom been duplicated. It would be not only a forum where property interests might be defended against leveling tendencies of the representatives, but also an honorable place whither demagogues might be banished by election to render their ambition safe to and their abilities conserved for an empire of liberty. Adams' advocacy of coördinate but independent executive, judicial, and legislative branches of government causes no surprise. He advocated a single executive in order for it to be censorable for administrative abuse. By these forms, he contended, America would realize a practical government of laws and not of men.

Less hopeful of mankind and distrustful of a supposed passion for democracy, Adams denied Turgot's assertion that "a love of democracy is the love of equality,"

862

saying that "every man hates to have a superior . . . [and] no man is willing to have an equal," that "democracy signifies nothing more or less than a nation of people without any government at all, and before any constitution is instituted." Adams deemed "reason, conscience, a regard for justice, and a sense of duty and moral obligation" the only defenses against "desire for fame, and the applause, gratitude, and rewards of the public" as well as "the real friends of equality." He was so confident of the beneficent effects of a republic of mixed characteristics that he averred it would make honest men of knaves from having one rogue to watch another.

Believing that "God and nature" ordained inequalities of wealth, birth, and ability among men, Adams declared there was a natural aristocracy. Not dangerous in itself, he believed it would transform an omnipotent unicameral legislature into an oligarchy or monarchy, destroying *all equality and liberty, with the consent and acclamation of the people themselves.* Believing man more selfish than public-spirited, he would no more trust all of an omnipotent, unicameral legislature than any one man's ambition for gold or power or acclaim. Unless "the rich and the proud" and the representatives of the masses were thrown into separate, coequal assemblies, each could do mischief and neither check the other or an executive.

He declared that "conviction," not "habit," caused Americans to retain their English inheritance of preserving governmental equilibrium by division of powers between executives, two-house legislatures, and a separate judiciary. Only in such institutions did he find hope for avoiding the hypocrisy, superstition, flattery, and corruption which had overturned earlier republics. Advancing from the individual states to the federal government, Adams dismissed the continental congresses under the Articles of Confederation as "only a diplomatic assembly," necessitating that the states themselves have balanced governments to check the aristocratical traits of the congressmen. "Mixing the authority of the one, the few, and the many confusedly into one assembly," said he, created a train of events which would proceed from aristocratical wrangling over offices to "division, faction, sedition, and rebellion." He observed political parties in every country, controlled only by monarchial armies or by "a balance in the constitution." Thinking virtue "too precarious a foundation for liberty," he declared that governments needed power to compel "all orders, ranks, and parties" to "prefer the public good before their own," but that power was surest if based on "reverence and obedience to the laws."

With enthusiasm for the proposed federal constitution, Adams hailed the old confederation as inadequate and the new frame of government, so similar to Adams' own views, to be the "greatest single effort of national deliberation that the world has ever seen."

DEIRDRE

Type of work: Novel
Author: James Stephens (1882-1950)
Type of plot: Legendary romance
Time of plot: The Heroic Age
Locale: Ireland
First published: 1923

Principal characters:
CONACHÚR MAC NESSA, King of Ulster
CLOTHRU, his first wife
MAEVE, his second wife
CATHFA, his father, a magician
LAVARCHAM, his conversation-woman
FERGUS MAC ROY, his stepfather
NESSA, his mother
FELIMID MAC DALL, his story-teller
DEIRDRE, Felimid's daughter, ward of Conachúr
UISNEAC, Conachúr's brother-in-law
NAOISE,
AINNLE, and
ARDAN, Uisneac's sons

Critique:

James Stephens was a brilliant Irish writer of poetry and prose, whose best work was grounded in the early literature of his own country. Just as he attempted to bring Irish folklore to life in *The Crock of Gold,* so he tried to revitalize ancient Gaelic legend in *Deirdre.* In this novel he wrote of the beautiful and mystical Deirdre, of brave and handsome Naoise, and of strong and willful Conachúr, who was loved by all his people and who was almost great. But it is not only the people in the story that are remembered afterward; there are also memorable scenes, like the one of Maeve taking her goods and chattels back to her father's kingdom, or the fight in the Red Branch fortress, or the picture of Deirdre falling dead over Naoise's body just as Conachúr is ready to claim her. *Deirdre* is a novel of legend and fantasy, but there is also a core of realism at its center.

The Story:

The King of Ulster had a daughter who was called Assa, the Gentle. She loved knowledge and had many tutors. One day, returning from a visit to her father and finding her tutors killed, she buckled on her armor and set out to find the murderer. Henceforth her name was Nessa, the Ungentle. While she was bathing in the forest, Cathfa, the magician, saw and loved her. He offered to spare her life only if she would marry him. Their son was Conachúr mac Nessa. After a while Nessa left Cathfa, taking her son with her.

When Conachúr was sixteen, Nessa was still the most beautiful woman in the land. Fergus mac Roy, the new King of Ulster, was only eighteen, but he fell in love with Nessa as soon as he saw her. She promised to marry him only if Conachúr could be king for a year while she and Fergus lived away from court. Fergus agreed, but after the year was up Conachúr kept the throne and Fergus became one of his most trusted followers.

Nessa arranged a marriage between Conachúr and Clothru, daughter of the High King of Connacht. On a visit to her father, Clothru was killed by her sister Maeve. Conachúr's first son was born just before she died.

Bent on vengeance, Conachúr went to

Connacht. There he saw Maeve and, changing his mind, married her against her wishes. When she went to Ulster with him, she took along great riches and also a guard of one thousand men.

During one of his journeys at a time when Maeve had refused to accompany him, he stopped at the house of Felimid mac Dall, his story-teller. That night Conachúr sent a servant to say that Felimid's wife should sleep with him. The servant returned to say that Felimid's wife could not accommodate him as she was then in childbed. Soon the men heard the wail of the newborn infant. Conachúr asked Cathfa, his father, to interpret the wail and other evil omens that men had seen recently. Cathfa prophesied that the child then born, a girl, would be called The Troubler and that she would bring evil and destruction in Ulster. When one of his followers suggested that Conachúr have the child killed immediately, he sent for the infant. But he decided it was not becoming a prince to evade fate, and he let the child live. Deirdre was her name.

Conachúr had Deirdre brought up at Emania by Lavarcham, his conversation-woman, who let the girl see no one but women servants and a guard of the oldest and ugliest swordsmen in Ulster. Lavarcham could adapt herself to any situation or group of people and, while acting as a spy for Conachúr, she also learned everything that had to be taught to Deirdre to prepare her for the place Lavarcham had decided she should have in the kingdom.

Lavarcham reported regularly to Conachúr so that, while he never saw Deirdre, the king knew how she progressed month by month. He refused to believe Lavarcham's glowing reports; besides, at that time, he was well satisfied with Maeve. On the other hand, Lavarcham reported at length to Deirdre about Conachúr until the child knew all his whims, his boldness, and his majesty.

Maeve, who had never forgiven Conachúr for marrying her against her will, finally decided to leave him. She was so unforgiving that she refused to leave behind one thread of her clothes or one bit of her riches. Since some of those riches included great herds of cattle, flocks of sheep, heaps of silver and jewelry, and pieces of furniture, she had to make careful plans to get everything away when Conachúr was not looking. She trusted no one entirely, but she had a spy, mac Roth, who was even more diligent than Conachúr's Lavarcham. He discovered that Conachúr was to take a trip to Leinster; he even followed Conachúr's company for two full days until he felt the group was far enough away to be unable to get back in time; then he returned to help Maeve in her flight. Only Lavarcham guessed that something might happen, but her messengers did not reach Conachúr before Maeve had fled.

Conachúr grieved for Maeve, but he was unable to bring her back to Ulster. In the meantime, Lavarcham began to brood about the matter. The whole kingdom wanted the king to remarry, and Deirdre was sixteen. Lavarcham persuaded the king to come to see Deirdre.

Although Lavarcham had taught Deirdre all that she needed to know about Conachúr, she did not realize that the child thought of the king as an ancient and feared him a little. Nor did Lavarcham know that Deirdre, longing for people of her own age, had learned how to escape the guards around Emania.

Deirdre was first tempted to go beyond the walls to investigate a campfire. Around it she saw three boys: Naoise, who was nineteen; Ainnle, who was seventeen; and Ardan, who was fourteen. They were the sons of Uisneac, who had married Conachúr's sister. Deirdre startled them when she first appeared in the light of the fire, but they all laughed and told so many good stories that she knew she would have to go back again. The younger boys insisted that Naoise would soon be the champion of Ulster, and Deirdre did not doubt it.

When Conachúr went to see Deirdre, he found her the most beautiful girl in Ulster, and he intended to marry her immediately. Lavarcham made him wait a week, after which he would have a three-month feast. Deirdre, in love with Naoise, was horrified at the idea of marrying one so old and huge, but several nights passed before she could make her way to the campfire again. At her pleading, the brothers took her out of the country.

Six years later Conachúr decided that Deirdre and the sons of Uisneac should be brought back from Scotland, where they had found refuge, but the boys would not return except under the protection of one of Conachúr's trusted men. Fergus and his sons were sent to Scotland with assurances of safety. Deirdre had a dream and begged Naoise not to leave, but he declared that Fergus was honorable.

When the travelers reached the coast of Ulster, Fergus was detained by one of Conachúr's men, and Fergus' sons took Deirdre and the sons of Uisneac under their protection. Arriving at Conachúr's court at night, they were lodged in the fortress called the Red Branch. Then Deirdre knew there would be trouble because Conachúr had not received them under his own roof.

Conachúr sent his men to batter down the doors and to bring Deirdre to him. The sons of Uisneac and Fergus made quick sallies, dashing out one door and in another, and killed so many of Conachúr's warriors that at last the king ordered the fortress set afire. As Deirdre and the boys fled, Conachúr asked Cathfa to stop them. Cathfa cast a spell which made the boys drop their arms, and they were captured. Conachúr had Fergus' and Uisneac's sons killed. When Deirdre knelt over Naoise's dead body, she sipped his blood and fell lifeless.

DEIRDRE OF THE SORROWS

Type of work: Drama
Author: John Millington Synge (1871-1909)
Type of plot: Romantic tragedy
Time of plot: The legendary past
Locale: Ireland
First presented: 1910

Principal characters:
DEIRDRE, a heroine of Gaelic legend
NAISI, Deirdre's lover
CONCHUBOR, High King of Ulster
FERGUS, Conchubor's friend
LAVARCHAM, Deirdre's nurse
AINNLE, and
ARDAN, Naisi's brothers
OWEN, Conchubor's attendant and spy

Critique:

Deirdre of the Sorrows, Synge's last play, was never performed until after his death. The play deals with the Irish legendary past, dramatizing an account of the beautiful Irish heroine who preferred death along with her lover to life as the wife of the king. The play is full of this romantic dedication, fully developed in Synge's rich Irish idiom. The language of the Irish peasant is given both power and dignity as it is shaped into the tragic movement of the play. And the play is not without touches of humane characterization. The king is not simply the cruel ruler; he is also a sad and lonely man who deeply regrets the deaths he has caused. Naisi is not simply the martyred hero, but also the husband who rants that his wife has caused him to be a softer man and allowed him to desert the ways of his brothers and his companions in arms. The play contains both the rich warmth of Synge's local and distinctively Irish characterizations and the romantic quality of the legendary.

The Story:

King Conchubor had been keeping Deirdre, the beautiful young girl whom he had resolved to make his bride, at the home of Lavarcham, the old nurse, on Slieve Fuadh. One rainy evening, Conchubor and his friend Fergus arrived to find that Deirdre, to the king's displeasure, was still out gathering nuts and sticks in the woods. Lavarcham warned the king that Deirdre would not be anxious to see him, and she repeated the old prophecy that Deirdre had been born to bring destruction into the world. When Deirdre came in, the king presented her with rings and jewels and remonstrated with her for staying out in the woods. Deirdre defended her behavior and said that she had no desire to go to Emain to become queen.

Conchubor pleaded with her, talking of his loneliness, his love for her, the rooms he had prepared for her in his castle at Emain, but Deirdre insisted that in spite of the fact that she was pledged to Conchubor she would prefer to remain in the simple cottage with Lavarcham as long as possible. Conchubor, growing impatient, insisted that she be ready to go to Emain and become his queen within a few days.

After he left, Lavarcham urged Deirdre to be sensible and bend to Conchubor's wishes, but Deirdre kept talking about other defiant legendary heroines and about the hero, Naisi, and his broth-

DEIRDRE OF THE SORROWS by John Millington Synge, from THE COMPLETE WORKS OF JOHN M. SYNGE. By permission of the publishers, Random House, Inc. Copyright, 1935, by Random House, Inc.

ers, the bravest men in the woods. Deirdre went to dress elegantly for the last night or so of her freedom.

In the meantime Naisi and his brothers arrived at the cottage to take refuge from the storm. Lavarcham was not eager to let them in, but they claimed that a beautiful lady whom they had met in the woods had promised them refuge from the storm. They entered, but Lavarcham, sensing trouble, tried unsuccessfully to get rid of them. They were still in the room when Deirdre returned. Deirdre provided food for Ainnle and Ardan. When they left the cottage she asked Lavarcham to leave also. Alone with Naisi, she told him of Conchubor's imminent suit. Deeply in love by this time, they decided to marry and run away in spite of their knowledge of the troubles foretold. They asked Ainnle, who had returned to the cottage, to marry them before they fled into the night.

Seven years passed during which Deirdre and Naisi, with Ainnle and Ardan, lived happily beside the sea in Alban. One day Lavarcham arrived to announce that Fergus was on his way with peace offerings from King Conchubor and to plead with Deirdre to accept the king's offer. Deirdre insisted on her loyalty to Naisi. Owen, Conchubor's trusted man, arrived with word that Naisi and Fergus were already talking on the path below; he rudely advised Deirdre to leave Naisi and return to the king, for Owen thought that seven years of love were more than enough and that Deirdre would one day be old and yearn for the comfort of the royal palace. The messenger also revealed that he was jealous of Naisi and hated him because he had killed Owen's father some time before.

Fergus, on his arrival, said that Conchubor in his peace offering had invited both Naisi and Deirdre back to Emain in peace. Naisi and Deirdre wondered if they should accept the offer. They talked of age, the possible death of love, and the happiness of their seven years, despite some difficult times, at Alban.

Because they had experienced such perfect years, they decided to accept Conchubor's offer and return to Emain, for they felt they would never know such complete happiness at Alban again. Owen returned, screaming that it was all a plot, and then ran out and split his head against a stone. Believing Owen mad, Naisi and Deirdre accepted Fergus' promise that no trick was involved, and they set out for Emain to meet Conchubor again.

Lavarcham, arriving first to speak with Conchubor, found him a lonely old man. After assuring the king that he could never gain Deirdre's love, she reported that Owen, despairing of ever gaining Deirdre, had run mad and destroyed himself. Conchubor's warriors arrived and reported that they had separated Naisi and Deirdre from Naisi's brothers. When Naisi and Deirdre arrived, they found themselves in a tent. A freshly-dug grave was concealed by curtains next to the tent. They spoke mournfully, for they strongly suspected a plot against them. Conchubor returned, welcomed them, and seemed, in spite of the evidence of the tent, the grave, and warriors lurking nearby, to mean his offer of peace seriously. Then, as he and Naisi were about to clasp hands of friendship, Naisi heard his brothers cry for help. Naisi started to leave, although Deirdre pleaded with him to stay. Naisi cursed the softness of women and ran out. The king's warriors killed Naisi, as they killed his brothers.

Conchubor urged Deirdre to end her mourning for Naisi and become his queen. But Deirdre continued to lament and would have nothing to do with Conchubor. Fergus appeared and announced that he had burned Emain because the king had gone back on his pledge not to harm Naisi. Fergus, who had acted in good faith, tried to protect Deirdre, but Deirdre used Naisi's knife to commit suicide and join him in another world without defiling their love. After Deirdre's death, all mourned. Conchubor, old and broken, was led away by Lavarcham.

DELPHINE

Type of work: Novel
Author: Madame de Staël (Baronne de Staël-Holstein, 1766-1817)
Type of plot: Romantic tragedy
Time of plot: Late eighteenth century
Locale: France
First published: 1802

Principal characters:
DELPHINE D'ALBEMAR, a rich, talented young widow
MATILDA DE VERNON, her kinswoman, daughter of Madame de Vernon
MADAME DE VERNON, Delphine's close friend and confidante
LÉONCE MONDEVILLE, affianced to Matilda de Vernon
MADAME D'ERVIN, a friend of Delphine
MONSIEUR DE SERBELLANE, Madame d'Ervin's lover
MONSIEUR DE VALORBE, in love with Delphine

Critique:

In terms of world literature, this novel is an anachronism. It appears in the form of letters, the epistolary form which, although prevalent seventy years before, was almost outmoded by the time of Madame de Staël. In addition, the tone of the novel is in the sentimental vein of many French and British novels of the first rank in the first half of the eighteenth century. The origin of the sentiment was undoubtedly Rousseau, for whom Madame de Staël had a very high regard. In *Delphine* there is constant reflection of the ideas of Rousseau and other advanced political thinkers and philosophers of the late eighteenth century, for such doctrines as the education of women, political equality, freedom of religious conscience, anti-clericism, and devotion to reason appear constantly in the letters written by Delphine to the other characters in the novel. The novel is, therefore, an index to the temper of Madame de Staël's circle at the time.

The Story:

Delphine d'Albemar was a rich young widow who had been married to her guardian after her father's death. Her husband, who had been her tutor in childhood, had instilled in her the best of sentiments and virtues. As a result of her education, however, she did not wish to submit to the dogmas of society or church. Although she was a member of the French nobility, she was a believer in revolutionary doctrine, a dangerous way of thinking in France during the years immediately preceding the French Revolution. In addition, she, unlike most women of her time and position, refused to let men do her thinking for her. After her husband's death, which occurred in her twentieth year, Delphine was emotionally, intellectually, and financially independent.

Shortly after her husband's death, Delphine proposed giving away a large part of her fortune to Matilda, a relative of her husband and the daughter of Delphine's close friend, Madame de Vernon. Despite the warnings of Mademoiselle d'Albemar, Delphine's sister-in-law, that Madame de Vernon was a very treacherous person, the gift was made so that Matilda could marry Léonce Mondeville, a Spanish nobleman. No one had met Léonce Mondeville, for the marriage had been arranged by Matilda's mother, a long-time friend of the proposed bridegroom's mother.

When Mondeville arrived in Paris, he met his future wife and Delphine. Much to Delphine's dismay, she fell in love with him and he with her. To Delphine, who had bestowed on Matilda the fortune which was making the marriage possible, it seemed that fate had played its worst trick of irony. For a time it seemed as if the two lovers might find a way out of the difficulty. As her confidante in the problem, Delphine took Matilda's own mother, Madame de Vernon. Matilda's mother had no intention of allowing so advantageous a match to slip through her and her daughter's fingers, and she plotted to turn Mondeville against Delphine.

Delphine, meanwhile, had been aiding Madame d'Ervin in a love affair with Monsieur de Serbellane. Because de Serbellane was seen going into Delphine's house late at night, scandal linked her name with his, although he had actually gone there to see Madame d'Ervin. A short time later Madame d'Ervin's husband surprised the two lovers in Delphine's home. When de Serbellane killed the husband in a duel, scandal named Delphine as the woman in the case. Delphine, desiring to keep her friend's honor, did not relate the true cause of the quarrel which had precipitated the duel. Anxious to clear herself with Mondeville, however, Delphine asked Madame de Vernon to act as her friend. Instead of telling what had really happened, the older woman told him that Delphine and de Serbellane were lovers and that Delphine was about to leave France to join de Serbellane in Italy.

Mondeville prepared to marry Matilda, although he did not love her. Although Delphine realized that someone had misrepresented her to her lover, she could find no way to prevent the marriage. Only after the marriage had taken place did Delphine learn that Madame de Vernon's duplicity had caused the rift between herself and Mondeville. At that time, anxious not to hurt Matilda, Delphine promised herself not to see Mondeville and to try to forget her passion for him. Unfortunately, they continued to love one another greatly. A few months later Madame de Vernon, on her deathbed, confessed her guilt.

Feeling themselves cheated, the lovers decided to continue seeing each other, even though their course was dangerous to their honor and unfair to Matilda. Society was soon whispering that Delphine and Mondeville were lovers. Actually, there was nothing immoral in their affair, but society assumed the worst.

De Valorbe, a friend of Delphine's late husband, learned of the state of affairs and resolved to marry her in order to remove her from a compromising situation. His intention aroused Mondeville's jealousy, even though Delphine protested that she did not love de Valorbe and would never marry him. One night de Valorbe went to Delphine's house in the hope that she would hide him from the police. Mondeville saw him there and challenged him to a duel. De Valorbe, hoping to escape from the country before he was imprisoned on political charges, refused to fight. A witness set scandal going once again. Soon everyone believed that the two men had accidentally met while both going to assignations with Delphine, and so her name was publicly dishonored. In addition, de Valorbe's refusal to meet Mondeville placed him in disgrace.

Learning at last that her husband and Delphine were in love, Matilda went to Delphine and revealed that she was to have a child. Delphine, moved by Matilda's pleas, decided to leave France. She went to Switzerland and became a pensionary at a convent which was under the direction of Mondeville's aunt. De Valorbe followed her there and caused her name to become common gossip. When he offered to clear her name by marriage, Delphine refused his proposal and decided to remain in the convent. De Valorbe, moved to distraction, caused his own death, but before he died he cleared Delphine's reputation with Mondeville.

Word came to Mondeville's aunt that Matilda was dying. She, in league with Mondeville's mother, persuaded Delphine to become a nun. They were able to have the pope waive the required year's novitiate. By the time Mondeville went to the convent to claim Delphine, she had already taken her vows.

Meanwhile the republican government had taken over in France and had disallowed the vows of religious orders. Friends persuaded Delphine that she should renounce the vows and return to France to marry her lover. She left the convent, only to discover that public opinion condemned her action. Rather than make her lover live a life of misery, she refused to marry him.

Mondeville went to join the royalist forces fighting against the republican French government, but before he could join them he was captured and sentenced to death as a traitor. Delphine tried unsuccessfully to secure his pardon. When she failed, she took poison and then joined him when he went to the execution ground. She died on the spot where he was to be executed. At first the soldiers refused to shoot Mondeville. Having no desire to live, he taunted them until they picked up their muskets and killed him. Friends took the bodies of Delphine and her lover and buried them side by side, so that they, kept apart in life, might be close in death.

DELTA WEDDING

Type of work: Novel
Author: Eudora Welty (1909-
Type of plot: Regional realism
Time of plot: Early 1920's
Locale: Mississippi
First published: 1946

Principal characters:

LAURA McRAVEN, cousin to the Fairchilds
DABNEY FAIRCHILD, a bride-to-be
ELLEN, her mother
BATTLE, her father
SHELLEY, her sister
GEORGE FAIRCHILD, her uncle
ROBBIE, George's wife
TROY FLAVIN, a plantation manager

Critique:

Delta Wedding is the chronicle of a remarkable family living in Mississippi in the early 1920's. The Fairchilds seemed to draw excitement to them just by doing nothing. Although the plot centers around the preparations for the wedding of one of the Fairchild daughters to a man considered in all ways her inferior, the main theme of the story is in reality the portrayal of this unusual family and a regional way of life. Through the eyes of a child we see the cousins and aunts and great-aunts, all criticizing the others but uniting against any outsider. Life on the Delta is a thing apart from that in other sections of the country, and Eudora Welty has shown in her novel a superb picture of this segment of America.

The Story:

Nine-year-old Laura McRaven made her first journey alone from Jackson to the Delta, to visit her dead mother's people, the Fairchilds. One of her cousins, Dabney Fairchild, was to be married, and Laura's chief regret was that she could not be in the wedding party because of her mother's recent death. She remembered Shellmound, the Fairchild plantation, and knew that she would

have a wonderful time with her exciting cousins and aunts. The Fairchilds were people to whom things happened, exciting, unforgettable things.

At Shellmound, Laura found most of the family assembled for the wedding. Although children her age were her companions, she was aware also of the doings of the grownups. It was obvious that the family was not happy about Dabney's marriage. Her husband-to-be was Troy Flavin, the manager of the plantation, whose inferior social position was the main thing against him. Uncle Battle, Dabney's father, was most of all reluctant to let one of his family go from him, but he could not bring himself to say anything to Dabney, not even that he would miss her. In fact, that seemed to Laura to be a strange thing about her cousins. They seldom talked as a united family, but they always acted as one.

There were so many members of the family that it was hard for Laura to keep them straight. Uncle Battle's wife was Aunt Ellen, and their oldest daughter was Shelley, who was going to be a nun. Again the whole family disapproved of her plan, but there was hardly ever any attempt to get her to change her mind. The obvious favorite was Uncle George,

Battle's brother. Uncle George had also married beneath himself. He and his wife Robbie lived in Memphis, where everyone knew poor Uncle George could never be happy.

When George arrived for the wedding festivities, he was alone and miserable. Robbie had left him, and he had come down alone to see his family. Not wanting to make Dabney unhappy, they did not tell her of Robbie's desertion. The children and the aunts and great-aunts were not told either, although one by one they began to suspect that something was wrong. Ellen could have killed Robbie for making George unhappy, but she kept her feelings to herself except when she was alone with Battle, her husband.

Robbie's anger at her husband began on the afternoon of a family outing. George had risked his life to save one of the cousins, a feeble-minded child caught in the path of a train as they crossed a railroad trestle. After that incident Robbie was never the same with George. She seemed to want him to prove that he loved her more than he loved his family.

Probably Shelley understood the family best. She knew that they had built a wall against the outside world. But she suspected that they were more lonely than self-sufficient. Most people took the family as a group, loving or hating them all together. Only Uncle George seemed to take them one by one, loving and understanding each as an individual. Shelley thought that this was why they all loved Uncle George so much.

Dabney herself seemed to wish for more than she had in her love for Troy. Sometimes she felt left out, as if she were trying to find a lighted window but found only darkness. She loved Troy, but she wanted to feel even more a part of him. She wished also that her family would try to keep her with them, wanted to make certain of their love.

Preparations for the wedding created a flurry. The dresses had been ordered from Memphis, and when some of the gowns failed to arrive there was the usual hubbub among the women, a concern that the men could not appreciate. One of the children fell sick at the last minute, so that Laura was made one of the wedding party after all. Troy's mother sent some beautiful handmade quilts from her mountain shack. Troy felt proud, but the Fairchilds were even more self-consciously and unwillingly ashamed of his background.

After their wedding Dabney and Troy would live at Marmion, an estate owned by the family. Dabney rode over to see the house. Looking at the stately buildings and the beautiful old trees, she knew that best of all she would love being inside it looking out on the rest of the world. That was what she wanted the most, to be inside where she was a part of the light and warmth. That was what marriage must give her.

All the time, unknown to any of the family but Shelley, Robbie was not far away. She had come after George in hopes that he was looking for her. What had almost defeated Robbie was the fear that she had not married George but the whole Fairchild family. It was that fear which had made her angry at the affair on the railroad trestle. Wanting desperately to come first with George, she knew instinctively that he could never set her apart from or above the family. Contrite and humble, she went to Shellmound. The fact that George was not even there at the moment hurt her even more, for she wanted very much for him to be miserable without her. He was, of course, but it was not the Fairchild way to let anyone see his true feelings.

Robbie probably hit the secret of the family when she said that the Fairchilds loved each other because in so doing they were really loving themselves. But of George that fact was not quite true. He was the different one. Because of his gentleness and his ability to love people as individuals, he let Robbie see his love for her without ever saying the words she had longed to hear.

The wedding was almost an anticlimax, a calm scene following gusty storms of feeling. Troy and Dabney took only a short trip, for Troy was needed to superintend the plantation. While they were gone Battle worked the hands hard to get Marmion ready for them. Dabney was anxious to move in, but the move was not so necessary after her marriage as it had seemed before; she no longer felt left out of Troy's life. She thought her life before had been like seeing a beautiful river between high banks, with no way to get down. Now she had found the way and she was at peace. Indeed, the whole family seemed to have righted itself.

When Aunt Ellen asked Laura to live with them at Shellmound, her being wanted by the Fairchilds seemed too wonderful for her belief. Laura knew that she would go back to her father, but still feeling that she really belonged to the Fairchilds seemed like a beautiful dream. She clung briefly to Aunt Ellen, as if to hold close that wonderful moment of belonging.

DESIRE UNDER THE ELMS

Type of work: Drama
Author: Eugene O'Neill (1888-1953)
Type of plot: Romantic tragedy
Time of plot: 1850
Locale: The Cabot farmhouse in New England
First presented: 1924

Principal characters:
EPHRAIM CABOT, a farmer
SIMEON,
PETER, and
EBEN, his sons
ABBIE, his third wife

Critique:

Desire Under the Elms was the last of O'Neill's naturalistic plays and one of his most effective. The structural set, showing the entire farmhouse with one wall removed, was an innovation in its day. In this play O'Neill's daring reduction of human motives to the simple impulses of love, hate, lust, and greed gives an impression of human nature as convincing and complete as the more complex studies of his later, longer plays.

The Story:

When the news of gold discoveries in California reached New England, Simeon and Peter Cabot, who had spent their lives piling up stones to fence their father's farm, became restless. In the summer of 1850 they were ready to tear down the fences which seemed to hem them in, to rebel against their close-fisted old father, and for once in their lives to be free. One day Ephraim Cabot hitched up his rig and drove off, leaving the farm in charge of his three sons, Sim, Peter, and their younger half-brother, Eben. All three sons cordially hated their father because they saw him for what he was, a greedy, self-righteous old hypocrite. The older brothers hated old Ephraim for what he had done to them, but Eben had a further grievance. He hated his father because he had stolen the land which had belonged to his mother, and had then

worked her to death on the farm. Eben felt the farm belonged to him, and he meant to have it. He had inherited some of old Ephraim's stony implacability, as well as his sensuality, and he gave expression to the latter on his trips down the road to visit Minnie, the local prostitute who had belonged to his father before him.

Realizing that Sim and Peter wanted to go to California, yet had no money to take them there, Eben thought up a plan to get rid of them once and for all. During old Ephraim's absence he offered them three hundred dollars apiece in gold if they would sign a paper renouncing all claims to the farm. The money had belonged to Eben's mother, and Eben had found it buried beneath the floorboards of the kitchen. The brothers accepted Eben's offer and set off for California.

Shortly afterward old Ephraim drove home with his third wife. He was seventy-six, she was thirty-five. But Abbie Putnam had decided that she wanted a home of her own. When old Ephraim offered to marry her she accepted him at once, and when she moved into the Cabot homestead she was already determined that whatever happened the farm would be hers someday. She tried unsuccessfully to make friends with Eben. But the thought of another woman's coming to take his mother's place and the farm which rightfully belonged to him made him hate Abbie at first.

After a time Eben began to notice that life on the farm was easier since his stepmother had arrived. But the realization that Abbie could influence his father as she desired only strengthened Eben's determination to resist her attempts to conciliate him. Finally some of his taunts became so pointed that Abbie complained to Ephraim. When she falsely hinted that Eben had been making advances toward her, the old man threatened to kill his son. Realizing that she had gone too far, and that she must make a different approach, Abbie subtly built up in Ephraim's mind the idea that a son and heir who would inherit the farm upon his death would be a better way of getting back at Eben than to kill him outright. The thought that at the age of seventy-six he might have a son flattered the old man, and he agreed to let Eben alone.

One night, after Ephraim had gone out to sleep in the barn, Abbie saw her opportunity to make her hold on the farm secure. She managed to lure Eben into his mother's parlor, a room which had not been opened since her death, and there she seduced him, breaking down his scruples with the suggestion that by cuckolding his father he could get revenge for Ephraim's treatment of his mother.

The result of this move on Abbie's part was the son whom Ephraim wanted as an heir. To celebrate the child's birth, Ephraim invited all the neighbors to a dance in the kitchen of the farmhouse. Many of the guests suspected the true circumstances and said so as openly as they dared. Ephraim paid no attention to the insinuations and outdanced them all until even the fiddler dropped from sheer exhaustion.

While the revelry still was going on the old man stepped outside to cool off. There he and Eben, who had been sulking outside, quarreled over the possession of the farm. Spitefully Ephraim taunted his son with a revelation of how Abbie had tricked him out of his inheritance. Furious, Eben turned on Abbie, threatening to kill her, and telling her he hated her and the child he had fathered when she tricked him with her scheme. But by this time Abbie was genuinely in love with Eben, and, thinking the child was the obstacle which was keeping them apart, she smothered it in an effort to prove to her lover that it was he and not the child she wanted. When he discovered what had happened, Eben was both enraged and shocked, and he set off to get the sheriff for Abbie's arrest.

When Ephraim discovered that Abbie had killed the child that was not his, he too was shocked, but his heart filled with contempt at his son's cowardice in giving Abbie over to the law.

On his way to the farm Eben began to realize how much he loved Abbie, and the great love she had shown for him in taking the child's life. When the sheriff came to take Abbie away, he confessed that he was an accomplice in the crime. The two were taken off together, both destined for punishment, but happy in their love. Ephraim Cabot was left alone with his farm, the best farm in the county. It was, the sheriff told him, a place anybody would want to own.

DESTINY BAY

Type of work: Short stories
Author: Donn Byrne (Brian Oswald Donn-Byrne, 1889-1928)
Type of plot: Regional romance
Time of plot: Early twentieth century
Locale: Ireland
First published: 1928

Principal characters:
SIR VALENTINE MACFARLANE, lord of Destiny Bay
JENEPHER, his blind sister
KERRY, his nephew and heir
JAMES CARABINE, his valet and friend
JENICO HAMILTON, Kerry's cousin
ANN-DOLLY, Jenico's wife
PATRICK HERNE, Jenepher's husband
COSIMO, Sir Valentine's brother
ANSELO LOVERIDGE, Cosimo's friend

Critique:

Reading Donn Byrne's short stories is like being lifted up out of a flat country and being set down in a wonderfully clean, colorful, and powerful land. There the characters are courtly, their stories full of courage, humor, and skill. *Destiny Bay* is a series of nine of these stories, differing greatly in length, told by Kerry Macfarlane, heir to Destiny Bay, a house and a district in the north of Ireland. This place is a region of high hills, wild ocean, sun, and heather; the characters are equally bold, wild, warm, and beautiful.

The Story:

Kerry's uncle, Sir Valentine Macfarlane, lord of Destiny Bay, with his great fan-shaped red beard that came to his waist, was the courtliest and most hospitable of men. In twenty minutes he had persuaded the old Duke of la Mentera and his grandson that he could not allow Spanish royalty to stay at the Widow McGinty's village hotel when there was room and plenty at Destiny Bay. With the simplicity which comes with great age, the duke said that his life had been full of many turnings; now he was on the last path and he had come hoping to find a treasure chest, said to have been lost when one of his ancestors was killed off the Irish coast after Drake's defeat of the Armada. His grandson must be provided for; he had nowhere else to turn.

Aunt Jenepher, beautiful, blind, but seeming to see people better than anyone, said the duke and Don Anthony, his grandson, were noble and good, and she treated them with that kindness of hers which went straight to the heart.

A short time later the duke died, leaving his girlish-looking grandson to the Macfarlanes' several cares—the courtliness of Uncle Valentine, the trust of his valet, James Carabine, the kindness of Aunt Jenepher, and Kerry's companionship. That friendship was not always pleasing to Don Anthony, since he could not bear to see their prize fights or cock fights, though he was beside himself with joy at their horse races. But it was Jenico for whom the boy conceived a hero worship.

Jenico was not a large man like Uncle Valentine, but he had that look of burnished strength which made women try to get his attention, and he was innately courteous, though his mind might be a thousand miles away. His home was near Destiny Bay and nearer Spanish Men's Rest, that spot where the Spaniards were buried after their ships had been wrecked.

For a long time the bees and birds had shunned the place, and it was a chill on the heart to go there. But when Jenico and Kerry took Don Anthony to Spanish Men's Rest, they heard the bees and birds again and the place seemed sunnier.

Jenico, trying to get the boy's mind off the settlement of the grandfather's estate, finally asked him to take off with him on a trip to the Atlas Mountains. The boy was flattered and obviously wanted to go, but begged off. Shortly after, as the three walked near the river, Jenico and Kerry decided to go swimming. Jenico went on ahead and Kerry could see his head like that of a sleek seal in the waves. When Kerry started to strip, Don Anthony begged him not to take off his clothes. Jenico laughed and told Kerry to strip the boy and throw him in. Kerry headed for the boy. Don Anthony flashed a knife, then ducked away. As Kerry turned to follow him, there was Uncle Valentine, roaring that there was once a time when a lady could be trusted amongst Irishmen.

With a change of clothes, Ann-Dolly, as she asked to be called, was one of the loveliest girls they had ever seen, and there was a new spirit in her. So that she would feel free to stay, they made her companion to Aunt Jenepher. At that time her relations with Jenico were strained, but whenever they were in a room together she would look at him when he was not looking, and then he would look at her when she had turned away.

Jenico tried a fool scheme of planting treasure for her to find, but he and Kerry had a fight about that and he never told her. Finally she had enough of the Macfarlanes and ran away in the night. Jenico and James Carabine and Kerry used horses, bicycles, and even bloodhounds to follow her. At last they found her huddled in an old ruin. She was deathly white and scared, and nothing they did could make her move. James

Carabine plucked Kerry's sleeve, suggesting that they return the horses, the bicycles, the dogs they had borrowed, but Kerry brushed him off. Finally Carabine picked Kerry up like a feather and forcibly carried him out, to leave Jenico and Ann-Dolly together.

After Ann-Dolly became mistress of Jenico's house, the birds always sang and the bees knew it was a fair and happy home.

One never knew what or whom Uncle Valentine might bring back from a trip. One of the kindest of men was Patrick Herne, a man who looked like a double for Digory Pascoe, who was to have married Aunt Jenepher after he made his fortune. Digory had died in a fight, but Uncle Valentine had kept him alive for twelve years by writing letters from him, until he found Patrick Herne and brought him home as Digory. Aunt Jenepher played along for a while until she had to ask who the man really was who thought just as she did. Theirs was a happy wedding.

One time Uncle Valentine went off to America to find James Carabine, who had once saved his life. James Carabine was the Irish champion in the prize ring when he had an urge to sail to America to take care of a drunken friend. Because the friend died at sea, he was lonesome in New York and married a hard-faced and, as it turned out, two-faced singer whose friends ran illegal fights in and around the city. When Uncle Valentine found him, he had taken to drink after losing a bad fight and his wife; but he regained his self-respect and rewon his title before Uncle Valentine took him home. There was no more devoted valet and friend in Ireland than Uncle Valentine's James Carabine.

It was not only Uncle Valentine who traveled distances to help a friend. Anselo Loveridge, the gipsy whom Uncle Valentine's brother Cosimo saved from the hangman's noose, worried about Uncle Cosimo's heavy drinking, brought on,

Uncle Cosimo told him, because of a Chinese girl he called the Fair Maid of Wu, whom he had seen three times and never spoken to. Anselo disappeared for six years, and when he came back he brought the Chinese girl as a present to Uncle Cosimo. Having lost his heart in those hard years, he would not wait to see Uncle Cosimo, but continued his wanderings. Uncle Cosimo was happy, his pocket bulging with his big flask, when he went to see what Anselo had brought. After one look his head cleared and he turned on his heel and left the country. From that day he worked to reclaim drunks in the slums of London and became so straight-laced that he was made Bishop of Borneo.

THE DEVIL'S ELIXIR

Type of work: Novel
Author: Ernst Theodor Amadeus Hoffmann (1776-1822)
Type of plot: Psychological fantasy
Time of plot: Eighteenth century
Locale: Germany and Italy
First published: 1815-1816

Principal characters:
MEDARDUS, a monk
AURELIA, a young noblewoman
FRANCESCO, a painter
PRINCE VON ROSENTHURM
COUNT VICTORIN, Medardus' brother
LEONARDUS, a prior
AN ABBESS
PIETRO BELCAMPO, a hairdresser

Critique:

E.T.A. Hoffmann was a writer, musician, and artist whose stories will be remembered for their presentation of the bizarre as an ironic facet of the natural. Hoffmann took evident pleasure in creating odd situations and weaving out of them a confusing and fantastic web of associations, intimations, and recapitulations, all made grotesque, of what had gone before. For example, Medardus is an insane priest who finds himself in a devilish hall of distorted mirrors. As soon as a reasonable pattern begins to emerge from the course of events, a new mystery rises to destroy it. The story deals with an innocent who has sinned and who is then confronted by all the devices of the powers of darkness.

The Story:

Francis was born at the Convent of the Holy Lime-Tree in Prussia, at the very moment that his father lay dying. At Kreuzberg, the abbess of the Cistercian convent made him her pupil. When he was sixteen he became a monk at the Capuchin convent in Königswald and took the name of Medardus.

Medardus was put in charge of the relics of the convent. Among them was a strange elixir. Legend said that all who drank of the potion would belong to the devil, and that if two persons drank of it, they would share the same thoughts and desires but secretly wish to destroy each other.

On St. Anthony's Day Medardus preached a sermon about the elixir. While he was talking he saw in the audience a painter whom he had once seen at the Convent of the Holy Lime-Tree. The sight disturbed him so much that he began to rave like a madman. Later, in an attempt to regain his full senses, he drank some of the elixir.

One day, during the confessional a beautiful woman, in appearance exactly like a painting of St. Rosalia, told Medardus that she loved him, and then left. Medardus determined to run away to find her. Before he could escape from the convent, however, Prior Leonardus sent him on an errand to Rome.

On the way to Rome Medardus saw an officer leaning over a precipice. When Medardus tried to save him, the officer fell over the ledge. Just then a page appeared and told Medardus that his disguise was very good. Medardus, hardly knowing what he did, went to the nearby castle, where he met an old man, Reinhold, who seemed to be expecting him. Reinhold told him that Baron von F———, the owner of the castle, had a son, Hermogen, and a daughter, Aurelia, by an Italian wife who later died. The baron

880

had then married Euphemia, a sinister woman who was carrying on an affair with Count Victorin, an ex-suitor. The count was in the habit of disguising himself in order to gain entrance to the castle.

Medardus became convinced that he was Victorin. When he saw that Aurelia was the mysterious lady who looked like St. Rosalia, he felt that fate was guiding him. He tried to approach Aurelia, but she ran away. Because Hermogen had witnessed the incident, Medardus killed him. As Medardus fled from the castle, he heard that Euphemia was dying of a poison she had intended for him. Taking refuge in the woods, Medardus cut off his beard and changed into clothes that Victorin's page had brought him.

When Medardus arrived in Frankenburg, he recognized the painter who had disturbed his sermon on St. Anthony's Day. After he had tried to kill the man with a stiletto, Medardus was rescued from an angry mob by Pietro Belcampo, an odd hairdresser.

At the forest house of the Prince von Rosenthurm, Medardus met a monk who looked like him and who drank some of his elixir. Medardus later went to the castle, where the court physician showed him a picture of a person who again looked just like him. The man was Francesco, who, together with a strange painter, had been brought to the court by the prince's brother, the Duke of Neuenburg. The duke had become engaged to an Italian countess and married her, but on their wedding night the duke had been found murdered by a stiletto wound. The bride claimed, however, that the groom had come to the bridal chamber without a light, consummated the marriage, and left. The painter, accused of the murder, escaped, and the countess went to live in a distant castle.

Francesco was engaged to the sister of the princess. During the marriage ceremony the painter reappeared. Francesco, trying to kill the painter with a stiletto, fainted. The next day he left, still un-

wed. It was later learned that the Italian countess had given birth to a son named Victorin. Francesco's intended bride left to become the abbess at Kreuzberg.

Hearing these tales, Medardus realized that Francesco must be his father. At a party that night Medardus was astonished to see that the princess was accompanied by Aurelia. When Aurelia recognized him, he was charged with the murder of Hermogen and imprisoned. Later he was released because his double, a mad monk who greatly resembled him, had confessed to the crime. Medardus also learned that he and Victorin were stepbrothers.

Medardus became engaged to Aurelia. On the day that he was to marry her he saw the mad monk being taken to the scaffold. Suddenly Medardus began to rave. In his frenzy he stabbed Aurelia, rescued the monk from the cart, and escaped into the woods. When he regained consciousness he found himself, dressed as a monk, in an Italian madhouse. He had been taken there by Belcampo, the hairdresser, who said that he had found Medardus in the woods, naked, with a monk's robe lying beside him.

Medardus went next to a Capuchin convent near Rome. While there, he learned that Aurelia was alive. He also saw a strange book that a mysterious painter left at the convent. It contained sketches of paintings Medardus had seen at the Convent of the Holy Lime-Tree and the history of the artist. He was Francesco, a painter who had drunk of St. Anthony's elixir.

Among his works, according to the account, was a painting of the martyrdom of St. Rosalia. One day he had met a woman who looked just like the painting. They married, but his wife died soon after their son was born. Then Francesco, accused of sorcery, fled with his child, whom he nourished on the elixir. From Francesco's son the family branched out and included the Princess von Rosenthurm, the abbess, the first

Baroness von F——, Euphemia, and Victorin.

Medardus, now repenting his past, punished himself so much that he became known to the Pope, who spoke of making the monk his confessor. Having incurred the antagonism of the papal confessor in this manner, Medardus, realizing that his life was in danger, left Rome.

He returned to the Cistercian monastery and saw Prior Leonardus, who said that Victorin had come there, claimed to be Medardus, and then disappeared. By piecing together the strange sequences of events, Medardus and Leonardus realized that Medardus and Victorin, two brothers who had drunk of the elixir, had tried to destroy each other.

Leonardus also told Medardus that Aurelia was to become a nun that day, taking the conventual name of Rosalia. This news so disturbed Medardus that while Aurelia was taking her vows he had an impulse to stab her, but after an inward struggle he conquered his demon and had peace in his soul. Suddenly there was a disturbance in the church. Medardus' double, dressed in rags, ran to the altar, shouted that Aurelia was his intended bride, stabbed her in the heart, and escaped. Medardus rushed to Aurelia's side. Close by he saw the mysterious painter, who said that Medardus'

trials would soon end. Aurelia regained consciousness, told Medardus that he and she were destined to expiate the guilt of their family, and then died. The people in the church, having seen the painter emerge from a picture over the altar, believed that a miracle had occurred; they regarded Aurelia, now called Rosalia, as a saint.

Medardus, having fully recovered, could clearly tell truth from falsehood, and from Leonardus and the abbess he received forgiveness for his past deeds. Leonardus then asked him to commit his life story to writing. Having completed this task, he was awaiting the time when he would join Aurelia in Heaven.

Father Spiridion, the librarian of the Capuchin monastery at Königswald, appended a note to Medardus' manuscript. He wrote that one night, hearing strange sounds from Medardus' cell, he investigated and saw a tall man who said that the hour of fulfillment would come soon. Then Medardus died, one year to the minute from the time of Aurelia's death. Father Spiridion added that the painting of St. Rosalia, which the monastery had acquired, bore, on the day of Medardus' funeral, a wreath of roses. The wreath had been put there by Pietro Belcampo, who later joined the order and became Brother Peter.

THE DEVOTION OF THE CROSS

Type of work: Drama
Author: Pedro Calderón de la Barca (1600-1681)
Type of plot: Religious tragedy
Time of plot: Seventeenth century
Locale: Siena, Italy
First presented: c. 1633

Principal characters:
EUSEBIO, a foundling
JULIA, his sister
LISARDO, his brother
CURCIO, their father
GIL, a peasant
MENGA, a peasant woman
ALBERTO, a priest

Critique:

To understand a religious play like *The Devotion of the Cross*, one must always keep in mind that Spain was, and still is, a deeply religious nation, and that Calderón most truly expressed its feelings and ideas in the seventeenth century. The most popular of Spanish playwrights after the death of Lope de Vega in 1635, he wrote both secular and religious dramas until he took holy orders in 1651. From that time until his death he wrote only religious plays, including two Corpus Christi plays a year. *The Devotion of the Cross* is one of his early works. Since the characters and the setting are Italian, some critics assign it to the period when he was a soldier in Italy. Another version called *The Cross in the Sepulchre* has been found in a rare "suelta," or play printed separately, undated but signed "Ivan de Alarcón." Its discoverer believes that Calderón used it as a basis for his improved version. Valbuena Prat, on the other hand, wonders whether it may be a later version of Calderón's play, done by a less skilled dramatist. Another version of it, assigned—as was practically every other unclaimed play during the Golden Age—to Lope de Vega, can be found in a collection dated 1634. All that is definite is that Calderón claimed it under its present title in his *Primera Parte* of 1636. The plot is less complicated than is usual in Calderón's work.

The Story:

Two rustics, Gil and Menga, were looking for a lost donkey when they spied two men preparing to fight a duel. One was Lisardo, angry that anyone as low-born as Eusebio should aspire to marry his sister Julia.

Eusebio explained by telling a miraculous story. He had been one of two infants abandoned beneath a wayside cross. Taken home by a shepherd, the famished baby bit the breast of his foster mother, who threw the child into a well where his rescuers found him floating safely with arms crossed. Later the house in which he was living burned, but the fire broke out on the Day of the Cross, and once more he survived unharmed. More recently, in a shipwreck, he had floated to safety on a raft of two crossed planks. He explained that since he had obviously acquired nobility by devotion to the cross, he deserved the girl. Lisardo denied the claim and they fought. Again nothing could harm Eusebio. As Lisardo lay dying of his wound, he begged in the name of the cross for Eusebio to save him. The amazed peasants reported that they had seen Eusebio pick up his dying enemy and carry him to a convent.

Back in Siena, Julia was fearful of her father's discovery of letters she had received from Eusebio. When her lover appeared, wanting to take her away with him before she learned about her brother's death, her father's arrival forced him to hide and listen to Curcio as he voiced his long-held suspicions of his wife's infidelity. Curcio was interrupted by the arrival of four peasants carrying the body of Lisardo. Julia, grieving, ordered the killer out of her life forever.

Eusebio, broken-hearted, turned bandit and through his cruelty rose to command a troop of outlaws. Only captives mentioning the cross escaped death at his hands. One day a bullet-creased prisoner was brought in carrying a volume titled *Miracles of the Cross*. He was Father Alberto, and in gratitude for having his life spared the priest promised Eusebio that he would be on hand to hear the bandit's last confession.

News arrived that Lisardo's father, having put Julia into a convent, was pursuing Eusebio with soldiers. Scorning danger, Eusebio let his passion for Julia take him to the convent, where he found the girl in bed. Before he could take her, he saw on her breast the same sign of the cross that was on his own skin. The mark told him that she had been the other child left beside the cross, his sister, and so he ran away. Julia, who had tried to fight him off in her cell, now pursued him in masculine attire; she did not know why he refused to love her.

When the soldiers overtook him, Curcio wounded Eusebio fatally. Then the cross on the young man's body revealed to Curcio that he had slain his own son, exposed with his twin sister because of the father's baseless suspicions of his wife's unfaithfulness.

With his dying breath, Eusebio called for Father Alberto. Four shepherds arrived to bury his body. The priest also appeared as he had promised. He explained that because of God's pleasure in Eusebio's devotion to the cross, his soul had been left in his body long enough for him to make his confession and be redeemed.

LE DIABLE BOITEUX

Type of work: Novel
Author: Alain René Le Sage (1668-1747)
Type of plot: Picaresque romance
Time of plot: Early eighteenth century
Locale: Madrid
First published: 1707

Principal characters:
DON CLEOPHAS LEANDRO PEREZ ZAMBULLO, a student
ASMODEUS, the demon in the bottle
DON PEDRO DE ESCOLANO, a Spanish nobleman
DONNA SERAPHINA, his daughter

Critique:

Le Sage is chiefly remembered today for his long picaresque novel, *Gil Blas* (1715-1735), but his early publication of *Le Diable boiteux* (*Asmodeus; or, The Devil on Two Sticks*), with its extensive revision and enlargement in 1725, created far more excitement in his own day and is still an interesting example of the early realistic novel of manners. As he did in most of his prose fiction, Le Sage worked from a Spanish original in this work, borrowing his title and some of the early incidents from *El Diablo Cojuelo* (1641), by Luis Vélez de Guevara. Once started, however, Le Sage drew further and further away from his Spanish beginnings and thereby entertained his contemporaries by introducing a wealth of anecdotes and reminiscences, portraits and sketches of some of the most prominent of Parisian personages, under the guise of Spanish names. His satire is trenchant and ironical, though never gross or vulgar. Le Sage saw humanity with a sharp and critical eye, and he was particularly successful in his witty portrayals of authors, actors, lawyers, the social world, and "persons of quality." Like most picaresque fiction, the novel is loosely plotted; within a central narrative concerning the fortunes of Don Cleophas, a young Spanish cavalier, Le Sage introduced scores of other tales, ranging from brief summaries of a few sentences to short stories running for several pages or chapters. But the major plot remains in evidence throughout the book, and the author concludes his tale with a suitably romantic ending.

The Story:

On a dark October night in Madrid, Don Cleophas Leandro Perez Zambullo, a student of Alcala, was in dreadful trouble. While visiting Donna Thomasa, his inamorata, in her apartment, three or four hired bravos set upon him, and when he lost his sword in the ensuing struggle, he was forced to take flight over the rooftops of the neighboring houses. Spying a light in a garret, he entered through a window and discovered an empty room furnished with all manner of a magician's strange gear. As he was taking stock of the place, he heard a sigh. Soon he realized that he was being addressed by a demon in a bottle. To the student's questionings the spirit replied that he was neither Lucifer, Uriel, Beelzebub, Leviathan, Belphegor, nor Ashtaroth, but Asmodeus, the Devil on Two Sticks, who always befriended hapless lovers.

Welcoming the help of this creature, Cleophas broke the vial, and out tumbled a monstrous dwarf, with the legs of a goat, a stature of less than three feet, and a grotesque and grimacing face. Half concealed by extraordinary clothing and a curiously embroidered white satin cloak were the two crutches on which the dwarf hobbled about.

Since Cleophas was eager to escape his pursuers and Asmodeus wished to avoid his captor, the magician, the two did not

885

linger in the attic. Cleophas grasped the edge of the demon's cloak, and off they flew into the sky over Madrid. For the remainder of their association together, Asmodeus entertained his companion with views of all that was happening in the city, explaining the circumstances and characteristics of those into whose houses they looked.

At first they peered into the houses immediately beneath them. Asmodeus showed Cleophas some ridiculous views of a coquette and her artifices, a nobleman, a poet, and an alchemist. At last they came to a mansion where cavaliers and their ladies were celebrating a wedding. The demon proceeded to tell the story of the Count de Belflor and Leonora de Cespedes.

The Count de Belflor, a gallant of the court, fell in love with Leonora de Cespedes and wished to make her his mistress. By guile, the gift of a well-filled purse, and the promise of another thousand pistoles when he had accomplished his design, he secured the aid of her duenna, Marcella, who at last prevailed on the girl to admit the young nobleman to her chamber at night. One morning, as the count was making a hasty departure, for the dawn was breaking, he slipped and fell while descending the silken ladder lowered from Leonora's bedchamber, and the noise awakened Don Luis de Cespedes, her father, who slept in the room above. Uncovering the truth and affronted by this stain upon his family honor, the old don confronted his daughter's lover. The count offered to provide for Don Pedro, the son of the insulted father, but refused to marry the daughter, giving as his false excuse a marriage which the king had already arranged for the young courtier.

Later, after reading a reproachful letter written by Leonora, the count was moved to repentance. About the same time Don Pedro played truant from his studies at Alcala to pay court to an unknown young beauty whom he was meeting in secret. In a street brawl his life was saved by the count, who happened to be passing by. The count asked the young man to go with him to act as a watchman and guard while Belflor had an interview with Leonora. The truth being revealed when Don Luis confronted his son, the count asked for the hand of Leonora and bestowed that of his sister, Donna Eugenia, on his new friend and brother. Don Pedro was overjoyed when he in turn discovered that his secret love was the sister of the Count de Belflor. The two couples were married, and Cleophas, guided by the demon, witnessed the festivities of their double wedding. Only Marcella, the treacherous duenna, had no part in the mirth; Don Luis sent her to a nunnery where she could spend her ill-gotten pistoles and prayers to win pardon for her wickedness.

Directing Cleophas' attention to other homes in the city, Asmodeus showed him the plight of an impoverished marquis, a plagiarizing author, a procurer of young men for rich widows, and a printer of anti-religious books. At Cleophas' request, the dwarf secured revenge for his mortal companion on the faithless Donna Thomasa. As she was entertaining the assassins she had hired to attack Cleophas, Asmodeus put the men into a jealous rage over her and set them to fighting. So great was the disturbance they caused that neighbors summoned the police, who on their arrival found two of the men slain. The assassins were thrown into the city dungeon and Donna Thomasa was eventually sentenced to be transported to the colonies. Thus proud Cleophas had his revenge.

Next, Asmodeus revealed the circumstances of the wretches in the nearby prison and madhouse. Poisoners, assassins, servants falsely accused and servants deserving imprisonment, a dishonest surgeon, and others were all displayed in their cells. At the madhouse, Cleophas saw political and religious fanatics, as well as those maddened by jealousy, grief, and the ingratitude of their relatives. Asmodeus also took the opportunity of showing Cleophas other people who should have been confined in an insane asylum, for their brains were addled by avarice, egotism, and the uncontrollable pangs of love.

Suddenly from their vantage point above the city, the two glimpsed a raging fire in a house beneath them. To everyone's horror, the beautiful Donna Seraphina, daughter of Don Pedro de Escolano, was trapped in an upstairs room. Asmodeus, at the entreaties of Cleophas, assumed the shape and appearance of the young student and brought the girl out of the burning building safely. After the rescue Asmodeus told Cleophas that he had suddenly decided upon a grand design: the young man was ultimately to marry the lovely Donna Seraphina, whose noble father already believed himself deeply indebted to the handsome young cavalier.

Asmodeus continued this strange tour of Madrid with portrayals of the unrevealed secrets of those buried in the tombs of a churchyard and with glimpses of bedside death scenes of true grief, avarice, jealousy, and self-seeking. For contrast, he then told Cleophas a long and circumstantial tale of true friendship and love.

Having slain his false wife's lover, Don Juan de Zarata, a gallant of Toledo, fled to Valencia. Near the outskirts of that city he stopped a duel between Don Alvaro Ponzo and Don Fabricio de Mendoza, rivals for the hand of the beautiful young widow, Donna Theodora de Cifuentes. On the advice of Don Juan, the lady was allowed to choose between her suitors; her choice was Don Fabricio. Through that meeting the young Toledan and Don Fabricio became inseparable companions. The latter, however, could not understand his friend's seeming indifference to the charms of Donna Theodora. What he did not suspect was that the Toledan had been greatly attracted to the lady and she to him, but that out of regard for friendship Don Juan made every effort to repress his passion. Un-

happy in her own unrealized love for Don Juan, the lady finally decided to return to her estate at Villareal. When the Toledan confessed the truth to Don Fabricio, that gentleman was so moved by Don Juan's delicacy of feeling that he vowed no rivalry in love could ever part them.

Meanwhile, Donna Theodora had been kidnapped by Don Alvaro's ruffians and put on a vessel bound for Sardinia. Don Fabricio and Don Juan set out in pursuit, but the ship on which they sailed was overtaken by Tunisian pirates and the two were made prisoners. Separated in their captivity, they were in despair. Don Juan, sold to the Dey of Algiers, was made a gardener. At length the dey, impressed by the bearing and courtesy of his Christian slave, made him his confidant. The dey had in his harem a Spanish lady whose grief appeared inconsolable; he asked Don Juan to speak to her as a countryman and assure her of her master's tender regard. To Don Juan's surprise, the lady proved to be Donna Theodora, also taken captive when her abductors were killed by Algerian pirates.

From that time on Don Juan planned to deliver Donna Theodora from her captivity, and at last, aided by an unknown accomplice, they made their escape. Their unknown benefactor turned out to be Don Fabricio, who had been rescued aboard a French privateer. Mistaking Don Juan for the false Don Alvaro, Don Fabricio stabbed his friend and then, discovering his error, plunged his sword into his own breast. The condition of Don Fabricio grew worse and he died soon after the arrival of the fugitives in Spain. Torn between their mutual love and grief for their friend, Donna Theodora and Don Juan were at last free to marry. A short time later Don Juan was mortally injured in a fall from his horse. Half mad with grief, Donna Theodora would soon follow him to the grave.

At length the sleeping city awoke. Protesting that he was not weary, Cleophas urged the little demon to let him see more. Asmodeus directed his glance to the activities in the streets of beggars, artisans, a miser, a philosopher. Then they came upon the throngs of people gathering for the king's levee: faithless and forgetful noblemen, those seeking their own good fortune, gamblers, an honest magistrate, and others awaited their turn to appear before the king. But Cleophas could not be shown into the king's presence, since the royal cabinet, as Asmodeus carefully explained, was under the exclusive control of other devils.

For diversion, Asmodeus took Cleophas to see the arrival of ransomed slaves at the Monastery of Mercy. Each captive had his own fears and hopes to realize, and Asmodeus recounted the past and future of scores of these wretches. A few met with happy circumstances upon gaining their freedom, but most of them found grief, loneliness, and disappointment for their reward.

At that point Asmodeus became aware that his master, the magician, had missed him, and he departed swiftly after making the student promise that he would never reveal to mortal ears all that he had seen and overheard that night.

Returned to his own apartment, Cleophas sank into a deep slumber that lasted a day and a night. When he awoke, he went to call on Donna Seraphina, where he was welcomed by the grateful Don Pedro, her father. During a later visit in the house where he was now an honored guest, Cleophas confessed that it was not he who had rescued the girl from the flames. Although overcome by astonishment, Don Pedro waved the explanation aside. After all, it was at Cleophas' insistence that Donna Seraphina had been brought from the blazing house unharmed. A few weeks later the wedding of Donna Seraphina and Cleophas was celebrated with much magnificence, and the happy bridegroom never had occasion to regret the night of freedom he had provided for the devil on two sticks.

DIALOGUE DES HÉROS DE ROMAN

Type of work: Literary criticism in the form of satiric dialogue
Author: Nicolas Boileau-Despréaux (1636-1711)
First published: 1713

Principal characters:
MINOS,
PLUTO,
RHADAMANTHUS,
DIOGENES, and
MERCURY, judges of the heroes
CYRUS,
TAMYRIS,
HORATIUS COCLES,
CLÉLIE,
BRUTUS,
SAPHO, and
FARAMOND, heroes and heroines of French romances

The French literary scene of the late seventeenth and early eighteenth centuries was blessed with the corrective vigorous activity of two writers endowed with unsurpassed wit and common sense—Molière and Boileau. It was an age that desperately needed the scourge of satire. Life and letters were thoroughly corrupt; the topmost level of society rode like a gaudy, grinning monkey on the back of the miserable, millipedic populace, and the amusements of the idle betrayed clearly their innocent or deliberate unawareness of reality and the bizarre lengths to which they were willing to go in their futile attempt to conquer an enormous boredom.

One of their most fantastic solitary diversions was the writing and reading of romantic novels that often ran to a dozen or more volumes. Beginning with Honoré d'Urfé's *Astrée* (1607-1627), this papier-mâché fantasy went through a tortuous evolution in de Gomberville's *La Carithée* (1621) and *Polexandre* (1629-1637), Jean Desmarets' *Ariane* (1623), La Calprenède's *Cassandre* (1642-1650), *Cléopâtre* (1647-1658), and *Faramond* (1661-1670), and, finally, reached an apogee in the four romances of Mademoiselle Madeleine de Scudéry, darling of the famous Hôtel de Rambouillet salon before establishing her own popular Saturday nights. These novels probably constitute

the most valueless literature of all time. Mlle. de Scudéry insisted that the language of her characters (like that of the dramatists Racine and Corneille) reproduce exactly the language of society, a carefully cultivated, artificial speech striving for novelty and preciosity and inevitably tumbling into absurdity. It is precisely this affectation that Molière made such hilarious fun of in his farce, *Les Précieuses Ridicules* (1659), but apparently the institution was so well-established and so satisfying to its practitioners that not even the blows of the great Molière could strike it down. Boileau soon joined his friend in the attack, composing in 1664 his *Dialogue des héros de roman*, which he enjoyed reciting with great zest and elaborate mimicry to his friends. However, as he says in the preface to his first published version, he was unwilling to publish or even to circulate his satire in manuscript while Mlle. de Scudéry was still alive, "since she was after all a woman of considerable merit and honor even if her writing did not reflect those attributes." Even after her death, the satire would probably not have appeared in print with Boileau's blessing had not a pirated version been published anonymously in Prussia in 1687. Boileau's devoted young friend Brossette, who discovered and reported the piracy to him in 1704, urged him to add this to the nine satires which had already contributed to his fame. Although Madame de Lafayette had established a basis for a change to the modern novel of sentiment with *La Princesse de Clèves* in 1678, there was still a large target of fantasy-romance for Boileau's *Dialogue,* since romantic literary faddism had spread not only across France but in England as well. Addison recommended *Faramond* and *Cassandre* to the readers of the *Spectator Papers;* multi-volume translations found a fascinated public; imitations (such as Aphra Behn's *The Young King*) rolled off the presses, and stage adaptations like Dryden's *Almanzor and Almahide* (1670-1672) hastened the vogue of neo-classic tragedy.

It is impossible to present in a short space any satisfactory vision of the enormous tedium of the seventeenth-century French romances. Even Desmarets' *Ariane,* remarkable for its unusual brevity, runs to well over a thousand pages. Shepherds, guided by gods and goddesses, make fleshless love in stilted prose and verse; characters from Greek, Roman, and Celtic tradition roam across fairy wonderlands in pursuit of or in escape from monsters or powerful enemies in disguise. Elaborate allegorical dreams, involuted love letters, intensely polite conversations, portraits in enameled prose, and grandiose heraldry and tournaments pad out complex, disorganized plot lines that make Italian opera classically simple by comparison. Boileau declared himself unable to stomach "their precious affectation of language, frivolous and pointless conversations, flattering portraits at every turn, of obviously mediocre persons, endless verbiage about love leading nowhere." But the leading practitioner of that romantic nonsense, Mlle. de Scudéry, gained an astonishing international fame —gifts from the Queen of Sweden, membership in the Italian academy, homage from English writers, as well as pensions from Cardinal Mazarin and the King of France.

Witty and polished conversation in writing as well as in society was a favorite seventeenth-century art, witness Mlle. de Scudéry's own ten volumes of model *Conversations.* For this reason Boileau, like many another critic of his day, adopted the dialogue: "I have taken as a point of departure in this attack on the novel . . . the manner of Lucian" (the greatest of the second-century Sophists, who also used humor and buffoonery to attack manners and ideas of his time). Although Boileau says that this is "the least frivolous work to issue from my pen," the *Dialogue* is hilarious good fun. Like Lucian, he sets his scene in Hades. Minos comes running frantically to Pluto with a report that hell has suddenly become populated with idiots afflicted with a "fury to talk . . . a certain language they call gallantry":

"One even assured me that this pestilent gallantry had infected all the infernal countries and even the Elysian fields so that the heroes and, above all, the heroines who live there today are the most foolish people in the world, thanks to certain authors who have taught them that fine language and have made them bashful lovers."

As Pluto resolves to examine these strange people, Rhadamanthus arrives with the news that the fiercest criminals in Hades—Prometheus, Tantalus, Ixion, and Sisyphus—have revolted. While preparations are being made for war, Diogenes arrives to contribute his walking stick to the arsenal. He warns Pluto not to expect much help from the newly arrived heroes: "They are a troop of madmen . . . I've never seen anything so effeminate and gallant!" But Pluto, eager for heroic aid, summons them. He is delighted when the first hero turns out to be the great Cyrus, the Persian warrior-king who had conquered the Medes and ravaged more than half the world. But his delight quickly turns to dismay when he learns that Cyrus has adopted the [Scudérian] name of Artimin and is engaged in an eternal quest to find his kidnapped princess, though he fears that even if he finds her she will not return to him because he is so unworthy. "Chase away this rain-bucket, this great sobber!" cries Pluto as he turns to welcome Tamyris, savage queen of the Massagetes who had plunged the great Cyrus' head into a bucket of human blood. Tamyris, however, is now distraught because she has lost the madrigal which she had composed to woo Cyrus. Next comes Horatius Cocles, the Roman warrior who alone had held off an entire army at the bridge. He is now a shepherd troubadour singing a song he had made from an echo for Clélie. "The nut! the nut!" cries Pluto, dismissing him; "to amuse himself with such trifles he must have entirely lost his senses!"

The mad parade continues. Clélie, once the audacious hero of Titus Livius, is now completely absorbed with the map of Tendre-Land, tracing the path from Constant Love along Inclination River, through Billet Doux and Sincerity to New Amity. Lucretia, who once killed to defend her chastity, now babbles of love; and Brutus, savior of Rome against the Tarquins, also prattles of love. Diogenes tries unsuccessfully to explain to Pluto:

"Lucretia who is in love with and loved by Brutus says to him in transposed words: 'How sweet it would be to love, if one loved always! But alas, there are no eternal loves.' And Brutus answers: 'Permit me to love, marvel of

our days. You will see that one can have eternal loves.'"

To which Pluto shouts, "By these bagatelles I recognize that they're possessed with infinite folly. Chase them away!" Then Mlle. de Scudéry herself arrives in the person of Sapho, once a famous Lesbian, now a poser of elaborate parlor-game questions on friendship: "Define for me what a tender heart is, what tenderness in friendship, tenderness in love, tenderness of inclination, and tenderness of passion." As indignant Pluto is about to send for the Fury Tisiphone, the "impertinent wench" subjects him to a ridiculous, flattering character sketch of that deadly harridan.

At last, after several more of these impossible heroes of the novel have passed in review, Mercury (one of the most frequently invoked gods of the romance) arrives to denounce them all as fakers. He has brought with him a Frenchman who identifies them as the common bourgeoisie of his quarter. Pluto wrathfully summons all the demons and furies of hell to skin alive these chimerical heroes. "The last act of the comedy is over!" he cries as the heroes call in vain upon the authors who created them.

Thus Boileau, whose epitaph rightly names him the "not unequal rival of Horace," redeemed the reputation of the French mind for common sense, clarity, and wit from one of the greatest threats in France's literary history.

THE DIALOGUES OF PLATO

Type of work: Philosophical dialogues
Author: Plato (427-347 B.C.)
Time: About 400 B.C.
Locale: Greece, principally Athens
First transcribed: c. 387-347 B.C.

Principal personages:
SOCRATES, the Athenian philosopher
GORGIAS, a Sophist
PROTAGORAS, a Sophist
CRITO, Socrates' contemporary, an aged friend
PHAEDRUS, a defender of rhetoric
ARISTOPHANES, a poet and playwright
THEAETETUS, hero of the battle of Corinth
PARMENIDES, the philosopher from Elea
PHILEBUS, a hedonist
TIMAEUS, a philosopher and statesman
PLATO, Socrates' pupil

The Platonic *Dialogues* rank with the extant works of Aristotle as the most important collection of philosophical works so far produced in the Western world. Although Plato's influence is partly due to the fact that his works have survived, unlike many writings of earlier Greek philosophers, and also to the fact that at various times in the history of the Christian church his ideas have been utilized in one form or another in the process of constructing a Christian theology—although Aristotle's influence in this respect has been greater—the principal cause of his past and present effect on human thought is the quality of his work.

The distinctive character of Platonic thought finds adequate expression in the dialogue form. Although Plato, like all philosophers, had his favored perspectives from which he interpreted and, consequently, saw the world, he realized better than most philosophers that philosophy is more an activity of the mind than the product of an investigation. This is not to say that philosophy does not, in some legitimate sense, illuminate the world; it means that in the process of making sense out of experience the philosopher is restless: no one way of clarifying an idea or a view is entirely satisfactory, and there is always much to be said for some alternative mode of explanation. When distinctive Platonic conceptions finally become clear, they do so against a background of penetrating discussion by means of which alternative ideas are explored for their own values and made to complement the conception which Plato finally endorses. As an instrument for presenting the critical point counterpoint of ideas, the dialogue is ideal; and as a character in control of the general course and quality of the discussion, Socrates is unsurpassed.

Socrates was Plato's teacher, and it was probably out of respect for Socrates the man and philosopher that Plato first considered using him as the central disputant in his dialogues. Reflection must have enforced his decision, for Socrates was important more for his method than for his fixed ideas, more for his value as a philosophical irritant than as a source of enduring wisdom. The Socratic method is often described as a question-answer method designed to bring out the contradictions and omissions in the philosophical views of others; but it is better understood as a clever technique for so playing upon the ambiguities of claims as to lead others into changing their use of terms and, hence, into *apparent* inconsistency.

The question concerning the extent to which Plato uses the dialogues to record the ideas of Socrates and the extent to which he uses Socrates as a proponent of his own ideas will probably never be conclusively answered. The question is, of course, historical; philosophically speaking, it makes no difference whose ideas find their way into the dialogues. A fairly safe assumption is that Socrates emphasized the importance of philosophical problems of value, knowledge, and philosophy itself. He probably did argue that it is important to know oneself, that the admission of one's own ignorance is a kind of wisdom possessed by few men, and that virtue is knowledge.

Certainly Socrates must have had a devotion to his calling as philosopher and critic: no man who regarded philosophy as a game would have remained in Athens to face the charge that by philosophy he had corrupted the youth of Athens, nor would he have refused a chance to escape after having been condemned to death. The courage and integrity of Socrates are recorded with poignant power in the *Apology*, the dialogue in which Socrates defends himself and philosophy against the charges brought against him; the *Crito*, in which Socrates refuses to escape from prison; and the *Phaedo*, in which Socrates discusses the immortality of the soul before he drinks the hemlock poison and dies.

Of the ideas presented in the dialogues, perhaps none is more important than Plato's theory of Ideas or Forms. This idea is most clearly expressed in the *Republic* (q.v.), the dialogue in which the problem of discovering the nature of justice in man is resolved by considering the nature of justice in the state. Plato distinguished between particular things, the objects we experience in our daily living, and the characters that things have, or could have. Goodness, truth, beauty, and other universal characters—properties that can affect a number of individual objects—are eternal, change-less, beautiful, and the source of all knowledge. Although some critics have claimed that Plato was speaking metaphorically when he talked, through Socrates, about the reality of the Forms, speaking as if they enjoyed a separate existence, the dialogues leave the impression that Plato considered the Forms (Ideas) to be actually existing, in some sense peculiar to themselves, as universals or prototypes which things may or may not exemplify.

If one reviews, however inadequately, the range of questions and tentative answers to be found in the dialogues, a bare inkling of Plato's power as a philosopher is then realized. But the dialogues must be read before the depth of Plato's speculative mind and the skill of his dialectic can be appreciated. Furthermore, only a reading of the dialogues can convey Plato's charm, wit, and range of sympathy. Whether the final result may be in good part attributed to Socrates as Plato's inspiring teacher is not important. Socrates as the subject and Plato as the writer (and philosopher—in all probability more creative than Socrates) combine to leave us with an unforgettable image of the Hellenistic mind.

Although many of the dialogues concern themselves with more than one question, and although definitive answers are infrequent so that discussions centering about a certain subject may crop up in a number of different dialogues, it may be helpful to indicate the central problems and conclusions of the dialogues:

Charmides centers about the question, "What is temperance?" After criticizing a number of answers, and without finally answering the question, Socrates emphasizes the point that temperance involves knowledge. *Lysis* and *Laches* consider, respectively, the questions, "What is friendship?" and "What is courage?" The former discussion brings out the difficulty of the question and of resolving conflicts of values; the latter distinguishes courage from a mere facing of danger and makes the point that courage, as one of the virtues, is a kind of knowledge involving willingness to act for the good. The *Ion* exhibits Socratic irony at work on a rhapsode who is proud of his skill in the recitation of poetry. Socrates argues that poetry is the result of inspiration, a kind of divine madness. In the *Protagoras* Socrates identifies virtue and knowledge, insisting that no one chooses evil except through ignorance. One of a number of attacks of the Sophistical art of fighting with words is contained in the *Euthydemus*.

In the *Meno* the philosopher Socrates and his companions wonder whether virtue can be taught. The doctrine that ideas are implanted in the soul before birth is demonstrated by leading a slave boy into making the correct answers to some problems in geometry. At first it seems that since virtue is a good and goodness is knowledge, virtue can be taught. But since there are no teachers of virtue, it cannot be taught; and, in any case, since virtue involves right opinion, it is not teachable.

"What is piety?" is the question of the *Euthyphro*. Euthyphro's idea that piety is whatever is pleasing to the gods is shown to be inadequate.

The *Apology* is the most effective portrait of Socrates in a practical situation. No moment in his life had graver consequences than the trial resulting from the charge that he had corrupted the youth of Athens by his teachings, yet Socrates continued to be himself, to argue dialectically, and to reaffirm his love of wisdom and virtue. He pictured himself as a gadfly, stinging the Athenians out of their intellectual arrogance. He argued that he would not corrupt anyone voluntarily, for to corrupt those about him would be to create evil that might harm him.

Socrates is shown as a respecter of the law in the *Crito*; he refuses to escape after having been pronounced guilty. In the *Phaedo* he argues that the philosopher seeks death because his whole aim in life is to separate the soul from the body. He argues for the immortality of the soul by saying that opposites are generated from opposites; therefore, life is generated from death. Also, the soul is by its very nature the principle of life; hence, it cannot itself die.

The dialogue *Greater Hippias* does not settle the question, "What is beauty?" but it does show, as Socrates points out, that "All that is beautiful is difficult."

The subject of love is considered from various philosophic perspectives in the *Symposium*, culminating in the conception of the highest love as the love of the good, the beautiful, and the true.

Gorgias begins with a discussion of the art of rhetoric, and proceeds to the development of the familiar Socratic ideas that it is better to suffer evil than to do it, and it is better to be punished for evil-doing than to escape punishment.

The *Parmenides* is a fascinating technical argument concerning various logical puzzles about the one and the many. It contains some criticism of Plato's theory of Ideas. Plato's increasing interest in problems of philosophic method is shown by the *Cratylus*, which contains a discussion of language beginning with the question whether there are true and false names. Socrates is not dogmatic about the implications of using names, but he does insist that any theory of language allow men to continue to speak of their knowledge of realities.

The *Phaedrus* is another discourse on love. It contains the famous myth of the soul conceived as a charioteer and winged steeds. In the *Theaetetus* Socrates examines the proposal by Theaetetus that knowledge is sense perception. He rejects this idea as well as the notion that knowledge is true opinion.

The *Sophist* is a careful study of sophistical method with emphasis on the problem of Being and Not-being. In the *Statesman* Plato continues the study of the state he initiated in the *Republic*, introducing the idea—later stressed by Aristotle—that virtue is a mean.

Socrates argues in the *Philebus* that neither pleasure nor wisdom is in itself the highest good, since pleasure that is not known is worthless and wisdom that is not pleasant is not worth having; only a combination is wholly satisfactory.

A rare excursion into physics and a philosophical consideration of the nature of the universe are found in the *Timaeus*. Here Plato writes of God, creation, the elements, the soul, gravitation, and many other matters.

The *Critias*, an unfinished dialogue, presents the story of an ancient and mythical war between Athens and Atlantis; and with the *Laws*, the longest of the dialogues, Plato ranges over most of the areas touched on in his other dialogues, but with an added religious content: Soul is the source of life, motion, and moral action; and there is an evil soul in the universe with which God must deal.

DIANA OF THE CROSSWAYS

Type of work: Novel
Author: George Meredith (1828-1909)
Type of plot: Psychological realism
Time of plot: Nineteenth century
Locale: England
First published: 1885

Principal characters:

DIANA MERION WARWICK, a woman of beauty and charm
AUGUSTUS WARWICK, her husband
LADY EMMA DUNSTANE, Diana's friend
THOMAS REDWORTH, Diana's friend and admirer
LORD DANNISBURGH, another friend
SIR PERCY DACIER, a young politician in love with Diana

Critique:

Any novel by George Meredith requires attention not only to the book in question but also to the wider aspects of the technique of fiction, for Meredith, always an original, was a writer of deep concentration and mature force. His Diana is a character head and shoulders above most heroines in nineteenth-century English novels. She offers the charm of femininity, perplexed by convention and yet aware of its force. Her predicament is at once an error in judgment and a glory to her. Her career compels our belief that a life which will not let go its harvest of errors until they are thoroughly winnowed is a human drama of deepest interest, for that life extracts the wisdom experience can offer. Diana, beautiful, witty, skeptical of social convention and moral expediency, is the embodiment of Meredith's philosophy and art.

The Story:

All of fashionable London was amazed and shocked when Diana Warwick suddenly left her husband's house. Society should not have been surprised at her action, however; the marriage had been ill-fated from the start. For Augustus Warwick, a calculating, ambitious politician, his marriage to the beautiful and charming Diana Merion had been largely one of convenience. Diana, in her turn, accepted his proposal as a refuge from unwelcome attentions to which her own position as an orphan had exposed her.

Diana Merion had first appeared in society at a state ball in Dublin, where her unspoiled charm and beauty attracted many admirers. Lady Emma Dunstane introduced Diana to Thomas Redworth, a friend of her husband, Sir Lukin Dunstane, and Redworth's attentions so enraged Mr. Sullivan Smith, a hot-tempered Irishman, that he attempted to provoke the Englishman to a duel. Redworth pacified the Irishman, however, to avoid compromising Diana by a duel fought on her account.

Later, while visiting Lady Emma at Copsley, the Dunstane country home in England, Diana was forced to rebuff Sir Lukin when he attempted to make love to her. Leaving Copsley, she went to visit the Warwicks. Meanwhile, Thomas Redworth announced to Lady Emma that he loved Diana. His announcement came too late. Diana was already engaged to Augustus Warwick.

In London the Warwicks took a large house and entertained lavishly. Among their intimates was Lord Dannisburgh, an elderly peer who became Diana's friend and adviser. While Warwick was away on a government mission, the two were often seen together, and Diana was so indiscreet as to let Lord Dannisburgh accompany her when she went to visit Lady Emma. Gossip began to circulate. On his return Warwick, who was incapable of understanding his wife's innocence and charm, served Diana with a process in suit. Accusing her of infidelity, he named Lord Dannisburgh as correspondent. Diana disappeared from Warwick's house and from London. In a letter to Lady Emma she had said that she intended to leave England. Her friend, realizing that flight would be tantamount to confession, felt sure that Diana would go to Crossways, her father's old home, before she left the country. Determined that Diana should remain and boldly defend the suit, Lady Emma sent Redworth to Crossways with instructions to detain Diana and persuade her to go to stay with the Dunstanes at Copsley.

Lady Emma had guessed correctly; Diana was at Crossways with her maid. At first Diana was unwilling to see Lady Emma's point of view, for she thought of her flight as a disdainful stepping aside from Warwick's sordid accusations; but at last she gave in to Redworth's arguments and returned with him to Copsley.

Although the court returned a verdict of not guilty to the charge Warwick had brought against her, Diana felt that her honor had been ruined and that in the eyes of the world she was still guilty. For a time she was able to forget her own distress by nursing her friend, Lady Emma, who was seriously ill. Later she left England to go on a Mediterranean cruise. Before her departure she had written a book, *The Princess Egeria*.

In Egypt she met Redworth, now a brilliant member of Parliament. He was accompanied by Sir Percy Dacier, Lord Dannisburgh's nephew and a rising young politician. Falling in love with Diana, Sir Percy followed her to the continent. He was recalled to London by the illness of his uncle. Diana followed him a short time later, to learn on her arrival in London that Redworth had been active in making her book a literary triumph. He had stirred up interest among the critics because he knew that Diana was in need of money.

Lord Dannisburgh died, with Diana at his bedside during his last illness. He had been her friend, and she paid him that last tribute of friendship and respect regardless of the storm of criticism it created. When Lord Dannisburgh's will was read, it was learned that he had left a sum of money to Diana.

In the meantime Diana had made an enemy of the socially ambitious Mrs. Wathin, who thought it her social duty to tear Diana's reputation to shreds. Part of her dislike was motivated by jealousy that Diana should be accepted by people who would not tolerate Mrs. Wathin. Some of her actions were inspired by Warwick, Mrs. Wathin's friend, who, having lost his suit against Diana, was trying to force his wife to return to him.

Sir Percy's attentions were also distressing to Diana. Half in love with him, she was not free to marry again. She faced a crisis in her affairs when Mrs. Wathin called to announce that Warwick, now ill, wanted Diana to return and to act as his nurse. Diana refused. Warwick then threatened to exercise his legal rights as her husband. Sir Percy, who informed her of Warwick's intention, asked her to elope with him to Paris. She agreed. She was saved from that folly by the appearance of Redworth, who arrived to tell her that Lady Emma was ill and about to undergo a serious operation at Copsley. Diana went with him to be at her friend's side.

Lady Emma nearly died, and the gravity of her condition restored Diana's own sense of responsibility. She ordered Sir Percy to forget her, but in spite of her protests he continued to follow her about. One day he confided a tremendous political secret to her—the prime minister was about to call upon Parliament to pass some revolutionary reform measures. Having told her his secret, he attempted to resume his former courtship. Diana refused to listen to his pleadings. After he had gone, she felt broken and cheated. If she would not have Sir

Percy as a lover, she felt, she could not keep him as a friend. Diana was desperately in need of money. She had been forced to sell Crossways to pay her debts and her later novels had been failures. Feeling herself a complete adventuress, she went to the editor of a paper which opposed the government party and sold him the information Sir Percy had given her.

When the paper appeared with a full disclosure of the prime minister's plan, Sir Percy accused her of betraying him and broke with her. A short time later he proposed to a young lady of fortune. About the same time Warwick was struck down by a cab in the street and killed. Diana had her freedom at last, but she was downcast in spirit. She knew that she was in public disgrace. Although she had burned the check in payment for the information she had disclosed, it was common knowledge that she had betrayed Sir Percy and that he had retaliated by his marriage to Constance Asper, an heiress. When Sullivan Smith proposed for her hand, Diana refused him and sought refuge in the company of her old friend, Lady Emma. Her stay at Copsley freed her of her memories of Sir Percy, so much so that on her return to London she was able to greet him and his bride with dignity and charm. Her wit was as sharp as ever, and she took pleasure in revenging herself upon those who had attempted to destroy her reputation with their gossip and slander.

On another visit to Copsley she again encountered Redworth, now a railroad promoter and still a distinguished member of Parliament. When he invited her and Lady Emma to visit Crossways, Diana learned that it was Redworth who had bought her old home and furnished it with her own London possessions, which she had been forced to sell in order to pay her debts. He bluntly told Diana that he had bought the house and furnished it for her because he expected her to become his wife. Not wishing to involve him in the scandals which had circulated about her, she at first pretended indifference to his abrupt wooing. Lady Emma, on the other hand, urged her to marry Redworth, who had loved her for many years, so that he could protect her from social malice. At last, knowing that she brought no real disgrace to Redworth's name, she consented to become his wife.

DIARY

Type of work: Diary
Author: John Evelyn (1620-1706)
Time: 1620-1706
Locale: England and the Continent
First published: 1818-1819

Principal personages:
JOHN EVELYN
CHARLES I
CHARLES II
JAMES II
OLIVER CROMWELL
SAMUEL PEPYS
QUEEN MARY
WILLIAM OF ORANGE
QUEEN ANNE
JEREMY TAYLOR, English divine

An intimate of people in high places, John Evelyn was able to observe at first hand many of the significant events and developments of his time. To his observation, he brought a mind remarkable in a turbulent era for its calmness, balance, and acuity. His diary is a contribution of exceptional value to our understanding of seventeenth-century England.

Evelyn, the son of a large landowner, was a royalist and an Anglican. He served briefly in the army of Charles I, but, after the king's retreat in 1641, he resigned, believing that further service would mean financial ruin for himself and would little aid the royalist cause. Finding it difficult to maintain a neutral position, he left England in 1643 for the Continent, where he spent most of the next nine years traveling and studying European culture. After his return to England in 1652, he occupied himself with gardening and with improving his estate. He refused a position under Cromwell and maintained secret correspondence with Charles II. From the Restoration until his death in 1706, he enjoyed the favor of the crown and held several important minor positions in the government.

Evelyn lived in an era of unrest and calamity. Three times he saw the existing English government overthrown; he observed the Dutch war from the vantage point of an official position; he remained in London during the plague of 1665; he watched the progress of the Great Fire from its start to its engulfment of the city; he noted with disapproval the licentiousness of the court of Charles II; he attended the spectacular trials of the men accused of complicity in the Popish Plot. In religion, he witnessed the shifting fortunes of the various sects; in politics, he saw the rise and the fall of a multitude of favorites.

The diary, in addition to providing an inside view of these major events, reveals the ordinary conditions of existence in the seventeenth century. Life was filled with hazards. On voyages, pirates were frequently a threat, Evelyn himself barely escaping them on one occasion. For travel on the Continent, an armed escort was often necessary for protection against highwaymen. Within a brief period, Evelyn was robbed three times; and once, in England, he was robbed and bound, and narrowly missed being killed. Also in the seventeenth century, many barbarous practices were still sanctioned by law. Evelyn tells of beheadings that required several blows of the ax, of men put on the rack to elicit confessions, of the public display of bodies that had been hanged, then drawn, and quartered. The plague, smallpox, and other diseases constantly reminded men of their mortality. Evelyn made frequent references in his diary to death among his friends and his children, seven of whom never reached adulthood.

Amid the public tumult and private insecurity, Evelyn was throughout a truly civilized man. While many were dominated by the emotions that religious and political controversy aroused, he retained his sanity. Of a compassionate nature, he deplored acts of cruelty, and expressed his opposition to many accepted practices, such as the harsh treatment of criminals and the baiting of animals. During the Dutch war he served as commissioner for the care of the sick, wounded, and prisoners of war. He was not deterred from his duties by the plague or by the frustrating difficulties involved in securing funds.

At a time when apostasy was commonplace, Evelyn remained firm in his religious and political convictions. His life was guided, first, by his belief in the Church of England and, secondly, by his belief in the monarchy. A large part of the diary is concerned with church affairs, ranging from discussions of major issues to records of fasting days. A devoutly religious man, he based his conduct upon his conception of the Christian ideal, and accepted blessings and misfortunes alike as the will of God. Although he feared rival sects—the Jesuits, in particular— and believed that certain laws were necessary to protect the Church of England, he was a generally tolerant man and opposed punitive laws against Catholics and Nonconformists.

As a monarchist, he felt that the execution of Charles I was the blackest spot on English history. He regarded the Restoration as the greatest blessing God could bestow, and he continued to celebrate its anniversary even after King James II was deposed in 1688. Initially, he had misgivings about the Glorious Revolution, but, probably because of its preservation of the Church of England, he came to approve of it.

However unwavering he may have been in his royalist sympathies, he was no absolutist, nor did he hesitate to criticize the actions of royalty. When the king overstepped his traditional authority—as Charles II did, for example, in revoking the charter of London, and as James II did in dispensing with the Test Act—Evelyn was firm in his objections. He frequently protested against the profligacy of the court; and once, after having observed some disabled soldiers, he wrote: "What confusion and mischief do the avarice, anger, and ambition of Princes, cause in the world!"

Evelyn apparently could have aspired to higher positions than he attained, but he enjoyed his "private condition" and cared not for "the extreme slavery and subjection that courtiers live in." There was in him none of the sycophant. Generally he avoided offices that might beget a clash between his personal interests and his principles. In one position which did create such a conflict, he followed his principles. As a commissioner of the Privy Seal, he twice refused, against the wishes of James II, to license the illegal sale of Catholic literature.

His independent nature can also be seen in his loyalty to friends. When Samuel Pepys was placed in the Tower on suspicion of treason, Evelyn immediately went to see him. He was the last person to visit Clarendon before that deposed official fled England to escape the wrath of Parliament and king. Many others found in Evelyn a friend who was unmoved by the tergiversations of courtly favor.

Despite the heavy demands of private business and public service, Evelyn found time to acquire a vast amount of knowledge. His range of interests was prodigious, with the novel as well as the important attracting his attention. Amid more weighty topics, such subjects as fire-eating and knife swallowing are soberly discussed in the diary. Much of his intellectual curiosity, however, was directed toward practical matters. His concern with the depletion of forests in England led him to write *Sylva* (1664), a highly significant book on afforestation. His knowledge of gardening was considerable, and his gardens at Saves Court attracted thousands of visitors. The smoke nuisance in London was attacked by Evelyn as early as 1661. After the Great Fire he drew up plans for rebuilding the city. His publications include works on government, education, English customs, horticulture, science, chalcography, and architecture.

Evelyn was also active in promoting the work of others. He was closely associated with England's creative leaders, men such as Robert Boyle and Christopher Wren. A patron of the arts, he introduced Grinling Gibbons to the notice of Charles II, and he persuaded the Duke of Norfolk to present the Arundel marbles to Oxford University. His most productive efforts of this kind were those connected with the Royal Society, of which he was an original promoter and, for many years, an active member.

Unlike the other great diarist of the seventeenth century, Samuel Pepys, Evelyn had little talent for bringing warm, personal touches to his writing. In reading the objective, factual presentation of the earlier part of the diary—with its absence of feeling and with little, even, of personal opinion—one wishes that more of John Evelyn were in the work. In the later part of the diary there is greater freedom of expression. Never, however, is Evelyn able truly to share his emotional experiences with the reader. He was a man of reason, and his writing is formal, dignified, and cerebral.

DIARY

Type of work: Day-to-day journal
Author: Samuel Pepys (1633-1703)
Time: 1660-1669
Locale: London
First published: 1825; first complete edition, 1848-1849

Principal personages:

SAMUEL PEPYS, Clerk of the Acts of the Navy Board, the diarist
ELIZABETH ST. MICHEL PEPYS, his wife
SIR EDWARD MONTAGUE, the First Earl of Sandwich, his patron
CHARLES II, King of England
THE DUKE OF YORK, his brother, later James II
SIR WILLIAM PENN, a Commissioner of the Navy Board
EVERY OTHER IMPORTANT STATESMAN, POLITICIAN, COURTIER, MUSICIAN, POET, PLAYWRIGHT, ENTERTAINER, SYCOPHANT, ROYAL MISTRESS, AND CHARLATAN THAT INHABITED THE LONDON OF 1660-1669

The *Diary* of Samuel Pepys is a unique document in the annals of English literature—perhaps of all literature. There are other fascinating day-to-day accounts of interesting and momentous times, and some of these were written by men of genius; but there is only one other autobiographical collection—the recently discovered journals of James Boswell—which combines fascinating subject matter and genius of composition with the intriguing detective-story discovery that is associated with the *Diary* of Pepys.

The author of the greatest of all biographies must bow to this lesser Samuel in one respect: Boswell, as his editors admit, was writing for posterity; Pepys was not. Pepys' *Diary* was written for himself only, apparently for the sole purpose of allowing its author to savor once more, at the end of each day, the experiences of the preceding twenty-four hours. There is no evidence of revision of any kind, and it was written in a shorthand which protected it from posterity for over a hundred years after its author's failing eyesight had forced him reluctantly to give it up.

Pepys' method of composition gives the *Diary* an immediacy that makes Boswell's *Journals* appear sedulously organized. And the protective coloration of the shorthand allows for admissions of personal animosities and revelations of scandalous behavior that otherwise would not

be found in the confessions of a responsible public official. Also, the point that Pepys was a responsible public official is the last factor that contributes to the importance of his work. Boswell was the scion of an important Scottish family and a member of the Scottish bar, but (aside from his Corsican experience) the only history he was involved in was literary history. Pepys was involved with the history of a nation at a very important time.

The *Diary* is important in a number of ways. First, it is of great value as a document of the Restoration period. No writer of a historical novel based on the history of the time could possibly create a character familiar with as many important events as was that opportunistic busybody, Samuel Pepys. One of the most influential figures in bringing about the return of the Stuarts in 1660 was the former Cromwellian, Sir Edward Montague, who was assisted by his able cousin and protégé, Samuel Pepys. It was Sir Edward who commanded the fleet that sailed from Holland and returned triumphantly with the king. On board the flagship, kissing the king's hand, firing a cannon to salute the new monarch (and burning an eye in the process), commenting on the plainness of the queen, taking charge of the king's dog in the landing at Dover was, again, Samuel Pepys. Later, made Clerk of the Acts of the Navy Board because of his assistance to the

Stuarts (Sir Edward Montague was made Earl of Sandwich), he remained at his post in London and wrote down his observations of the terrible plague from which most members of his class fled in panic. It was Pepys, again, who did his best to keep the English Navy afloat during the Dutch Wars, and Pepys who defended the Navy in a brilliant speech before Parliament in the investigation that followed (1668). Earlier (September 2, 1666), when the great fire of London broke out, it was Pepys who rushed to the king to inform him of the catastrophe and to suggest the blowing up of houses to prevent the spread of the fire. Pepys, who had a part in all these events, tells of them in a straightforward, unself-conscious account unvarnished by fear of what his contemporaries would have thought or of what posterity would think.

Along with vivid pictures of the major events of Restoration history are day-to-day accounts of the less earthshaking but equally revealing activities in the life of the London that Pepys shared, accounts that make the Diary a document of social, cultural, and artistic history as well. Here Pepys' concern with—his actual delight in—detail brings a particular world of the past to life. We see the crowded, unsanitary, and often impassable London streets. At times, during trips to Pepys' father's house in Brampton or during excursions into the country, we catch glimpses of rural existence in the days of Charles II. We see life in the houses of the well-to-do and the noble and, occasionally, at court. On a more mundane scale, there is Pepys' concern with clothes (his father was a tailor and he reflects a professional knowledge) and his greater concern with managing his own household. Unfortunately for revelations on this score, Pepys had no children, but his problems in household management included his handling of the affairs of his rather shiftless parents, brothers, and sister, the maintenance of a staff of servants that grew as his own wealth increased, and domestic supervision of his beautiful but erratic—sometimes docile, sometimes temperamental—young wife. In regard to the arts, there is a wealth of material on the theater and on music. Pepys was an inveterate playgoer. Though his frequent attendance bothered his basically Puritan conscience and though he made intermittent vows to refrain, it is seldom that many entries go by in which some play that he has seen is not commented on. So frequent are these comments, in fact, that the Diary is an invaluable source of information to the student of Restoration drama. It is equally valuable to the specialist in the history of music: Pepys was not only an accomplished musician but also a composer, and the delight in music which he expresses gives an insight into a particularly musical age.

Nor was artistic beauty the only kind that captivated the practical and mercenary Pepys. Since he was equally attracted to beauty in its carnal manifestations, his pursuit of beauty in feminine form and his diligent (but finally unsuccessful) attempts to hide these pursuits from his wife provide an insight into the mores of the Restoration period. These accounts of the diarist's philanderings—honest, but hidden by the elaborate code—are a part of the personal revelation that the work provides.

In spite of its importance as historical and social document, the Diary is, on its most intriguing level, the portrait of a man, a self-portrait drawn in strong and certain lines with no detail, however uncomplimentary, however compromising, omitted. That it is the portrait of a man active in the affairs of his day adds to its interest; but the main value comes from its unstinting wealth of circumstantial detail. Yet the detail and the man cannot be separated: the love of detail and the love of life that inspired the keeper of the Diary make up the essence of the man himself. The Diary is a celebration of the things of this world and a portrait of the man who praised them.

THE DIARY OF A COUNTRY PRIEST

Type of work: Novel
Author: Georges Bernanos (1888-1948)
Type of plot: Psychological realism
Time of plot: The 1920's
Locale: France
First published: 1937

Principal characters:
A PARISH PRIEST, the diarist
THE CURÉ DE TORCY, a superior of the narrator
DR. MAXENCE DELBENDE, the narrator's friend
SERAPHITA DUMOUCHEL, a young parishioner
MONSIEUR DUFRETY, a former classmate of the narrator
THE COUNT, a wealthy resident of the parish
THE COUNTESS, his wife
MADEMOISELLE CHANTAL, their daughter
MADEMOISELLE LOUISE, governess at the chateau

Critique:

Meager of plot because Bernanos is interested more in showing a man's thoughts and basic principles than in picturing human behavior, *The Diary of a Country Priest* is fictional presentation of priestly attitudes, functions, and tribulations. Through this philosophical and realistic treatment of life in a small French parish, it is easy to see Bernanos' high regard for Joan of Arc as the symbol of France. In their simplicity the Maid's peasantry and saintliness are not unlike those phases of the diarist's life. Fittingly, compassion and tenderness characterize the writing, which, in translation, sustains the poetic charm and fluency of the original. Mankind's holiness is Bernanos' keynote.

The Story:

A young priest, thirty years old, in charge of the Ambricourt Parish in France, recorded in his diary his impressions and activities over a period of one year. His purpose in keeping the diary was to maintain frankness with himself in his relationships with his parishioners and in his service to God.

The priest was a man of marked humility, sympathy, simplicity, and great loneliness. Son of a poor family in which there had been much suffering and hardship, he planned to raise the scale of living in his parish. His plans for a village savings bank and for coöperative farming were discussed at his first monthly meeting with the curates, but his plans were disapproved because of their pretentious scope and his lack of personal influence in the parish. This saddening blow, which caused him to question whether God would use his services as He did the services of others, was intensified by the words of his superior and ideal, the Curé de Torcy, and of his friend, Dr. Maxence Delbende, who soon afterward committed suicide because of his disappointment at not receiving a legacy he expected.

These two men thwarted the young priest's ambition with their opinions that the poor were not to be raised from their low level because of religious and social reasons. God gave the poor a dignity, the Curé de Torcy said, which they do not wish to lose in His sight. According to the doctor, poverty served as a social bond and a mark of prestige among the poor. In the eyes of the Church, the curate believed, the rich are on the earth to protect the poor.

Undaunted and hopeful, the priest accepted an invitation to the chateau, where he hoped to get financial help from the

Count for his parish projects. Thwarted in his attempt, he gave his physical energy, which was limited because of insomnia and a chronic stomach disorder, to the spiritual advancement of his parish. But his efforts in this direction were ill-spent. He questioned his success in teaching a catechism class, for the children did not respond as he had hoped, and he was tormented and plagued by the unsavory attentions of Seraphita Dumouchel, a young student in the class, who discomfited him by her suggestive questions and remarks to the other children and by her scribbled notes left about for the young priest to find.

Seraphita later befriended him, when on a parish visit he suffered a seizure and fell unconscious in the mud. A few days later Seraphita, bribed by sweets, offset her beneficence to the priest by telling Mademoiselle Chantal, the Count's strong-willed, jealous daughter, that the priest had fallen in drunkenness. The story was believed because it was known generally among the parishioners that the priest drank cheap wine, and because his physical condition was growing progressively worse.

The priest's spiritual strength was shown in his theological dealings with the Count's family. Mademoiselle Chantal had told, in conversation and in confession, that her father was having an affair with Mademoiselle Louise. The daughter, believing that she was to be sent to England to live with her mother's cousin, declared that she hated everyone in her household—her father and the governess for their conduct, and her mother for her blindness to the situation. After asserting that she would kill Mademoiselle Louise or herself and that the priest would have to explain away her conduct to God, she got his promise that he would discuss the girl's problems with her mother.

The priest went to the chateau to confer with the Countess regarding her daughter's spiritual state. There he found the mother in a more pronounced atheistic frame of mind than that of her daughter.

Her spiritual depression resulted from the death of her baby son, twelve years before. During a prolonged philosophical discussion the Countess, after ridiculing the priest for his theological idealism and his lack of vanity and ambition, described with bitterness the hateful selfishness of her daughter, and related with indifference the Count's many infidelities.

Before he left the chateau, the priest sensed a spiritual change in his wealthy parishioner when she threw into the fire a medallion containing a lock of her son's hair. The priest, always humble, tried to retrieve the locket. In a letter delivered to him at the presbytery later in the day the Countess informed him that he had given her peace and escape from a horrible solitude with the memory of her dead child.

The Countess died that night. The priest's success in helping to redeem her soul left him with an uncertain feeling. He did not know whether he was happy or not.

If his reaction was happiness, it was short-lived. When the details of his session with the Countess became common knowledge, for Mademoiselle Chantal had eavesdropped during the interview, criticism and derision were heaped upon him. The canon reprimanded him because he had assumed the role of her confessor, and the Curé de Torcy ridiculed his approach in dealing with the Countess. Members of the family, unstable as they were in their relationships, accused him of subversive tactics to realize a childish ambition.

His social ineptness, his personal inadequacies, and his professional inaptitude—deficiencies repeatedly mentioned in his introspective moods—seemed to increase as his physical condition grew worse. His hemorrhages continuing, he decided to consult Dr. Lavigne in Lille.

His last major bungle was in connection with this medical aid. Because he forgot the name of the doctor recommended to him, in Lille he turned to the directory and mistakenly chose the name of Dr. Laville. The physician, a drug addict, bluntly diagnosed the priest's ailment as cancer of the stomach.

From the doctor's office, the priest went to the address of his old schoolmate at the seminary, Monsieur Dufrety, who had long been urging his friend to visit him. There he died that night.

In a letter from Monsieur Dufrety to the Curé de Torcy, details of the priest's death were described. In great suffering and anguish, following a violent hemorrhage, the priest held his rosary to his breast. When he asked his old friend for absolution, his request was granted and the ritual performed in a manner, Monsieur Dufrety wrote, that could leave no one with any possible misgivings. The priest's last words affirmed his great faith in the whole scheme of things, because of God's existence.

DIGBY GRAND

Type of work: Novel
Author: George J. Whyte-Melville (1821-1878)
Type of plot: Picaresque romance
Time of plot: Early nineteenth century
Locale: England
First published: 1853

> *Principal characters:*
> DIGBY GRAND, a spirited young Englishman, officer in the Guards
> SIR PEREGRINE GRAND, Digby's father
> SHADRACH, a money-lender
> TOM SPENCER, Digby's friend
> CAPTAIN LEVANTER, a fellow officer
> COLONEL CARTOUCH, Digby's commanding officer
> FLORA BELMONT, loved by Digby

Critique:

Because George J. Whyte-Melville's works have been catalogued as sporting fiction, they have never been given their rightful place in the history of English literature, and most scholars pass them by completely. It is true that Whyte-Melville wrote particularly for the sporting world, but his novels, especially *Digby Grand*, have interested wider audiences in their time. His writings have an air of liveliness, a note of authenticity, and an ineffable freshness. *Digby Grand* was Whyte-Melville's first novel, and it was truly termed by the novelist an autobiography, for the author's own early career as an officer in a Highland regiment and the Guards is mirrored in the novel. Digby Grand is, in fact, partly young Whyte-Melville. Considered in his time an authority on fox hunting, the author refers to the sport frequently in *Digby Grand*, as in his other novels.

The Story:

Digby Grand's father, Sir Peregrine Grand, of Haverley Hall, had one fond wish with respect to his son: he wanted Digby to be a man of fashion and to know his position in society. With that in mind, he decided that when Digby, then a youngster at Eton, should finish school he would be commissioned in the British Army. Digby, taken with the idea, wished to have his appointment made at once.

As luck had it, Digby met General Sir Benjamin Burgonet, who, pleased with the young man, made every effort to secure Digby's commission. Within a matter of weeks Digby received a letter announcing his commission in the army as an ensign in a regiment of infantry.

Digby Grand reported to his regiment's headquarters in Scotland, where he rapidly adjusted himself to military life. Being of an adventurous turn and liking sports and gambling, he quickly became a sought-out addition to any party. He soon discovered, however, that the slim allowance made him by his father and his small pay as an ensign did not cover his large expenditures, and so he fell into the habit of gambling on horses, cards, and billiards to augment his income. Most of his fellow officers existed in much the same fashion.

While in Scotland, Digby had a narrow escape from marriage when an officer's daughter, a woman in her thirties, induced Digby to become engaged. His friends saw through the woman's plot, however, and rescued him from his predicament. He had the satisfaction of seeing her become instead the wife of Dubbs, the regimental drum major.

Shortly after that incident Digby was sent to Canada for a tour of duty. Memorable events of that short tour were the slaughter of a huge bull moose and a love affair with a French-Canadian girl named

Zoë. Colonel Cartouch, Digby's commanding officer, having taken a liking to the high-spirited young man, prevented him from marrying the girl because he felt that the teen-age ensign was not yet ready for marriage.

Upon his return to England, Digby found himself with a new commission in Her Majesty's service; his father had purchased a lieutenancy in the Life Guards for him during his absence in Canada. Digby was now in the most honored and most social brigade in the service, the Guards being the units which were stationed in London. Within a short time Digby had once again won for himself a place in fashionable London life. He was voted into several of the choicest gambling clubs, appeared in the best society, and was taken up by some well-known people. One of his friends was a youthful peer named St. Heliers; another was an officer named Levanter; a third was Mrs. Mantrap, a woman who basked in the attentions of young men.

To keep up his life of ease, including gambling for high stakes, maintaining good rooms, drinking only the best wines, and buying expensive horses, required all of Digby's resourcefulness. Because his resourcefulness was not enough at times, his friend Levanter introduced him to a money-lender named Shadrach, who was quite willing to lend Digby money at a high rate of interest, the principal to be repaid when Digby inherited the family estates. Not once but many times Digby borrowed from Shadrach.

One day, while in charge of a small group of military police at parade, Digby met Flora Belmont, who had attended the parade with her father, a retired colonel. Immediately Digby fell in love, in spite of the fact that the colonel had little or nothing to pass on to his daughter in the way of a fortune.

On his twenty-first birthday, spurred on by his own love and that which Flora Belmont had declared for him, Digby went home to Haverley Hall to request a definite income of size from his father so that he and Flora could be married. Sir Peregrine, instead of being happy, was furious that Digby would even think of marrying anyone but an heiress, for the Grand estate was in poor financial condition and Sir Peregrine had been counting on a brilliant marriage by his son to recoup the family fortunes.

Downhearted, Digby returned to duty in London. To while away the time he continued his old life, living beyond his means and borrowing money to pay his expenses. He even borrowed from Shadrach when his boyhood chum, Tom Spencer, who was studying for holy orders at Oxford, had to sign the notes with him. For a time Digby had an affair with Coralie de Rivolte, a famous dancer, but that romance ended, though only after Digby had made an enemy of a scarfaced Spaniard who seemed to be the dancer's relative.

Eventually Digby got so deeply into debt that only a change of regiments could help him. As an officer in the Guards he had too many social responsibilities, and he exchanged commissions with an officer in a dragoon regiment stationed in Kent, at some distance from London. Within a few weeks he made still another move. Old General Sir Benjamin Burgonet, who had secured Digby's original commission, made him his aide, and Digby prepared to go with the general to India. He was somewhat aghast, however, to learn that the girl who had married the drum major was now Lady Burgonet.

In spite of his precautions, Digby was unable to leave England without falling into the hands of Shadrach and other creditors, who had him imprisoned for debt. To satisfy his creditors, Digby had to sell his commission and give up all he owned. At that black hour word came that Sir Peregrine had died, leaving Digby with the title and the estate. When the will was settled, however, it became apparent that the estate was too heavily in debt to be of any use to the new heir. To salvage himself, Digby had to sell the land; he inherited only the title.

He was saved by a meeting with Tom Spencer, who had been prevented from finishing his degree at Oxford by an arrest made for a note he had signed on Digby's behalf. Spencer, far from being downcast, had become a successful wine merchant. He took Digby into the business with him and the two built up a flourishing trade. Digby had, by that time, acquired a great deal more discretion and a few gray hairs.

After some years Digby ran across his old commanding officer, Colonel Cartouch. The colonel was engaged in prosecuting a man who had forged checks on his name, and the two discovered that the man was married to Coralie de Rivolte, Digby's old love. That surprise was not the end, for the colonel discovered also that Coralie was his own daughter by a Spanish woman who had run away from him after killing her sister, whom she believed in love with Cartouch.

The appearance of Coralie reminded Digby of Flora Belmont, the girl whom his father had forbidden him to marry because she lacked a fortune. Digby found her in mourning for her father but still single. Through friends Digby learned that she had remained faithful to him. In a short time they had made plans for their approaching marriage. Digby Grand was ready to be tamed.

THE DISCIPLE

Type of work: Novel
Author: Paul Bourget (1852-1935)
Type of plot: Psychological realism
Time of plot: Late nineteenth century
Locale: Paris and Riom
First published: 1889

> *Principal characters:*
> ADRIEN SIXTE, a philosopher
> ROBERT GRESLOU, his disciple
> M. DE JUSSAT, a hypochondriac nobleman
> CHARLOTTE, his daughter
> LUCIEN, her younger brother
> ANDRÉ, her older brother

Critique:

Bourget represents in some ways the transition in French letters from naturalistic materialism to the more traditional religious and moral disciplines, and *The Disciple* is the mid-point in the work of this distinguished critic, novelist, and academician. This novel is a psychological study of the moral bases in abstract learning. Bourget has written an impeccable novel which combines solid psychological analysis with a sensational murder story.

The Story:

Adrien Sixte grew up in a peculiar way. His hardworking father wanted him to study for one of the professions, but despite the boy's early promise in school he never went to a university. His indulgent parents allowed him to spend ten lonely years in study. In 1868, at the age of twenty-nine, Adrien Sixte published a five-hundred-page study of *The Psychology of God.* By the outbreak of the Franco-Prussian War, Adrien had become the most discussed philosopher in the country. He followed his first study with two books even more provocative, *The Anatomy of the Will* and *The Theory of the Passions.*

Soon after the death of his parents, Adrien settled down to a well-regulated life in Paris. So regular was he that the inhabitants of the quarter could set their watches by his comings and goings. He spent eight hours of the twenty-four in work, took two walks each day, received callers, chiefly students, one afternoon a week, and on another afternoon made calls on other scholars. By patient labor and brilliant insight he developed to his complete satisfaction his deterministic theory that each effect comes from a cause, and that if all causes are known, results can be predicted accurately. He applied his theory to all forms of human activity, to vices as well as virtues.

One day the neighbors were startled to see Adrien leave his apartment hurriedly at an unusual hour. He had received, to his great consternation, a notice to appear before a magistrate in the affair of Robert Greslou, one of his students, and he had also a letter from Robert's mother saying that she would visit him that very day at four on an urgent matter.

The sophisticated judge was incredulous when he learned that Adrien never read the papers. The celebrated savant had not heard of Greslou's imprisonment after being charged with the murder of Charlotte de Jussat. Adrien soon learned that the suspect had been arrested on purely circumstantial evidence, that the proof of his guilt or innocence might well be only psychological. Hence Adrien, the master, must testify as to his disciple's ideas on multiplied psychological experience. Adrien explained that if a chemist can analyze water into hydrogen and oxygen, he can synthesize hydrogen and oxygen into water. Similarly, if a psychological result can be analyzed into its causes, the result can be reproduced by those same causes; that is, by scientific method one can predict human behavior. The judge was much interested and inquired if his theory applied to vices. Adrien said that it did, for psychologically vices are forms of behavior as interesting and valid as social virtues.

When he returned home, Adrien found Robert's mother waiting for him. She protested her son's innocence and begged Adrien to save her boy. Adrien remembered Robert as a precocious student of philosophy, but he really knew little of him as a person. The mother begged Adrien to help and gave him a manuscript written by Robert while in jail. On the outside of the manuscript was a note. If Adrien read the document, he must agree not to try to save Robert; if the condition were unacceptable, he must burn the manuscript immediately. With many misgivings Adrien took the document and read it. It was a minute and detailed account of Robert's upbringing, his studies, and his experiences in the de Jussat home.

Robert was always brilliant. He did outstanding work in school and early in his studies showed a pronounced talent in psychology. Most of his time was devoted to study, but a developing sensuality showed itself sporadically. Since he grew up at Clermont, he lacked some of the polish imparted at Paris; in consequence he failed an examination. While waiting another opportunity to enter the university, Robert accepted a year's appointment as tutor to Lucien de Jussat. At the de Jussat country home Robert found an interesting household. Lucien, his pupil, was a fat, simple boy of thirteen. André, the older brother, was an army officer fond of hunting and riding.

The father was a hypochondriac and a boor. But Charlotte, the daughter of the family, was a beautiful girl of nineteen.

Robert soon began the studied seduction of Charlotte. He had three reasons for such a step. First, he wanted to have some sort of revenge against the wealthy family. In the second place, his developed sexuality made the project attractive. Also, and probably more important, he wanted to test his theory that if he could determine the causes leading to love and sexual desire, he could produce desire by providing the causes. Robert kept careful notes on procedures and results.

He knew that pity is close to love. Consequently he aroused the pity of Charlotte by mysterious allusions to his painful past. Then, by carefully selecting a list of novels for her to read, he set about inflaming her desire for passionate, romantic love. But Robert was too hasty. He made an impassioned avowal to Charlotte and frightened her into leaving for Paris. Just as Robert began to despair of ever accomplishing his purpose, the illness of Lucien recalled Charlotte. Robert wrote her a note telling her he would commit suicide if she did not come to his room by midnight. He prepared two vials of strychnine and waited. When Charlotte came, he showed her the poison and proposed a suicide pact. Charlotte accepted, provided she could be the first to die. They spent the night together. Robert had triumphed.

Robert repudiated the pact, prompted in part by a real love for Charlotte. The next day she threatened to call her brother if Robert attempted to stop her own attempt at suicide, for she had read Robert's notes and knew she was simply the object of an experiment. After writing to her brother André a letter telling him of her intended suicide, she drank the strychnine. Robert was arrested soon afterward on suspicion of murder.

When Adrien Sixte came to the end of the manuscript, he began to feel a moral responsibility for his disciple's act. Disregarding the pledge implicit in his reading, he sent a note to André asking him if he intended to let Robert be convicted of murder by concealing Charlotte's letter. André resolved to tell the truth, and in a painful courtroom scene Robert was acquitted.

Immediately after the trial, André went to look for Robert. Scarcely able to resist, since he had been ready to die with Charlotte's secret safe, Robert went with André willingly. On the street, André pulled out a gun and shot Robert in the head. Robert's mother and Adrien mourned beside the coffin, Adrien because he accepted moral responsibility for the teachings that had prompted his disciple's deed.

THE DIVAN

Type of work: Poetry
Author: Hāfiz (Shams ud-din Mohammed, c.1320-c.1388)
First transcribed: c.1350

The *Divan* of Hāfiz is one of the glories of Persian literature in its Golden Age and a classic of Eastern literature. Hāfiz was the pen name of Shams ud-din Mohammed, a Persian who early in life turned to the serious study of philosophy, poetry, and theology. The pen name he adopted means "a man who remembers," a title normally bestowed upon persons who have committed the Koran to memory. In Hāfiz' case the title was not unwarranted, for he was a dervish who taught the Koran in an academy founded by his patron, the Vizier Haji Kiwam-ud-din.

The *Divan* is the best known of Hāfiz' works. In addition, he wrote in various other patterns common to Persian poetry. The *Divan* itself is a collection of short poems, lyric in quality, in the form known as *ghazals*. In the original Persian these poems consist of from five to sixteen couplets (called *baits*), and the particular poetical form has been compared to the ode and the sonnet in English-language poetry because of the lyric qualities, the length, and the subject matter. One curious feature of Hāfiz' *ghazals* is that the last two lines normally contain the poet's name. The first line of each *ghazal* introduces the rhyme, which is repeated in every other succeeding line within the poem.

Although relatively little known in the Western world, Hāfiz' *Divan* has remained the most popular poetry ever written in his native land. It has even been considered oracular, and Persians sometimes consult it by opening the book and placing a finger on a chance passage, hoping to have an answer thereby to whatever question has arisen. Such a procedure, or a variation of it, was supposedly done at the death of the poet. Because of exception taken to some of his poems, his corpse was at first denied the usual burial rites. To settle the question, some of his *ghazals* were written on slips of paper and placed in an urn, one to be drawn out by a child. According to legend, the verse drawn by chance from the urn said that Hāfiz should be given appropriate funeral rites, as he would enter Paradise; thus the question was settled.

Through the centuries there has been debate over whether his poetry should be taken literally or symbolically, with those who want to see in the *Divan* a serious work by a great Persian philosopher and student of the Koran taking one side of the question, those who wish to see in the work a fine expression of a warmly alive human being taking the other. Western readers who cannot see anything religious in these superficially hedonistic poems should call to mind the religious expression, veiled in imagery though it is, of such poetry as that of John Donne and Richard Crashaw in England and Edward Taylor in America.

Whether one may wish to take it literally or on a symbolic level, the imagery of Hāfiz' poetry is warm, human, even passionate. There is no escaping, even in translation, the sincerity of the poet. Like most Eastern poetry, the imagery may even seem lush to Western readers, as in the following example:

The east wind at the dawn of day
brought a perfume from the tresses
of my beloved, which immediately
cast my foolish heart into fresh agitation.

THE DIVAN by Hāfiz. Translated by Henry Bertram Lister. Published by La Boheme Club, San Francisco, Calif. Excerpts reprinted by permission of the Executors of the Estate of Henry B. Lister. Copyright, 1950, by Henry B. Lister.

I imagined that I had uprooted that flower from the garden of my heart, for every blossom which sprang up from its suffering bore only the fruits of pain.

From fear of the attacks of her love, I set my heart free with bloody strife; my heart dropped gouts of blood which marked my footsteps.

I beheld from her terrace how the glory of the moon veiled itself in confusion, before the face of that dazzling sun.

In his poems Hāfiz praises love between man and woman, and he praises also the beauty of women, their eyes, their lips, their hair, their features, their forms. He also sings of wine and men, as in these lines:

O Cupbearer! bring the joy of youth; bring cup after cup of red wine.

Bring medicine for the disease of love; bring wine, which is the balm of old and young.

Do not grieve for the revolution of time, that it wheeled thus and not thus. Touch the lute in peace.

Wisdom is very wearisome; bring for its neck the noose of wine.

When the rose goes, say, "Go gladly," and drink wine, red like the rose.

If the moan of the turtle does no remain, what matter? Bring music in the jug of wine.

Whether one can interpret this praise of wine as symbolic of spiritual substance is open to question. That there is passion, grace, and charm in the lines is, however, undeniable. The same is true of the following, also typical of Hāfiz:

O interpreter of dreams! give good tidings because last night the sun seemed to be my ally in the joy of the morning sleep.

At the hour when Hāfiz was writing this troubled verse, the bird of his heart had fallen into the snare of love.

An interesting legend about one of Hāfiz' poems in the Divan has come down through the ages. In the poem he offered willingly to exchange both the rich cities of Bokhara and Samarkand for the mole on the cheek of his beloved. When the great conqueror Tamerlane learned of the poem and had an opportunity, he sent for the poet and rebuked him, saying that Hāfiz should not have offered to give away what did not lay in his power to bestow. Not entirely subdued, even in the presence of the great Tamerlane, Hāfiz is supposed to have replied that it was through such generosity that he came to the attention of the mighty conqueror. Over and over again in the Divan another city is mentioned, his own native city of Shiraz, which he loved greatly. ("Hail, Shiraz! incomparable site! O Lord, preserve it from every disaster!") From the fame of Hāfiz and his poems, Shiraz came to be a symbol of poetic inspiration among poets who followed him.

The reader of the Divan will find himself making comparisons between Hāfiz' lyrics and those of Omar Khayyám, an earlier Persian poet and one whose work is more widely known among English-speaking readers through the adaptation by Edward FitzGerald. The works of the two poets have much in common. The apparent hedonism, the similar imagery, and the same flowing mellifluousness are found in the work of both men. The obvious difference is the superficial one of form, Omar Khayyám having written in quatrains, as the word "Rubáiyát" indicates, Hāfiz in the form of the ghazal. But a more important difference lies in the attitudes expressed in the poems. Hāfiz is the more serious of the two, despite an apparent hedonism. There is a greater inclination on the part of Hāfiz to be religious, to place his faith in Allah and his wisdom, inscrutable as the poet may find it. One result is that it is easier to think of Hāfiz growing old gracefully than of Omar Khayyám facing inevitable old age with equanimity.

THE DIVINE COMEDY

Type of work: Poem
Author: Dante Alighieri (1265-1321)
Type of plot: Christian allegory
Time of plot: The Friday before Easter, 1300
Locale: Hell, Purgatory, Paradise
First transcribed: c. 1307

Principal characters:
DANTE
VIRGIL, his guide
BEATRICE, the soul of Dante's beloved

Critique:

No words can describe the greatness of this work, a greatness both of theme and poetry. As a poet, Dante takes his place in the ranks of the foremost artists the world has ever known. The theme which he treats is universal; it involves the greatest concepts which man has ever attained. Only a master could find the loftiness of tone and the splendor and variety of images and scenes which are presented in *The Divine Comedy*.

The Story:

Dante found himself lost in a dark and frightening wood, and as he was trying to regain his path, he came to a mountain which he decided to climb in order to get his bearings. Strange beasts blocked his way, however, and he was forced back to the plain. As he was bemoaning his fate, the poet Virgil approached Dante and offered to conduct him through Hell, Purgatory, and blissful Paradise.

When they arrived at the gates of Hell, Virgil explained that here were confined those who had lived their lives without regard for good or evil. At the River Acheron, where they found Charon, the ferryman, Dante was seized with terror and fell into a trance. Aroused by a loud clap of thunder, he followed his guide through Limbo, the first circle of Hell. The spirits confined there, he learned, were those who, although they had lived a virtuous life, had not been baptized.

At the entrance to the second circle of Hell, Dante met Minos, the Infernal Judge, who warned him to take heed how he entered the lower regions. Dante was overcome by pity as he witnessed the terrible punishment which the spirits were undergoing. They had been guilty of carnal sin, and for punishment they were whirled around without cessation in the air. The third circle housed those who had been guilty of the sin of gluttony. They were forced to lie deep in the mud, under a constant fall of snow and hail and stagnant water. Above them stood Cerberus, a cruel monster, barking at the helpless creatures and tearing at their flesh. In the next circle, Dante witnessed the punishment of the prodigal and the avaricious, and realized the vanity of fortune.

He and Virgil continued on their journey until they reached the Stygian Lake, in which the wrathful and gloomy were suffering. At Virgil's signal, a ferryman transported them across the lake to the city of Dis. They were denied admittance, however, and the gates were closed against them by a multitude of horrible demons. Dante and Virgil gained admittance into the city only after an angel had interceded for them. There Dante discovered that tombs burning with a blistering heat housed the souls of heretics. Dante spoke to two of these tormented spirits and learned that although they had the power to predict the future, they had no way of knowing what was occurring in the present.

The entrance to the seventh circle was guarded by the Minotaur, and only after Virgil had pacified him could the two travelers pass down the steep crags to the base of the mountain. There they discerned a river of blood in which those who had committed violence in their lifetimes were confined. On the other side of the river they learned that those who had committed suicide were doomed to inhabit the trunks of trees. Beyond the river they came to a desert in which were confined those who had sinned against God, or Art, or Nature. A stream flowed near the desert and the two poets followed it until the water plunged into an abyss. In order that they might descend to the eighth circle, Virgil summoned Geryon, a frightful monster, who conducted them below. There they saw the tortured souls of seducers, flatterers, diviners, and barterers. Continuing along their way, they witnessed the punishment accorded hypocrites and robbers. In the ninth gulf were confined scandalmongers and spreaders of false doctrine. Among the writhing figures they saw Mahomet. Still farther along, the two discovered the horrible disease-ridden bodies of forgerers, counterfeiters, alchemists, and all those who deceived under false pretenses.

They were summoned to the next circle by the sound of a trumpet. In it were confined all traitors. A ring of giants surrounded the circle, one of whom lifted both Dante and Virgil and deposited them in the bottom of the circle. There Dante conversed with many of the spirits and learned the nature of their particular crimes.

After this visit to the lowest depths of Hell, Dante and Virgil emerged from the foul air to the pure atmosphere which surrounded the island of Purgatory. In a little while, they saw a boat conducted by an angel, in which were souls being brought to Purgatory. Dante recognized that of a friend among them. The two poets reached the foot of a mountain, where passing spirits showed them the easiest path to climb its slope. On their way up the path they encountered many spirits who explained that they were confined to Purgatory because they had

delayed their repentance too long. They pleaded with Dante to ask their families to pray for their souls when he once again returned to earth. Soon Dante and Virgil came to the gate of Purgatory, which was guarded by an angel. The two poets ascended a winding path and saw men, bent under the weight of heavy stones, who were expiating the sin of pride. They examined the heavily carved cornices which they passed, and found them covered with inscriptions urging humility and righteousness. At the second cornice were the souls of those who had been guilty of envy. They wore sackcloth and their eyelids were sewed with iron thread. Around them were the voices of angels singing of great examples of humility and the futility of envy. An angel invited the poets to visit the third cornice, where those who had been guilty of anger underwent repentance. Dante was astonished at the examples of patience which he witnessed there. At the fourth cornice he witnessed the purging of the sin of indifference or gloominess. He discussed with Virgil the nature of love. The Latin poet stated that there were two kinds of love, natural love, which was always right, and love of the soul, which might be misdirected. At the fifth cornice, avarice was purged. On their way to the next cornice, the two were overtaken by Statius, whose spirit had been cleansed and who was on his way to Paradise. He accompanied them to the next place of purging, where the sin of gluttony was repented, while voices sang of the glory of temperance. The last cornice was the place for purging by fire of the sin of incontinence. Here the sinners were heard to recite innumerable examples of praiseworthy chastity.

An angel now directed the two poets and Statius to a path which would lead them to Paradise. Virgil told Dante that he might wander through Paradise at his will until he found his love, Beatrice. As he was strolling through a forest, Dante came to a stream, on the other side of which stood a beautiful woman. She explained to him that the stream was called Lethe, and helped him to cross it. Then Beatrice descended from heaven and reproached him for his unfaithfulness to her during her life, but the virgins in the heavenly fields interceded with her on his behalf. Convinced of his sincere repentance and remorse, she agreed to accompany him through the heavens.

On the moon Dante found those who had made vows of chastity and determined to follow the religious life, but who were forced to break their vows. Beatrice led him to the planet Mercury, the second heaven, and from there to Venus, the third heaven, where Dante conversed with many spirits and learned of their virtues. On the sun, the fourth heaven, they were surrounded by a group of spirits, among them Thomas Aquinas. He named each of the spirits in turn and discussed their individual virtues. A second circle of blessed spirits surrounded the first, and Dante learned from each how he had achieved blessedness.

Then Beatrice and Dante came to Mars, the fifth heaven, where were cherished the souls of those who had been martyred. Dante recognized many renowned warriors and crusaders among them.

On Jupiter, the sixth heaven, Dante saw the souls of those who had administered justice faithfully in the world. The seventh heaven was on Saturn, where Dante found the souls of those who had spent their lives in meditation and religious retirement. From there Beatrice and her lover passed to the eighth heaven,

the region of the fixed stars. Dante looked back over all the distance which extended between the earth and this apex of Paradise and was dazzled and awed by what he saw. As they stood there, they saw the triumphal hosts approaching, with Christ leading, followed by Mary.

Dante was questioned by the saints. Saint Peter examined his opinions concerning faith; Saint James, concerning hope, and Saint John, concerning charity. Adam then approached and told the poet of the first man's creation, of his life in Paradise, and of his fall and what had caused it. Saint Peter bitterly lamented the avarice which his apostolic successors displayed, and all the sainted host agreed with him.

Beatrice then conducted Dante to the ninth heaven, where he was permitted to view the divine essence and to listen to the chorus of angels. She then led him to the Empyrean, from the heights of which, and with the aid of her vision, he was able to witness the triumphs of the angels and of the souls of the blessed. So dazzled and overcome was he by this vision that it was some time before he realized Beatrice had left him. At his side stood an old man whom he recognized as Saint Bernard, who told him Beatrice had returned to her throne. He then told Dante that if he wished to discover still more of the heavenly vision, he must join with him in a prayer to Mary. Dante received the grace to contemplate the glory of God, and to glimpse, for a moment, the greatest of mysteries, the Trinity and man's union with the divine.

917

THE DIVINE FIRE

Type of work: Novel
Author: May Sinclair (1870?-1946)
Type of plot: Psychological romance
Time of plot: The 1890's
Locale: England
First published: 1904

Principal characters:
SAVAGE KEITH RICKMAN, the genius
HORACE JEWDWINE, a literary editor
LUCIA HARDEN, loved by Rickman
FLOSSIE WALKER, betrothed to Rickman
MR. PILKINGTON, a financier

Critique:

Written by a popular English author of the early twentieth century, The Divine Fire is the chronicle of a gifted but unknown poet. His story was one of conflict between the genius and the man. First one, then the other was supreme, and he fought unsuccessfully to reconcile the two. It was only through the help of a good and inspiring woman that he was at last able to find himself.

The Story:

Horace Jewdwine, a literary editor, had a problem. He thought he had discovered a genius in Savage Keith Rickman, a young and unknown poet who earned his living by making catalogs for his father, a bookseller. But Jewdwine was afraid to say openly that Rickman was a genius, afraid for his reputation if he called Rickman a genius publicly and then the young man proved otherwise. He encouraged Rickman privately but failed to give him the public recognition that would have meant so much to the young writer.

Rickman himself cared little for fame or money. He knew too that he was a genius. That is, part of him was a genius. He was also a student, a young man about town, a journalist, a seeker after simple home life, and sometimes a drunk. It was hard to have so many facets to one's nature. One part warred constantly with the others. But no matter in what form he found himself, honor never left him. Even when drunk he continued to be honorable.

Rickman's intelligence and his ability to judge books were the foundations upon which the elder Rickman had built his financial success as a book dealer. The father and son could never understand each other. Money was the father's god; the muse was Rickman's. The father was backed by and supported by Mr. Pilkington, a financier of questionable ethics but great success. When Pilkington informed him that the Harden library might soon be on the market, the old man sent his son to evaluate it. At the same time Miss Lucia Harden, daughter of the owner of the library, asked for someone to catalog it for her. Rickman was sent because his knowledge of old books was infallible.

Rickman was awed by Lucia. She was the daughter of a baronet, so far above him that he could never hope to have her return his affection, but from the first he knew that she was destined to be his inspiration. Lucia was Jewdwine's cousin, and he was unhappy when he learned of her association with Rickman. He knew Rickman was beneath her, but he knew too that his cousin was moved by poetry. In addition, Jewdwine himself thought he would one day marry Lucia and inherit the library and the country estate. However, he could not bring himself to ask for her hand; decisions were almost impossible for Jewdwine.

Rickman soon learned, as he worked for Lucia, that his father and Pilkington were planning to pay a ridiculously low price for the Harden library. In order to help the girl, he wrote to Jewdwine and asked him to buy the library at a fair figure. Jewdwine failed to answer the letter. When Lucia's father died suddenly, leaving her indebted to Pilkington, Rickman went to his father and tried to persuade him to change the offer. The old man refused, and Rickman left the bookshop forever, refusing to compromise his honor in return for the partnership his father offered him if he would stay. Not wanting to hurt Lucia, he told her little of what had happened. He even tried to excuse Jewdwine's failure to buy the library and so salvage some of her father's estate.

Pilkington took the Harden house and furniture and Rickman's father the library. After Rickman left him the old man's business began to fail, and he had to mortgage the library to Pilkington. The books were stored, pending redemption. Rickman left Lucia and returned to his rooming-house, not to see her again for five years.

Back in London, Rickman continued to write for various journals. Jewdwine gave him a junior editorship on the journal which he edited, and the job allowed Rickman to live fairly comfortably. His serious writing he had put away in a drawer. The product of his genius, it would bring no money. Meanwhile he was trapped into a proposal by little Flossie Walker, a fellow boarder. Flossie was a girl who could never understand the ways of genius; her proper world was a house in the suburbs, decorated with hideous furniture. Rickman found himself with the house bought and the wedding date set.

Chance was to save him. Lucia, after five years, visited a friend in Rickman's boarding-house and the two met again. No word of love was spoken, for Lucia, even without her fortune, was still above him. And Rickman had no desire to hurt Flossie, who had waited two years for him to make enough money for their marriage. But he and Lucia found inspiration and comfort in renewed acquaintance. The real blow to Flossie's dreams came when Rickman's father died, leaving him a small inheritance. With it, Rickman could possibly redeem from Pilkington the mortgaged Harden library and return it to Lucia. To do so would mean a wait of at least two more years for Flossie. This she could not understand. A legal debt was one thing, a debt of honor another. With great relief Rickman learned that she refused to wait. She quickly married another boarder and found her house in the suburbs, complete with nursery.

Rickman lived through years of the most killing labor he would ever know. He worked all night, starved himself, lived in an unheated attic in order to redeem the complete library. He got extensions from Pilkington, who enjoyed the sight of genius chasing an impossible goal. His friends lost track of him. He lost his job with Jewdwine because he would not compromise his honor even in his desperate need to help Lucia. At last he seemed doomed to fail, for his lack of food and his feverish work made him desperately ill. Friends found him and took him, unconscious, to a hospital. Later, going through his things, they found the work of his genius. When it was published, Rickman's fame was assured. Poor Jewdwine! How he wished now that he had had the courage to claim Rickman in time. But Jewdwine had by that time sacrificed his own principles, and success was beyond hope for him.

Recovered, Rickman went to Lucia. He found her ill, unable to walk. When she learned that his illness had been caused by work for her, the gift was almost more than she could bear. With his aid she arose from her bed. Cured of the

malady which she knew now was only genius and the man fused at last.
heartbreak, she saw Rickman whole, the

DIVINE LOVE AND WISDOM

Type of work: Theosophical treatise
Author: Emanuel Swedenborg (1688-1772)
First published: 1763

During the earlier part of his life Emanuel Swedenborg established for himself a lasting reputation as a man of science, doing research in many scientific fields, including physics, astronomy, mathematics, engineering, and human anatomy. His research in several of these fields culminated in important publications which showed him well in advance of his time. His work in anatomy, for example, anticipated some of the theories of modern physiology, including those involving the functions of the ductless glands.

With respect to his later writings in religion and theosophy Swedenborg's reputation is a mixed one. Between 1743 and 1745 he suffered a mental and religious crisis which changed his life and his work. During the crisis, according to his own report, he underwent mystical experiences during which he was given access to the spiritual world, enjoying visions of that world, hearing and taking part in celestial conversations, and receiving divine instruction. In 1745, during a third great spiritual experience, reported Swedenborg, he witnessed the second advent of Christ and was instructed to establish a "New Church." From his visions and the instructions he purportedly received grew Swedenborg's theosophical writings, written in Latin. Although he wrote voluminously on his doctrines, Swedenborg did not himself found a sect, for he believed that members of any church could follow his doctrines. Later his followers did constitute the Church of the New Jerusalem, or New Church.

Like all theosophical writings, those of Swedenborg depend for their importance on how seriously one is willing to take the author's reports of divine inspiration and revelation. If acceptance is granted by the reader, then the writings assume tremendous, even cosmic, significance, for

Swedenborg did not attempt to disguise or conceal the supernatural source of his doctrines. He stated as actual fact that his doctrines were the results of visions granted to him by God, and he calmly and routinely noted certain facts and points either overheard in conversations among the angels or witnessed during the times he was transported spiritually to heaven. He regarded his mission seriously, sincerely believing that he had been commanded to interpret the spiritual world and explicate the Bible's true spiritual intent to mankind.

Swedenborg's most important theosophical work is the Divine Love and Wisdom, in which he stated his system most comprehensively and succinctly. The premises of his doctrine are that God is Man (or God-Man) and that God is Love. He reported that the conception of God as Man is held in all the heavens, the reason he vouchsafed being that heaven as a whole and in every part resembles the human form, and the Divine itself, together with the angels (who are also human in form) constitutes heaven. Swedenborg added that all angels and other heavenly spirits are men in perfect form. The essence or being of God, according to Swedenborgian doctrine, is love, an infinite love which mankind knows only as existing and not through an acquaintance with its nature, inasmuch as mankind is, without God, held to the natural world.

For Swedenborg, the manifestation of God and His infinite love is a sun, in the spiritual world a living sun. That spiritual sun corresponds in heaven to the "dead" sun of the natural world, and is the source of spiritual life. The sun of the natural world, according to Swedenborg, is the source of life in nature, which is but a receptacle of life, not a source. Just as the spiritual sun and the

921

natural sun are distinct but analogous in part and whole, so are heaven and earth distinct but analogous. Swedenborg warned, however, that space and time are concepts only of the natural world and are not to be found in the structure of the infinite and perfect realm of heaven. In heaven, according to the cosmology expounded in *Divine Love and Wisdom,* are three uncreated, distinct, and eternal degrees, corresponding to which in the natural world there are three finite degrees. Swedenborg did not describe in *Divine Love and Wisdom* how these degrees exist, but only stated that they are love, wisdom, and use, or to put it another way, end, cause, and effect. The three degrees exist, said Swedenborg, in every man at birth, although as a creature of the natural world the human being is unaware of them. As the degrees are opened successively to the individual, so is God in man and man in God, according to the doctrine. Light from the spiritual sun flows into man as he shuns evil, meaning that he can gain in wisdom; but the "heat" of the spiritual sun, or love, man cannot receive. The natural mind of the lowest degree, said Swedenborg, is a hell in itself, while the mind which is spiritualized becomes a heaven. In other words, by love and the opening of each of the successive degrees man can rise toward God. According to *Divine Love and Wisdom,* the end of creation, both spiritual and natural, is to become perfectly the image of God-Man.

Swedenborg undertook to answer the question of creation that has bothered countless numbers of theologically-minded persons in every generation: Did God create the universe out of nothing, or did He form a cosmos from the stuff of chaos? He wrote:

Every one of enlightened judgment sees that the universe was not created out of nothing, because it is impossible to make anything out of nothing; for nothing is nothing, and to suppose anything to be made out of nothing is absurd and therefore contrary to the light of truth, which comes from the divine Wisdom; and whatever is inconsistent with the divine Wisdom is also inconsistent with the divine Omnipotence. Everyone of enlightened judgment also sees that all beings were created out of self-existent substance, the very BEING out of which all things that exist come forth: and as God is the only self-existent Substance, and thus is essential BEING, it is plain that this is the source of all things that exist. Many have seen this because it is consistent with reason; but they have not dared to confirm it, fearing to be led to suppose that the created universe is God, because it exists from Him, or that nature is self-existent, and thus that what is called God is only nature in her utmost recesses.

Swedenborg suggests that there are pairs in all parts of the body in order that every man may achieve the love and wisdom of divinity. He notes that the eyes, ears, nostrils, hands, loins, and feet exist in pairs, that the heart, brain, and lungs are divided into two parts. The right-hand parts, according to his views, have a relation to love and the left-hand parts a relation to wisdom.

The doctrine propounded in *Divine Love and Wisdom* grants to all human beings the means of achieving the spiritual heaven, for in the Swedenborgian view it is a false doctrine that the Lord admits or excludes members of the human race arbitrarily from salvation.

DOCTOR FAUSTUS

Type of work: Novel
Author: Thomas Mann (1875–1955)
Type of plot: Philosophical chronicle
Time of plot: 1885-1945
Locale: Germany
First published: 1947

Principal characters:
ADRIAN LEVERKÜHN, an arrogant, sickly musical genius
SERENUS ZEITBLOM, his lifelong friend, the narrator
WENDELL KRETSCHMAR, Adrian's music teacher
EHRENFRIED KUMPF, and
EBERHARD SCHLEPPFUSS, teachers of theology
RÜDIGER SCHILDKNAPP, a poet, Adrian's friend
RUDOLF SCHWERDTFEGER, a violinist befriended by Adrian
INEZ INSTITORIS, in love with Schwerdtfeger
CLARISSA RODDE, her sister
MARIE GODEAU, loved by Adrian
NEPOMUK SCHNEIDEWEIN, Adrian's young nephew

Critique:

Doctor Faustus: The Life of the German Composer Adrian Leverkühn as Told by a Friend offers several approaches to an understanding of Mann's purpose and narrative pattern. On one level, it may be taken simply as the biographical story of a strange and fascinating genius, written in simple, honest prose by his lifelong friend and admirer, Serenus Zeitblom, a retired professor of philology. Again, it may be regarded as an excursion into a field which present-day fiction has neglected, a story of the destruction of a human soul in that demon-haunted world of the imagination which modern science has almost destroyed. Or it may be read as a study of the problem of the artist in contemporary society, of the conflict between his love of beauty and his moral responsibility to the kind of world in which he lives today. Beneath and beyond these levels of meaning, however, the novel is a political and philosophical allegory deeply charged with suggestion and purpose. Leverkühn, who gave his soul to the devil for twenty years of creative genius, symbolizes the German break-through to world power, the tortured nationalism of the Nazi state. As the narrator digresses to comment on the progress of the war the reader perceives that the rise and collapse of the Nazi dream runs side by side with Leverkühn's tragic story, like musical counterpoint creating a mood of increasing shame and community guilt, and a realization of inescapable doom. The novel is intricately constructed, profoundly serious, and beautifully written, with meanings which extend beyond the purely national and the temporal.

The Story:

At the outset Serenus Zeitblom doubted his ability to make understandable the life story of his friend Adrian Leverkühn, a musical genius whose strange, doomed career had much in common with the fated course of German history in the twentieth century. A former professor of philology, living in retirement and out of sympathy with the Hitler regime, greatly concerned for the future of his country, Zeitblom hesitantly began his task in May, 1943.

Adrian Leverkühn was born in 1885

on a farm near Kaiseraschern, in Thuringia. His family was of superior yeoman stock, and his father, a man interested in curious natural phenomena, did everything in his power to stimulate his son's intellectual curiosity. Adrian's boyhood friend was Serenus Zeitblom, a frequent visitor in the Leverkühn household. Years later Zeitblom could remember his friend's absorbing interest in a book filled with pictures of exotic lepidoptera. One in particular, *Heræra Esmeralda*, fascinated the boy because of its unusual beauty and protective coloring. Adrian had his introduction to music from a hired girl who taught him old folk songs.

A boy of brilliant mind and arrogant disposition, Adrian was educated to become the scholar of the family, since the farm was intended for an older brother. When he was ten he entered the gymnasium in Kaiseraschern. Living in the house of his uncle, a dealer in musical instruments, he had the run of the shop and began to play chords on an old harmonium. His uncle, overhearing his efforts, decided that the boy ought to have piano lessons. Adrian began to study under Wendell Kretschmar, the organist at the cathedral. His chief interest at that time, however, was theology, and he entered the University of Halle with the intention of preparing himself for the clergy. Zeitblom, certain that his friend's choice was dictated by the arrogance of purity, went with Adrian to his theological lectures. One of the teachers was Ehrenfried Kumpf, a forthright theologian who enlivened his classes by insulting the devil with epithets that Martin Luther might have used. Another instructor was Eberhard Schleppfuss, whose lectures were filled with anecdotes and sly undertones of demonism and witchcraft.

Because of the variety of his talents Adrian was soon ready for a career in scholarship, theology, or music. At last, unable to reconcile his interest in philosophy and science with theological precepts, he turned to music and began, still under Kretschmar's training, experiments in theory and technique which were to determine the highly original nature of his art. Before long the pupil had surpassed the instructor. Then Zeitblom was called up for a year of military duty, service from which Adrian was exempt because of his frail constitution, and the two friends separated for a time.

Adrian went to Leipzig for further study. With Kretschmar's encouragement he began to compose music of his own. A new friend was Rüdiger Schildknapp, an Anglophile poet whose enthusiasm for Shakespeare led to Adrian's decision to plan an opera based on *Love's Labor's Lost*. One night a sinister guide, somewhat like Schleppfuss in appearance, lured Adrian to a brothel. When a girl in the house—an Esmeralda, he called her—approached him, he ran from the place. Later he tried to see the girl again, but she had gone to Pressburg. Adrian followed her and there voluntarily contracted the venereal infection which was to account for the strange flowering of his genius and the eventual wreckage of his life. Several years afterward, during a holiday in Italy, he imagined a medievalistic, hallucinated encounter with the devil, who in return for his soul promised him twenty-four years in which to fulfill his powers as an artist.

Before his Italian journey Adrian had lived for a time in Munich. There his friends were artists and young intellectuals, including Rüdiger Schildknapp, the poet; Jeanette Scheurl, a novelist; Rudolf Schwerdtfeger, a young violinist; several actors, and the daughters of his landlady, Inez and Clarissa Rodde. Through Adrian, Zeitblom met these people and became interested in them. In 1912 Zeitblom married. A short time later, on his return from Italy, Adrian retired to a Bavarian farm presided over by motherly Frau Else Schweigestill. In his retreat, during the next twenty years, he composed the music that established his fame. Zeitblom went to teach at Freising, not far away, and from that time on the friends saw each other frequently. Zeitblom wrote the libretto for *Love's Labour's Lost*.

In 1914 Zeitblom went into the army and served until invalided home with typhus. Adrian, in retirement, wrote *Marvels of the Universe* and a composition based on the *Gesta Romanorum*. During the war Inez Rodde married Dr. Helmut Institoris. Secretly in love with Rudolf Schwerdtfeger, however, she kept up an adulterous relationship with the violinist for years. Adrian's health began to improve after the war. His great work of that period was an oratorio, *Apocalypse*. As his fame grew he acquired a patroness, Madame de Tolna, a wealthy Hungarian widow whom Zeitblom never met. Schwerdtfeger, in the meantime, had broken off his love affair with Inez. Their first meeting after their separation was at the funeral of Clarissa Rodde, an actress driven to suicide by a blackmailing lover.

Adrian yielded at last to Schwerdtfeger's urging and composed for the musician a violin concerto. About that time Adrian met attractive Marie Godeau. Hoping to marry her, he sent Schwerdtfeger to act as his emissary in his courtship, but the violinist fell in love with the girl and wooed her for himself. Shortly after the engagement had been announced Inez Institoris boarded a streetcar in which Schwerdtfeger was riding and shot her former lover. Adrian blamed himself for his friend's death.

Fate had one more blow in store for the composer. Adrian had a nephew, Nepomuk Schneidewein, of whom he was paternally fond. While convalescing from an illness, little Echo, as his uncle called him, went to stay with Adrian at the Schweigestill farm. Taken suddenly ill with cerebrospinal meningitis, the child died. It seemed to Adrian that he had lost the child he himself might have had. He was never to recover completely from his grief.

Meanwhile he was at work on his masterpiece, a symphonic cantata called *The Lamentation of Doctor Faustus*. In the early summer of 1930 he invited a number of his friends and some critics to hear excerpts from the work, but his explanation of his composition was so disordered and blasphemous that many of the guests left before he sat down to begin playing the score. As he struck the first chords he fell senseless to the floor.

Adrian Leverkühn lived in madness for the next ten years, and he died, tenderly cared for by his aged mother, at his Thuringian birthplace in 1940. Serenus Zeitblom was among the few old friends present at the funeral. It seemed to him then, and the certainty grew upon him while he was writing the story of Adrian's life, that his friend had somehow reflected the destiny of the German nation, a land arrogant, isolated, dehumanized, and at last reeling to that destruction which was the price of its power as the old philologist penned his final pages in April, 1945.

925

DOCTOR FAUSTUS

Type of work: Drama
Author: Christopher Marlowe (1564-1593)
Type of plot: Romantic tragedy
Time of plot: Sixteenth century
Locale: Germany
First presented: c. 1588

Principal characters:
FAUSTUS, master of all knowledge
WAGNER, his servant
LUCIFER, the fallen angel
MEPHOSTOPILIS, a devil
GOOD ANGEL
EVIL ANGEL

Critique:

This drama should be regarded as a skeletal structure of the play written by Marlowe, for the surviving manuscripts are so interspersed with comic scenes and the lines themselves so often revised according to whims of the actors that the original writing must be culled out of the surviving version. Even so, *The Tragical History of Doctor Faustus* is worth reading and study because of the many remaining examples of the poet's skill it contains. In addition to the adulterated poetry in this play there is also the problem of the tainted characterization and symbolism; for while the personality of Mephostopilis is often caricaturized and while the exploits of Faustus are frequently rendered pure low comedy, still the Marlowe version of the two principal characters is evident in the sober and more consistent moments of the play. As an added contribution to existing Faustian literature, Marlowe's *Doctor Faustus* is an artistic effort, although not comparable in depth or scope to the treatment given this theme in Goethe's *Faust*.

The Story:

Faustus nad been born of base stock in Rhodes, Germany. In his maturity, while living with some relatives in Wittenberg, he studied theology and was called a doctor. However, Faustus was so swollen with conceit that, Daedalus-like, he strove too far, became glutted with learning, con-

spired with the devil, and finally fell, accursed.

At the outset of his downward path Doctor Faustus found himself complete master of the fields of knowledge which men at that time studied. As a medical doctor he had already achieved huge success and great renown. But after obtaining good health for men no challenge remained in medicine except immortality. Law, Faustus concluded, was nothing but an elaborate moneymaking scheme. Only divinity remained, but theology led to a blind alley. Since the reward of sin was death and since no man could say he was without sin, then all men must sin and consequently die.

Necromancy greatly attracted Faustus. Universal power would be within his reach, the whole world at his command, and emperors at his feet, were he to become a magician. Summoning his servant Wagner, Faustus ordered him to summon Valdes and Cornelius, who could teach him their arts.

The Good Angel and the Evil Angel each tried to persuade Faustus, but Faustus was in no mood to listen to the Good Angel. He exulted over the prospects of his forthcoming adventures. He would get gold from India, pearls from the oceans, tasty delicacies from faraway places; he would read strange philosophies, cull from foreign kings their secrets, control Germany with his power,

926

reform the public schools, and perform many other fabulous deeds. Eager to acquire knowledge of the black arts, he went away to study with Valdes and Cornelius. Before long the scholars of Wittenberg began to notice the doctor's prolonged absence. Learning from Wagner of his master's unhallowed pursuits, the scholars lamented the fate of the famous doctor.

Faustus' first act of magic was to summon Mephostopilis. At sight of the ugly devil, he ordered Mephostopilis to assume the shape of a Franciscan friar. The docile obedience of Mephostopilis elated the magician, but Mephostopilis explained that magic had limits in the devil's kingdom. Mephostopilis claimed that he had not actually appeared at Faustus' behest but had come, as he would have to any other person, because Faustus had cursed Christ and abjured the Scriptures. Whenever a man is on the verge of being doomed, the devil will appear.

Interested in the nature of Lucifer, Faustus questioned Mephostopilis about his master, the fallen angel, and about hell, Lucifer's domain. Mephostopilis was wary. He claimed that the fallen spirits, having been deprived of the glories of heaven, found the whole world hell. Mephostopilis urged Faustus to give up his scheme, but Faustus scorned the warning, saying that he would surrender his soul to Lucifer if the fallen angel would give to Faustus twenty-four years of voluptuous ease, with Mephostopilis to attend him.

While Faustus indulged in a mental argument concerning the relative merits of God and the devil, the Good Angel and the Evil Angel, symbolic of his inner conflict, appeared once again, each attempting to persuade him. The result was that Faustus was more determined than ever to continue his course.

Mephostopilis returned to assure Faustus that Lucifer was agreeable to the bargain, which must be sealed in Faustus' blood. When Faustus tried to write, however, his blood congealed and Mephostopilis had to warm the liquid with fire.

Significantly the words, "Fly, man," appeared in Latin on Faustus' arm. When Faustus questioned Mephostopilis about the nature of hell, the devil claimed that hell had no limits for the damned. Intoxicated by his new estate, Faustus disclaimed any belief in an afterlife. Thus he assured himself that his contract with Lucifer would never be fulfilled, in spite of the devil's warning that he, Mephostopilis, was living proof of hell's existence.

Faustus, eager to consume the fruits of the devil's offering, demanded books that would contain varied information about the devil's regime. When the Good Angel and the Evil Angel came to him again, he realized that he was beyond repentence. Again the opposing Angels insinuated themselves into his mind, until he called on Christ to save him. As he spoke, wrathful Lucifer descended upon his prospective victim to admonish him never to call to God. As an appeasing gesture Lucifer conjured up a vision of the Seven Deadly Sins.

Faustus traveled extensively throughout the world, and Wagner marveled at his master's rapid progress. In Rome, at the palace of the Pope, Faustus, made invisible by his magic arts, astounded the Pope by snatching things from the holy man's hands. Like a gleeful child Faustus asked Mephostopilis to create more mischief. When Faustus returned home the scholars questioned him eagerly about many things unknown to them. As his fame spread, the emperor invited him to the palace and asked him to conjure up the spirit of Alexander the Great. Because a doubtful knight scoffed at such a preposterous idea, Faustus, after fulfilling the emperor's request, spitefully placed horns on the head of the skeptical nobleman.

Foreseeing that his time of merriment was drawing to a close, Faustus returned to Wittenberg. Wagner sensed that his master was about to die when Faustus gave his faithful servant all his wordly goods.

As death drew near, Faustus spoke with

his conscience, which, assuming the form of an Old Man, begged him to repent before he died. When Faustus declared that he would repent, Mephostopilis cautioned him not to offend Lucifer. Faustus asked Mephostopilis to bring him Helen of Troy as a lover to amuse him during the final days of his life.

In his declining hours Faustus conversed with scholars who had loved him, and the fallen theologian revealed to them his bargain with Lucifer. Alone, he uttered a final despairing plea that he be saved from impending misery, but in the end he was borne off by a company of devils.

THE DOCTOR IN SPITE OF HIMSELF

Type of work: Drama
Author: Molière (Jean Baptiste Poquelin, 1622-1673)
Type of plot: Farce
Time of plot: Seventeenth century
Locale: Paris
First presented: 1666

Principal characters:
SGANARELLE, a woodcutter
MARTINE, his wife
GÉRONTE, a gentleman of means
LUCINDE, his daughter
VALÈRE, his attendant
LÉANDRE, Lucinde's lover

Critique:

This drama, ordinarily considered one of Molière's less important works, nevertheless demonstrates his ability to ridicule the fads of his day, in this case the vogue, not wholly extinct three centuries later, of showing obsequious deference to men of science no matter what their real qualifications may be. Exposing the fact that ignorance often hides behind a smattering of superficial learning, he levels his barbs against the doctors of his time. The comedy was an immediate success and has always been popular. Sixty-five years after its first presentation, Henry Fielding, English novelist and dramatist, adapted the basic plot in a play presented at the Drury Lane Theatre under the title of *The Mock Doctor; or, the Dumb Lady Cur'd.*

The Story:

Sganarelle, a faggot gatherer, was driven to extremes because Martine, his nagging wife, accused him of always being drunk instead of working, and finally he took a stick and beat her soundly. When their neighbor M. Robert sought to interfere, Martine boxed his ears and declared she liked to have her husband beat her. But as Sganarelle went off to the woods after promising to bring back a hundred faggots that day, Martine itched for wifely revenge.

Géronte's daughter Lucinde had feigned illness and loss of speech in order to escape marriage to a wealthy suitor her father had chosen for her; she herself was in love with Léandre, who returned her love. Her father had summoned many physicians to treat her, but all had failed to find a cure. At last Géronte sent his attendants, Valère and Lucas, in search of a specialist.

When they encountered the offended Martine and confided in her the reason for their journey, she saw in their search an opportunity to get even with her husband. She told them that he was a marvelous curer of any illness, a doctor who pretended to be a woodcutter who dressed absurdly and pretended complete ignorance of his art, so that it might actually be necessary to thrash him violently to gain from him admission of his real talents. Her boasts of the wonderful cures he had performed so impressed her listeners that they set off in immediate search of this medical prodigy. They found Sganarelle in the wood, relaxing with his bottle, and, being rebuffed by him after their first ceremonious introduction, they thrashed him severely and finally forced him to say he was a doctor and to follow them to see Lucinde.

The attendants persuaded Géronte that Sganarelle, though he loved a joke and seemed to be off his head, was really the greatest doctor in the world. When Sganarelle was introduced to Géronte, he inquired, as he himself had been

929

asked, if the other man were a doctor. Géronte replied that he was not, whereupon Sganarelle, following the pattern applied to him, gave him a sound thrashing. The attendants thereupon explained to the bewildered Géronte that this was merely an example of the great doctor's eccentricity, a sure sign of his greatness.

When Géronte brought in his daughter, she replied to Sganarelle's questions by signs, gestures, and grunts. From these noises Sganarelle diagnosed Lucinde as dumb, a malady caused by loss of speech because of an impediment in the action of her tongue, on which subject Aristotle said—thus and so. Using some learned-sounding Latin words which meant nothing at all, he prescribed that the patient be put to bed and given plenty of bread soaked in wine; his explanation was that in this manner parrots were induced to speak.

Géronte, overwhelmed by the brilliance of Sganarelle's diagnosis and vast medical knowledge, felt absolute confidence in the ability of this eccentric to cure his daughter of her strange action. What pleased Sganarelle most was the generous fee Géronte gave him.

Léandre came to the fake physician to ask his help in carrying out a plan by which the young man hoped to see Lucinde; but Sganarelle pretended to be beyond influence in such matters, until the lover offered him a handsome fee. Léandre then told him that Lucinde's illness was put on and that its cause was not the brain, the spleen, or intestines, but love. Sganarelle and the young man plotted to disguise Léandre as an apothecary's assistant so that he could speak with Lucinde. Sganarelle also confided that he was not really a doctor but had been forced to appear one in spite of himself, for a reason he did not know. Once the error had spread, however, everyone had taken him for a man of great reputation, and so he had made up his mind to stick to his new calling, for it paid very well.

As if to substantiate his story, Thibaut and his son Perrin, country fellows who had heard of Sganarelle's powers, asked him to prescribe for Thibaut's ailing wife; but Sganarelle gave no ear to their troubles until they gave him gold crowns. As a cure, he prescribed a piece of cheese, which, he said, was made of mixed gold, coral, pearls, and other precious things, and must be used as directed. He also warned them that if the patient died they should bury her as decently as possible.

Géronte reported to Sganarelle that his patient had grown worse since taking his remedy. When the nurse brought in Lucinde, Sganarelle asked his disguised assistant to feel her pulse, meanwhile keeping Géronte occupied in conversation in order to keep him from overhearing the lovers' plans. But Géronte caught a few words spoken by Lucinde and exclaimed in surprise and in praise of the doctor. Lucinde approached her father and acknowledged that she had now recovered her speech, but only to tell him that she would marry no one except Léandre and that nothing would shake her resolution.

Géronte stubbornly insisted that she must marry Horace, the man of his choice, that very evening. When Lucinde declared she would rather die, Sganarelle stepped in and assured the father that her actions were merely a sign of additional madness and that the apothecary was the man who could effect a cure. Summoning Léandre, and, sprinkling his instructions with Latin polysyllables to mislead the others, he urged the lover to fly with Lucinde immediately. Sganarelle engaged Géronte in conversation while Lucinde and Léandre made their escape. When their flight was reported to the irate father, he threatened Sganarelle with hanging for aiding in his daughter's elopement.

In the midst of this predicament Martine overtook her husband. On being told he was about to hang for helping his master's daughter elope, she bewailed the fact but added she would have been somewhat comforted if only he had finished chopping their wood. Sganarelle told her to leave, but she said she preferred to stay and see him hanged.

At that critical moment Lucinde and Léandre returned to confront Géronte with the news that Léandre's uncle had just died and named the young man heir to a considerable fortune. Géronte, overjoyed at the turn of events which would bring him a rich son-in-law, gave the couple his blessing. Martine insisted that since Sganarelle was not to be hanged he could thank her for having achieved the honor of being a doctor; but Sganarelle pointed out that this distinction had gained him innumerable thwacks with a stick. He forgave the beatings, however, because of his new dignity as a doctor. But he took occasion to remind his shrewish wife that henceforth she must show greater respect for a man of his consequence, one whom the world now looked up to and honored—in spite of himself.

DR. JEKYLL AND MR. HYDE

Type of work: Novelette
Author: Robert Louis Stevenson (1850-1894)
Type of plot: Fantasy
Time of plot: Nineteenth century
Locale: London
First published: 1886

Principal characters:
DR. HENRY JEKYLL, a London physician
MR. UTTERSON, counselor for Dr. Jekyll
POOLE, Dr. Jekyll's manservant
DR. HASTIE LANYON, Dr. Jekyll's close friend

Critique:

The *Strange Case of Dr. Jekyll and Mr. Hyde* has steadily maintained the popularity which it had originally. The story is basically one of romantic adventure and fantasy, of the type currently found in paper pulps. Yet by merit of Stevenson's understanding of human nature and his mastery of English prose, the story holds subtle values as an illustration of man's dual nature. It is not necessary to believe the story in order to understand and believe the symbolism.

The Story:

Mr. Richard Enfield, and his cousin, Mr. Utterson, a lawyer, were strolling according to their usual Sunday custom when they came upon an empty building on a familiar street. Mr. Enfield told that some time previously he had seen an ill-tempered man trample down a small child at the doorway of the deserted building. He and other indignant bystanders had forced the stranger, who gave his name as Hyde, to pay over a sum of money for the child's welfare. Enfield remembered the man Hyde with deep loathing.

Utterson had reasons to be interested in Hyde. When he returned to his apartment he reread the strange will of Dr. Henry Jekyll. The will stipulated that in the event of Dr. Jekyll's death all of his wealth should go to a man named Edward Hyde.

Utterson sought out Hyde, the man whom Enfield had described, to discover if he were the same who had been named heir to Dr. Jekyll's fortune. Sus- picious of Utterson's interest, Hyde became enraged and ran into his house. Questioned, Dr. Jekyll refused to discuss the matter, but insisted that in the event of his death the lawyer should see to it that Mr. Hyde was not cheated out of his fortune. The lawyer believed that Hyde was an extortioner who was getting possession of Dr. Jekyll's money and who would eventually murder the doctor.

About a year later Hyde was wanted for the wanton murder of a kindly old man, Sir Danvers Carew, but he escaped before he could be arrested. Dr. Jekyll presented the lawyer and the police with a letter signed by Hyde, in which the murderer declared his intention of making good his escape forever. He begged Dr. Jekyll's pardon for having ill-used his friendship.

About this time Dr. Lanyon, who had been for years a great friend of Dr. Jekyll, became ill and died. Among his papers was a letter addressed to Utterson. Opening it, Utterson discovered an inner envelope also sealed and bearing the notice that it was not to be opened until after Dr. Jekyll's death. Utterson felt that it was somehow associated with the evil Hyde, but he could in no way fathom the mystery.

One Sunday Enfield and Utterson were walking again in the street where Enfield had seen Hyde mistreating the child. They now realized that the strange deserted building was a side entrance to the house of Dr. Jekyll, an additional wing used as a laboratory.

Looking up at the window, they saw Dr. Jekyll sitting there. He looked disconsolate. Then his expression seemed to change, so that his face took on a grimace of horror or pain. Suddenly he closed the window. Utterson and Enfield walked on, too overcome by what they had seen to talk further.

Not long afterward Utterson was sitting by his fireside when Poole, Dr. Jekyll's manservant, sought entrance. He related that for a week something strange had been going on in Dr. Jekyll's laboratory. The doctor himself had not appeared. Instead, he had ordered his meals to be sent in and had written curious notes demanding that Poole go to all the chemical houses in London in search of a mysterious drug. Poole was convinced that his master had been slain and that the murderer, masquerading as Dr. Jekyll, was still hiding in the laboratory.

Utterson and Poole returned to Dr. Jekyll's house and broke into his laboratory with an ax. Entering, they discovered that the man in the laboratory had killed himself by draining a vial of poison just as they broke the lock. The man was Edward Hyde.

They searched in vain for the doctor's body, certain it was somewhere about after they discovered a note of that date addressed to Utterson. In the note Dr. Jekyll said he was planning to disappear, and he urged Utterson to read the note which Dr. Lanyon had left at the time of his death. An enclosure contained the confession of Henry Jekyll.

Utterson returned to his office to read the letters. The letter of Dr. Lanyon described how Dr. Jekyll had sent Poole to Dr. Lanyon with a request that Dr. Lanyon search for some drugs in Dr. Jekyll's laboratory. Hyde had appeared to claim the drugs. Then, in Dr. Lanyon's presence, Hyde had taken the drugs and had been transformed into Dr. Jekyll. The shock of this transformation had caused Dr. Lanyon's death.

Dr. Jekyll's own account of the horrible affair was more detailed. He had begun early in life to live a double life. Publicly he had been genteel and circumspect, but privately he had practiced strange vices without restraint. Becoming obsessed with the idea that people had two personalities, he reasoned that men were capable of having two physical beings as well. Finally, he had compounded a mixture which transformed his body into the physical representation of his evil self. He became Hyde. In his disguise he was free to haunt the lonely, narrow corners of London and to do the darkest acts without fear of recognition.

He tried in every way to protect Hyde. He cautioned his servants to let him in at any hour; he took an apartment for him, and he made out his will in Hyde's favor. His life proceeded safely enough until he awoke one morning in the shape of Edward Hyde and realized that his evil nature had gained the upper hand. Frightened, he determined to cast off the nature of Hyde. He sought out better companions and tried to occupy his mind with other things. However, he was not strong enough to change his true nature. He finally permitted himself to assume the shape of Hyde again, and on that occasion Hyde, full of an overpowering lust to do evil, murdered Sir Danvers Carew.

Dr. Jekyll renewed his effort to abandon the nature of Hyde. Walking in the park one day, he suddenly changed into Hyde. On that occasion he had sought out his friend Dr. Lanyon to go to his laboratory to obtain the drugs which would change him back to the personality of the doctor. Dr. Lanyon had watched the transformation with horror. Thereafter the nature of Hyde seemed to assert itself constantly. When his supply of chemicals had been exhausted and could not be replenished, Dr. Jekyll, as Hyde, shut himself up in his laboratory while he experimented with one drug after another. Finally, in despair, as Utterson now realized, he killed himself.

933

DOCTOR PASCAL

Type of work: Novel
Author: Émile Zola (1840-1902)
Type of plot: Naturalism
Time of plot: Late nineteenth century
Locale: The south of France
First published: 1893

Principal characters:
DOCTOR PASCAL, a doctor interested in heredity
CLOTILDE, his niece
MARTINE, their devoted old servant
FÉLICITÉ ROUGON, Dr. Pascal's mother
DOCTOR RAMOND
MAXIME, Clotilde's brother

Critique:

Doctor Pascal is the twentieth and last volume of the Rougon-Macquart series, in which Zola intended to apply the methods of the experimental sciences to the social novel. Dr. Pascal, himself a Rougon, is doing research on the problem of heredity. Using experimental methods, he has chosen his own family as his field of investigation. Thus the novel affords Zola a double opportunity: to conclude the whole series with flashbacks to the former volumes, and to expose his own conception of reality through Dr. Pascal's exposition of his theories. When Dr. Pascal remarks that his files on the family contain the materials for a fresco of life during the Second Empire, the parallel is obvious. What Dr. Pascal has meant to do on the subject of heredity, Zola intended to do on the subject of social life. As in the preceding volumes, a dominant characteristic of the book is its objectivity. Although Zola has often been accused of insensibility, Dr. Pascal seems to testify more to his great passion for truth, whether pleasant or not.

The Story:

The July afternoon was extremely hot, but the room was well protected from the heat by heavy wooden shutters. In front of a huge carved oak armoire, Dr. Pascal was patiently looking for a paper. The search was not easy. For some thirty years, the doctor had been amassing manuscripts related to his work on heredity.

A smile came over his face as he found the paper and handed it to his niece, asking her to copy it over for their friend, Dr. Ramond. Clotilde took it without interrupting her pastel drawing of some flowers intended to provide illustration plates for the doctor's work.

Martine, the housekeeper, came in to repair the tapestry on an armchair. She had been with the doctor for thirty years, ever since he had come to Plassans as a young doctor. Thirteen years later, Dr. Pascal's brother, following the death of his wife, had sent Clotilde, then seven years old, to live with him. Martine had cared for the child according to her own zealous religious conviction.

For his part, Dr. Pascal completed Clotilde's instruction by trying to give her clear and healthy ideas on everything. The three had lived in peaceful happiness, although a certain uneasiness was now beginning to grow out of their religious conflicts. Martine considered it a pity that such a kind man as her master refused to go to church; the two women had agreed that they would force him to attend services.

Toward the end of the afternoon old Madame Rougon came for a visit, but under a false pretext; she was actually there to inspect everything. Hearing her son in the next room, she appeared quite displeased that he was again doing what she called his "devilish cooking." She told Clotilde of the unpleasant rumors going around about the doctor's new drug. If only he could try spectacular cures on the famous people of the town, she declared; but he was always treating the poor. She had always wanted him to be a success, like his two brothers or his nephew, Clotilde's brother. But Dr. Pascal was most unlike the rest of his family. He had practiced medicine for only twelve years; then he had invested his money with a private broker and was now living on its returns. Martine was getting the money every three months and using it to the best advantage. When his patients paid him, Dr. Pascal would throw the money in a drawer, taking it only as he needed it. When he visited a poor patient he often left money there instead of receiving payment. He was completely lost in his research work, his faith in life, and his fight against suffering.

Madame Rougon was upset most by the fact that the big oak armoire contained detailed information on each member of the family. Afraid that the doctor's papers might fall in the hands of a stranger, she asked Clotilde to give her the key. She opened the cupboard, but as she was reaching for the famous files, Dr. Pascal entered; she left demurely as if nothing had happened. It was Clotilde who received the explosion of the doctor's anger.

From that time on Dr. Pascal felt that he was being betrayed by the two human beings who were dearest to him, and to whom he was dearest. He kept all the drawers of his desk tightly locked.

One day Maxime came for a visit. He was still young, but worn out by a dissolute way of life. Seeing that his sister was not planning to get married, he asked her to come to Paris with him. Clotilde was frightened at the idea of leaving Dr. Pascal's home, but she promised to go to her brother if some day he really needed her.

After Maxime's visit the house returned to its state of subdued tension un-

til a Capuchin came to Plassans to preach. Clotilde, deeply shaken by his preaching, asked Dr. Pascal to burn all his papers. He refused. He also had another fruitless discussion with his mother, who was constantly begging the young girl to destroy his files.

One night, after Clotilde had taken the key to the armoire, he found her trying to steal the papers. While she was helping him replace them, he made a last attempt to convince her of the value of his work. He showed her the files and explained the use he was making of them. Clotilde, almost convinced, asked for time to think about the matter.

One day the doctor returned in an upset state from a call he had made. A patient had died of a heart attack while he was giving the man an injection. After Dr. Pascal had refused Clotilde's attempted comfort, his mother hinted that he might be going insane. and he nearly believed the suggestion. He felt he might be suffering from the same insanity as his grandmother, who had never been well-balanced and who was still in a sanitarium at the age of one hundred and four. Anxious and helpless, Clotilde and Martine watched over him.

When Dr. Ramond came to ask Clotilde to marry him, she said that she needed time to consider his proposal but that she would answer him soon. In the meantime she wanted to learn from him what he thought about her uncle's condition. Dr. Pascal overheard the conversation, and from that time on his health became worse. Although he allowed Clotilde to take care of him, he would not let her come into his room when he was in bed. She finally persuaded him to try some of his own injections, as Dr. Ramond had suggested. As he began to show improvement she tried to restore his faith in his research. He was overjoyed when she found the key to the armoire and brought it to him.

At last Dr. Pascal declared that he felt greatly improved, and he told Clotilde that she should begin to think about a

935

date for her marriage. Clotilde did not seem concerned. One day, as they were coming back from a walk, she asked him to help untie her hat. Suddenly, as he bent close to her, he realized how greatly he desired her. Disturbed by the strength of his feelings, he insisted that she give Dr. Ramond a definite date for the wedding. A short time later he bought her an extravagant present of lace, which he put on her bed. That night Clotilde came running to his door and told him that if her marriage was the occasion for the gift, she was not going to marry Dr. Ramond. He, Pascal, was the man she loved. That night she was his.

A period of extreme happiness for both followed. Martine, after disappearing for a full day to show her disapproval, continued her faithful service.

One day Martine returned with the news that the broker had embezzled the doctor's funds and fled. She performed miracles in preparing meals, using the money accumulated in the drawer, but at last their situation became really desperate. Dr. Pascal and Clotilde seemed quite unconcerned, however, and waited patiently for the matter to be settled in court.

Meanwhile, Madame Rougon kept busy. She produced a letter from Max-
ime, now disabled, in which he asked for his sister; she shamed Dr. Pascal for keeping this young girl without even marrying her and for not being able to feed her properly. Dr. Pascal was happy when Clotilde refused to go to her brother. Then, feeling guilty, he tried working hard in order to keep his mind busy. Finally, pretending that he needed time to devote himself to his research, he insisted that she should go. Clotilde, deeply hurt, obeyed.

Dr. Pascal went on working, waiting, meanwhile, for the painful joy of Clotilde's letters. In poor health, he suffered two heart attacks. Dr. Ramond brought him the news that some of his money had been recovered. About the same time he received a letter from Clotilde saying that she was pregnant. He immediately wired her to return. She left at once, but two hours before she arrived he died. However, he had gathered enough strength at the end to complete his files concerning himself, Clotilde, and their unborn child.

While Clotilde was in Dr. Pascal's room, Madame Rougon, with the help of Martine, burned all his papers. Later on, Clotilde used the shelves to store her baby's clothes.

DOCTOR THORNE

Type of work: Novel
Author: Anthony Trollope (1815-1882)
Type of plot: Domestic realism
Time of plot: Mid-nineteenth century
Locale: "Barsetshire," England
First published: 1858

Principal characters:
DOCTOR THORNE, a country doctor
MARY THORNE, his niece
SQUIRE GRESHAM, owner of Greshamsbury Park
LADY ARABELLA, his wife
FRANK GRESHAM, their son
ROGER SCATCHERD, a stonemason, later a barone.
LOUIS PHILIPPE, his son
MISS DUNSTABLE, an heiress

Critique:

The third in the series of Barchester Novels, Doctor Thorne continues the chronicling of clerical and county life begun in The Warden and Barchester Towers. The usual Trollopian theme of making money and a successful marriage is here portrayed against the background of an English country estate and the life connected with it. There is, as in other books of the series, a mixture of sentiment, humor, romance, and fidelity to human nature and experience. The chief value of these novels lies in their authentic depiction of middle-class country life in nineteenth-century England. The Barchester Novels do not contain the whole of Victorian society, but in them Trollope reflected, better than any other writer of his time, the manners and morals of the period.

The Story:

Greshamsbury Park, in the county of Barsetshire, dominated the life of the surrounding countryside. Unfortunately, Greshamsbury's lord, Squire Gresham, was rapidly spending himself into poverty. Most of his financial troubles resulted from the desire of his wife, Lady Arabella De Courcy Gresham, to get him into politics. The squire had inherited his father's seat in Parliament. He had lost favor, however, because of his Whig leanings. Barsetshire, overwhelmingly Tory, did not approve of Gresham's Whig friends or the

fact that his wife's aristocratic family, the De Courcys, were aggressively Whig in sentiment. Having lost his seat in the Parliamentary elections, Gresham twice tried to regain it. These attempts were stimulated by his wife, who fancied being the wife of a member of Parliament. But Gresham was not successful, and he lost a great deal of money in financing his campaigns.

Consequently, when his son Frank came of age, Squire Gresham had not much to offer him in the way of financial security. Lady Arabella saw as their only hope the possibility of Frank's marriage to a wealthy heiress. That he might do such a thing seemed rather doubtful, however, for, much to the distress of his mother and her family, young Frank was highly enamored of Mary Thorne, niece of the local doctor. Frank and Mary had known each other all their lives, and Mary had been educated along with the young Greshams at Greshamsbury Park. Hers was an interesting history.

She had been brought to live with her uncle, Doctor Thorne, when she was a mere infant. The real circumstances of her birth—that she was the illegitimate child of Doctor Thorne's brother and Mary Scatcherd, a village girl—were known only to the doctor. Even Mary Scatcherd's brother Roger, who had killed his sister's betrayer, did not know that Doctor Thorne had adopted the child. Roger

937

Scatcherd, a poor stonemason, had been sentenced to six months in prison for his crime. When his term was up, he was told that the child had died. Since the doctor stood in high favor with Squire Gresham and daily attended Lady Arabella, it was natural that his niece should visit the estate. Because she was an attractive child and near the age of the Gresham children, she soon took her lessons with them. By the time Frank was of age, Mary Thorne seemed part of the family. But Lady Arabella was determined that this was not to be the literal state of affairs; Mary had no money.

One of Squire Gresham's greatest misfortunes was the loss of a particularly choice part of his estate, land sold to pay off his numerous and most pressing debts. Doctor Thorne, acting as agent for the squire, found a buyer in Sir Roger Scatcherd, a wealthy baronet. Sir Roger was the former stonemason, who had prospered well after his jail term and was now the possessor of a title, a seat in Parliament, and a large fortune. Although he knew nothing of the existence of his sister's illegitimate child, Sir Roger was in close contact with Doctor Thorne. Sir Roger was a chronic alcoholic, and Doctor Thorne was often called on to attend him during his sprees.

To the Gresham family the loss of this piece of property was indeed a tragedy, for the sale greatly diminished the estate Frank would someday inherit. Nervously, Lady Arabella began to plan for the future of her family. Fortunately, one of the daughters was engaged to marry money, a politician who wanted the Gresham and De Courcy position and family connections. Another daughter would marry the local vicar and so would be assured of a respectable position, though one without much money. But Frank was his mother's real hope. If he could make a wealthy marriage, their troubles would be over. But Frank, in love with Mary Thorne, had no lofty matrimonial ambitions. Lady Arabella's family, to save him from an unfortunate romance, invited Frank to De

Courcy Castle for a visit.

It was the Countess De Courcy's plan to make a match between Frank and Miss Dunstable, a family friend. Miss Dunstable was considered the wealthiest heiress in England, but she was wary and sharp-tongued. Mostly to humor his aunt, Frank pretended to woo the heiress, and to his surprise he found her rather good company. Miss Dunstable, ten years his senior and much more worldly-wise, soon uncovered his little plot. Thereafter they became the best of friends, and she acted as an adviser to Frank in his affair with Mary Thorne.

Meanwhile Sir Roger Scatcherd was in such poor health from excessive drinking that he decided to make his will, leaving everything to Louis Philippe, his equally alcoholic son. When Dr. Thorne learned the terms of the will, he told Sir Roger that Mary Scatcherd's child was still living. Sir Roger made her his second heir in the event of his son's death.

Otherwise matters were not going well for Mary. Lady Arabella, finding Frank's attachment for Mary unchanged, would not allow the girl to visit Greshamsbury. When Frank arrived home and became aware of the shabby treatment she had received, he was furious. But the family insisted that he had to marry wealth, particularly after his sister, who was to marry money, had been jilted.

Sir Roger was also in difficulties. Having discovered a fraud in his election, the committee unseated him, and the shock was too great for the old man. He went on one final drinking bout and died from the effects. Louis Philippe, having inherited the estate, also formed an attachment for Mary, but she remained true to Frank. Dr. Thorne's only hope for the happiness of Mary and Frank lay in the possible death of Louis Philippe. Meanwhile that young man was well on his way to fulfilling the doctor's half-wish. Having paid a visit to the squire for the purpose of foreclosing on some debts, Louis Philippe went on a drinking spree that rivaled any of his father's. Weak and very ill, he was finally sent home.

Soon afterward, in a stormy interview, Lady Arabella demanded that Mary end her engagement to Frank. Mary refused to break her promise, but she did ask the young man to release her because of the hopelessness of the situation in which they found themselves. Frank refused, insisting that they loved each other. Then it was that Louis Philippe died. Doctor Thorne jubilantly told Mary the news of her inheritance, news which opened the way for her marriage to Frank. With Mary now an heiress in her own right, not even the proud De Courcys could object to so excellent a match. For the first time in years an atmosphere of rejoicing hung over Greshamsbury Park.

DODSWORTH

Type of work: Novel
Author: Sinclair Lewis (1885-1951)
Type of plot: Social criticism
Time of plot: The 1920's
Locale: United States and Europe
First published: 1929

Principal characters:
SAM DODSWORTH, an American manufacturer
FRAN DODSWORTH, his wife
KURT OBERSDORF, Fran's lover
EDITH CORTRIGHT, Sam's friend, later his fiancée
CLYDE LOCKERT, Fran's admirer
EMILY, the Dodsworths' daughter
BRENT, the Dodsworths' son

Critique:

Dodsworth is a successful novel in spite of its sprawling and sometimes rambling style. It describes convincingly the degeneration and unmasking of the shallow, snobbish Fran Dodsworth, and the disillusion and final rebellion of her idealistic husband. One of the last in the tradition of American novels on American materialism and European cultivation, the book contains brilliant insights into the relationships of the two cultures.

The Story:

In 1903, Sam Dodsworth married Fran Voelker whom he had met at the Canoe Club while he was assistant superintendent at the Zenith Locomotive works. Five years after their marriage Sam became vice-president and general manager of production for the Revelation Automobile Company. By 1925, the Dodsworths had two children, Emily, about to be married, and Brent, in school at Yale. When Sam sold his factory to the Unit Automotive Company, they decided to go to Europe for a leisurely vacation, a second honeymoon.

The first night out on the S.S. Ultima, Major Clyde Lockert seated himself at Sam's table in the smoking room. Lockert, who said he was growing cocoa in British Guiana, quickly became friends with Fran Dodsworth, and while Sam looked on like an indulgent parent, he squired her about, censuring and selecting the new friends she made. He continued to see the Dodsworths after they arrived in London.

Fran was snobbishly pleased when he took them to see his cousins, Lord and Lady Herndon. Between them Fran and Lockert made Sam feel almost like an outsider. He was a failure at the dinner party the Herndons gave, for he knew nothing about cricket or polo, and he had no opinions about the Russian situation.

One evening Hurd, manager of the London branch of the Revelation Motor Company, invited Sam to a get-together, along with about thirty representatives of American firms. Sam was surprised to learn that few of them wanted to go back to the United States except, perhaps, for a visit. They all preferred the leisureliness, the freedom from imposed moral restraint, which their adopted land afforded. These arguments made Sam see Europe in a different light.

When he returned to the hotel, he found Fran in tears. Lockert had taken her out that evening, and on their return had tried to make love to her. Fran, ashamed of the situation in which she had

DODSWORTH by Sinclair Lewis. By permission of the publishers, Harcourt, Brace and Co., Inc. Copyright 1929, by Harcourt, Brace and Co., Inc.

placed herself and sure that Lockert would be laughing at her, asked that they leave for France as soon as possible. They started four days later.

France was a new experience for Sam Dodsworth. When Fran was willing to go sightseeing, he was able to see Paris and observe its people. When she chose to be fashionable and take tea at the Crillon with other American tourists, he was less fortunate. But the more he saw, the more convinced Sam became that he could not understand Frenchmen. In the back of his mind he was afraid that his inability to accept foreign ways, and Fran's willingness to adopt them, would finally drive them apart. He felt lonely for his old friend Tubby Pearson, president of the Zenith bank.

Before long Fran had many friends among expatriate Americans of the international set. With her constant visits to dressmakers and her portrait painter, her outings with the leisured young men who escorted her and her friends, she and Sam saw less and less of each other. When he went home for his college class reunion that summer, he left Fran to take a villa with one of her new friends. He was to join her again in the fall, so that they might go on to the Orient together.

Back in New York, Sam felt, at first, as if he had become a stranger to the life of noise and hurry which he had previously taken for granted. Nor was he interested in the newest model Revelation which had been, quite competently, developed without his aid. He discovered also that he and his son no longer had common ground. Brent was planning to sell bonds. The newly-married Emily, her father observed, was the very capable manager of her own home, and needed no assistance. Even Sam's best friend, Tubby Pearson, had gone on without him to new poker-playing and golfing companions.

At first his letters from Fran were lively and happy. Then she quarreled with the friend who shared her villa over one of their escorts, Arnold Israel, a Jew. Sam grew increasingly anxious as he realized that the man was trailing Fran from one resort to another and that their relationship was becoming increasingly more intimate. He made sailing reservations and cabled his wife to meet him in Paris.

Sam had no difficulty discovering that his wife had been unfaithful to him; she admitted as much during their stormy reunion in Paris. With the threat that he would divorce her for adultery if she did not agree to drop Israel, he forced her to leave for Spain with him the following day.

The Dodsworths wandered across Spain into Italy, and finally on to Germany and Berlin, and Sam had ample time to observe his wife. Increasingly he noted her self-centeredness, her pretentiousness, and his pity for her restlessness made him fonder of her.

At the home of the Biedners, Fran's cousins in Berlin, the Dodsworths met Kurt Obersdorf, a ruined Austrian nobleman. Kurt took them to places of interest in Berlin and became Fran's dancing companion.

When the news came that the Dodsworths were grandparents, for Emily now had a boy, they did not sail for home. In fact, they did not tell their friends of the baby's birth because Fran feared that as a grandmother she would seem old and faded to them. When Sam went to Paris to welcome Tubby Pearson and his wife, abroad for the first time, Fran remained in Berlin.

Sam and Tubby enjoyed themselves in Paris. Then Sam, driven by a longing to see his wife, flew back to Berlin. That night Fran announced that she and Kurt had decided to marry, and that she wanted a divorce. Sam agreed, on the condition that she wait a month before starting proceedings.

Sadly, Dodsworth left for Paris and later went on to Italy. While he was sitting on the piazza in Venice and reading one of Fran's letters, he saw Edith Cortright, a widow whom the Dodsworths had met during their earlier trip to Italy. Mrs. Cortright invited Sam home to tea with her, and on his second visit he told her about his separation from Fran.

Sam spent most of the summer with Edith and her Italian friends. He began to gain a new self-confidence when he found that he was liked and respected by these new acquaintances, who admired him and were satisfied with him as he was. He grew to love Edith, and they decided to return to America together. Then Sam received a letter from Fran telling him that she had dropped divorce pro-ceedings because Kurt's mother objected to his marriage with a divorced American.

Without saying goodbye to Edith, Sam rejoined Fran, homeward bound. He tried patiently to share her unhappiness and loneliness. But before long Fran became her old self, implying that Sam had been at fault for the failure of their marriage and flirting with a young polo player aboard ship. After breakfast, one morning, Sam sent a wireless to Edith, making arrangements to meet her in Venice. When the boat docked in New York, Sam left his wife forever. Three days later he sailed again to Italy and Edith Cortright.

A DOLL'S HOUSE

Type of work: Drama
Author: Henrik Ibsen (1828-1906)
Type of plot: Social criticism
Time of plot: Nineteenth century
Locale: Norway
First presented: 1879

Principal characters:
 TORVALD HELMER, a bank manager
 NORA HELMER, his wife
 MRS. LINDE, Nora's old school friend
 KROGSTAD, a bank clerk
 DR. RANK, a friend of the Helmers

Critique:

A *Doll's House* is the best known and one of the most popular of Ibsen's works. A classic expression of the theme of woman's rights, the play shocked Ibsen's contemporaries, because in the end Nora leaves her husband and children. In the character of Dr. Rank there is a foreshadowing of the heredity theme later to be developed by Ibsen in *Ghosts.*

The Story:

On the day before Christmas, Nora Helmer was busying herself with last minute shopping, for this was the first Christmas since her marriage that she had not had to economize. Her husband, Torvald, had just been made manager of a bank and after the New Year their money troubles would be over. She bought a tree and plenty of toys for the children, and she even indulged herself in some macaroons, her favorite confection, but of which Torvald did not entirely approve. He loved his wife dearly, but he regarded her very much as her own father had seen her, as an amusing doll—a plaything.

It was true that she did behave like a child sometimes in her relations with her husband. She pouted, wheedled, and chattered because Torvald expected these things; he would not have loved his doll-wife without them. Actually, Nora was not a doll but a woman with a woman's loves, hopes, and fears. This was shown seven years before, just after her first child was born, when Torvald had been

ill, and the doctor said that unless he went abroad immediately he would die. Nora was desperate. She could not seek Torvald's advice because she knew he would rather die than borrow money. She could not go to her father, for he himself was a dying man. She did the only thing possible under the circumstances. She borrowed the requisite two hundred and fifty pounds from Krogstad, a moneylender, forging her father's name to the note, so that Torvald could have his holiday in Italy.

Krogstad was exacting, and she had to think up ways and means to meet the regular payments. When Torvald gave her money for new dresses and such things, she never spent more than half of it, and she found other ways to earn money. One winter she did copying, but she kept this work a secret from Torvald, for he believed that the money for their trip had come from her father.

Then Krogstad, who was in the employ of the bank of which Torvald was now manager, determined to use Torvald to advance his own fortunes. But Torvald hated Krogstad, and was just as determined to be rid of him. The opportunity came when Christina Linde, Nora's old school friend, applied to Torvald for a position in the bank. Torvald resolved to dismiss Krogstad and hire Mrs. Linde in his place.

When Krogstad discovered that he was to be fired, he called on Nora and informed her that if he were dismissed he

943

would ruin her and her husband. He reminded her that the note supposedly signed by her father was dated three days after his death. Frightened at the turn matters had taken, Nora pleaded unsuccessfully with Torvald to reinstate Krogstad in the bank. Krogstad, receiving from Torvald an official notice of his dismissal, wrote in return a letter in which he revealed the full details of the forgery. He dropped the letter in the mailbox outside the Helmer home.

Torvald was in a holiday mood. The following evening they were to attend a fancy dress ball, and Nora was to go as a Neapolitan fisher girl and dance the tarantella. To divert her husband's attention from the mailbox outside, Nora practiced her dance before Torvald and Dr. Rank, an old friend. Nora was desperate, not knowing quite which way to turn. She had thought of Mrs. Linde, with whom Krogstad had at one time been in love. Mrs. Linde promised to do what she could to turn Krogstad from his avowed purpose. Nora thought also of Dr. Rank, but when she began to confide in him he made it so obvious that he was in love with her that she could not tell her secret. However, Torvald had promised her not to go near the mailbox until after the ball.

What bothered Nora was not her own fate, but Torvald's. She pictured herself as already dead, drowned in icy black water. She pictured the grief-stricken Torvald taking upon himself all the blame for what she had done and being disgraced for her sake. But the reality did not quite correspond with Nora's picture. Mrs. Linde, by promising to marry Krogstad and look after his children, succeeded in persuading him to withdraw all accusations against the Helmers, but she realized that Nora's affairs had come to a crisis and that sooner or later Nora and Torvald would have to come to an understanding.

This crisis came when Torvald read Krogstad's letter after their return from the ball. He accused Nora of being a hypocrite, a liar, and a criminal, of having no religion, no morality, no sense of duty. He declared that she was unfit to bring up her children. He informed her that she might remain in his household but she would no longer be a part of it.

Then another letter arrived from Krogstad, declaring that he intended to take no action against the Helmers. Torvald's whole attitude changed, and with a sigh of relief he boasted that he was saved. For the first time Nora saw her husband for what he was—a selfish, pretentious hypocrite with no regard for her position in the matter. She reminded him that no marriage could be built on inequality, and announced her intention of leaving his house forever. Torvald could not believe his ears and pleaded with her to remain. But she declared she was going to try to become a reasonable human being, to understand the world—in short, to become a woman, not a doll to flatter Torvald's selfish vanity. She went out and with irrevocable finality, slammed the door of her doll house behind her.

DOMBEY AND SON

Type of work: Novel
Author: Charles Dickens (1812-1870)
Type of plot: Sentimental romance
Time of plot: Early nineteenth century
Locale: England
First published: 1846-1848

Principal characters:
MR. DOMBEY, a rich London merchant
PAUL, his son
FLORENCE, his daughter
EDITH GRANGER, his second wife
MR. CARKER, his trusted agent
WALTER GAY, in love with Florence

Critique:

Dombey and Son, which appeared after *Martin Chuzzlewit*, was an effort by Dickens to regain popularity he had lost with the publication of his previous novel. *Martin Chuzzlewit*, which had heavily satirized America and Americans, had caused Dickens to lose a great deal of favor, a loss which greatly irritated Dickens, who was by that time in something of a competition for the public's attention with another great Victorian novelist, William Makepeace Thackeray. *Dombey and Son* is also a milestone in Dickens' work in that he placed the story at a higher social level that he had done in his previous novels. For the first time he indicated an interest and a sympathy in the upper middle classes and the aristocracy. The story is a very serious one, involving the downfall of a dignified and pompous merchant and his learning of the power of love as compared to the lesser power of money. In typical Dickensian style, however, there is a whole catalog of characters to provide a humorous background.

The Story:

Mr. Dombey was a stiff and dignified man who rarely showed emotion. But the birth of an infant son, who was named Paul, was cause for rejoicing, as Mr. Dombey had longed many years for a child who would fill the second part of the mercantile firm of Dombey and Son. Even

the fact that Mrs. Dombey died shortly after the boy's birth did not particularly concern him; he was centered entirely on the little infant who he hoped would someday take over the business. Mr. Dombey also had a daughter, Florence, but she meant almost nothing to him, for she could not take a place in the firm.

Little Paul was first given over to a wet nurse, but the woman proved to be unreliable and was dismissed. After her dismissal little Paul was cared for by Mr. Dombey's sister and a friend of hers. Despite their vigilant care, however, little Paul's health was poor. He was listless and never cared to play. At last Mr. Dombey made arrangements to have him sent to a home, together with his sister, at Brighton, there to gain the benefits of the sea air.

Paul, in spite of his father's dislike for little Florence, loved his sister very much, and they were constant companions. Paul's love for Florence only made Mr. Dombey dislike the girl more, for the father felt that his daughter was coming between himself and his son.

One weekend, while Mr. Dombey was visiting at Brighton, Walter Gay, a young clerk in the firm, came to the inn where Mr. Dombey and his children were having dinner. Some time before the clerk had rescued Florence from an old female thief. Now his uncle was about to become a bankrupt, and Walter had come to ask for a loan to save his uncle's shop. Mr.

Dombey let little Paul, who was then six years old, make the decision. Paul asked Florence what he should do; she told him to lend the money, and he did.

Shortly afterward, little Paul was placed in a private school at Brighton, where he was to be educated as quickly as possible. The pace of his studies proved too much for him, and before the year was out his health broke down. He never seemed to grow any better, even after his father took him home to London. Before many months had elapsed, little Paul died, mourned by his father and his sister, though for different reasons.

Mr. Dombey took his son's death as a personal blow of fate at his plans. His sister and her friend became so concerned about him that they planned to have him take a trip with Major Bagstock, a retired officer, to Leamington. While they were there, they met Edith Granger, a young widow whose mother the major had known. Mr. Dombey, seeing in Mrs. Granger a beautiful, well-bred young woman who would grace his household, immediately began to court her. Mrs. Granger, coaxed by an aged mother who was concerned for her daughter's welfare, finally accepted Mr. Dombey, although she was not in love with him.

Florence Dombey had seen young Walter Gay several times since their meeting at Brighton, and after her brother's death she came to look upon young Walter as a substitute brother, despite his lowly station. Then their friendship was broken temporarily when Mr. Dombey sent Walter on a mission to the West Indies. Weeks passed, but no word was heard of the ship on which he had sailed. Everyone believed that it had sunk and that Walter had been drowned.

After Mrs. Granger had accepted Mr. Dombey's suit, they began to make plans for the wedding and for reopening the Dombey house in London. It was at the house that Edith Granger first met Florence. The two immediately became fast friends, even though Mr. Dombey dis-

liked his daughter and made it plain that he did not want his wife to become too fond of the girl.

Mr. Dombey's second marriage was unsuccessful from the start. Edith Granger was too proud to give in to Mr. Dombey's attempts to dictate to her and to his claim upon her as a piece of merchandise, and she resisted him in every way. Dombey, who was too dignified to argue with her, sent his business manager, Mr. Carker, to tell his wife that he was dissatisfied with her conduct. Carker warned Mrs. Dombey that, unless she obeyed Mr. Dombey, Florence would be the one to suffer. Edith Dombey then became outwardly cool to her stepdaughter, but still she resisted her husband. Mr. Carker was once more dispatched to tell her that Mr. Dombey meant to be obeyed in everything.

The wife then openly revolted. She felt that she could get complete revenge by running off with Carker, her husband's most trusted employee, who was also so far below Mr. Dombey socially that the blow would hurt even more. After she and the employee disappeared, Florence was only rebuffed in her attempts to comfort her father. When he struck her, she ran away from the house and went to the shop owned by Walter Gay's uncle, Sol Gills. There she found that Gills had disappeared and that an old ship's captain named Cuttle was in charge. Captain Cuttle recognized Florence and took her in.

Mr. Dombey at last learned the whereabouts of his wife and Carker from a young woman whom Carker had seduced and deserted. Mr. Dombey followed the pair to France but failed to locate them. Carker, meanwhile, returned to England. Mrs. Dombey had refused to have anything to do with him. She had her revenge, she said, in ruining him and her husband. Carker, trying to escape into the English countryside, met Mr. Dombey at a railway station. An accident occurred, and Carker was killed by a train.

Florence, staying with Captain Cuttle, hoped that Walter would return, even though everyone had given him up for dead. Her faith was at last rewarded. Walter had been picked up by a China-bound vessel and so had not had the opportunity to send back word of his safety. Shortly after his return he revealed to Florence that he no longer felt as a brother toward her, since she had become a woman during his absence. Realizing that she, too, had fallen in love with him, she accepted his proposal. Walter had found work as clerk on a ship, and after their marriage they sailed on a ship bound for the Orient.

The failure of his marriage had broken Mr. Dombey's spirit, and he took little interest in his firm from that time on. His lack of interest was unfortunate, for the firm had been placed in a difficult position by certain dealings of Carker's while he had been Dombey's trusted agent. As a result of Carker's mismanagement and Dombey's lack of interest, the firm went bankrupt. After the bankruptcy Mr. Dombey stayed alone in his house, saw no one, and gradually drifted into despair.

On the very day that Mr. Dombey had decided to commit suicide, Florence returned to London from the Orient with her year-old son, who was named Paul, after his dead uncle. Florence and the baby cheered up Mr. Dombey, and he began to take a new interest in life. Reconciled to his daughter, he realized that she had always loved him, even though he had been exceedingly cruel to her. Walter Gay succeeded in business, and all of them lived together happily, for his misfortunes had made a changed man of the almost indomitable Mr. Dombey.

DOMINIQUE

Type of work: Novel
Author: Eugène Fromentin (1820-1876)
Type of plot: Psychological romance
Time of plot: Nineteenth century
Locale: France
First published: 1862

Principal characters:
DOMINIQUE DE BRAY, a gentleman
MADELEINE DE NIÈVRES, his beloved
AUGUSTIN, his tutor
OLIVIER D'ORSEL, his friend

Critique:

Although Fromentin was primarily a painter, his writings quickly won the respect of the most distinguished of his contemporaries. In *Dominique* he drew from the experiences of his own youth; the powerful and permanent hold that the French countryside and the seacoast exerted upon his mind is evident throughout the book. The love theme is the old one of the moth being drawn to the flame, despite morality, orthodoxy, or common sense. The hero is also torn in a choice between the rigors of excellence and the pleasures of mediocrity. The psychology of personality is deftly explored in polished prose style.

The Story:

The narrator of the book first met Dominique de Bray at Villeneuve. Dominique lived at the large Château des Trembles with his wife and two children. The mayor of the commune, he was shy, unpretentious, and a friend to all in the community.

On St. Hubert's Day Dominique was visited by Olivier d'Orsel, a wealthy, solitary man with captivating manners and a passion for luxury, who had suddenly retired from social life. A few days after his visit Olivier tried to commit suicide. This event led Dominique to tell the narrator about himself.

Orphaned at an early age, Dominique grew up at Villeneuve. In his youth he

became a lover of the outdoors. He was cared for by Madame Ceyssac, his aunt, who provided him with a tutor named Augustin. The two differed greatly in temperament. Dominique was emotional and wild and loved nature; Augustin was well-read, exact, practical, and apparently oblivious to nature. When he was not tutoring Dominique, he would remain in his room, writing plays and letters. After four years the time came for Dominique to go away to school. Augustin went to Paris with high hopes of his own success.

Dominique went to live with Madame Ceyssac in her mansion at Ormesson. At school he befriended young Olivier d'Orsel, who also had an estate near Les Trembles. Dominique, who was a good student, helped Olivier with their schoolwork. Too shy to admit it, Dominique fell in love with Madeleine, Olivier's cousin. At night he would spend his time writing poetry. He also kept up a correspondence with Augustin, who warned him against confusing Olivier's love of pleasure with the true goals in life.

Dominique was surprised when Madeleine married M. de Nièvres, a well-established gentleman. After the ceremony Dominique was in despair because he realized that he loved a married woman.

After graduation, Dominique and Olivier went to Paris. There they saw

DOMINIQUE by Eugène Fromentin. Translated by Edward Marsh. By permission of the publishers, The Cresset Press. Copyright, 1948, by The Cresset Press.

Augustin, who grew to like Olivier but had no esteem for him. Olivier, in turn, esteemed Augustin without liking him.

Dominique, trying to forget his love for Madeleine, buried himself in his literary work. He went to libraries and lectures, and he read through the small hours of the night in the belief that the austere routine was good for him. After a few months, however, he burned his writings because he thought them stale and mediocre. Olivier, who saw what Dominique had done, told him to find other amusements and affections. Augustin, on the other hand, simply said that he would have to begin again. Augustin, who had experienced setbacks of his own, never complained. Having guessed Dominique's love problem, he told him to solve it by plunging into continuous work.

In spite of Augustin's advice and example, Dominique found it impossible to settle to his work. Through Olivier, he met a woman whom he saw steadily for two months. Then he learned that Nièvres and Madeleine were going to Ormesson, and he invited them to Les Trembles for the holidays. Although he never told Madeleine about his love for her, those were happy months for Dominique. That winter Nièvres and Madeleine decided to go to Paris.

Eventually Dominique wanted to make Madeleine admit that they loved each other, but the harder he tried to draw an admission from her the more she pretended to be quite unaware of his intention. One day, when he was determined to tell her of his love, he saw tears in her eyes; he understood then that there was nothing more to be said.

After that day their relationship became relaxed and natural, and Madeleine, wanting to encourage Dominique in his work, began to meet him at the risk of compromising her reputation. After a time Dominique realized that Madeleine was about to surrender herself to him. He then stopped seeing her, and she became gloomy and irritable. Her re-

actions made Dominique realize that he had deeply troubled her conscience.

Meanwhile, Augustin had married. Visiting Augustin in his home, Dominique saw the near-poverty but great happiness in which his former tutor lived. At the same time Olivier, deeply involved with the women he had been seeing, began to hate the world and himself. It became evident that Julie, Madeleine's younger sister, loved Olivier. But Olivier, who claimed that happiness was a myth, refused to think of marrying her, and his attitude led to a loss of confidence between Dominique and Olivier.

One night, while Dominique and Madeleine were attending the opera, Dominique caught the glance of his former mistress. Madeleine saw the exchange and later told Dominique that he was torturing her and breaking her heart.

That night Dominique, determined to deal honestly with Madeleine, decided to claim her. For the next three weeks, however, she was not at home to him. Frustrated, Dominique moved to new quarters and, as a final effort, tried to escape the life of emotions and concentrate on the logical disciplines of the mind. He read much, saved his money, and published anonymously two volumes of his youthful poetry. He also wrote some political books which were immediately successful. When he evaluated his talents, however, he concluded that he was a distinguished mediocrity.

Several months later Olivier told Dominique that there was unhappiness at Nièvres, where Madeleine was staying. Julie was ill and Madeleine herself was not well. Dominique went to Nièvres at once and there found Julie recovering. No longer needed as her sister's nurse, Madeleine, with disregard for propriety, shared with Dominique three days of supreme happiness.

On impulse, after Madeleine had led him in a dangerous ride on horseback, Dominique decided to leave as he had come, without premeditation or calculation. When he was helping her to fold a large shawl that evening, Madeleine half-fainted into his arms, and they kissed. Dominique felt very sorry for her and let her go. After dinner Madeleine told him that, although she would always love him, she wanted him to go away, to get married, to take up a new life. That was the last Dominique saw of Madeleine. He returned to Les Trembles and settled down to quiet country life.

Dominique told the narrator that the years had brought forgiveness and understanding. Augustin, he said, had become a respected figure in Paris. Dominique himself had never repented his early retirement; he felt, in fact, that his life was merely beginning.

DON CARLOS

Type of work: Drama
Author: Johann Christoph Friedrich von Schiller (1759-1805)
Type of plot: Historical tragedy
Time of plot: Sixteenth century
Locale: Spain
First presented: 1787

Principal characters:
DON CARLOS, heir to the Spanish throne
PHILIP II, King of Spain and Don Carlos' father
ELIZABETH DE VALOIS, Queen of Spain, Don Carlos' stepmother
MARQUIS DE POSA, Don Carlos' friend
DOMINGO, confessor to the king
DUKE OF ALVA, Philip II's trusted general and minister
PRINCESS DE EBOLI, attendant to the queen

Critique:

This drama by Schiller was based chiefly on a historical novel of the same title published by the Abbe de Saint-Réal at Paris in 1672. The play, an exceedingly long one, was written in blank verse and represented a distinct advance over Schiller's earlier dramas, which had been written in prose. Within this play the reader finds Schiller's own ideas of humanity and liberty expressed in words spoken by Don Carlos and the Marquis de Posa. Although the title indicates that the hero was to be Don Carlos, heir to the Spanish throne, the marquis usurps the central position, as he did in Schiller's own mind while the play was being written. This was Schiller's last play before he turned to writing in the fields of aesthetics, ethics, and literary criticism.

The Story:

Philip II of Spain did not wish to trust his son, Don Carlos, with any of the crown's affairs, even though Don Carlos was twenty-three years old. Philip's ostensible reason was that Don Carlos was too hot-blooded. Probably the real reason was Philip's fear of his son, fear springing from the fact that Philip himself had forced his father, Charles V, from the throne. To aggravate the differences and the coldness between the king and his son, Philip was married to Elizabeth de Valois, with whom Don Carlos had been

in love. Indeed, both France and Spain had given permission for the courtship between the two, until Philip had decided to take Elizabeth for himself.

Don Carlos hid his love for his stepmother until the Marquis de Posa returned from Flanders, at which time Don Carlos revealed his secret to his friend. The marquis was horrified, but swore upon their boyhood friendship to help the prince, if the prince in turn would try to help the people of Flanders escape from the heavy and tyrannic policies forced upon them by Philip through his emissary, the Duke of Alva.

Stating that he could be more humane than the duke, Don Carlos went to his father and pleaded that he be made the king's agent in Flanders. Philip, refusing to listen, sent the duke over Don Carlos' protests. He did, however, ask the duke to be more friendly with the prince. When the duke went to speak to the prince, he found Don Carlos in the queen's antechamber. They had words and fought, until the queen intervened.

From one of the queen's pages Don Carlos received a mysterious note and a key to a room in the queen's apartments. Hoping against hope that the queen had sent it to him, he went to the room, an act for which his jealous father would have punished him severely. He found, instead of the queen, the Princess de Eboli. Having fallen in love with the

951

prince, she had sent him the note. Loving Don Carlos, she asked his help in evading the importunities of the king, who sought her for his mistress. Don Carlos repelled the advances of the princess and thus incurred her anger. When he left, he took with him a letter which the king had sent to her. Hoping to use the letter as proof that the king was a tyrant and an evil man, he showed it to the Marquis de Posa. The marquis tore up the letter, saying that it was too dangerous a weapon and might hurt Don Carlos and the queen more than the king.

In the meantime the Princess de Eboli, infuriated at Don Carlos' refusal of her love, went to Domingo, the king's confessor and pander, and told him of her decision to become Philip's mistress. She also told about her meeting with the prince and his obvious hope that he was to meet the queen. That information pleased Domingo and the Duke of Alva, who wanted to rid the kingdom of both Don Carlos and the queen.

With the help of the princess, the duke and the confessor laid a trap for Don Carlos and the queen. Becoming suspicious of the conspirators' motives, Philip called in a man he thought would be completely honest in solving the problem. The man was, ironically, Don Carlos' friend, the Marquis de Posa. He quickly gained the king's confidence, even though some of his religious ideas were heretical, and he did his best to help Don Carlos. Having to work in secret, the marquis seemed to Don Carlos to be a traitor to his friend. Other courtiers reported to Don Carlos that a file of letters he had given to the marquis had been seen in the king's chamber. What Don Carlos heard was true, for the marquis had found it necessary to tell the truth about the letters to clear Don Carlos of the charge of illicit relations with the queen.

Don Carlos, not knowing the truth concerning the marquis' activities, went to the Princess de Eboli to seek her help.

The Marquis de Posa, learning of Don Carlos' visit to the princess, entered immediately after the prince. Using the authority given him by the king to arrest Don Carlos, the marquis had him put incommunicado in prison, lest he talk to others who could do him harm. The easiest way to keep Don Carlos safe would have been to murder the Princess de Eboli, but the marquis did not have the heart to kill her, even when his dagger was at her breast.

Instead of assuming the guilt of murder, the marquis resolved to make himself the victim. The king had been convinced that Don Carlos and the queen had been involved in a treasonable plot against the crown in Flanders. To clear them, the marquis sent a letter he knew would be put into the king's hands. In it he stated that he, the marquis, was the real conspirator. Afterward the marquis had only enough time to go to the prison and reveal his true actions to Don Carlos. As he spoke, a shot was fired through the gratings by an assassin sent by Philip.

Popular wrath and the indignation of the grandees forced Philip to release his son, but Don Carlos refused to leave the prison until his father came in person to give him back his sword and his freedom. When Philip arrived, in the company of the grandees of the council, Don Carlos confronted him with the marquis' corpse and told him that he had caused the murder of an innocent man. Philip, seeing the truth of the accusation, and filled with remorse, became ill in the prison and was carried away by the grandees.

A friend reported to Don Carlos that the king and the Duke of Alva had been enraged by public reaction in favor of the imprisoned prince. Hoping to lift the yoke of tyranny his father and the Duke of Alva had placed upon that country and its people, Don Carlos decided to leave Spain immediately and go to Flanders. Before he left, he planned to see the queen once more and tell her of his plans. Donning a mask and the garb of a monk, he went through a secret passage to the wing of the castle in which the queen lived. There he went through open corridors to her rooms, able to do so because of a superstition that Charles V, garbed in like manner, haunted the castle. The superstitious soldiers let him pass.

The king, meanwhile, had sent for the Cardinal Inquisitor. Asked for his advice, the churchman rebuked Philip for his waywardness in letting the heretic marquis escape proper punishment for so long and then having him killed for political reasons. They discussed also the heresy of the young prince, and Philip resolved to turn his son over to the Inquisition for punishment. In person, Philip led the cardinal to the queen's apartments, for the king, having heard reports of the ghost, guessed who really was beneath the disguise. Don Carlos was found with the queen and handed over to the authorities of the Inquisition.

THE DON FLOWS HOME TO THE SEA

Type of work: Novel
Author: Mikhail Sholokhov (1905-   )
Type of plot: Historical chronicle
Time of plot: 1918-1920
Locale: Russia
First published: 1933, 1938

Principal characters:
GREGOR MELEKHOV, a soldier
PIOTRA, his brother
AKSINIA, his mistress
NATALIA, his wife
KOSHEVOI, a Communist

Critique:

The Don Flows Home to the Sea is a sequel to *And Quiet Flows the Don.* Here the fortunes of the Cossacks are lengthily and vividly portrayed after the peace with the Central Powers in 1917 up to the dominance of the Reds in 1920. Although *The Don Flows Home to the Sea,* published in two parts in 1933 and 1938, was written under the Soviet regime, the insurgent Cossacks are sympathetically portrayed. The beginnings of Soviet autocratic ruthlessness are seen as base and inhuman but probably inevitable. In scope the work is vast. It deserves to be ranked among the best Soviet productions.

The Story:

The Germans were still carrying off white flour, butter, and cattle. Every day their trucks rolled from the Don through the Ukraine. Various sections of Russia, however, were fighting each other. To the north of the Don Basin the White Army was driving back the Bolsheviks. Most of the Cossacks were in the White forces, although some were with the Reds.

Gregor and Piotra Melekhov were leaders in the White Army. Piotra, the elder brother, was decidedly anti-Red and waged battle viciously. Gregor was of two minds; perhaps the Reds would bring stable government. Gregor was opposed

to pillaging civilians and killing prisoners. As best he could he kept his men in hand. When his father and his sister-in-law Daria visited him at the front, he was furious when they took home a wagon load of loot.

Back in Tatarsk the Whites were trying to win over the Cossacks to full support of the insurgent cause. In the spring of 1918 there had been a great defection of northern Cossacks to the Reds, and the southern Cossacks were only half-hearted in throwing back the Red tide. Koshevoi, a Red sympathizer, was caught when he returned to his home in Tatarsk. His companions were killed, but he was let off to join the drovers in the steppes.

Eugene Listnitsky, a rich Cossack from the district, spent a furlough with a brother officer. Eugene was attracted to Olga, the man's wife. After the officer was killed, Listnitsky married the widow. When he got home, invalided out with a missing arm, Aksinia, his former mistress, was still there, waiting for him. Eugene wanted nothing more to do with her after his marriage. He made love to her briefly under a currant bush and offered her money to go away. Aksinia was pained but stayed on in service. Her husband Stepan, miraculously alive after years in prison, tried in vain to get her to come home.

Gradually the Cossacks returned home;

THE DON FLOWS HOME TO THE SEA by Mikhail Sholokhov. Translated by Stephen Garry. By permission of the publishers, Alfred A. Knopf, Inc. Copyright, 1940, by Alfred A. Knopf, Inc.

farmers, they had to till the land. The advancing Red Army passed through the village of Tatarsk. After them came the political men and the Red government took charge. Gregor, glad to be home, had little longing now for Aksinia, who had been his mistress before she became Eugene's. After years of fighting Germans and Reds, he was content to be a little reconciled to Natalia, his wife.

Koshevoi was put in charge of the government of Tatarsk, and soon Stockman, a professional Red, came to help him. They began gradually, seizing a man here and there and spiriting him off to death or imprisonment. They wanted to arrest both Piotra and Gregor. A little afraid to take Piotra, who was friendly with Fomin, a Red commander, they did decide to take Gregor. Learning of their intentions in time, Gregor left Tatarsk and escaped.

As the political imprisonments and executions increased, the Cossacks revolted. Their wrongs were so great that in a comparatively short time the rebellion was succeeding. Piotra was made a commander immediately. He was a ferocious fighter and ruthless to the Reds. In a skirmish, however, he was captured by the enemy. Koshevoi, now a Communist, stepped out from a patrol and killed Piotra without compunction.

Gregor, after serving under Piotra, rose to command a division. He was cold with fury toward the Communists and had the reputation of never keeping live prisoners for long. Yet when the Cossacks began to imprison Red sympathizers from among the civilians, he dissented strongly. On one occasion he even forced open a prison and released old men and women who were suspected of helping the Reds.

Stockman and the others who had been the political rulers of Tatarsk were captured when a Red regiment deserted. Stockman was killed outright, and the others were returned to run a terrible gantlet at Tatarsk. Daria herself killed the man she thought responsible for the death of Piotra, her husband. Koshevoi

was unsuspected at the time.

Daria recovered from Piotra's death rather speedily and soon was carrying on various affairs. When Gregor came home on furlough, she even made tentative love to him. But Gregor was tired from fighting and carousing, and he still had bitter memories of Aksinia. Natalia, who had heard of Gregor's conduct on his sprees, was cold to him. The day before he was to return to the army, Gregor met Aksinia at the Don. He thought of their former love and of her affair with Listnitsky. But the old love was not dead, and he took Aksinia again.

The Soviet government, realizing by May of 1919 that they had a formidable task on their hands, increased their forces and slowly pushed back the insurgent Cossacks. The rebels retreated toward the Don, taking with them crowds of refugees. At last the Cossacks crossed the river and held their positions.

The Reds came through Tatarsk as Natalia was recovering from typhus. Koshevoi was with them; he was indignant that Dunia, Gregor's young sister, was across the Don, for he had long been in love with her. Koshevoi's own family was missing and his father's house had been destroyed. He took pride in firing the houses of all the rich landowners in and near Tatarsk.

Gregor, busy as a division commander, took time to send for Aksinia and she came to live near him. Stepan returned, to her embarrassment, and although she did not take him back as her husband, they preserved appearances among the refugee families.

With the arrival of the White Army, the Reds were driven back. Now that the insurgents were incorporated into a regular army, Gregor was demoted to the rank of squadron commander, for he was an uneducated man. The Whites sent punitive patrols to punish those who had aided the Reds. To the horror of the Melekhovs, all of Koshevoi's relatives were executed. Daria caught syphilis and drowned herself. Natalia, learning of

Gregor's return to Aksinia, refused to bear him another child. She had an unskillful abortion performed and bled to death.

With increasing Red pressure and desertion from the Cossack ranks, the White Army was going down in defeat. Gregor and Aksinia fled south to try to board a ship. On the way Aksinia fell ill with typhus and had to be left behind. She later made her way back to Tatarsk. Gregor could not leave the country. With nothing better to do, he joined the Reds and fought valiantly against the Poles.

In spite of family protests Dunia married Koshevoi, now commissar of the village. When Gregor returned home, Koshevoi at once set in motion plans to arrest him. But Gregor again escaped, joining up with Fomin, a deserter from the Red Army. Fomin tried to rally the Cossacks to revolt against the Communists for levying heavy taxes and collecting grain. The revolt, however, was short-lived. The rebels were killed, and only Gregor came back to Tatarsk. This time, when Gregor fled, he took Aksinia with him, but she was killed by a pursuing Red patrol. Gregor threw his arms into the Don and came back to his house. Only his son was left to him now and he would fight no more.

DON JUAN

Type of work: Poem
Author: George Gordon, Lord Byron (1788-1824)
Type of plot: Social satire
Time of plot: Late eighteenth century
Locale: Spain, Turkey, Russia, England
First published: By Cantos, 1819-1824

Principal characters:
DON JUAN, a young Spaniard
DONNA INEZ, his mother
DONNA JULIA, his first mistress
HAIDÉE, his second love
THE SULTANA, who coveted Juan
CATHERINE, Empress of Russia
LADY ADELINE AMUNDEVILLE, Juan's adviser
DUCHESS OF FITZ-FULKE, who pursued Juan
AURORA RABY, pursued by Juan

Critique:

Although Byron said that *Don Juan* was to be an epic, his story does not follow epic tradition but becomes a vehicle for digression on any and every subject and person that entered his mind as he wrote. The plot itself is almost a minor part of the poem, for much more interesting are Byron's bitter tirades on England, wealth, power, society, chastity, poets, and diplomats. For that reason, Juan's adventures being largely incidental, the poem holds a high place among literary satires, even though unfinished at Byron's death.

The Story:

When Don Juan was a small boy, his father died, leaving the boy in the care of his mother, Donna Inez. Donna Inez was a righteous woman who had made her husband's life miserable. She had her son tutored in the arts of fencing, riding, and shooting, and she herself attempted to rear him in a moral manner. But even though young Don Juan read widely in the sermons and lives of the saints, he did not seem to absorb from his studies the qualities his mother thought essential.

At sixteen, he was a handsome lad much admired by his mother's friends. Donna Julia, in particular, often looked pensively at the youth. Donna Julia was just twenty-three and married to a man of fifty. Although she loved her husband, or so she told herself, she thought often of young Don Juan. One day, finding herself alone with him, she gave herself to the young man.

The young lovers spent long hours together during the summer, and it was not until November that Don Alfonso, her husband, discovered their intrigue. When Don Alfonso found Don Juan in his wife's bedroom, he tried to throttle him. But Don Juan overcame Don Alfonso and fled, first to his mother's home for clothes and money. Then Donna Inez sent him to Cadiz, there to begin a tour of Europe. The good lady prayed that the trip would mend his morals.

Before his ship reached Leghorn a storm broke it apart. Don Juan spent many days in a lifeboat without food or water. At last the boat was washed ashore, and Don Juan fell exhausted on the beach and slept. When he awoke, he saw bending over him a beautiful girl who told him that she was called Haidée and that she was the daughter of the ruler of the island, one of the Cyclades. Her father, Lambro, was a pirate, dealing in jewels and slaves. Because she knew her father would sell Don Juan to the first trader who came by, Haidée hid Don Juan in a cave and sent her maids to

957

wait on him.

When Lambro left on another expedition, Haidée took Don Juan from the cave and they roamed together over the island. Haidée heaped jewels and fine foods and wines on Don Juan, for he was the first man she had ever known except her father and her servants. Although Don Juan still tried to think of Donna Julia, he could not resist Haidée. A child of nature and passion, she gave herself to him with complete freedom. Again Don Juan lived an idyllic existence, until Haidée's father returned unexpectedly. Don Juan again fought gallantly, but at last he was overcome by the old man's servants and put aboard a slave ship bound for a distant market. He never saw Haidée again, and he never knew that she died giving birth to his child.

The slave ship took Don Juan to a Turkish market, where he and another prisoner were purchased by a Negro eunuch and taken to the palace of a sultan. There Don Juan was made to dress as a dancing maiden and present himself to the sultana, the fourth and favorite wife of the sultan. She had passed by the slave market and had seen Don Juan and wanted him for a lover. In order to conceal his sex from the sultan, she forced the disguise on Don Juan. But even at the threat of death, Don Juan would not become her lover, for he still yearned for Haidée. Perhaps his constancy might have wavered, if the sultana had not been an infidel, for she was young and beautiful.

Eventually Don Juan escaped from the palace and joined the army of Catherine of Russia. The Russians were at war with the sultan from whose palace Don Juan had fled. Don Juan was such a valiant soldier that he was sent to St. Petersburg, to carry the news of a Russian victory to Empress Catherine. Catherine also cast longing eyes on the handsome stranger, and her approval soon made Don Juan the toast of her capital.

In the midst of his luxury and good fortune, Don Juan grew ill. Hoping that a change of climate would help her favorite, Catherine resolved to send him on a mission to England. When he reached London he was well received, for he was a polished young man, well versed in fashionable etiquette. His mornings were spent in business, but his afternoons and evenings were devoted to lavish entertainment. He conducted himself with such decorum, however, that he was much sought after by proper young ladies and much advised by older ones. Lady Adeline Amundeville, made him her protégé, and advised him freely on affairs of the heart. Another, the Duchess of Fitz-Fulke, advised him too, but her suggestions were of a more personal nature and seemed to demand a secluded spot where there was no danger from intruders. Because of the Duchess of Fitz-Fulke's attentions to Don Juan, Lady Adeline began to talk to him about selecting a bride from the chaste and suitable young ladies attentive to him.

Don Juan thought of marriage, but his interest was stirred by a girl not on Lady Adeline's list. Aurora Raby was a plain young lady, prim, dull, and seemingly unaware of Don Juan's presence. Her lack of interest served to spur him on to greater efforts, but a smile was his only reward from the cold maiden.

His attention was diverted from Aurora Raby by the appearance of the ghost of the Black Friar, who had once lived in the house of Lady Adeline, where Don Juan was a guest. The ghost was a legendary figure reported to appear before births, deaths, or marriages. To Don Juan, the ghost was an evil omen, and he could not laugh off the tightness about his heart. Lady Adeline and her husband seemed to consider the ghost a great joke. Aurora Raby appeared to be a little sympathetic with Don Juan, but the Duchess of Fitz-Fulke merely laughed at his discomfiture.

The second time the ghost appeared, Don Juan followed it out of the house and into the garden. It seemed to float before him, always just out of his reach.

Once he thought he had grasped it, but his fingers touched only a cold wall. Then he seized it firmly and found that the ghost had a sweet breath and full, red lips. When the monk's cowl fell back, the Duchess of Fitz-Fulke was revealed.

On the morning after, Don Juan appeared at breakfast, wan and tired. Whether he had overcome more than the ghost, no one will ever know. The duchess, too, came down, seeming to have the air of one who had been rebuked. . . .

DON JUAN

Type of work: Drama
Author: Molière (Jean Baptiste Poquelin, 1622-1673)
Type of plot: Social satire
Time of plot: Seventeenth century
Locale: Sicily
First presented: 1665

Principal characters:
DON JUAN, a philanderer
SGANARELLE, his valet
ELVIRE, his betrayed wife
DON LOUIS, his father
DON CARLOS, and
DON ALONSE, Elvire's brothers
STATUE OF THE COMMANDER

Critique:

Don Juan is not really representative of Molière's work, but it holds lasting interest for the modern reader for two reasons. Written to fatten the lean exchequer of his company's theater because of the enforced closing of Tartuffe, as well as to please his fellow actors, it is an excellent example of the skill and speed with which Molière could turn out a play. It also departs from his usual technique in making use of the melodramatic and supernatural elements which characterized the original Spanish drama from which it was adapted. Here, as in his other dramas, Molière holds to his genius as a revealer of the hypocrisies and manners of his day, and the play brought down on itself the harsh criticism of those who had been shocked by the boldness of Tartuffe. By the spectacle-loving Parisians it was hailed with delight.

The Story:

Don Juan's philandering habits filled Sganarelle, his valet, with apprehension that such scandalous behavior could only bring on him the wrath of heaven and an evil end; but Don Juan blatantly affirmed that any love he had for one fair face could not withhold his heart from others, and as for heaven, he was not afraid of divine wrath. His valet knew him for the greatest scoundrel on earth, a man who was ready to woo a fine lady or country lass at any time but who tired

of them in rapid succession. Through fear, however, he remained faithful to Don Juan and often applauded his master's acts, even though he really detested them.

In one of his many affairs Don Juan had killed a Commander. Though officially pardoned, he was believed not entirely free of guilt, and friends and relatives of the dead man sought revenge. They followed Don Juan on one of his philandering journeys to a town where he determined to separate a pair of lovers he had chanced upon and to gratify his passion for the lady. The happy pair had planned a sail on the sea, and he prepared to follow in another vessel manned by villains ready to do his bidding.

Meanwhile, Donna Elvire, whom Don Juan had seduced and carried off from a convent where her brothers, Don Carlos and Don Alonse, had placed her, had got wind of his escapade and followed him. She upbraided him for his desertion. Don Juan refused to admit that he was tired of her, but he wished her to believe that he repented his former madcap behavior in forcing her to marry him against her will. From this sin he would deliver her by allowing her to return to the convent and her former obligations. Elvire, seeing through this deception, threatened him with the anger of an injured woman and declared that heaven would punish him for the wrong he had done her.

Don Juan gave chase to the vessel which carried the object of his most recent infatuation. But his plans were upset when a sudden squall arose and both ships were wrecked. Don Juan was rescued by Pierrot, a country lad, and brought with his men to land. He made immediate love to Charlotte, Pierrot's sweetheart, and she, overwhelmed by his smooth talk and social bearing, promised to marry him. At that moment Mathurine, another country lass who had caught the philanderer's fancy, accosted Don Juan, but he cleverly led each girl to think she was his only love and the one he would marry.

When Don Juan heard that his pursuers were closing in on him, he changed clothes with his valet. Sganarelle devised a better disguise. Putting on the attire of a physician, he prescribed remedies at random for ailing country folk, not knowing whether his medicines would kill or cure.

In the wood through which they were traveling, Don Juan and Sganarelle sought to evade their pursuers. They discoursed on heaven, hell, the devil, and another life, Don Juan declaring himself a practical man who held no belief in such stupid and supernatural things. Deep in argument, they lost their way. Suddenly, through a clearing in the trees, they saw Don Carlos, Elvire's brother, being attacked by a band of robbers. Don Juan rushed to assist the stranger and succeeded in routing the attackers. Don Carlos, not knowing that his rescuer was his own sister's seducer, expressed his gratitude to Don Juan for saving his life. At this moment Alonse came upon them. Their friendly attitude horrified him, for he immediately recognized Don Juan and demanded of his brother that this betrayer of their sister be killed. Don Carlos pleaded for delay and won for Don Juan a day's respite, but he agreed that after this short delay justice would be done and vengeance satisfied.

As Don Juan and Sganarelle continued on their way, Don Juan gave voice again to the song that his heart belonged equally to all the fair sex and that his attraction to Elvire had entirely faded. Among the trees they came on a statue, part of the tomb which the Commander had been building when killed by Don Juan. On a sudden whim Don Juan insisted that the shocked Sganarelle approach the mausoleum and invite the Commander to dine with them. To their amazement the statue nodded its head in assent. Overwhelmed, they retreated hastily, although Don Juan boldly asserted that strong minds are not affected by a belief in anything supernatural.

Don Louis, father of Don Juan, threatened action to put an end to his son's irregularities, reproaching his son for his unworthy life and lack of virtue, from the consequences of which even a worthy name could not protect him. A tradesman and creditor, Monsieur Dimanche, also learned where Don Juan was hidden. Although he blandly acknowledged his indebtedness to the tradesman, Don Juan had no intention of meeting his obligations, and he put the honest man off with hypocritical words of solicitude and friendliness.

Elvire, veiled, let Don Juan know that her love for him was now wholly free from sensual attachment and that she would retire to the convent from which he had taken her. Fearing that he could not escape the wrath of heaven, she implored him to reform before he was utterly crushed.

Meanwhile, Sganarelle and Don Juan had forgotten their invitation asking the statue to dinner. When the meal was served, the statue knocked at the door and seated itself at their table. The statue challenged Don Juan to dine with it the next day.

These happenings led Don Juan to pretend conversion and penitence to his father, who was overjoyed. But his so-called reform was merely a sham to further another of his designs, for Don Juan still believed that hypocrisy was a fashionable and privileged vice. He would boldly don the clothes of hypocrisy, more relentlessly than ever continue to persecute his enemies, and, holding to a good opinion of himself alone, adapt himself to the vices of his age.

Don Carlos demanded that Don Juan recognize Elvire publicly as his wife, but Don Juan demurred, saying the matter was no longer in his hands as Elvire was resolved to go into retreat and he to reform. Sanctimoniously, he begged Don Carlos to leave everything to the will of heaven, but he also warned that if attacked he would fight.

Don Juan, in calling on heaven, had gone too far. A ghost in the form of a veiled woman warned him to repent of his sins immediately. Don Juan, thinking he recognized the voice, challenged the figure and raised his sword to strike, but the shape changed to that of Time with a scythe before vanishing. Later the statue returned, adding its threat of a terrible death if Don Juan persisted in his wickedness. Scorched by an invisible flame, Don Juan cried out, but amid lightning flashes and thunderous sounds, the earth opened up and swallowed him. Thus he who neglected debts, seduced his victims, dishonored friends, and violated all laws finally offended heaven. The things which he held in scoffing disbelief brought about his doom.

DON JUAN TENORIO

Type of work: Drama
Author: José Zorrilla y Moral (1817-1893)
Type of plot: Fantastic-religious comedy
Time of plot: c. 1545
Locale: Seville, Spain
First presented: 1844

Principal characters:
DON JUAN TENORIO, a nobleman of Seville
DON DIEGO TENORIO, his father
DON LUIS MEJIA, another Andalusian gentleman
DON GONZALO DE ULLOA, Comendador of Calatrava
INES DE ULLOA, his daughter
ANA DE PANTOJA, betrothed to Mejía
MARCOS CIUTTI, servant of Don Juan

Critique:

One of the best examples of Spain's romantic theater is this play in seven acts, four of which take place during a single night, the remaining three about five years later. The drama was written in twenty days for a theater owner threatened with bankruptcy. Though full of exaggeration and melodramatic improbabilities that even its author ridiculed, it has been popular in Spain since the time of its first presentation. Based on a well-loved Spanish legend, spiritedly written in excellent and varied poetry, traditionally it is produced all over the Spanish-speaking world for All Saint's Day, the first of November. Audiences see in it not only a play about a rollicking adventurer whom they would like to imitate, but also a story with a meaning deeper than that which appears on the surface. The implication of the drama seems to be that since God's love is infinite, a man can sin as much as he likes, provided at the end he wins the love of a pure woman. This combination of the romantic with the mystic has perennial appeal to the Latin temperament.

The Story:

It was the carnival season in Seville, and the Laurel Tavern was a strange place in which to find gallant young Don Juan Tenorio, when the streets outside were filled with masked merrymakers. But he was there with his servant, Mar-

cos Ciutti, to keep a rendezvous with Don Luis Mejía, another gallant. One year before each had wagered that he could do the most harm in the next twelve months. That night they were to decide the bet.

Don Gonzalo de Ulloa, father of the girl whom Don Juan hoped to marry, went masked to the inn, for he wanted to hear with his own ears an account of the wild and villainous deeds attributed to his prospective son-in-law. Don Diego, Juan's father, joined him, masked as well. Several officers, friends of Don Juan and Mejía, were also loitering in the tavern to learn the outcome of the wager, which had been talked about in the city for months. Mejía appeared promptly, just as the cathedral clock was striking eight.

With good-humored boasting the rivals compared lists of the men they had slain in duels and the women they had cruelly deceived during the year. Don Juan was easily the victor. Because his roster lacked only two types of women, a nun and the bride of a friend, he wagered that he could add both to his list within a week. Fearing that his rival had an eye on Ana de Pantoja, whom he was planning to marry, Mejía sent his servant to call the police. Angered by the evil deeds of which Don Juan had boasted, the comendador announced that he would never consent to the young scoundrel's marriage with his daughter Ines. Instead, the girl would be kept safe in a convent. Don Diego also disowned his son.

A patrol appeared to arrest Don Juan on Mejía's accusations. Other guards summoned by Ciutti took Mejía into custody at the same time.

Through the influence of powerful friends Mejía soon had himself freed. He hurried at once to the house of Ana de Pantoja, where he persuaded a servant to let him into the house at ten o'clock that night. His purpose was to keep Don Juan from attempting an entrance. When Ana appeared at the balcony, he told her his plan and got her acquiescence to it.

Don Juan, also released from custody, overheard their conversation, which gave him the idea of impersonating his rival in order to get into Ana's room. Ciutti had already bribed Ana's duenna to secure the key to the outer door. To make sure that Mejía was out of the way, Ciutti also hired several men to impersonate the police patrol. These bravos seized Mejía and bound him.

Don Juan next interviewed Brígida, the duenna of Ines, and bribed her to deliver a note to the girl in the convent. When the old woman reported that her charge was already in love with Don Juan, whom she had never seen, the gallant decided that he had time to go to the convent and abduct her before the hour for him to appear at Ana's house.

Meanwhile, at the convent, Ines listened abashed as the abbess praised the girl's godliness. Perhaps she had once been like that; now she no longer looked forward to taking holy orders. Half-frightened, half-eager, she kept thinking of Don Juan. The appearance of Brígida with the note upset her still more, so that when Don Juan himself appeared suddenly at the door of her cell she collapsed in a faint. In her unconscious state it was easy for him to carry her off. Don Gonzalo, worried by the young man's boasting and reports of conversations between him and Brígida, arrived at the convent too late to save his daughter.

Ines remained unconscious while Don Juan took her to his house beside the Guadalquiver River. When she came to, Brígida lied to her charge, saying that Don Juan had saved the girl's life when the convent caught on fire.

Later Don Juan returned, after he had successfully entered Ana's room. Mejía, seeking revenge, came in pursuit. Don Gonzalo, hoping to rescue his daughter, also appeared at the house. Enraged by their insults, Don Juan shot Don Gonzalo and stabbed Mejía. Then he jumped into the river to escape from police who were hammering at his front door. Abandoned by Don Juan, Ines returned to the convent and died of grief.

Five years later a sculptor was putting the finishing touches to the Tenorio pantheon. On Don Diego's orders the family mansion had been torn down and the grounds had been turned into a cemetery for his son's victims. Lifelike statues of the three chief ones, Mejía, Don Gonzalo, and Ines, gleamed in the moonlight. Patiently the sculptor explained his labors to a stranger who finally terrified the craftsman by revealing himself as Don Juan.

Repentant, Don Juan knelt before Ines' monument and begged her to intercede with God for mercy. When he looked up, her statue had disappeared from its pedestal and Ines herself stood beside him, sent reincarnate from Heaven either to bring him back with her to salvation or to be damned with him throughout eternity; he had until dawn to choose their fate. Don Juan, unable to believe that what was happening was real, thought it a trick of crafty priests.

When two officers who five years before had witnessed the outcome of his bet with Mejía came into the graveyard, he laughed at their fear of ghosts; fear had no entry to his heart. After inviting his old acquaintances to have supper with him and hear the story of his adventures, with rash bravado he also extended his invitation to the statue of Don Gonzalo. Only the comendador's presence at the table, Don Juan said, would convince him of a life beyond the grave. The statue kept its stony silence.

While the trio sat drinking at the table, they heard the sound of knocking, each time nearer, though all the doors were bolted. Then into the room stalked the statue of Don Gonzalo, to tell the skeptic about the life eternal that could be realized through God's mercy. The officers fainted, but Don Juan was so courteous a host that before the statue disappeared through the wall it invited him to a similar banquet in the cemetery.

Still unconvinced that one moment of repentance could wipe out thirty years of sin, Don Juan refused to be moved when Ines appeared to persuade him to make the right choice. Half believing that the whole affair was a joke concocted by the sleeping officers, he shook them back to consciousness and accused them of using him for their sport. They in turn charged him with drugging them. The argument ended in challenges to a duel.

In the half light of early morning the statues of Ines and Don Gonzalo were still missing from the pantheon of the Tenorio family when Don Juan, melancholy because he had killed his old friends in the duel, appeared to keep his appointment. His knock at the comendador's tomb transformed it into a banquet table that parodied his own bountiful spread of the night before. Snakes and ashes were the foods, illuminated by the purging fire of God, and ghostly guests crowded around the board. Although death was on his way, Don Juan still refused to repent as Don Gonzalo's statue once more told him about the redeeming power of Heaven.

As Don Juan's funeral procession approached, Don Gonzalo seized the sinner's arm and prepared to drag him off to Hell. At that moment Don Juan raised his free arm toward Heaven. Ines appeared and she and Don Juan, both saved, sank together into a bed of flowers scattered by angels. Flames, symbolizing their souls, mounted to Heaven.

DON QUIXOTE DE LA MANCHA

Type of work: Novel
Author: Miguel de Cervantes Saavedra (1547-1616)
Type of plot: Picaresque romance
Time of plot: Late sixteenth century
Locale: Spain
First published: Part I, 1605; Part II, 1615

Principal characters:
DON QUIXOTE DE LA MANCHA, a knight-errant
SANCHO PANZA, his squire
DULCINEA DEL TOBOSO, a village wench
PEDRO PEREZ, a village curate
MASTER NICHOLAS, a barber
SAMSON CARRASCO, a young bachelor of arts

Critique:

Macauley said that *Don Quixote* is "the best novel in the world, beyond comparison." This belief was, is, and certainly will be shared by lovers of literary excellence everywhere. Cervantes' avowed purpose was to ridicule the books of chivalry which enjoyed popularity even in his day. But he soared beyond this satirical purpose in his wealth of fancy and in his irrepressible high spirit as he pokes fun at social and literary conventions of his day. The novel provides a cross-section of Spanish life, thought, and feeling at the end of the chivalric age.

The Story:

A retired and impoverished gentleman named Alonzo Quixano lived in the Spanish province of La Mancha. He had read so many romances of chivalry that his mind became stuffed with fantastic accounts of tournaments, knightly quests, damsels in distress, and strange enchantments, and he decided one day to imitate the heroes of the books he read and to revive the ancient custom of knight-errantry. Changing his name to Don Quixote de la Mancha, he had himself dubbed a knight by a rascally publican whose miserable inn he mistook for a turreted castle.

For armor he donned an old suit of mail which had belonged to his great-grandfather. Then upon a bony old nag he called Rosinante, he set out upon his first adventure. Not far from his village he fell into the company of some traveling merchants who thought the old man mad and beat him severely when he challenged them to a passage at arms.

Back home recovering from his cuts and bruises, he was closely watched by his good neighbor, Pedro Perez, the village priest, and Master Nicholas, the barber. Hoping to cure him of his fancies, the curate and the barber burned his library of chivalric romances. Don Quixote, however, believed that his books had been carried off by a wizard. Undaunted by his misfortunes, he determined to set out on the road again, with an uncouth rustic named Sancho Panza as his squire. As the mistress to whom he would dedicate his deeds of valor he chose a buxom peasant wench famous for her skill in salting pork. He called her Dulcinea del Toboso.

The knight and his squire had to sneak out of the village under cover of darkness, but in their own minds they presented a brave appearance: the lean old man on his bony horse and his squat, black-browed servant on a small ass, Dapple. The don carried his sword and lance, Sancho Panza a canvas wallet and a leather bottle. Sancho went with the don because in his shallow-brained way he hoped to become governor of an isle.

The don's first encounter was with a score of windmills on the plains of Montiel. Mistaking them for monstrous giants, he couched his lance, set spurs to Rosinante's thin flanks, and charged full tilt against them. One of the whirling vanes lifted him from his saddle and threw him into the air. When Sancho Panza ran to pick him up, he explained that sorcerers had changed the giants into windmills.

Shortly afterward he encountered two monks riding in company with a lady in a coach escorted by men on horseback Don Quixote imagined that the lady was a captive princess. Haughtily demanding her release, he unhorsed one of the friars in an attempted rescue. Sancho was beaten by the lady's lackeys. Don Quixote bested her Biscayan squire in a sword fight, sparing the man's life on condition that he go to Toboso and yield himself to the peerless Dulcinea. Sancho, having little taste for violence, wanted to get on to his isle as quickly as possible.

At an inn Quixote became involved in an assignation between a carrier and a servant girl. He was trounced by the carrier. The don, insulted by the innkeeper's demand for payment, rode away without paying. Sancho, to his terror, was tossed in a blanket as payment for his master's debt.

The pair came upon dust clouds stirred up by two large flocks of sheep. Don Quixote, sure that they were two medieval armies closing in combat, intervened, only to be pummeled with rocks by the indignant shepherds, whose sheep he had scattered.

At night the don thought a funeral procession was a parade of monsters. He attacked and routed the mourners and was called the Knight of the Sorry Aspect by Sancho. The two came upon a roaring noise in the night. Quixote, believing it to be made by giants, wanted to attack immediately, but Sancho judiciously hobbled Rosinante so he could not move. The next day they discovered the noise came from the pounding of a mill.

Quixote attacked an itinerant barber and seized the poor barber's bowl, which he declared to be the famous golden helmet of Mambrino, and his packsaddle,

which he believed to be a richly-jeweled caparison.

Next, the pair came upon a chain-gang being taken to the galleys. The don interviewed various prisoners and decided to succor the afflicted. He freed them, only to be insulted by their remarks concerning his lady, the fair Dulcinea. Sancho, afraid of what would ensue from their releasing of the galleyslaves, led Quixote into the mountains for safety. There they came upon a hermit, a nobleman, who told them a long story of unrequited love. Quixote and the hermit fought over the virtues of their inamoratas. Deciding to do penance and to fast for the love of Dulcinea, Quixote gave a letter to Sancho to deliver to the maiden. When Sancho returned to the village Don Quixote's friends learned from Sancho the old man's whereabouts. They returned with Sancho to the mountains, in hopes that they could trick Don Quixote into returning with them. The priest devised a scheme whereby a young peasant woman would pose as a distressed princess. Don Quixote, all but dead from hunger and exposure, was easily deceived, and the party started homeward.

They came to the inn where Sancho had been tossed in the blanket. The priest explained the don's vagaries to the alarmed innkeeper, who admitted that he, too, was addicted to the reading of romances of chivalry. At the inn Don Quixote fought in his sleep with ogres and ran his sword through two of the innkeeper's precious wine-skins. The itinerant barber stopped by and demanded the return of his basin and packsaddle. After the party had sport at the expense of the befuddled barber, restitution was made. An officer appeared with a warrant for the arrest of the don and Sancho for releasing the galleyslaves. The priest explained his friend's mental condition and the officer departed.

Seeing no other means of getting Don Quixote quietly home, his friends disguised themselves and placed the don in a cage mounted on an oxcart. He was later released under oath not to attempt to escape. A canon, joining the party, sought to bring Quixote to his senses by logical argument against books of knight-errantry. The don refuted the canon with a charming and brilliant argument and went on to narrate a typical romance of derring-do. Before the group reached home, they came upon a goatherd who told them a story and by whom Quixote was beaten through a misunderstanding.

Sometime later the priest and the barber visited the convalescing Don Quixote to give him news of Spain and of the world. When they told him there was danger of an attack on Spain by the Turks, the don suggested that the king assemble all of Spain's knights-errant to repulse the enemy. At this time, Sancho entered despite efforts to bar him. He brought word that a book telling of their adventures had appeared. The sight of Sancho inspired the don to sally forth again. His excuse was a great tournament to be held at Saragossa.

Failing to dissuade Don Quixote from going forth again, his friends were reassured when a village student promised he would waylay the flighty old gentleman.

Don Quixote's first destination was the home of Dulcinea in nearby El Toboso. While the don awaited in a forest, Sancho saw three peasant girls riding out of the village. He rode to his master and told him that Dulcinea with two handmaidens approached. Frightened by the don's fantastic speech, the girls fled. Don Quixote swore that Dulcinea had been enchanted.

Benighted in a forest, the knight and his squire were awakened by the arrival of another knight and squire. The other knight boasted that he had defeated in combat all Spanish knights. The don, believing the knight to be mistaken, challenged him. They fought by daylight and, miraculously, Don Quixote unhorsed the Knight of the Wood, who was Carrasco, the village student, in disguise. His squire was an old acquaintance of Sancho. The don declared the resemblances were the work of magicians and continued on his way. Upset by his failure, Carrasco swore vengeance on Don Quixote.

Sancho filled Quixote's helmet with curds which he procured from shepherds. When the don suddenly clapped on his helmet at the approach of another adventure, he thought his brains were melting. This new adventure took the form of a wagon bearing two caged lions. Quixote, ever intrepid, commanded the keeper to open one cage—he would engage a lion in combat. Unhappily, the keeper obeyed. Quixote stood ready, but the lion yawned and refused to come out.

The don and Sancho joined a wedding party and subsequently attended a wedding festival at which the rejected lover tricked the bride into marrying him instead of the rich man she had chosen.

Next, the pair were taken to the Caves of Montesinos, where. Quixote was lowered underground. He was brought up an hour later asleep, and, upon awakening, he told a story of having spent three days in a land of palaces and magic forests where he had seen his enchanted Dulcinea.

At an inn Quixote met a puppeteer who had a divining ape. By trickery, the rascal identified the don and Sancho with the help of the ape. He presented a melodramatic puppet show which Don Quixote, carried away by the make-believe story, demolished with his sword. The don paid for the damage done and struck out for the nearby River Ebro. He and Sancho took a boat and were carried by the current toward some churning mill wheels, which the don thought were a beleaguered city awaiting deliverance. They were rescued by millers after the boat had been wrecked and the pair thoroughly soaked.

Later, in a forest, the pair met a huntress who claimed knowledge of the famous knight and his squire. They went with the lady to her castle and were welcomed by a duke and his duchess who had read of their previous adventures and who were ready to have great fun at the pair's expense. The hosts arranged an elaborate night ceremony to disenchant Dulcinea, who was represented by a disguised page. Sancho was told, to his great discomfort, that he would receive five hundred lashes as his part of the disenchantment. Part of the jest was a ride through space on a magic wooden horse. Blindfolded, the pair mounted their steed and servants blew air in their faces from bellows and thrust torches near their faces.

Sancho departed to govern his isle, a village in the domains of the duke and duchess, while the female part of the household turned to the project of compromising Quixote in his worship of Dulcinea. Sancho governed for a week. He made good laws and delivered wise judgments, but at the end of a week he yearned for the freedom of the road. Together he and his master proceeded toward Saragossa. Don Quixote changed their destination to Barcelona, however, when he heard that a citizen of that city had written a spurious account of his adventures.

In Barcelona they marveled at the city, the ships, and the sea. Don Quixote and Sancho were the guests of Moreno, who took them to inspect the royal galleys. The galley which they visited suddenly put out to sea in pursuit of pirates and a fight followed. Sancho was terrified.

There came to Barcelona a Knight of the White Moon, who challenged Don Quixote to combat. After the old man had been overcome, the strange knight, in reality the student Carrasco, sentenced him to return home. Don Quixote went back, determined next to follow a pastoral shepherd life. At home, the tired old man quickly declined. Before he died, he renounced as nonsense all to do with knight-errantry, not realizing that in his high-minded, noble-hearted nature he himself had been a great chivalric gentleman.

DON SEGUNDO SOMBRA

Type of work: Novel
Author: Ricardo Güiraldes (1882-1927)
Type of plot: Regional romance
Time of plot: Late nineteenth century
Locale: Argentina
First published: 1926

Principal characters:
DON SEGUNDO SOMBRA, a gaucho
FABIO, a young waif
DON LEANDRO GALVÁN, a rancher
PEDRO BARRALES, a gaucho
PAULA, a pretty young woman, loved by Fabio

Critique:

Don Segundo Sombra: Shadows on the Pampas has been called the South American counterpart of *Huckleberry Finn*. Like the hero of Mark Twain's novel, Fabio wanders on his own through youth in a new country, giving the author a chance not only to tell a story but also to present a vivid and varied documentation of details about the people, the customs, and the countryside. In Argentina itself, the book was immediately popular. It and the earlier gaucho epic, *Martín Fierro*, are the best narratives dealing with the gaucho, the South American cowboy. The hero of Güiraldes' novel was drawn from a real-life gaucho whom the author had known and loved in his own childhood on his father's ranch, La Portena, in the province of Buenos Aires. The novel reflects a pastoral form of life that has all but disappeared in Argentina, and the story will probably fascinate later generations much as Owen Wister's picturesque narrative of the North American cowboy, *The Virginian*, has caught the fancy of post-frontier readers.

The Story:

Fabio was a young lad who lived with his two maiden aunts in a small Argentine village. He disliked his aunts, who felt, in their turn, that he was simply a bother. He was not sure that the two women were truly his relatives, for they paid him little heed as long as he gave them no trouble. Don Fabio Cáceres, a rancher, occasionally came to see the boy and take him into the country for a day, but the man ceased coming about Fabio's eleventh year.

Fabio grew up to be a cheeky youngster who showed off for the worst element of the town. He knew all the gossip and spent most of his time hanging about the saloons; no one seemed to care that he never went to school. The village loafers hinted that he was an illegitimate, unwanted child. At best, he seemed destined to be a ne'er-do-well who carried a chip on his shoulder in defiance of the rest of the world.

One night a gaucho rode into the town as Fabio was going homeward from fishing. The man impressed the boy at sight, and a little later Fabio earned the gaucho's interest by warning him of an ambush laid by a knife-wielding bully. The kind words spoken by the gaucho, Don Segundo, went to the boy's heart, and Fabio immediately decided to follow the man when he left town. Gathering together his meager possessions, which fortunately included a saddle and two ponies, Fabio went quietly away without telling anyone where he was going, in order to escape his hated aunts. He rode to the ranch belonging to Don Le-

DON SEGUNDO SOMBRA by Ricardo Güiraldes. Translated by Harriet de Onís. By permission of the publishers, Rinehart & Co., Inc. Copyright, 1935, by Farrar & Rinehart, Inc.

andro Galván, where he knew Don Segundo was going to spend a few days breaking wild horses for riding.

When he arrived, the boy applied for work and was accepted. By the time Don Segundo was ready to leave the ranch on a cattle drive Fabio had convinced Don Leandro and Don Segundo that he was a willing worker, and they let Fabio go with the other gauchos on half pay. At the end of the drive Fabio was well along in his apprenticeship as a gaucho.

For five years Fabio continued under the tutelage of Don Segundo. Traveling from ranch to ranch, they worked for a number of landowners. From the older man Fabio learned to care for himself and his horses, to work cattle under various conditions, to live courageously, to get along with all kinds of people, and to have a good time singing songs, dancing, and telling stories. It was more than a way of making a living that the man passed on to the boy; it was an entire culture, a culture as old as the cattle industry and in some respects even older, going back as it did to the culture of Spain.

There were many incidents in their wanderings, including the time that Fabio won a large number of pesos by picking the winning bird in a cockfight when everyone else bet against the bird. That happened in the town of Navarro, a town which remained a lucky place in young Fabio's mind. He remembered also a long drive with cattle to a ranch on the seashore. There Fabio found a country he detested and a young woman he loved, as well as a great store of bad luck. He had picked up quite a respectable string of horses, the tools of the gaucho's trade, and he was very proud of them. But in working the cattle at the seashore ranch two of the horses were injured, much to the young gaucho's disgust. One of them was badly gored by a bull, and when Fabio came across the bull one evening while exploring with another young man he vowed to break its neck. He lassoed the beast and broke its neck with the shock, but in doing so he injured himself severely, breaking several bones.

While Fabio remained at the ranch convalescing from his injuries he fell in love, he thought, with Paula, a pretty young girl who lived on the place. Unfortunately, she led him on and also the rather stupid son of the rancher. The other lad took advantage of Fabio's crippled arm and attacked him with a knife. Fabio, not wanting to injure the owner's son, to fight over a woman, or to violate the father's hospitality, avoided the other fellow's thrusts until they became deadly. Then with a quick thrust Fabio slashed the boy's forehead slightly, taking the will to fight out of him very quickly. Paula, over whom the fight began, rebuked the crippled Fabio. Disgusted at her and at himself, Fabio, crippled as he was, mounted his horse and rode away to rejoin Don Segundo, who was working at a nearby ranch until Fabio could be ready to travel.

Don Segundo and Fabio happened into a small village on a day when people had gathered from miles around to race horses. Fabio bet and lost a hundred pesos, then another hundred, and finally the third and last hundred he possessed. Still not satisfied that he was a hopeless loser, he gambled five of his horses and lost them as well. He came out of the afternoon's activity a sad young man.

He and Don Segundo were hired to trail a herd of cattle from a ranch near the village to the city to be butchered. It was a long, hard drive, even for experienced gauchos. It was made even more difficult for Fabio by the fact that he had only three horses, for the animals soon became fatigued from the work of carrying him and working the cattle on the road. When the herd stopped to rest one afternoon, Fabio decided to see if he could somehow get another horse or two.

While looking about he found Pedro Barrales, a gaucho who had traveled with him and Don Segundo several times before. Pedro Barrales had a letter addressed to Señor Fabio Cáceres, a letter which he gave to Fabio. The lad looked blankly at the letter, not believing it was addressed to him, for he thought he had no surname. Don Segundo opened the letter to find that the maiden aunts had been truly Fabio's relatives and that Don Fabio Cáceres who had visited him at his aunts' home was really his father, from whom he had inherited a fortune and a large, well-stocked ranch. The news saddened Fabio because he saw that it would take him away from the life he loved. He was angered, too, because he had been left so long under the impression that his parentage was one to be ashamed of.

Acting upon the good advice of Don Segundo, Fabio returned to his native town, however, and from there to the ranch where he had begun work under Don Leandro Galván, who had now become his guardian. When Don Segundo agreed to remain with him for three years on his own ranch, Fabio was willing to settle down. But the three years passed all too swiftly, and at the end of that time Fabio was exceedingly sad when Don Segundo, answering the gaucho's call to wander, rode away.

DOÑA BARBARA

Type of work: Novel
Author: Rómulo Gallegos (1884-   )
Type of plot: Regional romance
Time of plot: Early twentieth century
Locale: The Arauca Valley of Venezuela
First published: 1929

Principal characters:
DOÑA BARBARA, a beautiful, unscrupulous mestiza
SANTOS LUZARDO, owner of the Altamira ranch
MARISELA, illegitimate daughter of Doña Barbara and Lorenzo Barquero
ANTONIO, a cowboy at the Altamira ranch
THE WIZARD, a rascally henchman of Doña Barbara
SEÑOR DANGER, an American squatter on the Altamira ranch
DON BALBINO, treacherous overseer at the Altamira ranch

Critique:

Seldom is the literary man a political leader, but Rómulo Gallegos is an exception to that rule. He was one of the founders of the Democratic Action Party in Venezuela in 1941 and was nominated by that party for the Venezuelan presidency in 1947. He was elected by the people to office and served until overthrown by a military dictatorship. Gallegos and his party stood for a liberal, social-minded government which would improve living conditions for the masses of Venezuela. Gallegos' national pride in his country and his people is reflected in his fiction. Although his fiction, like most of the books written in Latin America, is little known in the United States, it has a high reputation with readers who have come to know it either in Spanish or in translation.

The Story:

The Altamira ranch was a vast estate in the wildest section of the Arauca River basin of Venezuela, a ranch that had been established early in the history of the cattle business of that South American country. Late in the nineteenth century, however, it had been divided into two parts by the joint heirs of one of the owners. One part retained the old name and went to the male heir of the Luzardo family. The other part, going to a daughter who had married a Barquero, took its name from the new owner. As the years went by the two families carried on a feud which killed most of the men on both sides. In the years of the Spanish-American War, the owner of Altamira and his elder son quarreled; the father killed the son and then starved himself to death. Doña Luzardo took her only remaining son and went to Caracas, there to rear him in a more civilized atmosphere.

Years went by, and finally the son, Santos Luzardo decided to sell the ranch, which had been allowed to deteriorate to almost nothing under irresponsible overseers. In order to set a price upon his property he went into the back country to see it for himself. On his arrival he found that the neighboring ranch of the Barqueros had fallen into the hands of Doña Barbara, a mestiza who had been the mistress of the real owner before she ran him off his own property. Doña Barbara was in the process of taking over Altamira ranch with the help of several henchmen, including Don Balbino, the overseer of Altamira ranch. Santos decided to keep the ranch and try to make it a prosperous business, if he could only keep it out of Doña Barbara's hands.

To help him, Santos had a handful of loyal cowboys who had known him as a child, including Antonio, a cowboy who had been his playmate years before. Santos Luzardo's first move was to end the feud between himself and the Barqueros. He found Lorenzo Barquero living in a cabin in a swamp, the only land his mistress had not taken from him. After making his peace with Lorenzo and with his illegitimate daughter Marisela, Santos took them to live at Altamira ranch. Marisela was as beautiful as her mother, Doña Barbara, and Santos wished to retrieve her from barbarity.

Most of the cattle had been stolen from Altamira ranch, until only about a hundred head were left. But Antonio, the loyal cowboy, had seen to it that many hundreds more had been allowed to stray into wild country in order to save them from the depredations of Doña Barbara and Señor Danger, an American who had begun as a squatter and who was carving his own ranch out of Altamira land. Don Balbino, the treacherous overseer, was immediately discharged. Since he had been working for Doña Barbara and was her lover, he sought the mestiza's protection.

Santos, who had been trained as a lawyer, decided first to try legal means in order to repossess part of his ranch. He went to the local magistrate and through his knowledge of the law forced that official to call in Doña Barbara and Señor Danger. They were told to permit a roundup of his cattle and to help him, since their herds were intermingled with those from Altamira. They were also told to take action with respect to fences. Danger had to build fences, for according to the law he had too few cattle to let them run wild. Doña Barbara was to help build a boundary fence between her ranch and Altamira. Surprisingly, she took the decisions with good grace. Her henchmen were completely surprised, for previously she had ridden roughshod over all opposition. The answer lay in the fact that she was secretly in love with Santos Luzardo, and she thought she could command his love and his property by her beauty.

As weeks of deadening ranch routine passed, Santos was glad that he had brought Marisela to his house, for his efforts to teach her culture kept him from losing touch with civilization. Although his interest in her was only that of a friend and tutor, Marisela had fallen in love with the rancher.

Along the Arauca River there were thousands of herons. When the birds were moulting, the people of Altamira went out to collect the plumes and gathered fifty pounds of the valuable feathers, which were sent with two of the cowboys to market. Santos intended to use the money from the sale to fence his boundaries. On their way to market the cowboys were murdered and the feathers stolen. Their loss and the failure of the authorities to track down the culprit caused a great change in Santos. He determined to take the law into his own hands and to match violence with violence when he found it necessary.

His first act was to have three of Doña Barbara's henchmen captured and sent off to prison, for they had been long wanted for a number of crimes. A short time later he received word from Doña Barbara, who was pulled in two ways by her love for him and by her wish for power, that he would find in a certain canyon the thief who had taken the feathers. Santos went in the night and killed the Wizard, Doña Barbara's most trusted and bloodthirsty henchman. Meanwhile Don Balbino, the treacherous overseer who had been in charge of Altamira and who had been Doña Barbara's lover, became distasteful to her. She had him killed after discovering that it was he who had stolen the feathers. To aid Santos, she threw on Don Balbino the blame for killing the Wizard.

Recovering the feathers, Doña Barbara went to town to sell them for Santos.

At the same time she had documents made out to transfer the disputed lands to their rightful owner. When she returned to her ranch she found that her people had deserted her; they could not understand why she had turned on her trusted killers. Doña Barbara rode immediately to Altamira, where she found Santos talking to Marisela, whose father had recently died. Because the girl's love for Santos showed plainly on her face, Doña Barbara, unseen, drew her revolver to kill her daughter. Her own love for Santos prevented the deed, however, and she rode away without revealing her presence.

Doña Barbara was not heard from again. The next day a large envelope was delivered to Santos. In it he found a sheaf of documents giving back the property that had been stolen from him, and others transferring the Barquero ranch to Doña Barbara's daughter Marisela. Shortly afterward Santos and Marisela were married, and thus the two ranches which had been separated for many years were once again joined under one owner.

DOÑA PERFECTA

Type of work: Novel
Author: Benito Pérez Galdós (1843-1920)
Type of plot: Tragedy of religious bigotry
Time of plot: Late nineteenth century
Locale: Orbajosa, Spain
First published: 1876

Principal characters:
JOSÉ ("PEPE") REY
DOÑA PERFECTA REY, his aunt
ROSARIO, her daughter
DON INOCENCIO, canon of the cathedral
MARÍA REMEDIOS, his sister
JACINTO, María's son

Critique:

Pérez Galdós went to Madrid as a student of law in 1863; however, literature and the theater proved more interesting than the bar. Early in his literary career he wrote several novels about politics and social customs. Then, between 1875 and 1878, Galdós became interested in religion and published three novels dealing with its different aspects: *Doña Perfecta,* the story of a town dominated by the clergy; *Gloria* (1876-1877), a novel about a Jewish-Christian clash, and *The Family of León Roch* (1879), a story of religious fanaticism ruining a happy household. All are classified as belonging to the novelist's early period, though they represent a great technical advance over his first attempts. In *Doña Perfecta,* Galdós describes the clash of modern ideas against the walls of bigotry and prejudice in a small Andalusian town removed from the main current of life. Representative of the new order is the scientifically trained, clear-thinking, outspoken bridge builder. The old is represented by a wealthy woman so fanatically religious that to save her daughter's immortal soul she would even condone murder. The result is a suspense novel that has shown its popularity by translation into eight languages.

The Story:

The city of Orbajosa, with its 7,324 inhabitants, was proud of its religious atmosphere. It boasted a cathedral and a seminary, but it possessed nothing else to make it known to the rest of Spain. It had no manufacturing, and its only agricultural activity was the raising of garlic.

The leading citizen of Orbajosa was Doña Perfecta Rey, a widow whose wealth was the result of legal victories won over her husband's family by her brother, an Andalusian lawyer. Since she had a son, Pepe Rey, and she had a daughter, Rosario, the idea of marriage between the two young people seemed a natural arrangement to their elders. It was for this purpose that Pepe first came to Orbajosa.

In his busy life as a road construction engineer, Pepe had thought little about matrimony, but he began to do so after seeing the lovely Rosario. The girl was in turn attracted to her cousin. Doña Perfecta was also much taken with Pepe, but not for long.

Doña Perfecta, like the other inhabitants of Orbajosa, was under the domination of the Church, and as the town's most exemplary citizen she felt the need to be especially devout. At the same time Don Inocencio, canon of the cathedral, had other plans for Rosario. Urged on by his sister, María Remedios, who desired the Rey fortune for her son Jacinto, Don Inocencio, far less innocent than his name implied, began conniving to end all talk of marriage between the cousins.

Pepe, through his wide travel and training, was unorthodox, though not without regard for religion. Before long, however, Don Inocencio made him appear a heretic, and Doña Perfecta, forgetting her indebtedness to his father and ignoring the feelings of her daughter, refused him permission to see Rosario. The girl, made meek by education and dominated by her mother, lacked the courage to assert herself in declaring her love for her cousin.

Soon all the people of Orbajosa, from the bishop to the working man in the fields, were made to feel it a matter of religious and civic pride to rid their city of the heretic. The unsuspecting Pepe could not conceive of such intolerance. He tried to explain that he had no intention of attacking religion, but his attempts to make clear his position only made matters worse.

Finally, after several stolen interviews with Rosario in the family chapel, Pepe decided to take her away, and Rosario agreed to go with him. But the lovers had failed to reckon with the power of community opinion. While the conscience-stricken Rosario was revealing to her mother her plan to run away that night with Pepe, María Remedios, filled with hatred for the young man who was cheating her Jacinto out of the Rey fortune, arrived to warn Doña Perfecta that the heretic was entering the garden.

Warned now that Pepe was coming to take Rosario away, her mother ordered one of her acquaintances to shoot him. Pepe fell, mortally wounded. His death drove Rosario insane. Don Inocencio felt himself cut off from the world, and Doña Perfecta died of cancer. Nobody gained anything, but Orbajosa felt sure it had won a victory for the faith.

THE DOUBLE-DEALER

Type of work: Drama
Author: William Congreve (1670-1729)
Type of plot: Tragi-comedy
Time of plot: Seventeenth century
Locale: London
First presented: 1694

Principal characters:
MELLEFONT, an earnest young man
LORD TOUCHWOOD, his uncle
LADY TOUCHWOOD, in love with Mellefont
CYNTHIA, Mellefont's sweetheart
MASKWELL, Mellefont's false friend

Critique:

The *Double-Dealer,* Congreve's second play, failed at the time of its presentation. This failure probably can be explained by the play's departure from the established tradition of Restoration comedy. In spite of its firm construction and witty dialogue, *The Double-Dealer* contains some repulsive elements not relished by the play-going audience of Congreve's day. Yet its plot, characters, and light dialogue make it one of the best comedies of the period. The play also reflects the dramatic conventions of its time and type: the attack on Puritans and Puritanism, dissolute dandies, devastatingly witty maidens, faithless young wives of old men, rascally servants, and devious intrigue.

The Story:

Lady Touchwood was infatuated with her husband's nephew, Mellefont, who had pledged himself to Cynthia, daughter of Sir Paul Plyant. When she confessed her ardor to him, and he rebuked her, she attempted to end her life with his sword. Prevented in her attempt, she vowed revenge.

Fearing the designs of Lady Touchwood, Mellefont engaged his friend Careless to keep Lady Plyant, Cynthia's stepmother, away from Lady Touchwood. Careless also revealed his distrust of Maskwell, Mellefont's friend, who was under obligations to Lord Touchwood.

From sheer spite, Lady Touchwood gave herself to Maskwell. In return, Maskwell promised to help Lady Touch-wood by insinuating to Lady Plyant that Mellefont really loved her, not Cynthia.

Lady Touchwood's plan began to work. Old Sir Paul Plyant and Lady Plyant expressed indignation when they were told that Mellefont desired Lady Plyant. Actually, Lady Plyant was flattered and merely pretended anger, but she was nevertheless shocked that Mellefont intended to marry Cynthia for the ultimate purpose of cuckolding Sir Paul. Lady Plyant rebuked him, but at the same time she told the puzzled young man not to despair. Maskwell revealed to Mellefont that he was Lady Touchwood's agent in provoking trouble; Maskwell's real purpose was to create general confusion and to win Cynthia's hand.

Lord Touchwood, refusing to believe that his nephew played a double game, was scandalized when Lady Touchwood recommended cancellation of the marriage on the grounds that Mellefont had made improper advances to her. Maskwell, instructed by Lady Touchwood, ingratiated himself with Lord Touchwood by saying that he had defended Lady Touchwood's honor and had prevailed upon Mellefont to cease his unwelcome attentions.

Maskwell, in his own vicious behalf, told Mellefont that his reward for assisting in the breakup of Mellefont's marriage to Cynthia was the privilege of bedding with Lady Touchwood. Plotting Mellefont's ruin, the fake friend pretended that he wished to be saved from the shame of collecting his reward, and he asked the

978

credulous young man to go to Lady Touchwood's chamber and there surprise Maskwell and Lady Touchwood together.

When Lord Plyant, frustrated by Lady Plyant's vow to remain a virgin, complained to Careless that he did not have an heir, Careless waggishly promised to see what he could do in the matter.

Mellefont, to escape the evil that was brewing, impatiently urged Cynthia to elope with him. Although she refused, she promised to marry no one but him. When she challenged Mellefont to thwart his aunt and to get her approval of their marriage, he promised to get Lady Touchwood's consent that night.

Lady Plyant, meanwhile, had consented to an assignation with Careless. When Lord Plyant appeared, Careless had to give her, secretly, a note containing directions for their meeting. Lady Plyant, anxious to read Careless' letter, asked her husband for a letter which he had received earlier. Pretending to read her husband's letter, she read the one given her by Careless. By mistake she returned her lover's letter to her husband.

Discovering her mistake, she reported it in alarm to Careless. Lord Plyant, meanwhile, had read the letter. Lady Plyant insisted that it was part of an insidious plot against her reputation, and after accusing her husband of having arranged to have it written in order to test her fidelity, she threatened divorce. Careless pretended that he had written it in Lord Plyant's behalf to test his wife's virtue. As foolish as he was, Lord Plyant was not without suspicion of his wife and Careless.

That night Mellefont concealed himself in Lady Touchwood's chamber. When she entered, expecting to find Maskwell, Mellefont revealed himself. Lord Touchwood, informed by Maskwell, then appeared. When her husband threatened his nephew, Lady Touchwood

pretended that the young man was out of his wits.

Not suspecting Maskwell's treachery, Lady Touchwood later told him of her lucky escape. Maskwell, in a purposeful soliloquy, revealed to Lord Touchwood his love for Cynthia. Duped, the old man named Maskwell his heir and promised to arrange a marriage between Cynthia and the schemer.

Lady Touchwood learned of Maskwell's treachery when Lord Touchwood told her that he intended to make Maskwell his heir. Chagrined by her betrayal, Lady Touchwood urged her husband never to consent to Cynthia's marriage with anyone but Mellefont.

Maskwell, still pretending to be Mellefont's friend, made his final move by plotting with the unwary Mellefont to get Cynthia away from her house. His intention being to marry her himself, he privately told Cynthia that Mellefont would be waiting for her in the chaplain's chamber. Careless checked Maskwell's carefully laid plans, however, when he disclosed to the young lovers Maskwell's true villainy. Cynthia and Lord Touchwood, in concealment, overheard Lady Touchwood rebuke Maskwell for his betrayal of her. At last she tried to stab her lover but was overcome with emotion. Maskwell then revealed the meeting place where Mellefont, in the disguise of a parson, would be waiting for Cynthia. Lady Touchwood, planning to disguise herself as Cynthia, hurried away to meet him there.

Lord Touchwood, knowing of her plan, put on a chaplain's habit and confronted his wife when she came to make overtures to the man she supposed was Mellefont. The whole plot uncovered, and Maskwell, the double-dealer, unmasked, Mellefont, cleared of all suspicion, took Cynthia for his own.

DOWN THERE

Type of work: Novel
Author: Joris Karl Huysmans (Charles Marie Georges Huysmans, 1848-1907)
Time: Late nineteenth century
Locale: Paris
First published: 1891

Principal characters:
DURTAL, a writer
DES HERMIES, his friend and interlocutor
CARHAIX, bell ringer at Saint-Sulpice
CHANTELOUVE, a Catholic historian
HYACINTHE CHANTELOUVE, his wife and Durtal's mistress
CANON DOCRE, a Satanist
GILLES DE RAIS (1404-1440), Marshal of France, infamous murderer, sadist, and Satanist

Huysmans began his career as a novelist during the 1870's as a member of the naturalistic school of Zola, whose friend and disciple he then was. But in 1884 he broke with Zola by writing his most famous book, *À rebours (Against the Grain)*, which was vastly admired by the *fin-de-siècle* writers on both sides of the Channel.

Down There (Là-bas) was the first of a series of four novels, the purpose of which was to trace the spiritual autobiography of one Durtal (Huysmans himself) as he struggled from skepticism through spiritual despair to the final goal of faith. It was not the author's intention to "tell a story" but rather to analyze his own reactions to the faith that he had lost, but hoped to regain, and to various aspects of historical and contemporary Roman Catholicism; hence, the plots of the books are very slight, and Huysmans used the novels as a platform from which he could express his very decided views on a number of subjects and display his esoteric learning.

When the story opens, Durtal is engaged in writing a biography of Gilles de Rais, the infamous murderer of children, who lived in the fifteenth century. With his friend Des Hermies, whose sole function is to provide someone for him to talk with, Durtal visits the home of Carhaix,

the bell ringer of Saint-Sulpice, in the tower of the church. During these visits the conversation turns to Church history and especially to Satanism, a subject in which Durtal has become interested as part of the background for his study of de Rais. Des Hermies avers that Satanism is being practiced in Paris at that very time and he mentions a certain Canon Docre, a renegade priest. While Durtal is wondering how he can make the contacts necessary to observe modern Satanism at first hand, he receives a series of anonymous love letters. He eventually discovers that the writer is a Madame Chantelouve, whose receptions he has sometimes attended. After a few meetings she becomes his mistress; he learns that she knows Docre, and at length he persuades her to take him to a Black Mass. He witnesses the revolting spectacle, held in an abandoned Ursuline convent; afterwards, in a nearby tavern, Madame Chantelouve tricks him into committing sacrilege. Disgusted with her, he breaks off their relationship, and the novel comes to an end.

There is, however, a story within the story, for large sections of the book are devoted to Durtal's readings from his biography of de Rais. The material for this section Huysmans obtained from a work by the Abbé Bossard, published in

1884, which contained a transcript of the records of de Rais' trial preserved in the archives at Nantes. Although he made a number of mistakes, Huysmans traced, with reasonable accuracy and considerable drama, the career of the sinister marshal. The details are often horrifying, and Huysmans spares his readers none of them; but the ending of the story, with de Rais' trial and final repentance, gave him the opportunity for his most famous passages of description. He was attracted to this unsavory bit of history as others have been (for the literature in French on de Rais is considerable) by the problem in morbid psychology that it presents. De Rais had been in his youth a companion-in-arms of Jeanne d'Arc and had apparently shared the religious exaltation that had affected her followers. How, then, did he change into such a monster of butchery, Satanism, and sexual perversion that his name is remembered after the passage of five hundred years? In addition, Huysmans was a fervent medievalist; and all aspects of the period fascinated him, particularly the religious fervor that had been possible in an age of faith. He never tired of contrasting the ardent Catholicism of the Middle Ages, the splendor of its ritual and the beauty of its architecture, with the vulgar manifestations that he saw in his own day. Faith had been easy in the fifteenth century, he believed; the problem was to find it in the materialistic present.

The parts of the novel dealing with modern Satanism—weird as they appear —were taken from happenings in contemporary Paris. There was apparently a good deal of this disgusting hocus-pocus going on at the time, and several of the characters in *Down There* were drawn from life.

Huysmans, during his later period, never wearied of damning the nineteenth century and all its characteristic works. He begins the novel with an attack on Naturalism, the literary school to which he had once belonged. It has "made our literature the incarnation of materialism . . . 'appetite and instinct' seem to be its sole motivation and rut and brainstorm its chronic states." And throughout the book he continues to attack his own age for its shoddiness, crassness, and vulgarity.

But the core of the book is its contribution to the author's spiritual autobiography. Huysmans had spent his childhood quite literally in a religious atmosphere, under the shadow of Saint-Sulpice, but he confessed later that he had been completely indifferent to religion throughout his youth. He was converted between 1884 and 1892; *Down There* represents the first stage of this conversion. In this work Durtal-Huysmans has reached the stage, familiar enough in such cases, of being attracted by the externals of religion, such as the beauty of the liturgy and the fascination of Church history, and yet unable to accept the essentials. He had the true Romanticist's attitude: he could have been a devout Catholic in any period except the present. Because the Church fell artistically short of what he believed it to have been during the Middle Ages, he had difficulty in understanding that the underlying reality could have remained unchanged. Here his artistic nature interfered with his religious conversion because the undoubted ugliness of much nineteenth-century ecclesiastical art was a stumbling block. He had yet to understand that belief in a materialistic age is a greater triumph than during an age of faith.

THE DOWNFALL

Type of work: Novel
Author: Émile Zola (1840-1902)
Type of plot: Social criticism
Time of plot: 1870-1871
Locale: France
First published: 1892

Principal characters:
MAURICE LEVASSEUR, a private in the French Army
JEAN MACQUART, his corporal
DELAHERCHE, a textile manufacturer
WEISS, his secretary
HENRIETTE, twin sister of Maurice and wife of Weiss
FOUCHARD, a shrewd farmer
HONORÉ, his son
SILVINE, Fouchard's servant

Critique:

Zola's theme in this highly contrived novel would seem to be that France paid in full measure for the indulgences of seventy years in her wretched defeat at the hands of Bismarck and Von Moltke in 1870-71. Each character is a symbol of an economic or social group. Zola's account of Sedan, of the events leading up to Sedan, and of the insurrection in Paris, command admiration for his research. The plot makes even more dramatic the historical facts.

The Story:

Corporal Jean Macquart, a sturdy French peasant, led the squad of infantry of which Private Maurice Levasseur was a member. The squad was a part of the 106th Regiment of the Seventh Corps of the French Army. A state of war existed between France and Prussia; the year was 1870. At the outset it had been felt in France that the war would be nothing more than a quick promenade to Berlin, but shortages of equipment, the rivalry of the French commanders, and quick Prussian success made the outcome of the conflict doubtful.

Maurice, a scapegrace who had enlisted to get away from financial troubles in Paris, believed in the evolutionary necessity of war. As a member of the middle class, he loathed Jean, whose peasant common sense was unendurable to him.

Misinformation and lack of information led the leader of the Seventh Corps to order his divisions to fall back from their positions around Mulhausen, in Alsace. Defeat was in the air. Civilians, having heard that the Prussians were sweeping all before them, were fleeing westward. Demoralized, the troops threw away their packs and rifles. At Belfort the corps entrained for Rheims, where the retreating and disorganized French forces were regrouping.

Prussian victories cost Emperor Napoleon III his command of the French armies. But Napoleon, with his official entourage, remained with the troops. Maurice, in Rheims, learned from battle veterans that the Prussians were young, healthy, well-organized, and well-equipped. He lost all hope for France when he caught sight of the sickly emperor in Rheims.

The army was ordered to march to Verdun. Mendacious ministers and journalists lulled the French forces into a false sense of security. When the troops reached the Ardennes, there were marches and counter-marches, for the positions of the Prussian armies were not known by the French commanders. Regiments became mobs as the French

982

approached Sedan. By that time Maurice had become reconciled to his fate, and had even grown to admire Jean, whose steadiness had kept the squad together.

Near Sedan, Maurice, Jean, and Honoré, an artilleryman, rescued Honoré's father, old Fouchard, from pillaging soldiers. There Honoré also promised to marry Silvine, Fouchard's servant, who had had a baby by Fouchard's hired hand, Goliath. The hired man was suspected of being a Prussian spy, for at the beginning of hostilities he had disappeared from the Fouchard farm.

Sedan was a place of confusion, where men were separated from their units because there was no discipline and no organization. In the confusion, Jean and Maurice met at the house of Delaherche, a Sedan textile manufacturer, whose secretary, Weiss, was the husband of Maurice's twin sister, Henriette. After a rest Jean and Maurice rejoined their regiment. Napoleon III accompanied the troops to Sedan.

As the French poured into Sedan, it became evident that the Prussians were drawing a ring around the fortified town. Weiss and Delaherche went to Bazeilles, a village near Sedan, to check the safety of property which they owned there. Weiss, caught in a battle which took place in the village, joined the French forces against the Prussians. Delaherche hastened back to Sedan. Maurice, in the meantime, experienced his first artillery barrage.

At Bazeilles the Prussians closed in on inferior French forces. Weiss, in his house, was joined by a small group of French soldiers and one civilian to make a last ditch stand. Captured, Weiss was put up against a wall to be shot. Henriette appeared, and despite her plea to be shot with her husband, she was pushed aside while the Prussians shot Weiss. Henriette, nearly out of her mind with grief, wandered about the field where the battle was still going on.

The 106th Regiment was decimated in a futile attempt to retake a strategic hill. When Jean was wounded, Maurice carried him to safety. Honoré Fouchard was killed at his gun. Napoleon had a white flag raised over a city roof, but it was torn down. Delaherche's factory was converted into a hospital, soon filled to overflowing with French wounded. Napoleon sent General Reille to the Prussians with a letter of capitulation.

Maurice, Jean, and several survivors of the 106th made their way into Sedan, where Maurice met Henriette and learned of Weiss' gallant death. They were engaged in a fight with Prussian Guards commanded by an officer whom Maurice recognized to be his cousin Gunther. Henriette kept Maurice from shooting Gunther.

By nightfall all had become silent except for the turmoil created by the movement of thousands of French troops into Sedan. The French were forced to accept the demands of Bismarck and Von Moltke.

The next day Silvine went out to the battlefield and recovered the body of Honoré. Henriette learned that Weiss' body had been consumed in fires started by the Prussians at Bazeilles.

The surrendered French soldiers were herded together to await deportation to Germany. A few French officers who promised never to take up arms again were released. In the camp men were murdered for filthy scraps of bread and spoiled horseflesh. Maurice, who no longer believed in anything, nearly lost control of himself. Jean, a cool veteran of previous campaigns, placed himself and Maurice among soldiers of a regiment leaving for Germany. At a stop along the way, Jean procured civilian clothes from a sympathetic French girl who was selling bread. The pair changed quickly inside a tent and escaped into a forest. When they came to a Prussian outpost, Jean was wounded by rifle fire, but they managed to escape and make their way back to old Fouchard's farm, where they found Henriette. Maurice went on to aid in the defense of Paris;

Jean remained with Fouchard to be nursed back to health by Henriette.

The proclamation of the Second Republic was followed by the capitulation of Marshal Bazaine at Metz. Paris was invested by the Prussians while frantic attempts were made to organize new French armies in other parts of France.

Goliath, employed by the Prussians as a spy around Sedan, came to Silvine seeking her good graces. Upon her refusal, he threatened to expose Fouchard's connection with French partisans. When Goliath returned for his answer, two of the partisans, assisted by Silvine, killed him.

In Sedan Delaherche became friendly with Prussian Captain Von Gartlauben, who was billeted in the Delaherche house; he found the captain's friendship to be most advantageous in the matter of reëstablishing his textile works.

Jean, well again, joined the Army of the North. Maurice, meanwhile, took part in the defense of Paris. Sick of the Republic, he deserted after the capitulation of Paris and took a room near the boulevards. When the Commune took command in Paris and civil war broke out, Maurice joined the forces of the Commune to fight against the Republican forces, of which Jean's regiment was a part. The insurrectionists fired the city as they were pushed back. Maurice was bayoneted by Jean during night fighting in the streets. Jean disguised Maurice as a Republican soldier and took him to Maurice's lodgings, where Henriette, who had come to Paris to seek Maurice, was waiting. There Maurice passed the crisis safely, but a later hemorrhage killed him. Jean, broken-hearted at having been the cause of his friend's death, told Henriette goodbye, with the feeling that here was a pin-point of the desolation all France must know.

DRACULA

Type of work: Novel
Author: Bram Stoker (1847-1912)
Type of plot: Horror romance
Time of plot: Nineteenth century
Locale: Transylvania and England
First published: 1897

Principal characters:
JONATHAN HARKER, an English solicitor
MINA MURRAY, his fiancée
COUNT DRACULA, a mysterious nobleman
DR. SEWARD, head of a mental hospital
DR. VAN HELSING, a Dutch medical specialist
LUCY WESTENRA, Mina's friend
ARTHUR HOLMWOOD, engaged to marry Lucy

Critique:

This strange tale of vampires and werewolves has worn surprisingly well. It has been presented on the stage and its principal character, Dracula, has become a well-known figure of literary reference. Full of Gothic touches such as mysterious gloomy castles and open graves at midnight, the story is exciting even today. Although *Dracula* is not truly great literature, it is an excellent example of its type. Written with the rhetorical device of letters and diaries, its overall effect is one of realism and horror.

The Story:

On his way to Castle Dracula in the province of Transylvania, in Rumania, Jonathan Harker, an English solicitor, was apprehensive. His nervousness grew when he observed the curious, fearful attitude of the peasants and the coachman after they learned of his destination. He was on his way to transact business with Count Dracula, and his mission would necessitate remaining at the castle for several days.

Upon his arrival at the castle, Harker found comfortable accommodations awaiting him. Count Dracula was a charming host, although his peculiarly bloodless physical appearance was somewhat disagreeable to Harker's English eyes. Almost immediately Harker was impressed with the strange life of the castle. He and the count discussed their business at night, as the count was never available during the daytime. Although the food was excellent, Harker never saw a servant about the place. While exploring the castle, he found that it was situated high at the top of a mountain with no accessible exit other than the main doorway, which was kept locked. He realized with a shock that he was a prisoner of Count Dracula.

Various harrowing experiences ensued. While Harker half dozed in the early morning hours, three phantom women materialized and attacked him, attempting to bite his throat. Then the count appeared and drove them off, whispering fiercely that Harker belonged to him. Later Harker thought he saw a huge bat descending the castle walls, but the creature turned out to be Count Dracula. In the morning Harker, trying frantically to escape, stumbled into an old chapel where a number of coffin-like boxes of earth were stored. Beneath the cover of one which Harker opened lay the count, apparently dead. In the evening, however, the count appeared as usual, and Harker demanded that he be released. Obligingly the count opened the castle door. A pack of wolves surrounded the entrance. The count, laughing hysterically, left poor Harker a prisoner in his room.

The next day Harker, weak and sick from a strange wound in his throat, saw a pack cart loaded with the mysterious boxes drive from the castle. Dracula was gone and Harker was alone, a prisoner with no visible means of escape.

In England, meanwhile, Harker's fiancée, Mina Murray, had gone to visit her beautiful and charming friend, Lucy Westenra. Lucy was planning to marry Arthur Holmwood, a young nobleman. One evening, early in Mina's visit, a storm blew up and a strange ship was driven aground. The only living creature aboard was a gray wolf-like dog. The animal escaped into the countryside.

Soon afterward Lucy's happiness began to fade because of a growing tendency to sleepwalk. One night Mina followed her friend during one of her spells and discovered Lucy in a churchyard. A tall, thin man who was bending over Lucy disappeared at Mina's approach. Lucy, on waking, could remember nothing of the experience, but her physical condition seemed much weakened. Finally she grew so ill that Mina was forced to call upon Dr. Seward, Lucy's former suitor. Lucy began to improve under his care, and when Mina received a report from Budapest that her missing fiancé had been found and needed care, she felt free to end her visit.

When Lucy's condition suddenly grew worse, Dr. Seward asked his old friend, Dr. Van Helsing, a specialist from Amsterdam, for his professional opinion. Van Helsing, examing Lucy thoroughly, paused over two tiny throat wounds which she was unable to explain. Van Helsing was concerned over Lucy's condition, which pointed to unusual loss of blood without signs of anemia or hemorrhage. She was given blood transfusions at intervals, and someone sat up with her at night. She improved but expressed fear of going to sleep at night because her dreams had grown so horrible.

One morning Dr. Seward fell asleep outside her door. When he and Van Helsing entered her room, they found Lucy ashen white and in a worse condition than ever. Quickly Van Helsing performed another transfusion; she rallied, but not as satisfactorily as before. Van Helsing then secured some garlic flowers and told Lucy to keep them about her neck at night. When the two doctors called the next morning, Lucy's mother had removed the flowers because their odor might bother her daughter. Frantically Van Helsing rushed to Lucy's room and found her in a coma. Again he administered a transfusion and her condition improved. She said that with the garlic flowers close by she was not afraid of nightly flapping noises at her window. Van Helsing sat with her every night until he felt her well enough to leave. After cautioning her always to sleep with the garlic flowers about her neck, he returned to Amsterdam.

Lucy's mother continued to sleep with her daughter. One night the two ladies were awakened by a huge wolf that crashed through the window. Mrs. Westenra fell dead of a heart attack and Lucy fainted, the wreath of garlic flowers slipping from her neck. Seward and Van Helsing, who had returned to England, discovered her half-dead in the morning. They knew she was dying and called Arthur. As Arthur attempted to kiss her, Lucy's teeth seemed about to fasten on his throat. Van Helsing drew him away. When Lucy died, Van Helsing put a tiny gold crucifix over her mouth, but an attendant stole it from her body.

Soon after Lucy's death several children of the neighborhood were discovered far from their homes, their throats marked by small wounds. Their only explanation was that they had followed a pretty lady. When Jonathan Harker returned to England, Van Helsing went to see him and Mina. After talking with Harker, Van Helsing revealed to Dr. Seward his belief that Lucy had fallen victim to a vampire, one of those strange creatures who can live for centuries on the blood of their victims and breed their kind by attacking the innocent and making them vampires in turn. The only way to save Lucy's soul, according to Van Helsing, was to drive a stake through the heart of her corpse, cut off her head, and stuff her mouth with garlic flowers. Dr. Seward protested violently. The next midnight Arthur, Dr. Seward, and Van Helsing visited Lucy's tomb and found it empty. When daylight came they did as Van Helsing had suggested with Lucy's corpse, which had returned to its tomb.

The men, with Mina, tried to track down Dracula in London, in order to find him before he victimized anyone else. Their object was to remove the boxes of sterilized earth he had brought with him from Transylvania so that he would have no place to hide in the daytime. At last the hunters trapped Dracula, but he escaped them. By putting Mina into a trance Van Helsing was able to learn that Dracula was at sea, and it was necessary to follow him to his castle. Wolves gathered about them in that desolate country. Van Helsing drew a circle in the snow with a crucifix and within that magic enclosure the travelers rested safely. The next morning they overtook a cart carrying a black box. Van Helsing and the others overcame the drivers of the cart and pried open the lid of Dracula's coffin. As the sun began to set, they drove a stake through the heart of the corpse. The vampire was no more.

DRAGON SEED

Type of work: Novel
Author: Pearl S. Buck (1892-   )
Type of plot: Social chronicle
Time of plot: World War II
Locale: China
First published: 1942

Principal characters:
LING TAN, a Chinese farmer
LING SAO, his wife
LAO TA,
LAO ER,
LAO SAN, and
PANSIAO, their children
ORCHID, Lao Ta's wife
JADE, Lao Er's wife
WU LIEN, Ling Tan's son-in-law
MAYLI, a mission teacher

Critique:

The plot of this novel as a social chronicle is swiftly paced and convincing until the appearance of Mayli; then the emphasis shifts to the rather improbable love affair of Mayli and Lao San. Background and character remain superior to plot. As a result, the reader absorbs an excellent impression of these people of an alien culture, through colorful details woven into the pattern of the narrative. *Dragon Seed* also tells what World War II meant to the Chinese peasantry.

The Story:

Ling Tan's family all lived together in his ancestral home. Besides Ling Tan and his wife, Ling Sao, there were three sons, Lao Ta, Lao Er, and Lao San, and a daughter, Pansiao. Lao Ta and his wife Orchid had two children. Lao Er and his wife Jade as yet had none.

Jade was a strange woman who cared little for the old rules and customs governing Chinese wives. Her free manners and frank tongue were an embarrassment to Lao Er, for the men chided him about it. Then, too, he felt as if he did not really understand his wife. One evening, after they had both heard how the Japanese had begun war in the north, they unburdened their hearts to each other,

and Lao Er accepted the fact that he was married to a woman who was not like the others. He promised to go to the city and buy her a book so that she could learn what was happening in the world.

While Lao Er was in the city, he visited Wu Lien, a merchant who had married his older sister. Some Chinese students destroyed the Japanese merchandise that Wu Lien had for sale and branded him as a traitor. When Ling Sao heard this bad news, she too went to the city. Wu Lien was sick with worry over what had happened to him; he had also heard that the Japanese had landed on the coast nearby and were pushing inland. Ling Sao comforted him as well as she could and returned home.

The next morning Ling Tan was working in his fields when he saw Japanese aircraft approaching to bomb the city. He and the other farmers watched the planes, curious and unafraid. That night Wu Lien came to his father-in-law's house seeking refuge, for his shop had been hit by a bomb. Only then did Ling Tan's family learn the meaning of what had happened that day.

The next day Ling Tan and Lao San went to the city, where they were caught in the second air raid. Gravely, Ling Tan

DRAGON SEED by Pearl S. Buck. By permission of the author, her agent David Lloyd, and the publishers, The John Day Co., Inc. Copyright, 1941, 1942, by Pearl S. Buck.

asked his family how they were going to resist this enemy. Lao Er and Jade said that they must go westward into the hills, for Jade was now with child. The rest of the family decided to stay and hold the ancestral land at all costs.

Streams of refugees passed along the road toward the west, and Lao Er and Jade joined a group of students who were moving their school inland. Lao Er promised to send word when the baby was born. Other students passed through the village and stopped to tell of the atrocities of the Japanese, but the simple farmers could not believe the stories they heard. After a month or so Ling Tan and his family could hear the roar of the Japanese guns as they approached the city. Chinese soldiers deserted to the hills, leaving the inhabitants at the mercy of the enemy. For a few days after the city was taken all was peaceful. Then some Japanese marched to the village and demanded wine and women. Ling Tan hid his family in the fields. The soldiers discovered Wu Lien's mother, who was too old and fat to flee. When they found no other women, they attacked her and killed her. Then they wrecked the house and left.

Since he knew now that no woman was safe from the Japanese, Ling Tan put all of the women of his family with the white missionary lady in the city. The men remained at the farm, except for Wu Lien. He returned to his shop in the city and advertised for Japanese business.

Meanwhile the soldiers came again to Ling Tan's house in search of women. When they found none, they attacked Lao San, the youngest son. Humiliated and filled with hatred, the boy left to join the hill people who were fighting the Japanese.

Wu Lien ingratiated himself with the conquerors and was appointed to a job in the new city government. He took his family from the mission and moved into spacious quarters provided by the Japanese.

Orchid grew bored in the mission. She thought that the city was quiet now and nothing could happen to her. One day she went for a walk. Five soldiers captured her and killed her while they satisfied their lust. When her body was returned to the mission, Ling Sao sent for Ling Tan and Lao Ta. She could no longer stay in the city. She returned to the farm with Ling Tan, Lao Ta, and the two children of Orchid and Lao Ta. Pansiao was sent westward to a mission school in the hills, where she would be safe.

A message from Lao Er announced that Jade had a son. Ling Tan sent for Lao Er and his family to come and help with the farm. Lao Er obeyed the summons, for he could be useful as a messenger between the village and the guerilla warriors in the hills. He and Jade made a secret cavern under the house where they could store arms for the villagers. Meanwhile the children of Lao Ta died of flux and fever. Despondent, he left for the hills to join Lao San. Ling Tan worked his farm as best he could and held back from the enemy as much grain as he dared.

Lao San and Lao Ta returned from the hills with rifles to hide in the secret cavern. Whenever there were no witnesses, the farmers killed Japanese soldiers and secretly buried them. Jade succeeded in poisoning many Japanese leaders at a great feast in the city. A cousin of Ling Tan went to the city and stole a radio from Wu Lien. Afterwards he was able to report to the people the progress of the war. The people took heart from the knowledge that there were others fighting the Japanese.

Lao San had become a ruthless killer and Ling Tan thought that he needed a spirited wife to tame him. Jade wrote to Pansiao, asking her to find a wife for Lao San among the girls at the mission. Pansiao told one of her teachers, the daughter of a Chinese ambassador, about her brother. This girl, Mayli, traveled to see Lao San for herself. The young people fell in love at first sight, but Mayli returned to the hills to wait for Lao San to come after her. Lao Ta also returned home with a new wife. Ling Tan's house was full again, for Jade gave birth to twin boys.

The hardships continued. Losing all hope of conquering the Japanese, Ling Tan began to brood. Then one day Lao Er took the old man to the city to hear the news from the hidden radio. They heard that England and the United States were now fighting on their side. Ling Tan wept for joy. Perhaps some day there would be an end to the war. Once again there was hope.

DREAM OF THE RED CHAMBER

Type of work: Novel
Author: Tsao Hsueh chin (c. 1715-1763), with a continuation by Kao Ou
Type of plot: Domestic chronicle
Time of plot: c. 1729-1737
Locale: Peking
First published: 1792

Principal characters:

MADAME SHIH (the MATRIARCH), the living ancestress of the Chia family

CHIA SHEH, her older son, master of the Yungkuofu, or western compound

MADAME HSING, his wife

CHIA LIEN, their son

HSI-FENG (PHOENIX), Chia Lien's wife

YING-CHUN (WELCOME SPRING), Chia Sheh's daughter by a concubine

CHIA CHENG, the Matriarch's younger son

MADAME WANG, his wife

PAO-YU, their son

CARDINAL SPRING, their daughter, an Imperial concubine

CHIA HUAN, Chia Cheng's son by his concubine

TAN-CHUN (QUEST SPRING), Chia Cheng's daughter by his concubine

TAI-YU (BLACK JADE), the Matriarch's granddaughter, an orphan

HSIANG-YUN (RIVER MIST), the Matriarch's grandniece

PAO-CHAI (PRECIOUS VIRTUE), Madame Wang's niece

HSUEH PAN, Precious Virtue's brother, a libertine

CHIA GEN, master of the Ningkuofu, or eastern compound

YU-SHIH, his wife

CHIA JUNG, their son

CHIN-SHIH, Chia Jung's wife

HSI-CHUN (Compassion Spring), Chia Gen's sister

HSI-JEN (PERVADING FRAGRANCE),

CHING-WEN (Bright Design), and

SHEH-YUEH (Musk Moon), Pao-yu's serving maids

Critique:

Chinese scholars and readers consider the eighteenth-century *Hung Lou Meng* (*Dream of the Red Chamber*) the greatest of their novels. Published anonymously in 1792, and for a long time a matter of scholarly reference and dispute, the book is now ascribed to Tsao Hsueh-chin, who completed the first eighty chapters before his death in 1763, and Kao Ou, who added forty more as an expansion of Tsao Hsueh-chin's original notes. There is internal evidence to show that Tsao Hsueh-chin may have drawn on his own experience and family background in creating the character of

Pao-yu, the pampered younger son of an aristocratic and powerful family in gradual financial decline at the time of his birth. Like Pao-yu, Tsao Hsueh-chin was petted by his family and spoiled by luxury; unlike Pao-yu, he failed to pass the Imperial Examinations which would have raised him to some official position. *Dream of the Red Chamber* is within a single framework a long and extremely complicated domestic chronicle—the novel contains more than four hundred characters—that is both a lively comedy of manners and a realistic fable of moral seriousness. The title is capable of expressing several meanings. In the view of Professor Chi-Chen Wang, it may be translated as "Dreams of Young Maidens," since the younger women of the Chia clan lived in the traditional "red chamber" of a palace compound like those which housed wealthy or aristocratic Chinese families until fairly recent times. The term may also be interpreted as a reference to the metaphor "Red Dust," which in Buddhist usage is a designation for the material world with all its pleasures, follies, and vices. Manuscript copies of the first eighty chapters of the novel were apparently circulated before the publication of the complete 120-chapter version in 1792.

The Story:

Ages ago, in the realm of the Great Void, the Goddess Nügua whose task it was to repair the Dome of Heaven rejected a stone which she found unsuited to her purpose. Because she had touched it, however, the stone became endowed with life, so that thereafter it could move as it pleased. In time it chanced on a crimson flower in the region of the Ethereal, where each day it watered the tender blossoms with drops of dew. At last the plant was incarnated as a beautiful young girl. Remembering the stone that had showered the frail plant with refreshing dew, she prayed that in her human form she might repay it with the gift of her tears. Her prayers were to be granted, for the stone, too, had been given life in the Red Dust of earthly existence. At his birth the piece of jade was miraculously found in the mouth of Pao-yu, a younger son of the rich and powerful house of Chia, which by imperial favor had been raised to princely eminence several generations before.

At the time of Pao-yu's birth the two branches of the Chia family lived in great adjoining compounds of palaces, pavilions, and parks on the outskirts of Peking. The Matriarch, an old woman of great honor and virtue, ruled as the living ancestress over both establishments.

Chia Ging, the prince of the Ningkuofu, had retired to a Taoist temple some time before, and his son Chia Gen was master in his place. The master of the Yungkuofu was Chia Sheh, the older son of the Matriarch. Chia Cheng, her younger son and Pao-yu's father, also lived with his family and attendants in the Yungkuofu. A man of upright conduct and strict Confucian morals, he was a contrast to the other members of his family, who had grown lax and corrupt through enervating luxury and the abuse of power.

Pao-yu, the possessor of the miraculous jade stone and a boy of great beauty and quick wit, was his grandmother's favorite. Following her example, the other women of the family—his mother, aunts, sisters, cousins, and waiting maids—doted on the boy and pampered him at every opportunity, with the result that he grew up girlish and weak, a lover of rouge pots and feminine society. The traits of effeminacy he displayed infuriated and disgusted his austere father, who treated the boy with undue severity. As a result, Pao-yu kept as much as possible to the women's quarters.

His favorite playmates were his two cousins, Black Jade and Precious Virtue. Black Jade, a granddaughter of the Matriarch, had come to live in the Yungkuofu after her mother's death. She was a lovely, delicate girl of great poetic sensitivity, and she and Pao-yu were drawn to each other by bonds of sympathy and understanding that seemed to stretch back into some unremembered past. Precious Virtue, warm-hearted and practical, was the niece of Pao-yu's mother. She was a girl as good as her brother Hsueh Pan was vicious, for he was always involving the family in scandal because of his pursuit of maidens and young boys. Pao-yu's favorite waiting maid was Pervading Fragrance. She slept in his chamber at night, and it was with her that he followed a dream vision and practiced the play of cloud and rain.

When word came that Black Jade's

father was ill and wished to see her before his death, the Matriarch sent the girl home under the escort of her cousin Chia Lien. During their absence Chin-shih the daughter-in-law of Chia Gen, died after a long illness. By judicious bribery the dead woman's husband, Chia Jung, was made a chevalier of the Imperial Dragon Guards in order that she might be given a more elaborate funeral. During the period of mourning Chia Gen asked Phoenix, Chia Lien's wife, to take charge of the Ningkuofu household. This honor gave Phoenix a position of responsibility and power in both palaces. From that time on, although she continued to appear kind and generous, she secretly became greedy for money and power. She began to accept bribes, tamper with the household accounts, and lend money at exorbitant rates of interest.

One day a great honor was conferred on the Chias. Cardinal Spring, Pao-yu's sister and one of the emperor's concubines, was advanced to the rank of an Imperial consort of the second degree. Later, when it was announced that she would pay a visit of filial respect to her parents, the parks of the two compounds were at great expense transformed into magnificent pleasure grounds, called the Takuanyuan, in honor of the consort's visit. Later, at Cardinal Spring's request, the pavilions in the Takuanyuan were converted into living quarters for the young women of the family. Pao-yu also went there to live, passing his days in idle occupations and writing verses. His pavilion was close to that of Black Jade, who had returned to the Yungkuofu after her father's death.

Pao-yu had a half-brother, Chia Huan. His mother, jealous of the true-born son, paid a sorceress to bewitch the boy and Phoenix, whom she also hated. Both were seized with fits of violence and wild delirium. Pao-yu's coffin had already been made when a Buddhist monk and a lame Taoist priest suddenly appeared and restored the power of the spirit stone. Pao-yu and Phoenix recovered.

A short time later a maid was accused of trying to seduce Pao-yu. Dismissed, she drowned herself. About the same time Chia Cheng was told that his son had turned the love of a young actor away from a powerful patron. Calling his son a degenerate, Chia Cheng almost caused Pao-yu's death by the severity of the beating which the angry father administered.

As Phoenix became more shrewish at home, Chia Lien dreamed of taking another wife. Having been almost caught in one infidelity, he was compelled to exercise great caution in taking a concubine. Phoenix learned about the secret marriage, however, and by instigating claims advanced by the girl's former suitor she drove the wretched concubine to suicide.

Black Jade, always delicate, became more sickly. Sometimes she and Pao-yu quarreled, only to be brought together again by old ties of affection and understanding. The gossip of the servants was that the Matriarch would marry Pao-yu to either Black Jade or Precious Virtue. While possible marriage plans were being talked about, a maid found in the Takuanyuan a purse embroidered with an indecent picture. This discovery led to a search of all the pavilions, and it was revealed that one of the maids was involved in a secret love affair. Suspicion also fell on Bright Design, one of Pao-yu's maids, and she was dismissed. Proud and easily hurt, she died not long afterward. Pao-yu became even moodier and more depressed after her death. Outraged by the search, Precious Virtue left the park and went to live with her mother.

A begonia tree near Pao-yu's pavilion bloomed out of season. This event was interpreted as a bad omen, for Pao-yu lost his spirit stone and sank into a state of complete lethargy. In an effort to revive his spirits the Matriarch and his parents decided to marry him at once to Precious Virtue rather than to Black Jade, who continued to grow frailer each day. Pao-yu was allowed to believe, however, that Black Jade was to be his wife. Black Jade, deeply grieved, died shortly after the ceremony. Knowing nothing of the deception that had been practiced, she felt that she had failed Pao-yu and that he had been unfaithful to her. So the flower returned to the Great Void.

Suddenly a series of misfortunes overwhelmed the Chias as their deeds of graft and corruption came to light. When bailiffs took possession of the two compounds, the usury Phoenix had practiced was disclosed. Chia Gen and Chia Sheh were arrested and sentenced to banishment. The Matriarch, who took upon herself the burden of her family's guilt and surrendered her personal treasures for expenses and fines, became ill and died. During her funeral services robbers looted the compound and later returned to carry off Exquisite Jade, a pious nun. Phoenix died also, neglected by those she had dominated in her days of power. Through the efforts of powerful friends, however, the complete ruin of the family was averted, and Chia Cheng was restored to his official post.

But it was the despised son who in the end became the true redeemer of his family's honor and fortunes. After a Buddhist monk had returned his lost stone, Pao-yu devoted himself earnestly to his studies and passed the Imperial Examinations with such brilliance that he stood in seventh place on the list of successful candidates. So impressed was the emperor that he wished to have the young scholar serve at court. But Pao-yu was nowhere to be found. The tale was that he became a bodhisattva and disappeared in the company of a Buddhist monk and a Taoist priest.

DRINK

Type of work: Novel
Author: Émile Zola (1840-1902)
Type of plot: Naturalism
Time of plot: Second half of the nineteenth century
Locale: Paris
First published: 1877

Principal characters:
GERVAISE, a laundress
COUPEAU, a roofer, her husband
LANTIER, her lover and the father of her first two children
ADÈLE, Lantier's mistress
GOUJET, a neighbor secretly in love with Gervaise
NANA, the daughter of Gervaise and Coupeau
VIRGINIE, Adèle's sister

Critique:

Drink belongs to the series of the Rougon-Macquart in which Zola attempted to apply the methods of the experimental sciences to the social novel. This particular novel depicts with an extremely cruel precision the destructive effects of alcoholism among workers. At the time of publication it was received either with enthusiasm or with indignation, never with indifference. Actually, Drink might well be the one of Zola's novels in which there is the least prejudice and where the bare document is the most effective. Zola's visionary imagination communicates an intense life to the social group he describes as a whole; thus, a certain poetry evolves from the atmosphere of fatality in Drink, and it is this quality which makes the reading bearable.

The Story:

All night Gervaise had been waiting for her lover, Lantier, to come back to their quarters in Paris. When he finally came home, he treated her brutally and did not display the least affection toward Claude and Étienne, their two children. He stretched out on the bed and sent Gervaise off to the laundry where she worked.

When she was thirteen, Gervaise had left her country town and her family to follow Lantier; she was only fourteen when Étienne was born. Her family had been cruel to her, but until recently Lan-tier had treated her rather kindly. Gervaise knew that Lantier had come under the influence of the dram shop and at the same time of Adèle, a pretty prostitute.

Gervaise herself was rather pretty, but she had a slight limp which, when she was tired, became worse; the hard life she had lived also had put its mark on her face, although she was only twenty-two. She would have been perfectly happy working hard for her own home and a decent life for her children, but all she had ever known was endless hardship and insecurity.

At the laundry she found some relief in confiding her story to Madame Boche, an older woman who had become her friend. Suddenly the children came running in with word that Lantier had deserted the three of them to go away with Adèle and that he had taken with him everything they owned.

Gervaise's first thought was for her children, and she wondered what would become of them. Soon, however, she was roused in anger by the insults of Virginie, Adèle's sister; Virginie had come to the laundry for the sadistic pleasure of watching how Gervaise would take the triumph of her rival. Gervaise was quite frail and much smaller than Virginie; nevertheless, she jumped toward her, full of rage. A struggle followed, in which the two women used pieces of laundry equipment and wet clothes to beat each other. Sur-

995

prisingly, Gervaise, who had given all her strength, came out victorious. Virginie was never to forgive her.

Madame Fauconnier, proprietress of a laundry, gave Gervaise work in her establishment. There she earned just enough to provide for herself and her children. Another person interested in Gervaise was Coupeau, a roofer who knew all about her unhappy life. He would have liked to have her live with him. Gervaise preferred to devote herself entirely to her two small boys, but one day, when Coupeau proposed marriage to her, she was overcome by emotion and accepted him.

The situation was not very promising at first because the couple had no money. Coupeau's sister and brother-in-law, who were as miserly as they were prosperous, openly disapproved of his marriage. Slowly, perseverance in hard work made it possible for the Coupeaus to lead a decent life and even to put a little money aside. Gervaise had quite a reputation as a laundress and she often dreamed of owning her own shop. A little girl, Nana, was born to the couple four years later. Gervaise resumed working soon afterward.

This good fortune could not last. While he was working on a roof, Nana diverted her father's attention for a split second and he fell. Gervaise, refusing to let him be taken to the hospital, insisted on caring for him at home. Coupeau somehow survived, but his recovery was very slow. What was worse, inactivity had a bad effect on him. He had no more ambition, not even that of supporting his family. He also went more and more often to the dram shop.

Meanwhile, Gervaise was preparing to give up her dream of a little shop of her own when Goujet, a neighbor secretly in love with her, insisted that she borrow the five hundred francs he offered her as a gesture of friendship. She opened her shop and soon had it running quite well.

Goujet's money was never returned.

Instead, the family's debts kept progressively increasing, for Coupeau remained idle and continued his drinking. Gervaise herself had become accustomed to a few small luxuries, and she was not as thrifty as she had once been. Actually, she still felt quite confident that she would be able soon to meet her obligations: she had a very good reputation in the whole neighborhood.

At this point, Virginie returned, pretending that she had forgotten the fight in the laundry. Gervaise was a little startled at first to discover that her old enemy was going to be her neighbor once more. Being unprejudiced, however, she had no objection to being on friendly terms with Virginie.

Then Lantier came back. When Gervaise heard from Virginie that he had deserted Adèle and had been seen again in the neighborhood, she had been badly frightened. So far, however, her former lover had made no attempt to see her and she had forgotten her fears.

Lantier had waited to make a spectacular entrance. He chose to appear in the middle of a birthday party that Gervaise was giving. Most unexpectedly, Coupeau, who by that time was continuously drunk, invited him in. During the weeks that followed the two men became drinking companions. Later on, Lantier suggested that he might live and board with the Coupeaus. Gervaise's husband had reached such a state of degeneration that he welcomed the idea.

Although the agreement was that Lantier was to pay his share of the expenses, he never kept his promise, and Gervaise found herself with two men to support instead of one. Furthermore, Lantier had completely taken over the household and was running it as he pleased. Still a charming seducer, he was extremely popular with the women of the neighborhood.

Gervaise herself began to degenerate. Disgusted by her husband, she could not find the strength to refuse the embraces of her former lover. Before long her work suffered from such a state of affairs, and eventually she lost the shop. Virginie bought it and, at the same time, won the favors of Lantier.

Meanwhile, Nana had almost grown up, and she was placed as an apprentice in a flower shop. When she decided to leave home for the streets. Gervaise gave up all interest in life and joined Coupeau in the dram shop. After he finally died of delirium tremens, she tried walking the streets. but nobody would have her, wretched as she was. Goujet's timid efforts to help her were useless. Completely worn out by all the demands that had been made on her, she died alone.

DRUMS

Type of work: Novel
Author: James Boyd (1888-1944)
Type of plot: Historical romance
Time of plot: American Revolution
Locale: North Carolina and London
First published: 1925

Principal characters:
SQUIRE FRASER, a North Carolina planter
MRS. FRASER, his wife
JOHN FRASER, their son
SIR NAT DUKINFIELD, a sportsman
CAPTAIN TENNANT, Collector of the Port at Edenton
EVE TENNANT, his daughter
WYLIE JONES, a plantation owner
PAUL JONES, a sailor
SALLY MERRILLEE, a neighbor of the Frasers

Critique:

In Drums the author attempted to reproduce the feelings and actions of all classes of Americans during the Revolution, and he accomplished his purpose admirably, sometimes, however, at the expense of the movement of the plot. The episodes at the race track and on the sea stand out in vividness above the rest of the action. The book is a pleasing mixture of history and adventure, with little emphasis upon character.

The Story:

John Fraser lived with his mother and father in the backwoods of North Carolina. Squire Fraser, a strict but kind Scotsman, was determined that his son should have a gentleman's education, and so he sent John to the coastal town of Edenton to be tutored by Dr. Clapton, an English clergyman.

There John made many friends. Sir Nat Dukinfield, a young rake, asked John to go riding with him one afternoon. They parted close friends. Through Dr. Clapton, John met Captain Tennant, the Collector of the Port at Edenton. Captain Tennant took John home with him and introduced him to Eve, his daughter, who overwhelmed John and embarrassed him with her coquettish

manners. Captain Flood, a river boat skipper, was another of his friends. The old man taught him some sea lore and on his trips up and down the river acted as a messenger between John and his parents.

John went often to visit Captain Tennant and Eve. One evening two other gentlemen arrived at their house, Mr. Hewes, a shipbuilder, and Mr. Battle, a young lawyer. A bitter argument began among the gentlemen over the new tax on tea. Autumn came, and Squire Fraser sent for John to come home for a short vacation. Captain Flood took John up the river to Halifax. There he stayed overnight at the plantation of Wylie Jones, a rich young landowner.

After three years of schooling from Dr. Clapton, John became a young provincial gentleman. The only cloud on his horizon was the report of troubles with the British in Boston. Many people were angry; some predicted violence. But John thrust dark thoughts aside, for tomorrow was the day of the races. Sir Nat was to match his horse against a thoroughbred from Virginia. Everyone seemed to be excited over the holiday except Mr. Hewes, Mr. Battle, and Wylie Jones. The three sat apart at a table in the tavern and talked seriously among themselves while the rest of the company sang songs. At last Wylie Jones rose and announced that the ministers in Parliament had requested the king to declare the American Colonies in a state of rebellion.

The next day John rode to the races with Sir Nat; Eve was going with fat Master Hal Cherry, a repulsive boy, but rich. Sir Nat's horse was in perfect condition; his jockey, who had been drunk the night before, was not. He lost the first heat to the horse from Virginia. Then Sir Nat turned to John and asked him to ride. John rode the next two heats and won both of them. His friends celebrated the victory he had won for North Carolina.

Spring came. Sir Nat, putting no stock in rumors of war with the Colonies, volunteered for the English cavalry; he wanted to fight the French. The day after Sir Nat left for England, John learned of the battle fought at Lexington.

Squire Fraser sent a letter to his son with instructions to come home at once if British authority were overthrown at Edenton. John went to say goodbye to Captain Tennant and Eve, and then, following his father's instructions, he took leave of Dr. Clapton and went up the river with Wylie Jones. At Wylie's plantation he met Paul Jones, an adventurous seaman who had taken Wylie's last name. Mr. Battle, Paul Jones, and Wylie discussed a naval war against the British. They urged John to decide soon on which side he would be. He rode sadly home from Wylie's, but he brightened when he met Sally Merrillee, an old playmate. He suddenly decided that he liked her backwoods manners, so different from those of Eve Tennant. Later a company of militia camped on the Merrillee property, and the officers were billeted in Sally's house. John became angry at Sally's attentions to the militia officers and ceased courting her. Finally, Squire Fraser sent John to England to put the family money in a safe bank. John was

happy at a chance for an honorable escape from his problem. But when he went to say goodbye to Sally, she had only contempt for him. Her brother had gone with the militia.

In London, John became the clerk of an importing firm and again met Eve and Captain Tennant. He received a letter from Wylie Jones, who asked him to deliver some money to Paul Jones' mother in Scotland. John was staying at an inn on the Scottish coast the night American sailors made a shore raid. Suddenly homesick for America, he went back with them to their ship. The captain was Paul Jones. Grateful for the favor John had done for him in Scotland, he signed John on as a crew member.

After a naval engagement, the ship anchored in the French harbor of Brest. Then came long months of waiting while Paul Jones tried to get a larger ship from the French. Sir Nat arrived from England to visit John. One evening the two became involved in a tavern brawl, and Sir Nat was killed. At last Paul Jones obtained another ship, the *Bonhomme Richard*.

The ship put to sea with a motley crew and captured several British merchant vessels. Then, in a running fight with the Baltic Fleet, John was wounded in the left elbow. No longer fit for active duty and still feverish from his wound, he sailed home to North Carolina on a Dutch ship. As soon as his arm had healed, he volunteered in the militia, but they wanted no stiff-armed men. He helped out Sally's mother on her farm. Sally had gone north to nurse her brother, who had smallpox. Mr. Merrillee had been killed in the war.

When Sally returned, John went to call on her. But when he tried to tell her that he loved her, she wept. Thinking she was rejecting his love, he left disconsolately. He volunteered again for the militia and was accepted. In a skirmish with British troops he was wounded a second time.

His arm now useless, John spent his

days sitting on the front porch. One day Sally's mother came to call on him and scolded him for neglecting her daughter. Sally was in love with him; he had mistaken her reason for crying. John suddenly felt much better. He felt better still when his father heard that the British were retreating. As he sat on the porch, General Greene's victorious army passed along the road. John stumbled down to the fence and raised his stiff arm in an Indian salute as the last man of the rear guard came to the crest of a hill. The distant soldier, silhouetted against the sunset, raised his rifle over his head in answer. The war was over. In a few days he would be strong enough to visit Sally.

DRUMS ALONG THE MOHAWK

Type of work: Novel
Author: Walter D. Edmonds (1903-   )
Type of plot: Historical chronicle
Time of plot: 1775-1783
Locale: The Mohawk Valley.
First published: 1936

Principal characters:
GILBERT MARTIN, a young pioneer
MAGDELANA BORST MARTIN (LANA), his wife
MARK DEMOOTH, a captain of the militia
JOHN WOLFF, a Tory
BLUE BLACK, a friendly Oneida Indian
MRS. McKLENNAR, Captain Barnabas McKlennar's widow
JOSEPH BRANT, an Indian chief
GENERAL BENEDICT ARNOLD
NANCY SCHUYLER, Mrs. Demooth's maid
JURRY McLONIS, a Tory
HON YOST, Nancy's brother

Critique:

Drums Along the Mohawk depicts with great clarity the history of those stirring years from 1775 to 1783. Edmonds does not attempt a sweeping picture of the Revolutionary War. Instead, he shows how the times affected the farmers and residents of the Mohawk Valley in upstate New York. Realistically told, the novel gains added authenticity because its people, with some exceptions, actually lived during that period of American history. Edmonds lists his fictitious characters in an Author's Note.

The Story:

Magdelana Borst, the oldest of five daughters, married Gilbert Martin and together they started off from her home at Fox's Mill to settle farther west in their home at Deerfield. The time was July, 1776, and the spirit of the revolution was reaching into the Mohawk Valley, where settlers who sided with the rebels had already formed a company of militia commanded by Mark Demooth. Soon after he came to his new home Gil had to report for muster day. Some Indians had been seen in the vicinity. Also, the militia had decided to investigate the

home of John Wolff, suspected of being a king's man. Finding evidence that a spy had been hidden on the Wolff farm, they arrested John Wolff, convicted him of aiding the British, and sent him to the Newgate Prison at Simsbury Mines.

A few months after their arrival at Deerfield, Gil decided to have a log-rolling to clear his land for farming. The Weavers, the Realls, and Clem Coppernol all came to help with the work. When they were about half finished, Blue Black, a friendly Oneida Indian, came to warn them that a raiding party of Seneca Indians and whites was in the valley. The settlers immediately scattered for home to collect the few movable belongings which they might save, and then drove to Fort Schuyler. Lana, who was pregnant, lost her baby as a result of the wild ride to the fort. The enemy destroyed the Deerfield settlement. All the houses and fields were burned; Gil's cow was killed, and Mrs. Wolff, who had refused to take refuge with the people who had sent her husband to prison, was reported missing. Gil and Lana rented a one-room cabin in which to live through the winter. With spring coming on and needing a job to support himself and Lana, Gil became the hired man of Mrs. McKlennar, a widow. The pay was forty-five dollars a year plus the use of a two-room house and their food.

General Herkimer tried to obtain a pledge of neutrality from the Indian chief, Joseph Brant, but was unsuccessful. At the end of the summer, word came that the combined forces of British and Indians, commanded by General St. Leger, were moving down from Canada to attack the valley. The militia was called up and set out westward to encounter this army. But the attack by the militia was badly timed and the party was ambushed. Of nearly six hundred and fifty men, only two hundred and fifty survived. The survivors returned in scattered groups. Gil received a bullet wound in the arm. General Herkimer, seriously injured in the leg, died of his wounds.

After the death of General Herkimer, General Benedict Arnold was sent out to reorganize the army and lead 'it in another attack—this time against General St. Leger's camp.

When Nancy Schuyler, Mrs. Demooth's maid, heard that her brother, Hon Yost, was in the neighborhood with a group of Tories, she decided to sneak out to see him. On the way she met another Tory, Jurry McLonis, who seduced her. Before she was able to see Hon, the American militia broke up the band. Hon was arrested but was later released when he agreed to go back to the British camp and spread false reports of the American strength. As a result of her meeting with Jurry McLonis, Nancy became pregnant. About that same time John Wolff escaped from the prison at Simsbury Mines and made his way to Canada to join Butler and to look for his wife.

The following spring brought with it General Butler's destructives, raiding parties that would swoop down to burn and pillage small settlements or farms. Mrs. Demooth tormented Nancy constantly because of her condition and one night frightened the girl so completely that Nancy, in terror, packed a few of her belongings in a shawl and ran away. Her only idea was to try to get to Niagara and find her brother Hon, but she had not gone far before labor pains overtook her and she bore her child beside a stream. An Indian found her there and took her with him as his wife. Lana had her child in May. The destruction by the raiding parties continued all through that summer, and the harvest was small. Mrs. McKlennar's stone house was not burned, but there was barely enough food for her household that winter. In the spring Colonel Van Schaick came to the settlement with an army, and the militia headed west once again, this time to strike against the Onondaga towns.

Lana had her second child the following August. Because of the lack of food during the winter, she was still weak from nursing her first boy, Gilly, and after the birth of her second boy it took her a long while to recover. The next winter they all had enough to eat but the cold was severe. During that winter Mrs. McKlennar aged greatly and kept mostly to her bed. The destructives continued their raids through the next spring and summer. The men never went out to their fields alone; they worked in groups with armed guards. One day, after all the men had gone to the fort, Lana took the two boys for a walk and then sat down at the edge of a clearing and fell asleep. When she awoke, Gilly was gone. Two Indians were near the house. She put the baby, Joey, into a hiding place and then searched for Gilly. She found him at last and the two of them crawled into the hiding place also. Meanwhile the two Indians had entered the house and set it on fire. Overwhelmed by Mrs. McKlennar's righteous indignation, they carried out her bed for her. They fled when men, seeing the smoke, came hurrying from the fort. Gil and the two scouts, Adam Helmer and Joe Boleo, built a cabin to house them all during the coming winter.

With the spring thaws, a flood inundated the valley. As the waters receded, Marinus Willett came into the Mohawk Valley with his army, with orders to track down and destroy the British forces under General Butler. Butler's army already was having a difficult time, for British food supplies were running out and tracking wolves killed all stragglers. The militia finally caught up with Butler, harassed his army for several miles, killed Butler, and scattered the routed army in the wilderness. The Mohawk Valley was saved.

Three years later, the war over, Gil and Lana went back to their farm at Deerfield. They now had a baby girl and Lana and Gil felt content with their hard-won security, their home, their children, and each other.

THE DUCHESS OF MALFI

Type of work: Drama
Author: John Webster (1580-1638)
Type of plot: Romantic tragedy
Time of plot: Sixteenth century
Locale: Amalfi and Milan, Italy
First presented: c. 1613

Principal characters:
GIOVANNA, Duchess of Amalfi
ANTONIO, her second husband
FERDINAND, Duke of Calabria, jealous brother of the duchess
THE CARDINAL, another brother of the duchess
BOSOLA, the brothers' spy and executioner

Critique:

Webster's play is a blood-tragedy typical of the so-called decadent drama of the reign of James I of England. The melodrama of its scenes, however, is not enough to detract from the general dignity and tragedy of the play. A peculiarity of this play is that a year elapses between the first and second acts and another two years between the second and third acts, the passage of time made apparent to the audience by the birth of children to the duchess. As in most of the bloody tragedies, the setting is a Latin country.

The Story:

The Duchess of Malfi was a young widow whose two brothers, one a Cardinal and the other Ferdinand, the Duke of Calabria, were desperately jealous lest she marry again, for they planned to inherit her title and estates. Their spy in her household was Bosola, her master of horse.

In spite of the warnings of her brothers, the duchess fell in love with Antonio, her steward, and married him. Later, unknown to any person in the court except Antonio and Cariola, a servant girl, she had a child, a boy. Unfortunately, the happy father wrote out the child's horoscope according to the rules of astrology and then lost the paper. Bosola found the document and so learned about the duchess' child. He dispatched a letter immediately to Rome to inform the brothers. The duke swore that only her blood could quench his anger and threatened that once he knew

for certain the duchess' lover, he would be content only with her complete ruin.

The years passed and the duchess bore Antonio two more children, a second son and a daughter. Antonio told his friend Delio that he was worried because Duke Ferdinand was too quiet about the matter and because the people of Malfi, not aware of their duchess' marriage, were calling her a common strumpet.

Duke Ferdinand had come to the court to propose Count Malateste as a second husband for the duchess. She refused. Meanwhile Bosola had not been able to discover the father of the duchess' children. Impatient with his informer, the duke decided on a bolder course of action. He determined to gain entrance to the duchess' private chamber, and there to wring a confession from her. That night, using a key Bosola had given him, the duke went to her bedroom. Under threats she confessed to her second marriage, but she refused to reveal Antonio's name. After the duke left, she called Antonio and Cariola to her chamber. They planned Antonio's escape from Malfi before his secret became known to the duchess' brothers.

The duchess called Bosola and told him that Antonio had falsified some accounts. As soon as Bosola left, she recalled Antonio and told him of the feigned crime of which she had accused him to shield both their honors, and then bade him flee to the town of Ancona, where they would meet later. In the

1004

presence of Bosola and the officers of her guard she again accused Antonio of stealing money, and banished him from Malfi. Antonio replied that such was the treatment of stewards of thankless masters, and then left for Ancona. The duped Bosola upheld Antonio in an argument with the duchess. She then felt that she could trust Bosola with the secret of her marriage, and she asked him to take jewels and money to her husband at Ancona. Bosola, in return, advised her to make her own departure from the court more seemly by going to Ancona by way of the shrine of Loretto, so that the flight might seem a religious pilgrimage.

Bosola immediately traveled from Malfi to Rome, where he betrayed the plans of Antonio and the duchess to Duke Ferdinand and the Cardinal. They had the lovers banished from Ancona.

Bosola met the duchess and Antonio near Loretto with a letter from Duke Ferdinand bidding Antonio report to him, since now he knew Antonio as his sister's husband. Antonio refused and fled with his oldest son toward Milan. After Antonio's departure, Bosola took the duchess back to her palace at Malfi, a prisoner by Duke Ferdinand's command. At Malfi the duke again visited her in her chamber. He presented her with a dead man's hand, implying that it was from Antonio's corpse. Finally Bosola came to the duchess and strangled her. Cariola and the children were also strangled, though not with the quiet dignity with which the duchess was murdered. When

Bosola asked Duke Ferdinand for his reward, the hypocritical duke laughed and replied that the only reward for such a crime was its pardon.

In Milan, meanwhile, Antonio planned to visit the Cardinal's chamber during the night to seek a reconciliation with the duchess' brothers. He intended to approach the Cardinal because Duke Ferdinand had lost his mind after causing his sister's murder. The Cardinal ordered Bosola that same evening to seek out Antonio, who was known to be in Milan, and murder him. But when so ordered, Bosola accused the Cardinal of having plotted the duchess' murder and requested his reward. When a reward was again refused, Bosola swore to himself to join forces with Antonio to avenge the duchess' death.

That night all plans miscarried. In the dark Bosola accidentally murdered Antonio, the man he hoped to make an ally in his revenge on Duke Ferdinand and the Cardinal. A few minutes later, Bosola stabbed the Cardinal and was in turn stabbed by the mad Duke Ferdinand, who had rushed into the room. Bosola, with his last strength, stabbed the duke and they both died. Alarmed, the guards broke into the apartments to discover the bodies. Into the welter of blood a courtier led the young son of the Duchess of Malfi and Antonio, whom Antonio had taken to Milan. He was proclaimed ruler of the lands held by his mother and uncles.

DUINO ELEGIES

Type of work: Poetry
Author: Rainer Maria Rilke (1875-1926)
First published: 1923

For the reader who must rely on a prose translation of Rainer Maria Rilke's culminating work, the story and the man behind its appearance may overshadow the poem itself. Nothing of the elegiac quality of the original German can be translated which is as deeply affecting as the inspiration which produced the work, or the philosophy of the man who wrote it.

Often ranked with Yeats as one of the great poets of this century, Rilke is also called the great beginner. One might, however, better compare his poetic innovations with those of Gerard Manley Hopkins, though in the case of Rilke experimentation with rhythm and rhyme never took precedence over content. Like Yeats, he more often let the content find the form. Of the three, Rilke was the most intuitive, rhapsodic, and mystical; and he was perhaps the most consummate craftsman.

In October, 1911, the poet visited his friend, Princess Marie von Thurn und Taxis-Hohenlohe, at Schloss Duino, near Trieste. He remained at the castle, alone throughout the winter, until April, and there he composed the first, the second, and parts of several other elegies. The opening stanza, "Who, if I cried, would hear me among the angelic orders?" came to him while walking in a storm along a cliff two hundred feet above the raging sea, a romantic interlude worthy of an atmospheric passage in a Gothic novel. Rilke conceived the plan of all ten elegies as a whole, though ten years elapsed before the poem found its final form.

The First Elegy, like the first movement of a musical work, presents the central theme and suggests the variations that follow. From the opening line to the last, Rilke invokes the Angels, not those of Christianity but of a special order immersed in time and space, a concept of being of perfect consciousness, of transcendent reality. As a symbol appearing earlier in Rilke's poetry, the Angel represents to him the perfection of life in all the forms to which he aspired, as high above man as God is above this transcending one. Nearest to this angelic order are the Heroes—later he praises Samson—and a woman in love, especially one who dies young, as did Gaspara Stampa (1523-1554), whom Rilke celebrates as a near-perfect example. Like the lover, man must realize each moment to the fullest rather than be distracted by things and longings. With this contrast of Man and Angels, of Lovers and Heroes, and with the admission of life's transitoriness, the poet suggests the meaning of life and death as well as words can identify such profound things.

If the introduction or invocation is a praise of life, the Second Elegy is a lament for life's limitations. We moderns must, at best, content ourselves with an occasional moment of self-awareness, of a glimpse at eternity. Unlike the Greeks, we have no external symbols for the life within. In love, were we not finally satiated, we might establish communication with the Angels; but finally our intuitions vanish and we have only a fleeting glance at reality.

Rilke began the Third Elegy at Duino and completed it in Paris the following year; during an intervening visit to Spain he composed parts of the Sixth, Ninth, and Tenth Elegies. In the third section he confronts the physical bases of life, especially love. He suggests that woman

DUINO ELEGIES by Rainer Maria Rilke. Translated by J. B. Leishman and Stephen Spender. Excerpts reprinted by permission of the publishers, W. W. Norton & Co., Inc. Copyright, 1939, by W. W. Norton & Co., Inc.

is always superior in the love act, man a mere beginner led by blind animal passion, the libido a vicious drive. Sublime love is an end in itself, but often human love is a means to escape life. Even children have a sort of terror infused into their blood from this heritage of doubt and fear. From this view of mortality Rilke would lead the child away, as he says in powerful though enigmatic conclusion,

> . . . Oh gently, gently
> show him daily a loving, confident task
> done,—guide him
> close to the garden, give him those
> counter-
> balancing nights. . . .
> Withhold him. . . .

Perhaps the advent of war made the Fourth Elegy the most bitter of all, written as it was from Rilke's retreat in Munich in 1915. The theme of distraction, our preoccupation with fleeting time and time serving, makes of this part a deep lament over the human condition. We are worse than puppets who might be manipulated by unseen forces, Angels. Our attempts to force destiny, to toy with fate, cause us to break from heaven's firm hold. We must be as little children, delighted within ourselves by the world without, and with our attention and energies undivided, alone. Here, we will find our answer to death as the other side of life, a part of life and not the negation or end of it.

The Fifth Elegy, the last from the standpoint of time, written at the Château de Muzot in 1922, was inspired by Picasso's famous picture of the acrobats. Here again the circumstances of the writing overshadow the very real worth of the poem. Les Saltimbanques of Picasso was owned by Frau Hertha Koenig, who allowed Rilke the privilege of living in her home in 1915 in order to be near his favorite painting. Either the poet imperfectly remembered the details of the painting when the poem was finally writ-

ten or else he included recollections of acrobats who had so delighted him during his Paris years. Regardless of influences, however, this poem is remarkable in its merging of theme and movement with a painting, emphasizing Rilke's conviction that a poem must celebrate all the senses rather than appeal to eye or ear alone.

The acrobats, symbolizing the human condition, travel about, rootless and transitory, giving pleasure neither to themselves nor the spectators. Reality to the acrobat, as to man, is best discovered in the arduousness of the task; but routine often makes the task a mockery, especially if death is the end. If death, however, is the other side of life and makes up the whole, then life forces are real and skillfully performed to the inner delight of performers and spectators, living and dead alike.

The Hero, Rilke asserts in the Sixth Elegy, is that fortunate being whose memory, unlike that of long-forgotten lovers, is firmly established by his deeds. He, being single-minded and single-hearted, has the same destiny as the early departed, those who die young without losing their view of eternity. The great thing, then, is to live in the flower of life with the calm awareness that the fruit, death, is the unilluminated side of life. For the Hero, life is always beginning.

In the Seventh Elegy, the poet as the we and the you as well as the I, no longer worries about transitory decaying or dying. Now he sings the unpremeditated song of existence:

> Don't think that I'm wooing!
> Angel, even if I were, you'd never come.
> For my call
> is always full of 'Away!' Against such a
> powerful
> current you cannot advance. Like an
> outstretched
> arm is my call. And its clutching, upwardly
> open hand is always before you

as open for warding and warning, aloft there, Inapprehensible.

From this viewpoint, Rilke attempts in the Eighth Elegy, dedicated to his friend Rudolph Kassner, to support his belief in the "nowhere without no," the "open" world, timeless, limitless, inseparable "whole." "We," contrasted to animals, are always looking away rather than toward this openness.

The theme of creative existence Rilke continues in the Ninth Elegy, possibly begun at Duino but certainly finished at Muzot. Here he suggests that the life of the tree is superior in felicity to the destiny of man. We should, perhaps, rejoice in spite of the limiting conditions of man by overcoming this negation of the flesh with a reaffirmation of the spirit. Then death holds no fears since it is not opposite to life, not an enemy but a friend. This work possibly represents the author's own transformation from the negating, inhibiting conditions of the Great War to a renewed faith in life.

The Tenth Elegy, the first ten lines of which came to him in that burst of creativity at Duino, contains a satiric portrait of the City of Pain where man simply excludes suffering, pain, death, from his thoughts; where distractions, especially the pursuit of money, are the principal activities. This semi-existence the poet contrasts with that in the Land of Pain, Life-Death, where there is continuous progress through insights of a deeper reality to the primal source of joy.

And we, who have always thought
of happiness climbing, would feel
the emotion that almost startles
when happiness falls.

Perhaps Rilke means that by complete submission or attunement to universal forces one is suspended or even falls into the "open." This deeply realized philosophy he developed in the *Sonnets to Orpheus* (1923), a work which complements the *Duino Elegies,* though it does not surpass them in deep emotional undertones and sheer power of expression.

THE DUNCIAD

Type of work: Poem
Author: Alexander Pope (1688-1744)
Time: Eighteenth century
Locale: England, the underworld
First published: 1728-1743

Principal personages:
DULNESS, a goddess
TIBBALD, hero of the first edition, a Shakespearian scholar
COLLEY CIBBER, hero of the second edition, playwright, producer, and
poet laureate

When Alexander Pope set out to criticize the general literary climate of his time and to avenge the slights given his own work by other writers, he took the theme of John Dryden's *MacFlecknoe*, in which the poetaster Thomas Shadwell is crowned ruler of the Kingdom of Nonsense, and expanded it to make a true mock epic of three books. He added a fourth book when he rewrote the poem in 1742. *The Dunciad* acclaims the goddess Dulness, daughter of Chaos and Night, and her chosen prince: the scholar Lewis Theobald (Tibbald) in the first edition, Colley Cibber, playwright and poet laureate, in the second.

This poem lacks the close-knit quality of Pope's other fine mock epic, *The Rape of the Lock*. It is longer, and the fact that the hero appears only at intervals explains a certain disunity. Tibbald-Cibber appears at the middle of Book I, is present only as a spectator at the epic games described in Book II, and dreams the trip to the underworld, modeled on that of Aeneas in Book VI of the *Aeneid*. Thus, the action is limited. The important points in the poem are made in the descriptive passages in these episodes and in conversations which contain criticism of individuals and trends.

The general plan outlined above shows Pope's close reliance on the classical epic as his model. *The Dunciad*, like *The Rape of the Lock*, begins with a parody of the *Aeneid*:

The mighty Mother, and her Son, who
brings
The Smithfield Muses to the ear of
Kings,
I sing.

The invocation is appropriately directed not at a muse but at the Patricians, the patrons whose purses inspire dull writing. The dedication to the author's friend Jonathan Swift which follows is an eighteenth-century, rather than a classic convention.

Pope describes in detail the abode of Dulness and the allegorical figures gathered around her throne: Fortitude, Temperance, Prudence, and Poetic Justice, who is weighing truth with gold and "solid pudding against empty praise." The gods are notoriously interested in the affairs of mortals; Dulness looks out upon the ingredients of dull writing and the numerous creators of it. Her eye lights upon the hero, who is raising to her an altar of tremendous tomes of his writing. She anoints him as king of her realm, and the nation croaks Aesop's line, "God save King Log."

In the second book Pope designs appropriate contests for his various groups of enemies. The booksellers race to win a phantom poet. A patron is designated for the poet who tickles best, but he is carried off by an unknown sycophantic secretary. Journalists swim through the muck of the Thames River:

Who flings most filth, and wide pollutes
around
The stream, be his the Weekly Journals
bound;
A pig of lead to him who drives the
best;

1009

A peck of coals a-piece shall glad the rest.

As a final test the goddess promises her "amplest powers" to anyone who can remain awake as he listens to the verses of "Three College Sophs, and three pert Templars." The book ends with the whole company lying asleep.

Grandiose heroic couplets and numerous parallels with classical visits to the underworld fill the third book. John Taylor, the Water Poet, replaces the ferryman Charon; Elkanah Settle, a Restoration poet, takes Anchises' part in showing the hero the future of Dulness and her offspring. The high point of this book is the crowning of Tibbald-Cibber with a poppy wreath by Bavius, prototype of the worst of poets from ancient times.

The 1742 *Dunciad*, centering on the triumph of Dulness over England, reveals a slightly more mature outlook in the poet than does the earlier version. Tibbald was the object of a vindictive attack, occasioned by his criticism of Pope's edition of Shakespeare. Cibber is representative of the dull poet; as laureate he was well known for his poor occasional verse. The fourth book is far more concerned with the institutions promoting the rise of dullness than with individuals. The more frequent use of classical names, rather than personal ones, indicates the poet's movement toward universality.

The last book is almost an entity in itself. It opens with a new invocation, to Chaos and Night. The pseudo-learned notes, effective satire written by Pope himself, point out the precedents for a second invocation when important new matter is introduced. Evil omens presage the coming destruction as Dulness ascends her throne and Cibber reclines in her lap, making his only appearance in this book.

Around the goddess are Science, Wit, Logic, Rhetoric, and other abstractions in chains, reminiscent of several scenes in *The Faerie Queene*. Various personages

appear to tell of Dulness' victory over the many arts and institutions. First to come is a harlot representing the Italian opera; she rejoices in the banishment of Handel to Ireland and the supremacy of chaos in music.

Pope uses an epic simile to describe the nations clustering around the goddess:

Not closer, orb in orb, congloved are seen
The buzzing Bees about their dusky Queen.

Present are the passive followers of Dulness and those who lead the advance: pompous editors who make mincemeat of good poets with notes and commentary, patrons who set up a bust of a poet after he has died neglected.

A specter, the head of Westminster School, modeled on Milton's Moloch, speaks on the state of education:

As Fancy opens the quick springs of Sense,
We ply the Memory, we load the brain,
Bind rebel Wit, and double chain on chain,
Confine the thought, to exercise the breath;
And keep them in the pale of Words till death.

Pope criticizes the hair-splitting grammarians in Aristarchus' boasts that he has turned good verse into prose again. Science is also satirized as the study which loses itself in detail; but Dulness fears even that condition of affairs, for an object of nature is capable of awakening a mind. Religion does not escape; the poet says that it has degenerated into a belief in a mechanistic God, made in man's image.

Knowing the state of her kingdom, the goddess celebrates her mysteries, reflecting Pope's interest in ceremony. As the rites are concluded a state of dullness encompasses the country, schools, government, army. Truth, philosophy, and religion perish as "Universal Darkness buries All."

The Dunciad contains more of the true heroic spirit than most other mock epics, like Samuel Butler's coarse *Hudibras* or the delicate and sophisticated *The Rape of the Lock*. These poems are directed toward the amusement of the reader, while *The Dunciad* reveals Pope's passionate conviction that the triumph of dullness was a real danger to art, science, and learning. He chose to deliver his warning to England in the humorous mock-epic form, but his seriousness about his subject raises the latter part of the fourth book to the level of real heroic poetry.

There are many fine lines of poetry in *The Dunciad*, but it is more diffuse and less brilliant satire than either *MacFlecknoe* or Pope's own *Epistle to Dr. Arbuthnot*. Missing are the biting, succinct couplets like Dryden's

The rest to some faint meaning make pretense,
But Sh— never deviates into sense . . .

or Pope's lines on Addison:

Damn with faint praise, assent with civil leer,
And without sneering, teach the rest to sneer.

The greatest deterrent to the modern reader of *The Dunciad* is probably the fact that so much of the poet's contemporary criticism is almost unintelligible; few names die faster than those of the fifth-rate writers of an era. Yet the satirical comments on universal conditions remain fresh and pointed. *The Dunciad* is worthy of a high place among mock-heroic poems.

THE DYNASTS

Type of work: Dramatic poem
Author: Thomas Hardy (1840-1928)
Type of plot: Historical epic
Time of plot: 1806-1815
Locale: Europe
First published: 1903-1908

Principal characters:
NAPOLEON I
JOSEPHINE, his first wife
MARIE LOUISE, his second wife
KING GEORGE III OF ENGLAND
TSAR ALEXANDER OF RUSSIA
EMPEROR FRANCIS OF AUSTRIA
SIR WILLIAM PITT, Prime Minister of England
SPIRIT OF YEARS,
SHADE OF EARTH,
SPIRIT OF PITIES,
SPIRIT SINISTER, and
SPIRIT IRONIC, allegorical figures

Critique:

Written in various types of verse and in poetic prose, *The Dynasts,* a vast epic-drama of the tragedy of Napoleon, marks Hardy's greatest effort to portray Man as completely subject to a disinterested Destiny. Among his manifold points of view, shifting from a point somewhere above the earth to the courts of emperors or the cottager's fireside, that of the rural folk of southern England is the most effective. Long prose stage directions fill out the historical perspective of this sweeping panoramic treatment of the constant turmoil in Europe from 1805 to 1815. The array of allegorical spectators who comment on the events of the drama as they occur, and Hardy's device of switching the point of view, tend to make strikingly trivial the alarums and excursions of earth-bound humanity.

The Story:

The Spirit of Years, Shade of Earth, Spirit Sinister, Spirit Ironic, Spirit of Pities, and their accompanying choruses, forgathered somewhere above the earth to watch the larger movements of men in western Europe in 1805. The design of

the Immanent Will manifested itself at the time in Napoleon's preparations for the invasion of England.

Sir William Pitt, in England, contended with isolationist members of Parliament in order to secure proper defense against the invasion. Meanwhile Napoleon went to Milan to be crowned King of Italy. The spirits made light of the chicanery and pomp that attended the coronation. The Spirit of Pities descended to earth and disturbed Napoleon by reminding him of his original intention of championing liberty.

At sea, a Pyrrhic victory of the French and Spanish over the English prevented the support required for the planned invasion. On the south coast of England the Phantoms of Rumor caused great disturbance. A fleet of fishing craft was mistaken for the invasion fleet, and civilians fled from the coastal towns as signal fires flared upon the cliffs and hills.

When Napoleon learned that his admiral, Villeneuve, had returned to Cadiz, he discarded his invasion plan and moved eastward against Austria and Russia, countries which Pitt had enlisted in the

English cause. The Spirit of Years remarked that the ensuing campaign would be a model in tactics for all time.

At Ulm, Napoleon defeated the Austrians, who had hoped in vain that the English fleet would hold the French forces in northern France. In London, Pitt, unsuccessful in gaining permission from the king to form a coalition government, visibly declined in health under his terrible burden.

Villeneuve was ordered out of Cadiz. The British under Nelson met the French and Spanish off Trafalgar and defeated them. Nelson was killed in the engagement; Villeneuve subsequently ended his own life in an inn at Rennes.

Napoleon defeated the Austrians and Russians at Austerlitz. Then, hearing of the English victory at Trafalgar, he declared his intention of closing all continental ports to English ships. He dictated peace terms to Emperor Francis of Austria while attendant Austrian officers stood by in disgust at the sight of a nobody dictating to true royalty. In Paris the Spirit of Rumor commented on the way Napoleon was uprooting old dynasties and founding new ones.

Pitt having died and King George III being mentally ill, England, in the person of Charles James Fox, negotiated with Napoleon for peace; but the emperor used the negotiations as a screen for his real plans. He marched on Prussia and defeated the Germans at the Battle of Jena. In Berlin he decreed that all British ships were barred from continental ports. Next, Napoleon and Tsar Alexander of Russia met at the River Niemen, where the two drew up a Franco-Russian alliance. During this meeting Napoleon expressed the desire to cement his various alliances with blood ties. The Spirit of Years remarked ironically that Napoleon was one of the few men who could see the working of the Immanent Will.

Napoleon invaded Spain as a friend to help the Spanish gain Portugal. The Spanish Bourbons abdicated and Napoleon's brother, Joseph, was proclaimed king. When Bourbon partisans enlisted English aid, an English invasion fleet sailed for Portugal.

Back in Paris, Napoleon told his wife, Josephine, that he wished a divorce. Josephine had borne the emperor no children and he was anxious to perpetuate the dynasty he had founded. The British invasion of the Iberian Peninsula drew the emperor to Spain to direct the campaign there. Preparation for war in Austria caused Napoleon next to invade that country and to defeat its forces at Wagram. The British, under the Duke of Wellington, held their own against the French in Spain. At that point the Spirit Sinister reminded the Spirit Ironic not to sneer for fear Immanent Will would cut short the comedy that was taking place.

A British force was sent to the Scheldt, but the expedition ended disastrously when the army was decimated by miasmal fever. Napoleon, fearful of assassination and still anxious to perpetuate his line, negotiated with the Russians for the hand of a Russian princess, and with the Austrians for the hand of Princess Marie Louise. The tsar accepted the offer, but Napoleon had already arranged, through Metternich, for a marriage with the Austrian princess, Marie Louise. The marriage was performed in the conspicuous absence of many high clergy, and the Russians, incensed, prepared for war. In the meantime the British in Spain under the Duke of Wellington gained a decisive victory at Albuera.

In due time Marie Louise gave birth to Napoleon's heir. The insane King of England died after hearing of British successes in Spain. On the continent war became imminent between France and Russia.

Again on the banks of the Niemen, Napoleon received an evil portent when he was thrown from his horse. The Spirit of Pities foresaw misery for the French Grand Army in the Russian campaign. Wellington in Spain defeated the French at Salamanca. Napoleon gained a costly victory over the Russians at Borodino, and the French entered Moscow to find the city deserted and in flames. There followed a general retreat by the French across snow-covered Russian steppes to Lithuania. Thousands perished from the cold or were killed by harassing Russian cavalry. Napoleon deserted his army and raced back to Paris in order to arrive there before the news of his failure in Russia. His chief task now was to hold his empire together.

As the British continued their successes in Spain, Austria joined the allies. Napoleon met defeat at the hands of the Austrians and Prussians at Leipzig. The allies invaded France. Napoleon, forced to abdicate, was exiled to Elba, an island in the Mediterranean. Marie Louise and the infant King of Italy went to Austria to stay. The Bourbons reassumed the throne of France and a congress to deliberate on general peace in Europe met in Vienna.

Napoleon escaped from Elba and returned to Paris at the head of an army he had picked up on his way. The allies outlawed Napoleon and prepared to overthrow him again.

A private ball in Brussels was broken up by the news that the French army was nearing the Belgian frontier. . Almost overnight, Napoleon had organized and put into the field a large army. But he failed to separate the British and Prussians in Belgium, and he was brought to utter defeat on the fields south of Waterloo. The Hundred Days were ended.

The Spirit of Years pointed out to the Spirits assembled that the human beings below them behaved as though they were in a dream, as though they were puppets being drawn by strings manipulated by Immanent Will. The Spirit of Years pointed to Napoleon in defeat and compared him to a tiny insect on an obscure leaf in the chart of the Ages. When the Spirit of Pities asked for what purpose the events below had taken place, the Spirit of Irony answered that there was no purpose, for only a dumb thing turned the crank which motivated and directed human behavior.

EARTH

Type of work: Novel
Author: Émile Zola (1840-1902)
Type of plot: Social realism
Time of plot: 1860's
Locale: La Beauce, France
First published: 1887

Principal characters:
 FOUAN, an old peasant farmer
 ROSE, his wife
 HYACINTHE, called Jésus-Christ, his older son
 FANNY, his daughter
 BUTEAU, his younger son
 DELHOMME, Fanny's husband
 LISE, Fouan's niece, daughter of Old Mouche
 FRANÇOISE, Lise's sister
 JEAN MACQUART, a soldier and artisan, later a farm laborer in La Beauce

Critique:

Earth (*La Terre*), the fifteenth volume of the Rougon-Macquart series, is Zola's horrifying vision of the French peasantry before the Franco-Prussian War. In the relationships between Fouan and his family, Zola consciously adopted the theme of Lear, although the farmer drawn with realistic detail has none of the nobility of Shakespeare's king. Zola's introduction of Rabelaisian humor in the character Jésus-Christ was an innovation in literary realism. The earth itself dominates the novel, and its beauty and indifference contrast vividly with the peasants' passionate absorption in possessing the land and with the crimes they commit in order to do so. When the novel appeared, Zola was reproached for his lack of idealism and his lack of understanding of the peasants. Mallarmé, however, did not hesitate to see in it true poetry. *Earth* is now among the most widely read of Zola's novels.

The Story:

As Jean Macquart finished sowing each furrow with grain, he paused and gazed over the wide, rich plain. As far as he could see farmers were scattering their wheat, anxious to finish sowing before the frosts came. He met and talked with Françoise about the coming division of old Fouan's property.

In the notary's office, plans for Fouan's sons and son-in-law to divide and farm his land were angrily made. Fouan could not bear to lose the land which had taken all his strength to work and which he had loved more passionately than his wife. The rent and food he asked in return for his property seemed excessive to his children, who, now that the land was within their grasp, intended to keep as much of its yield as possible. Buteau declared that the old man had money saved in bonds. This claim so enraged Fouan that he exhibited some of his former ferocity and authority. Finally the notary completed the transaction and arranged for the division of land by the surveyor.

Buteau, having drawn the third lot of land, declared it was the worst, and he refused to take that part of the property. His refusal distressed Lise, Françoise's sister, for Buteau had been her lover and she was pregnant. She had hoped that when he got the land he would marry her.

Old Mouche, the sisters' father, had a stroke and died in his home. As the village women watched by his deathbed, a violent hail storm laid waste the village crops. The peasants examined the damage by lamplight, their animosities forgotten in their common anguish at this devastation and their fury at the destructiveness of heaven.

Lise and Françoise stayed in the house after their father's death. Lise's son had been born and still Buteau had not married her. Jean became a constant visitor in the household. Believing that he was attracted by Lise, he proposed to her. Before accepting him, she decided to consult Buteau because of the child.

At the autumn haymaking Jean and Françoise worked together. While the girl stood atop the growing rick, Jean forked up bales of hay to her. She was flushed and laughing and Jean found her violently attractive. Because he was years older than Françoise, he was greatly upset when he suddenly realized that it was she who had drawn him to the house and not Lise.

Jean and the sisters met Buteau at the market in Cloyes. Because Lise now had property of her own and because he had at last accepted his share of land, Buteau decided to marry Lise. Buteau, delighted now by possession of the land, plowed and sowed with vigor and passion, determined never to relinquish one inch of the earth. As the wheat grew, its rolling greenness covered La Beauce like an ocean. Buteau watched the weather as anxiously as a sailor at sea. Although Françoise wished to have her share of the land decided, Buteau managed to avoid a final settlement.

When Fouan's older son, nicknamed Jésus-Christ, took to buy brandy the money which Buteau had grudgingly given his parents as their allowance, Buteau was so infuriated that he struck his mother to the floor. Rose did not recover and in three days she was dead. Fouan was then left completely alone. Finally, much against his will, he decided to make his home with Delhomme, his son-in-law.

By harvest time the green sea of wheat had turned to a fiery gold, and the whole village worked at the harvest. Jean, meanwhile, was tormented by his desire for Françoise. Finally, exhausted by her struggle to resist the constant at-

tentions of Buteau as well, she yielded to him. Buteau, in his fear of losing both the girl and her land, asserted wildly that they could never be married while Françoise was under age.

Meanwhile, Fouan was bullied and restricted in Delhomme's home; he had no money for tobacco and he was allowed little wine. Completely miserable, he went to live with Buteau and Lise. There he was appalled by Buteau's pursuit of Françoise, whose resistance made Buteau so angry that even Lise expressed the wish her sister would surrender in order to have peace once more in the household. Françoise, continuing proudly to refuse Buteau, was gradually turned into a domestic drudge.

In desperation Françoise agreed to marry Jean when she was of age. Fouan, drawn into these household quarrels, was no happier than he had been with Delhomme. At last, because Buteau and his wife begrudged every mouthful of food that he ate, he accepted Jésus-Christ's offer of a home. Jésus-Christ was the only one of Fouan's children without a passion for land. Although it distressed Fouan to see his hard-won acres go to buy brandy for Jésus-Christ, he enjoyed the jokes and the occasional excellent meals cooked in the nearly ruined house by Jésus-Christ's illegitimate daughter.

Before the time of the vintage Jésus-Christ discovered that his father was spending his bonds on an annuity by which he hoped to acquire some land of his own once more. Amazed, first Fanny and then Buteau tried to bribe the old man to return to them. Fouan's relationship with Jesus-Christ was never close again after the discovery.

After a final explosion with Lise, Françoise left the house and went to live with her aunt. It was arranged that she should soon marry Jean and claim her full share of the property. The ill will between the sisters was intensified when the land was divided and Françoise secured the house at auction. Buteau and Lise moved to an adjacent house, where Fouan, fearing that Jésus-Christ would steal his bonds, joined them.

Jean and Buteau were forced to work side by side in the fields. One day, while Jean was manuring the earth, Lise told Buteau that Fouan had had a stroke and that she would bring the doctor. Surprisingly, the old man recovered. During his illness, however, Lise discovered his bonds. When they refused to return them, he left.

Homeless and desperate, Fouan wandered to Delhomme's farm, where he stayed wearily looking into the house. Next he went to Jésus-Christ's hovel, but fear and pride again prevented him from entering. That night, during a terrible storm, Fouan, wretched and exhausted, dragged himself around to look once more at the land he had owned. Finally his hunger became so great that he returned to Buteau, who jeeringly fed him.

Françoise was pregnant. Enraged by the fear that the property might not revert to him and by the fact that Jean's plow had cut into their land, Buteau, aided by Lise, at last raped Françoise. The girl then realized with revulsion that she had always loved him. Jealous, Lise knocked Françoise against a scythe in the field and the blade pierced her abdomen. As she lay dying Françoise refused to will her share of the farm to Jean; although he was her husband, she still regarded him as an outsider. After her death, Jean was evicted from the land.

Greedy for more money, and terrified that the old man would betray the manner of Françoise's death, Lise and Buteau murdered Fouan by smothering him with a pillow and then setting fire to his bed. Jean Macquart, having no further ties with La Beauce, decided again to become a soldier. After a final tour of the land he left the region for good. If he could not cultivate it, he would at least be able to defend the earth of France.

EAST OF EDEN

Type of work: Novel
Author: John Steinbeck (1902-   )
Type of plot: Regional chronicle
Time of plot: 1865-1918
Locale: California
First published: 1952

Principal characters:

ADAM TRASK, a settler in the Salinas Valley
CATHY AMES, later Adam's wife
CALEB, and
ARON TRASK, their twin sons
CHARLES TRASK, Adam's half-brother
SAMUEL HAMILTON, a neighbor of the Trasks
LEE, Adam's Chinese servant
ABRA BACON, Aron's fiancée

Critique:

East of Eden is an ambitious but not altogether successful attempt to present three themes simultaneously: a panoramic history of the Salinas Valley (and thus of America itself) around the turn of the century; a melodramatic chronicle of two families in the valley; a symbolic re-creation of the Cain and Abel story. Its expressed concern, however, is philosophic—the nature of the conflict between good and evil. In this conflict love and the acceptance or rejection it brings to the individual plays an important role, yet one has always the opportunity to choose the good. In this freedom lies man's glory. The book's defects stem from the author's somewhat foggy and sentimental presentation of its philosophy and his tendency to manipulate or oversimplify characters and events for symbolic purposes.

The Story:

The soil of the Salinas Valley in California is rich, though the foothills around it are poor and its life shrivels during the long dry spells. The Irish-born Hamiltons, arriving after American settlers had displaced the Mexicans, settled on the barren hillside. There Sam Hamilton, full of talk, glory, and improvident inventions, and Liza, his dourly

religious wife, brought up their nine children.

In Connecticut, Adam Trask and his half-brother Charles grew up, mutually affectionate in spite of the differences in their natures. Adam was gentle and good; Charles, roughly handsome with a streak of wild violence. After Adam's mother had committed suicide, his father had married a docile girl who had borne Charles. Adam loved his stepmother but hated his father, a rigid disciplinarian whose fanatic militarism had begun with a fictitious account of his own war career and whose dream was to have a son in the army. To fulfill his dream, he chose Adam, who could gain the greater strength that comes from the conquest of weakness as Charles could not. But Charles, whose passionate love for his father went continually unnoticed, could not understand this final rejection of himself. In violent despair, he beat Adam almost to death.

Adam served in the cavalry for five years. Then, although he hated regimentation and violence, he reënlisted, for he could neither accept help from his father, who had become an important figure in Washington, nor return to the farm Charles now ran alone. Afterward he wandered through the West and the

South, served time for vagrancy, and finally came home to find his father dead and himself and Charles rich. In the years that followed he and Charles lived together, although their bickering and inbred solitude drove Adam to periodic wanderings. Feeling that their life was one of pointless industry, he talked of moving west but did not.

Meanwhile, Cathy Ames was growing up in Massachusetts. She was a monster, born unable to comprehend goodness but with a sublimely innocent face and a consummate knowledge of how to manipulate or deceive people to serve her own ends. After a thwarted attempt to leave home, she burned her house, killing her parents and leaving evidence to indicate that she had been murdered. She then became the mistress of a man who ran a string of brothels and used his insatiable love for her to torment him. When he realized her true nature, he took her to a deserted spot and beat her savagely. Near death, she crawled to the nearest house—the Trasks'—where Adam and Charles cared for her. Adam found her innocent and beautiful; Charles, who had a knowledge of evil through himself, recognized the evil in her and wanted her to leave. Cathy, needing temporary protection, enticed Adam into marrying her, but on their wedding night she gave him a sleeping draught and went to Charles.

Feeling that Charles disapproved of Cathy, Adam decided to carry out his dream of going west. He was so transfigured by his happiness that he did not take Cathy's protests seriously; as his ideal of love and purity, she could not disagree. Adam bought a ranch in the richest part of the Salinas Valley and worked hard to ready it for his wife and the child she expected. Cathy hated her pregnancy, but she knew that she had to wait calmly to get back to the life she wanted. After giving birth to twin boys, she waited a week; she then shot Adam, wounding him, and walked out.

Changing her name to Kate, Cathy went to work in a Salinas brothel. Her beauty and seeming goodness endeared her to the proprietress, Faye, and Kate gradually assumed control of the establishment. After Faye made a will leaving Kate her money and property, Kate slyly engineered Faye's death. Making her establishment one which aroused and purveyed to sadistic tastes, she became legendary and rich.

Adam was like a dead man for a year after his wife left him, unable to work his land or even to name his sons. Finally Sam Hamilton woke him by deliberately angering him, and Sam, Adam, and Lee, the Chinese servant and a wise and good man, named the boys Caleb and Aron. As the men talked of the story of Cain and Abel, Lee concluded that rejection terrifies a child most and leads to guilt and revenge. Later, after much study, Lee discovered the true meaning of the Hebrew word *timshel*—thou mayest—and understood that the story meant in part that man can always choose to conquer evil.

Sam, grown old, knew that he would soon die. Before he left his ranch, he told Adam of Kate and her cruel, destructive business. Adam, disbelieving in her very existence, visited her and suddenly knew her as she really was. Though she tried to taunt him, telling him that Charles was the true father of his sons, and to seduce him, he left her a free and curiously exultant man. Yet he could not tell his sons that their mother was not dead.

Caleb and Aron were growing up very differently. Aron was golden-haired and automatically inspired love, yet he remained single-minded and unyielding; Caleb was dark and clever, a feared and respected leader left much alone. When Adam moved to town, where the schools were better, Aron fell in love with Abra Bacon. Abra told Aron that his mother was still alive, but he could not believe her because to do so would have destroyed his faith in his father and thus in everything.

About this time Adam had the idea of

1019

shipping lettuce packed in ice to New York, but the venture failed. Aron was ashamed of his father for failing publicly. Caleb vowed to return the lost money to his father.

As they faced the problems of growing into men, Aron became smugly religious, disturbing to Abra because she felt unable to live up to his idealistic image of her. Caleb alternated between wild impulses and guilt. Learning that Kate was his mother, he began following her until she, noticing him, invited him to her house. As he talked to her, he knew with relief that he was not like her; she felt his knowledge and hated him. Kate herself, obsessed by the fear that one of the old girls had discovered Faye's murder, plotted ways to destroy this menace. Although Caleb could accept Kate's existence, he knew that Aron could not. To get the boy away from Salinas, Caleb talked him into finishing high school in three years and beginning college. Adam, knowing nothing of Caleb's true feelings, was extravagantly proud of Aron.

World War I began. Caleb went into the bean business with Will Hamilton and made a fortune because of food shortages. With growing excitement, he planned an elaborate presentation to his father of the money once lost in the lettuce enterprise. First he tried to persuade Aron, who seemed indifferent to his father's love, not to leave college. Caleb presented his money to Adam, only to have it rejected in anger because Adam's idealistic nature could not accept money made as profit from the war. He wanted Caleb's achievements to be like his brother's. In a black mood of revenge, Caleb took Aron to meet his mother. After her sons' visit Kate, who was not disturbed by those she could hurt as she was by someone like Caleb, made a will leaving everything to Aron. Then, overburdened by age, illness, and suspicion, she committed suicide.

Unable to face his new knowledge of his parents' past, Aron joined the army and went to France. Adam did not recover from the shock of his leaving. Abra turned to Caleb, admitting that she loved him rather than Aron, whose romantic stubbornness kept him from facing reality. When the news of Aron's death arrived, Adam had another stroke. As he lay dying, Caleb, unable to bear his guilt any longer, told his father of his responsibility for Aron's enlisting and thus his death. Lee begged Adam to forgive his son. Adam weakly raised his hand in benediction and, whispering the Hebrew word *timshel*, died.

1020

EASTWARD HO!

Type of work: Drama
Authors: George Chapman (c. 1559-1634) with Ben Jonson (1573?-1637) and John Marston (1576-1634)
Type of plot: Realistic comedy
Time of plot: About 1605
Locale: London
First presented: 1605

Principal characters:
TOUCHSTONE, a goldsmith
MISTRESS TOUCHSTONE, his wife
GERTRUDE, his haughty daughter
MILDRED, his dutiful daughter
FRANCIS QUICKSILVER, his idle and prodigal apprentice
GOLDING, his diligent apprentice
SIR PETRONEL FLASH, a new-made knight
SECURITY, an old usurer
WINIFRED, his young wife
SINDEFY, Quicksilver's mistress

Critique:

Eastward Ho! is a remarkable example of successful collaboration. For three authors as different in temperament as Chapman, Jonson, and Marston to write together a smooth, unified, and amusing play is almost a miracle. It encompasses the heartwarming theme of the Prodigal Son and satirical thrusts at contemporary society. Scholars have tried to assign specific scenes and lines to the individual authors, but the general reader or playgoer need not trouble himself with problems of authorship. The play's rapid dramatic movement, in keeping with its apparently rapid composition, carries its audience through laughter and sentiment to an appropriate happy ending. The characters are amusing, and even the victims of the satire are treated without the bitterness or savagery that other works of Jonson and Marston might lead one to expect. It is a true comedy which should be as effective on the modern as on the Elizabethan stage.

The Story:

Touchstone, a goldsmith, had two daughters, Gertrude, a flutter-brained social climber, and Mildred, a modest, gentle girl. He also had two apprentices,

Francis Quicksilver, a fellow as unstable as his name, and Golding, who was steady and conscientious.

Caught while trying to slip away from the shop, Quicksilver made a spirited defense of his way of life, especially of his prodigality among the town gallants. Touchstone answered with a severe moral lecture and pointed out the exemplary behavior of his fellow apprentice. The lecture was interrupted by a messenger from Sir Petronel Flash, who wished to make arrangements to marry Gertrude. As soon as Touchstone was out of hearing, Quicksilver abused the old citizen; but Golding defended his master and warned and rebuked Quicksilver.

Mildred, with the help of a tailor and a maid, attired Gertrude elegantly to receive her knight, while Gertrude rattled away, full of herself and contemptuous of her bourgeois family. Touchstone brought in Sir Petronel and concluded the arrangements for the wedding, warning both Gertrude and the knight that they need not expect any gifts beyond the agreed dowry. Gertrude impudently flouted him and left with the knight, Mistress Touchstone fluttering in attendance on her soon-to-be-married daughter.

1021

After their departure Touchstone proposed a match between Mildred and Golding.

From the wedding feast Quicksilver returned to the shop drunk, hiccuping and quoting lines from popular plays like *Tamburlaine* and *The Spanish Tragedy*. Touchstone, losing patience with the fellow, released him from his indenture and discharged him. After Quicksilver's defiant and staggering exit, Touchstone told Golding that he too would no longer be an apprentice, but a full-fledged member of the guild and his master's son-in-law.

At' the home of old Security, where Quicksilver and his mistress Sindefy lived, the old usurer plotted with them to trap Sir Petronel and to gain possession of Gertrude's property. Quicksilver was to encourage the knight to borrow money for a proposed voyage to Virginia, and both Quicksilver and Sindefy, who was to become Gertrude's maid, were to encourage the bride to put up her land to cover the debt. Before leaving to set his plans in motion, Security delayed to bid farewell to his pretty young wife, Winifred.

Sir Petronel confessed to Quicksilver that he had no castle, but that he intended to send his bride on a wild-goose chase to an imaginary castle in the country in order to get her out of the way while he carried off old Security's young wife on the Virginia voyage. Security brought in Sindefy and placed her with Gertrude as a maid, then took Sir Petronel to his home for breakfast. Captain Seagull, Scapethrift, and Spendall joined Sir Petronel there to make the final plans for the voyage.

As Gertrude prepared for her ride into the country to see her husband's nonexistent castle, Touchstone entered with his other daughter and his new son-in-law, Golding. Gertrude heaped contempt on all three, and Sir Petronel made disparaging remarks about the groom's lack of nobility. Touchstone distributed a few ironical barbs and led away the newlyweds. After their departure, Security presented Gertrude with papers, supposedly to cover a loan for new furnishings for the country castle. At Sir Petronel's request she signed the papers without even reading them and set out ,in her coach after urging the knight to follow as soon as possible. Sir Petronel and Quicksilver convinced Security that the knight was planning to elope with a lawyer's wife; and Security, maliciously delighted at the chance to injure another man, promised to lend them his wife's gown as a disguise. He also felt that lending the gown would be a good way to make certain that his wife did not leave home.

Sir Petronel, the disguised Winifred, Quicksilver, and the other adventurers ignored storm warnings and set out in their boats for the ship. Security discovered his wife's absence and tried to follow them. Slitgut, a butcher coming to Cuckold's Haven to set up a pair of horns, saw from his elevated vantage point a boat overturned in the waves. A few minutes later old Security crawled ashore bemoaning the appropriateness of his place of shipwreck. As soon as he had crept away, the butcher saw a woman struggling in the waves and a boy plunging in to save her. The boy rescued a very repentant Winifred, brought her ashore, and offered her shelter and dry clothes. A third victim of the storm was washed ashore at the foot of the gallows—a bad omen, Slitgut thought. The man was Francis Quicksilver, who passed by cursing his fate. Finally, Sir Petronel and Captain Seagull reached shore and met Quicksilver. Sir Petronel, having lost his money in the water, had no hope of saving his ship, which he expected to be confiscated. Winifred, now dry and freshly dressed, convinced Security that she had not left home until she began to worry about him. Slitgut made a few wry remarks about marriage and went home, unobserved by any of the adventurers.

Touchstone, thoroughly angered by the knight's desertion and by his wife's and daughter's foolishness, turned out Gertrude and Sindefy to shift for themselves, but having borne his wife as a cross for thirty years, he felt he should continue to do so. Golding, made an alderman's deputy on his first day in the guild, reported that Sir Petronel and Quicksilver had been arrested and the ship attached.

Mistress Touchstone had learned her lesson; but Gertrude, in spite of her mother's entreaties that she beg forgiveness, treated her father with her customary contempt. Sir Petronel and Quicksilver were brought in by a constable, and Quicksilver was charged with the theft of five hundred pounds, a capital offense. A warrant was also sent out for old Security for his share in the business. Sir Petronel and Quicksilver reached a peak of repentance that made them the talk of the prison. Golding and the jailer joined Mistress Touchstone and her daughters in pleading with Touchstone to show mercy to the offenders; but Touchstone was adamant. Finally Golding had himself arrested, sent for Touchstone to come to release him, and arranged for the latter to overhear Quicksilver's ballad of repentance, sung for the edification of other prisoners to the tune of "I Wail in Woe, I Plunge in Pain." Touchstone's heart was moved, and he offered forgiveness to both prodigal son-in-law and prodigal apprentice. Old Security, hearing that a song of repentance had worked such wonders, rushed up howling a lamentable song in a most lamentable voice; he too received mercy. At Golding's urging, Quicksilver agreed to marry Sindefy. Security returned to Winifred. Even Gertrude forgave her erring husband and asked forgiveness from her father. Thus all differences were reconciled.

EBONY AND IVORY

Type of work: Short stories
Author: Llewelyn Powys (1884-1939)
Time: Early twentieth century
Locale: Africa and Europe
First published: 1923

Llewelyn Powys, the youngest of three brothers to achieve literary fame, was a rather gifted and remarkable British writer. He was educated at Cambridge, worked as a stock farmer in Kenya during World War I, and then moved to New York to work as a journalist for five more years. The stories in *Ebony and Ivory*, many of which were published in the best magazines of the time, were written during his stay in Kenya and New York. They present perhaps the best and most representative examples of his outlook and art.

Powys' outlook and art are very closely related. His vision of life informs every aspect of his art, while his art is an attempt to answer that vision. This tension between outlook and art, truth and style, content and form, provides Powys' stories with their intensity and force.

Powys' vision of life, the spirit that informs these stories, was grounded in pain and death, cruelty and mortality, vanity and doom, for Powys was obsessed with agony and fate, which for him were the sole absolutes of life. His stories dwell overwhelmingly on the tragic soul-destroying aspects of life and have much the same spirit as *Ecclesiastes*, the *Rubáiyát of Omar Khayyám*, and much of the fiction of Joseph Conrad. They show an intimate acquaintance with the terror, cruelties, and savagery that plague men. Powys knew the futility and mortality of humanity. This was the lesson he learned in Africa.

In this collection there are the Ebony stories and sketches, which take place in British East Africa, and the Ivory tales, which take place in Europe. The title obviously contains an ironic play on skin color, on black and white, but beyond this fact and far more important is the

reference to the Arab proverb: "On Ebony and Ivory the same dark doom is writ."

The Ebony stories provide the hard core of Powys' vision, for their total effect is that of hopelessness and despair. These sketches show the soul-killing effect of Africa on the European and African alike. The unrelenting sun, the harshness of color and noise, the voraciousness of animal and human life all reduce men to their naked, cruel selves. The European is demoralized and all of his illusions are destroyed. His rule is stripped of its benevolence in Africa and is shown to rest on brutality and cunning. Thus in "Black Parasites" a hardhearted, mediocre farmer sets fire to his brushland after tying up a native sheep thief in the middle of it. In "How It Happens" a sensitive boy arrives in British East Africa from England, and in his harsh, new surroundings he is demoralized by his mediocre associates, gets syphilis, and commits suicide. Powys' theme, the loss of innocence, was almost inevitable, given his outlook on life. In "Black Gods" he declared that the bottom of the well of life contains no hope, that the surface was all, the depth hollow and empty.

When Powys' heroes undergo any change, it is in the direction of shedding illusions, of descending to the bottom of the well of life and facing life without hope. This does not mean that they necessarily give up; Powys' most memorable heroes face life's savagery with a hopeless defiance. In "Dead Matter in Africa" a zebra guards his dead mate against the vultures, against all hope and reason, and against the universe. Again, in his Ebony story, "The Stunner," a dumb brute of a man rises from his deathbed and staggers miles to his sweetheart solely on strength of his love. But this kind of heroism, however admirable, is essentially futile; it means involving oneself in pain, in death, and in tragedy. Although Powys' stories are not Christian in outlook, the figure of the crucified Jesus runs through the majority of them, for Jesus is the epitome of this futile heroism, of this agonized defiance of fate.

As the Arab proverb suggests, Powys' Ivory tales elaborate the ideas and motifs of the Ebony section. In "Threnody," "Death," and "The Brown Satyr," Powys develops the same theme he used in "How It Happens," namely the loss of innocence and the problem of facing a world devoid of hope. In "Not Guilty," "Un Mufle," and "The Wryneck," Powys shows again the impossibility of love in a cursed and savage world devoid of meaning and full of doom.

In quality the Ebony stories seem slightly superior to the Ivory tales simply because Africa provided a more appropriate background for Powys' despairing vision, even though he does a fine job of conveying that vision in the Ivory section as well. For Powys the world was cursed and damned, and it was damned no matter where one was, whether in the heart of Africa or in the heart of civilization. To him it was as if some evil wizard had desolated the world and left it in agony and despair.

Needless to say, such a vision of life could easily become intolerable to the person who possessed it unless he had some means of protecting himself against it, some means of converting it into something productive. Powys' method of achieving release was through writing, through art which gave a tangible form to that vision. Powys sought his salvation through his stories and through observation. If participation in the world meant pain and tragedy, observation was a way of protecting oneself from pain and tragedy, a way of keeping the world at a distance. Art, for Powys, was a way of reshaping life's pain and thereby controlling it. Passive observation and active artistic creation were his way of protecting himself against his vision.

As one might expect, Powys wrote about pain and tragedy in a detached style that was both cool and evocative. Powys possessed a happy feeling for the right word, the precise expression, which contributed greatly to the crisp, cold, clear quality of his writing. This detached mode of writing, which at times approached cruelty, considerably heightened the horror of his tales. If Powys had written with sympathy for his characters the effect would have been reduced and the full power of his vision would not have come through.

Powys was essentially an ironist. His irony was engendered by the conflict between his vision and his art. On the one hand he saw the world as irrevocably damned and on the other he tried to escape this damnation through art; thus he wrote about cruelty, pain, and doom with detachment and reserve. Truth, for Powys, was only to be gained through passive observation. Through truth he hoped to gain a kind of salvation, but the truth proved to be just as ironic as himself. What Powys did gain through passive observation was the ability to transform horror into beauty. His stories possess a cruel, evocative beauty, but his beauty, like his truth, was essentially ironic, frigid and sterile in its revelation.

Powys' failings and virtues as a writer arise from his vision of life and his attempt to cope with that vision. He was a fine writer of short stories and sketches and had a remarkable ability to express himself with clarity, beauty, and force, but he paid for this ability in terms of agony and coldness. His stories are comparable with those of Poe, Bierce, and Hemingway in vividness, beauty, and power. One must be prepared to pay for these things.

THE ECCLESIAZUSAE

Type of work: Drama
Author: Aristophanes (c. 448-c. 385 B.C.)
Type of plot: Utopian comedy
Time of plot: Early fourth century B.C.
Locale: Athens
First presented: 392 B.C.

Principal characters:
PRAXAGORA, leader of the revolution
BLEPYRUS, her husband
CHREMES
A YOUNG MAN
THREE OLD WOMEN

Critique:

The *Ecclesiazusae* is not one of Aristophanes' best plays. Written late in his career, it lacks the wit and ingenuity of *Lysistrata*, the play which it most resembles. The scatological humor seems gratuitous, but the satire on the communistic Utopia enforced by the women of Athens is effective and the action moves swiftly, especially since the role of the chorus has been reduced to practically nothing. Although the play appeared some twenty years before Plato's *Republic*, some critics believe that the playwright is here deriding the philosopher's ideas as they circulated in discussion.

The Story:

Praxagora, who had stolen her husband's clothes and escaped from the house before dawn, was waiting in the street for her fellow conspirators to appear. As they arrived she inspected them to see if they had made all the preparations that had been agreed upon at the feast of the Scirophoria. Had they let the hair under their armpits grow? Had they darkened their complexions by rubbing themselves thoroughly with oil and standing all day in the sun? Had they prepared false beards? Had they stolen their husbands' shoes, cloaks, staffs, and clubs? Assured that they had done everything possible to disguise themselves as men, Praxagora opened the discussion of their plot to save Athens by taking over the government from the men. This was to be achieved by invading the assembly disguised as men and dominating the vote. The first problem was to select a spokesman. When woman after woman failed the practice test by invoking goddesses or addressing the audience in feminine terms, Praxagora herself took on the responsibility of speaking for them. At dawn they departed for the assembly.

Meanwhile, Blepyrus, Praxagora's husband, had awakened with a need to relieve himself, only to find both his wife and his clothes missing. His need was so great, however, that he dressed in his wife's saffron robe and rushed outdoors. Before he could return to the house, he was accosted by his friend Chremes, who gave him a detailed account of the strange proceedings at the assembly. He told how, after several citizens had proposed stupid suggestions for curing the economic plight of the city, a rather fair young man had taken the floor to urge that the government be hereafter entrusted to the women. The speaker had been enthusiastically applauded by a large crowd of strange shoemakers. Chremes himself was rather in favor of the idea, since it was the one and only solution that had hitherto not been tried.

After supervising a secret change back to feminine dress among the women, Praxagora returned to her husband with the excuse that she had been called during the night to aid a friend in labor and

1026

had taken his clothes for greater warmth. When Blepyrus described the decision of the assembly, Praxagora expressed great surprise and delight and immediately launched into a detailed list of the revolutionary reforms she intended to carry out. Every conceivable kind of private property—land, money, food, and even husbands and wives—was to be common to all. All cheating, bribery, and lawsuits would disappear, since no one would have to engage in such activities to achieve what he wanted. Robbery, gambling, and the exchange of money would be abolished. Prostitutes would be outlawed so that decent women could have the first fruits of the young men. Upon Blepyrus's protest that complete sexual freedom would result in chaos, Praxagora established the rule that all the youth would first have to satisfy the prior claims of the aged before mating with other young people and that all children would look upon the oldest people in the community as their parents. Blepyrus, thrilled, looked forward to the prospect of being known as the dictator's husband.

Chremes, also eager to coöperate, began to pack up all his belongings to contribute to the common store, despite the taunts of a skeptical citizen who reminded him that all previous decrees, such as the reduction of the price of salt and the introduction of copper coinage,

had failed. But Chremes insisted that the new reform was thoroughgoing and departed for the common feast, leaving the citizen to devise some scheme whereby he, too, might participate without abandoning all his goods.

The first great test of the new society occurred when a young man, about to enter the house of a voluptuous girl, was stopped by an old woman, a veritable hag, who insisted on her prior claim. The young man tried every conceivable stratagem to avoid relations with the aged flat-nose, but the old woman stubbornly insisted on her legal rights. At first the young man decided to do without sex altogether, rather than yield to the disgusting hag first; but, finding such renunciation impossible, he at last reluctantly submitted. Before the old woman could get him into her house, an even older and uglier hag appeared on the scene to demand her prior right to him. While he quarreled with her, a third and truly horrendous old woman seized him. He was last seen being carried off by two frightful old hags.

Praxagora's maid, returning from the great banquet, met Blepyrus, who had not yet dined, and regaled him with a frenzied account of the delicious viands that were being served there. Taking some young girls with him, Blepyrus hurried off to gorge himself on rich food and drink.

1027

EDMUND CAMPION

Type of work: Novelized biography
Author: Evelyn Waugh (1903-   )
Type of plot: Historical chronicle
Time of plot: Sixteenth century
Locale: Oxford, London, Douai, Rome, Prague
First published: 1935

Principal characters:
EDMUND CAMPION, an English martyr
DR. WILLIAM ALLEN, head of the English College at Douai
ROBERT PERSONS, Campion's classmate at Oxford
GEORGE ELIOT, a priest-hunter

Critique:

This book is an intelligent, sober, and admirably written biography of a man dear to the hearts of Anglo-Saxon Catholics. Evelyn Waugh has written a fine impressionistic portrait of the English martyr after whom Campion Hall at Oxford was named. Waugh warns that intolerance is a growing evil in our modern world, and martyrs may again be forced to die for their faith.

The Story:

Edmund Campion, born in 1540, was one of the most promising young men at Oxford. When Elizabeth visited the university in 1566, she was so impressed by him that she assured him of her patronage. Although there was a strong Protestant group in the university, Oxford then had a population of students who were mostly Catholic in religion, for laws against Catholics were not rigidly enforced. Campion, who as proctor held a responsible position, was suspected of Catholicism, however, and was asked to make a public declaration of his principles by delivering a sermon in a suitable church. He refused, and when his term was over he left for Dublin, where he was warmly received by the Stanihurst family. A university was to be built in Dublin, and he was waiting to accept a post on its faculty. Then rebellion threatened, and all Catholics were ordered arrested. Campion managed to escape

and make his way to Douai and the English College there.

The mild restrictions against Catholics turned into persecution when the Pope issued a Bull of Excommunication against Queen Elizabeth. Because of the fear of a French-Spanish alliance against England, the Bull caused grave anxiety in England and led to reprisals against Catholics. It became illegal to hear mass, to harbor a priest, or openly to profess Catholicism.

With the Catholic bishops imprisoned, thereby preventing the ordination of priests, and with all Catholic schools closed, the faith began to die out in England. The college at Douai sent young English priests into England to preserve the faith of the English Catholics.

Campion went to Douai and became a priest. Then he announced his intention of going to Rome and entering the Society of Jesus. Although Dr. Allen, the venerable head of the college, did not like to lose him to the Jesuits, he made no objection to Campion's plans. Admitted into the Society, Campion was sent to Bohemia, where he held important posts at the University of Prague.

Dr. Allen wrote Campion a letter informing him that he was to go to England. He and a few others, including Robert Persons, who had been an undergraduate at Oxford during the time of Campion's proctorship, were to be smug-

EDMUND CAMPION by Evelyn Waugh. By permission of the author, of Brandt & Brandt, and the publishers, Little, Brown & Co. Copyright, 1946, by Evelyn Waugh.

gled into England, there to carry on the work of the Church. They all realized that capture meant certain death. Campion demanded that Persons be made his superior before the group departed. Though the English government had learned of the group's intentions and had all the ports guarded, the priests succeeded in getting into England.

In disguise, Campion visited the homes of various Catholics, where he said mass and brought the sacraments to the faithful who had been long without them. He wrote his famous *Campion's Brag*, a defense of himself and his Church, which the best minds of the Anglican Church were called upon to answer. Persons wrote his own *Censure* of the Anglican reply. Later Campion wrote his equally famous *Ten Reasons*.

Persecution grew more intense, with Campion the prize the government most hoped to capture. During one of his tours Campion was persuaded to stop at Lyford Grange, the home of Mr. Yate, a well-known Catholic. He stayed there briefly, warning everyone not to tell the neighbors of his presence. After his departure some neighbors heard of his visit and were distressed that they had missed the visit of Father Campion. Father Ford was sent after him and reluctantly Campion returned.

A certain George Eliot, a professional priest-hunter, stopped at Lyford Grange. He was informed by a servant, who presumed Eliot to be Catholic, that Campion was there. He was shown into the room where Campion was saying mass. After receiving communion from Campion, Eliot went to notify the authorities. They came at once, but all evidence of the mass had been destroyed and the priests had been hidden behind a secret panel. The guards found nothing and were preparing to go when one of the searchers happened to tap a hollow-sounding portion of the wall. The priests were discovered in a secret room.

Months of imprisonment followed. Four conferences were held at which Campion and the Anglican clergy disputed points of doctrine. Campion was tortured and finally brought to trial with some other prisoners who were charged with having plotted to murder Queen Elizabeth and with conspiring with foreign powers. But Campion insisted that their only crime was their faith. They were tried by a court that was absolutely biased. Found guilty, they were sentenced to die by hanging, and their bodies to be drawn and quartered. Father Campion and the others went to the scaffold and died the death of martyrs on December first, 1581.

THE EDUCATION OF HENRY ADAMS

Type of work: Novelized autobiography
Author: Henry Adams (1838-1918)
Type of plot: Intellectual and social history
Time of plot: 1838-1905
Locale: America, England, France
First published: 1907

Principal characters:
HENRY ADAMS, an American
CHARLES FRANCIS ADAMS, his father
JOHN HAY, his friend
CLARENCE KING, whom he admired

Critique:

The theme of The Education of Henry Adams is the process of multiplication and acceleration of mechanical forces which, during his own lifetime, led to the breakdown of moral relationships between men and the degeneration of their pursuits into money-seeking or complete lassitude. The book is, too, an excellent autobiography, tracing Adams' thought processes intimately, and on an intellectual plane not generally achieved by most writers. Both for style and content this book ranks with the finest of American autobiographies.

The Story:

Henry Brooks Adams was born of the union of two illustrious Massachusetts families, the Brookses and the Adamses, and he was, in addition, the grandson and the great-grandson of presidents. His wealth and social position should have put him among the leaders of his generation.

Although the period of mechanical invention had begun in 1838, Henry Adams was raised in a colonial atmosphere. He remembered that his first serious encounter with his grandfather, John Quincy Adams, occurred when he refused to go to school, and that gentleman led him there by the hand. For Henry Adams, the death of the former president marked the end of his eighteenth-century environment.

Charles Francis Adams, Henry's father, was instrumental in forming the Free-

Soil party in 1848, and he ran on its ticket with Martin Van Buren. Henry considered that his own education was chiefly a heritage from his father, an inheritance of Puritan morality and interest in politics and literary matters. In later life, looking back on his formal education, he concluded that it had been a failure. Mathematics, French, German, and Spanish were needed in the world in which he found himself an adult, not Latin and Greek. He had opportunity to observe the use of force in the violence with which the people of Boston treated the anti-slavery Wendell Phillips, and he had seen Negro slaves restored to the South.

Prompted by his teacher, James Russell Lowell, he spent nearly two years abroad after his graduation from college. He enrolled to study civil law in Germany, but finding the lecture system atrocious he devoted most of his stay to enjoying the paintings, the opera, the theater in Dresden.

When he returned to Boston in 1860, Henry Adams settled down briefly to read Blackstone. In the elections that year, however, his father became a Congressman, and Henry accompanied him to the capitol as his secretary. There he met John Hay, who was to become his best friend.

In 1861 President Lincoln named Charles Francis Adams Minister to England. Henry went with his father to

THE EDUCATION OF HENRY ADAMS by Henry Adams. By permission of the publishers, Houghton Mifflin Co. Copyright, 1918, by Massachusetts Historical Society. Renewed, 1946, by Charles Francis Adams.

Europe. The Adams party had barely disembarked when they were met by bad news. England had recognized the belligerency of the Confederacy. The North was her undeclared enemy. The battle of Bull Run proved so crushing a blow to American prestige that Charles Francis Adams felt he was in England on a day-to-day sufferance. The Trent Affair and the second battle of Bull Run were equally disastrous abroad. Finally, in 1863, the tide began to turn. Secretary Seward sent Thurlow Weed and William Evarts to woo the English, and they were followed by announcements of victories at Vicksburg and Gettysburg. Charles Francis Adams remained in England until 1868, for Andrew Johnson had too many troubles at home to make many diplomatic changes abroad.

At the end of the war Henry Adams had no means of earning a livelihood. He had, however, developed some taste as a dilletante in art, and several of his articles had been published in the *North American Review*. On his return to America, Henry Adams was impressed by the fact that his fellow-countrymen, because of the mechanical energy they had harnessed, were all traveling in the same direction. Europeans, he had felt, were trying to go in several directions at one time. Handicapped by his education and by his long absence from home, he had difficulty in adapting himself to the new industrial America. He achieved some recognition with his articles on legal tender and his essays in the *Edinburgh Review,* and he hoped that he might be offered a government position if Grant were elected president. But Grant, a man of action, was not interested in reformers or intellectuals like Henry Adams.

In 1869 Adams went back to Quincy to begin his investigation of the scandals of the Grant administration, among them Jay Gould's attempts to obtain a corner on gold, Senator Charles Sumner's efforts to provoke war with England by compelling her cession of Canada to the United States, and the rivalries of Con-

gressmen and Cabinet members.

He decided it would be best to have his article on Gould published in England, to avoid censorship by the powerful financier. Gould's influence was not confined to the United States, however, and Adams was refused by two publications. His essay on Gould was finally published by the *Westminster Review.*

Adams became assistant professor of Medieval History at Harvard and taught at Cambridge for seven years. During that time he tried to abandon the lecture system by replacing it with individual research. He found his students apt and quick to respond, but he felt that he needed a stone against which to sharpen his wits. He gave up his position in 1871 and went west to Estes Park with a Government Geological Survey. There he met Clarence King, a member of the party, with whom he could not help contrasting himself. King had a systematic, scientific education and could have his choice of scientific, political, or literary prizes. Adams felt his own limitations.

After his flight from Harvard he made his permanent home in Washington, where he wrote a series of books on American history. In 1893 he visited the Chicago Exhibition. From his observations of the steamship, the locomotive, and the newly-invented dynamo, he concluded that force was the one unifying factor in American thought. Back in Washington, he saw the gold standard adopted, and concluded that the capitalistic system and American intervention in Cuba offered some signs of the direction in which the country was heading. During another visit to the Exhibition in 1900 Adams formulated an important theory. In observing the dynamo, he decided that history is not merely a series of causes and effects, of men acting upon men, but the record of forces acting upon men. For him, the dynamo became the symbol of force acting upon his own time as the Virgin had been the symbol of force in the twelfth century.

During the next five years Henry Adams saw his friends drop away. Clarence King was the first to go. He lost his fortune in the panic of 1893 and died of tuberculosis in 1901. John Hay, under McKinley, became American Minister to England, and then Secretary of State. He was not well when he accepted the President's appointments, and the enormous task of bringing England, France, and Germany into accord with the United States, and of attempting to keep peace, unsuccessfully, between Russia and Japan, caused his death in 1905.

Adams considered that his education was continuous during his lifetime. He had found the tools which he had been given as a youth utterly useless and he had to spend all of his days forging new ones. As he grew older, he found the moral standards of his father's and grandfather's times disintegrating, so that corruption and greed existed on the highest political levels. According to his calculations, the rate of change, due to mechanical force, was accelerating, and the generation of 1900 could rely only on impersonal forces to teach the generation of 2000. He himself could see no end to the multiplicity of forces which were so rapidly dwarfing mankind into insignificance.

EDWARD THE SECOND

Type of work: Drama
Author: Christopher Marlowe (1564-1593)
Type of plot: Historical chronicle
Time of plot: Fourteenth century
Locale: England and France
First presented: c. 1590

Principal characters:
EDWARD II, King of England
PRINCE EDWARD, his son
EDMUND, Earl of Kent, half-brother to the king
PIERCE DE GAVESTON, Earl of Cornwall
GUY, Earl of Warwick
THOMAS, Earl of Lancaster
LORD MORTIMER, the elder
LORD ROGER MORTIMER, the younger
HUGH SPENCER, Earl of Gloucester
QUEEN ISABELLA, wife of King Edward

Critique:

The Troublesome Reign and Lamentable Death of Edward the Second, the last play written by Marlowe before his untimely death, is a pre-Shakespearian chronicle in its highest form. In fact, the drama had in the past been assigned to Shakespeare himself. Unlike Marlowe's earlier work, this play is polished in form, sustained in theme, and consistent in characterization. Marlowe's first real success in the field of historical drama, Edward the Second sacrifices for a highly dramatic and tragic ending the lyrical beauty of language and metaphor present in his other plays. A further accomplishment to be noted here is Marlowe's use of a large group of dominant characters; in his earlier plays he had employed only two central figures.

The Story:

King Edward II having recalled his favorite from exile, Pierce de Gaveston joyfully returned to England. While hurrying to Westminster to rejoin his monarch, he came upon the king talking to his courtiers. Secretive, he hid from the royal assemblage and overheard the noblemen discussing his repatriation.

Edward, an immature and weak-minded yet stubborn man, nourished for Gaveston an unwholesome and unyielding love, in spite of the fact that Edward's

father had originally banished the man. The noblemen of England, sworn to uphold the decree of exile, hated the royal favorite. Most passionate in his fury was young Mortimer. But others were not far behind Mortimer in lusty dislike, and they threatened the king with revolt if Gaveston were permitted to remain in England. None but the king's brother Edmund would harbor Gaveston.

The fiery discussion ended, the nobles stalked off in haughty displeasure. Gaveston, still in hiding, rejoiced in his knowledge of the king's love, for Edward revealed his pettiness by his unconcern for the welfare of his kingdom as weighed against his desire to clasp Gaveston to his bosom once more. When Gaveston revealed his presence, Edward ecstatically rewarded him with a series of titles and honors, the scope of which caused even Edmund to comment wryly that Edward had outdone himself. Gaveston smirkingly claimed that all he desired was to be near his monarch. To add further salt to the kingdom's wounds, Edward sentenced the Bishop of Coventry, the instigator of Gaveston's exile, to die in the Tower of London.

This action, coupled with the titles and estates lavishly bestowed upon Gaveston, so incensed the rebellious nobility that

1033

under the leadership of the two Mortimers, Warwick, and Lancaster, they plotted to kill the favorite. The Archbishop of Canterbury, protesting the damage inflicted upon the Church by the king's folly, allied himself with the plot. Queen Isabella, who professed to love her lord dearly, complained to the noblemen that since Gaveston's return Edward had snubbed her beyond endurance. She agreed that Gaveston must be done away with, but she cautioned the angry noblemen not to injure Edward.

When the rebellious nobility seized Gaveston, Edward, yielding to the archbishop's threat to enforce his papal powers against the king, could do nothing but stand by and allow his beloved friend to be carried off. A bitter exchange of words between the king and his lords was tempered by the gentle sentiments of Gaveston as he bade Edward farewell. Driven by childish anger, perhaps incensed by an intuitive knowledge, Gaveston attacked the queen and accused her of a clandestine association with the younger Mortimer, a charge which she denied. Sensing his advantage, Edward seized upon the accusation as a wedge to undermine his enemies, and he compelled the queen to use her influence to save Gaveston. The queen, because of her love for Edward and her hopes for a reconciliation, resolved to mend the rift by abetting her husband.

At first the nobles disdainfully refused to hear her entreaties. Then, having prevailed upon young Mortimer's sympathy, she disclosed to him a plot whereby Gaveston could be overthrown and the king obeyed at the same time. Mortimer then convinced the other nobles that if Gaveston were allowed to remain in England, he would become so unpopular that the common people would rise in protest and kill him.

There was peace in England once more. Edward affected renewed love for his queen and the lords humbly repledged their fealty to Edward. An undercurrent of meanness prevailed, however, in the bosom of young Mortimer, whose sense of justice was outraged at the fact that Edward had chosen such a baseborn villain as his minion. He still believed that it would be a service to his king and country to unseat Gaveston, and thus he plotted secretly.

But at the ceremonial in honor of Gaveston's return the lords could not stomach the presence of the king's minion. Bitter sarcasm was showered upon Gaveston and young Mortimer tried to stab him. So outraged was Edward at this show of independence by his peers that he vowed vengeance for his dear Gaveston's sake. Even the loyal Edmund could not brook this display on the part of his brother; he deserted Edward to join the nobles.

Edward renewed the smoldering accusation against Isabella that she was Mortimer's lover. Defeated in battle, the king's forces, with Gaveston in flight, were split up to confuse the enemy. Warwick, Lancaster, and others succeeded in capturing the king's minion and ordered his death, but Arundel, a messenger from Edward, pleaded that Gaveston be allowed to say farewell to the king. One of the nobles, unable to scorn the king's wishes, arranged to escort Gaveston to Edward. With a servant in charge, Gaveston was conducted to a hiding place to spend the night. Warwick, driven by blind hatred and an irrational patriotism, kidnaped the prisoner.

Meanwhile Valois, King of France and Isabella's brother, had taken advantage of the revolt in England and had seized Normandy. Edward, displaying the corruption of his statesmanship, dispatched his son Prince Edward and Isabella to negotiate a parley with Valois. Arundel, meanwhile, reported to Edward that Warwick had beheaded Gaveston. Edward, in a wild rage against his lords, swore to sack their lands and destroy their families. Characteristically, having lost his beloved friend, he declared that henceforth young Spencer would be his favorite. He continued to resist the rebels, and before long Warwick, Lancaster, and Edmund were captured and sentenced to death.

In France, the Earl of Gloucester suspected that Isabella was gathering forces to place her son upon the throne. Isabella, in the meantime, had been rejected by Valois. Sir John of Hainault rescued the queen and prince by offering to keep the pair at his estate in Flanders until Edward had matured sufficiently to rule England. The young prince was already showing signs of royal character and a depth and magnitude of personality which promised to make him a suitable monarch.

The condemned Mortimer and Edmund escaped to France, where Sir John agreed to help them in levying forces to aid Isabella and the prince. Landing at Harwich, the forces of Mortimer and Edmund routed the king, who fled toward Ireland. Stalwart, sincere, and intellectually honest, Edmund, who had broken with his brother only after the king had driven him too far, relented in his feelings against Edward; he was further disturbed by a suspicion that Isabella was in love with Mortimer. Mortimer became a despot in his triumph. Edward was captured and sent to Kenilworth Castle, a prisoner. There he was prevailed upon to surrender his crown to the prince.

With the queen's consent Mortimer outlined a crafty scheme to kill Edward. He drew up an ambiguous note which ordered the king's death in one sense and abjured it in another. When Prince Edward, Isabella, Edmund, and Mortimer argued fiercely to decide upon the prince's protector, the prince revealed his distrust for Mortimer. Edmund, fearing greater disunion, resolved to rescue the imprisoned king. His attempt failed.

Prince Edward was crowned by the Archbishop of Canterbury. Shortly after the coronation the deposed Edward, tortured cruelly in a dungeon, was murdered by Mortimer's hireling. Edmund was beheaded. Thereupon Edward III, now monarch in his own right, ordered Mortimer to be hanged and Isabella, who was suspected of being the nobleman's accomplice in plotting her husband's death, to be taken to the Tower of London.

EFFI BRIEST

Type of work: Novel
Author: Theodor Fontane (1819-1898)
Type of plot: Domestic tragedy
Time of plot: Second half of the nineteenth century
Locale: Germany, Prussia
First published: 1895

Principal characters:
EFFI VON BRIEST, only child of the Briest family
FRAU VON BRIEST, her mother
RITTERSCHAFTSRAT VON BRIEST, her father
BARON VON INNSTETTEN, Effi's husband, a government official in Kessin
ANNIE, Effi's daughter
MAJOR VON CRAMPAS, District Commander in Kessin
ROSWITHA, Effi's maid

Critique:

Although he had been a writer for most of his life—poet, journalist, historian—Fontane did not begin to write fiction until he had gained a thorough knowledge of Prussian society. He was sixty when he completed his first novel, seventy-five when he wrote *Effi Briest.* His main subject was the human being entangled in a net of strict rules and principles of a society which felt secure in a Prussia stabilized by the "Iron Chancellor," Bismarck. Fontane did not raise a warning pedagogical finger when he described the merciless destruction of human happiness by the rigid rules of that society. He merely introduced his characters and left judgment to his readers. When, after the tragic death of Effi Briest, Effi's mother asks whether they might have done something wrong, the father waves the question aside because it is useless to discuss it. Fontane initiated in Germany the modern realistic novel, and in describing him the term "psychological novel" appears for the first time in German literature. The tragic tale of Effi Briest remains a perennial reprint favorite of German publishers.

The Story:

Effi Briest was sixteen years old when her mother cheerfully announced that Baron von Innstetten had asked for her hand in marriage. Effi had seen Innstetten only once, but she knew he had vainly tried to marry her mother years before. When Baron von Innstetten was absent for a long period, her mother had married Effi's father; at the time a match with Ritterschaftsrat von Briest had seemed too good an opportunity to forego. Innstetten was now a government official with a promising future.

Half an hour before, Effi had been sitting on a swing enjoying a happy childhood. Suddenly she was a bride to be. The situation seemed to her a new and welcome experience. In a few weeks she would be the wife of an important government official.

After the excitement of preparations, the wedding, and a honeymoon trip to Italy, the couple arrived in Kessin, a small town on the Baltic Sea. At first the completely new surroundings were interesting for Effi, but soon she felt ill at ease in the house. It was a strange house, formerly owned by a seafaring captain; his relics and souvenirs gave the place a bizarre character. A stuffed shark, stories about the captain's mysterious Chinese servant, and a mentally ill maidservant, who sat in the kitchen with a black chicken on her shoulder, brought nightmares to Effi, and she claimed that she heard noises in an unoccupied upstairs room. Considerate toward his young wife, Innstetten never failed to show his devotion, but being a practical-minded man, he paid no attention to Effi's tales of supernatural happenings in the house. He was convinced that his wife's childish imagination would soon return to normal. The obligatory social visits to the local aristocracy revealed to Effi that she would not have friends in their circle. At first her only friend was the town apothecary. Her second friend was Roswitha, her maid, whom she met in the graveyard where the girl was bemoaning the loss of her former mistress. Effi was pregnant and needed a maid. Learning that Roswitha was Catholic, she was convinced Roswitha's faith would conquer the ghostlike noises in the house. Roswitha never heard ghosts and her straightforward manner was a relief from the formal stiffness of Effi's social world. The birth of a daughter, Annie, gave Effi new activities, but her boredom with Kessin continued.

The new military commander in Kessin, Major von Crampas, was another addition to Effi's social world. The major's carefree behavior and witty conversation were quite a contrast to the well-disciplined and formal Innstetten, but both men respected each other and became friends. Visits to the Innstetten home, horseback riding along the seashore, and participation in community plays brought Effi and Crampas closer together. Effi, realizing the danger of this situation, made efforts to avoid him. During a sleighride Crampas overstepped the boundaries of their friendship.

One day Innstetten informed Effi that he had been promoted to a new post in a Berlin Ministry, a position which would take them to Berlin. Effi was happy to leave the strange house, the boring people, and above all to be separated from Crampas, for their relationship, although a well-kept secret, burdened her conscience increasingly. Innstetten, seeing Effi's great joy when he told her about the transfer to Berlin, felt guilty for not having considered leaving the disliked house sooner.

In Berlin, Innstetten made a special effort to have a cheerful house and an enjoyable social life. Though Innstetten's duties at the Ministry kept them from spending much time together, the years in Berlin were happy ones until Effi went to the Rhine country for recuperation after an illness. Meanwhile, Innstetten and Annie remained in Berlin. One day Annie fell on a stairway and cut her forehead, and Roswitha searched through Effi's belongings to find a bandage. Innstetten, trying to restore order in Effi's room, found a bundle of love letters from Crampas, written six years before. Innstetten did what he considered his duty regardless of his personal feelings: he called a friend to make the necessary arrangements for a duel with Crampas. Although his friend pointed out that the letters were more than six years old, Innstetten, who would have preferred to pardon Effi, decided to go through with the duel because he felt that the insult to his honor had not been diminished by time. In the duel, fought near Kessin, Crampas was shot fatally.

At the time Effi was still in the Rhine country waiting for Innstetten's letters, which used to arrive punctually every day. Instead, a letter from her mother informed her of the duel and of pending divorce. Annie was put in the custody of Innstetten. The Briest family was willing to assist Effi financially, but her conduct had made it impossible for her to return home. Heartbroken, she went back to Berlin and lived in a small apartment. As quickly as she had changed years ago from a child into a woman, she now became a social outcast. Only Roswitha remained faithful to her.

Effi's health declined rapidly. Once she accidentally saw Annie leaving school, but she avoided meeting the child. Finally, moved by a desire to see her daughter again, Effi asked for permission legally to have Annie visit her. When Annie arrived at the apartment, however, she gave only well-rehearsed and evasive answers. Discouraged, Effi sent the child home without the hope of seeing her again. Soon after this incident Effi's health became extremely poor and the family doctor reported her condition to her parents, hinting that their continued rejection could mean her death. Her health improved when she was finally permitted to return home. Aside from her parents and the local minister, however, there was nobody for Effi to speak to. Roswitha, concerned for her mistress' loneliness, wrote to Innstetten asking him to give Effi the family dog. Innstetten was glad to fulfill her desire. His career in the Ministry had been extremely successful, but no promotion would lessen the pain in his heart; he still loved his former wife.

After a beautiful summer at her parents' home, Effi died. In her last conversation with her mother she asked Frau von Briest to tell Innstetten that he had done the only correct thing possible for him. She wanted to die as Effi Briest, for she had not honored her married name.

EGMONT

Type of work: Drama
Author: Johann Wolfgang von Goethe (1749-1832)
Type of plot: Romantic tragedy
Time of plot: Sixteenth century
Locale: Brussels
First presented: 1788

Principal characters:
COUNT EGMONT, Lord of Gaure
CLÄRCHEN, his beloved
BRACKENBURG, a citizen in love with Clärchen
THE DUKE OF ALVA, emissary of Philip II
MARGARET OF PARMA, Regent of The Netherlands
WILLIAM, Prince of Orange

Critique:

This tragic account of the martyrdom of Egmont has remained constantly in favor, partly because of Beethoven's musical setting. Here Goethe has taken for his theme the undying love for liberty of oppressed peoples everywhere, and for his plot an episode in the struggle of The Netherlands to throw off Spanish rule. Egmont is warmly depicted as a brave and generous man, but the other characters are less fully developed. The action of the play is designed to bring out the theme of liberty, and in that design it succeeds admirably.

The Story:

The people of The Netherlands were unhappy in the state of their homeland. Philip II of Spain was tightening his absolute control of the Lowlands, particularly in religious matters, for Philip was the main instrument of the Inquisition. Recently a new regent had been appointed to administer his rule. The populace had hoped the office would go to Count Egmont, who, after his defeat of the French at Gravelines, had become a national hero. Besides, although Egmont was a Catholic, he treated the Protestants with kindness, and he had even gone to Madrid to plead with Philip to lessen the strictures of Catholic repression.

The king, however, had given the office to Margaret, his half-sister. She, like Philip, tolerated no dissidence from the established church, yet by firmness and tact she had pacified the sturdy burghers who stubbornly resisted any laws but their own. She had even managed to conciliate Egmont and William of Orange, so that outwardly at least there was harmony among the nobility.

Margaret summoned Machiavel, her secretary, to hear his account of new uprisings. He told her how throughout Flanders mobs were breaking into cathedrals and despoiling the monuments of the hated foreign religion. He counseled Margaret to be firm but not cruel toward the Protestants. Margaret told him that her efforts toward conciliation would mean little, for it was rumored that the cruel Duke of Alva was on his way to assume control of the provinces. Machiavel reminded her that as regent she would hold the final power, but Margaret was wise in the ways of kings. Officially or not, Alva would rule The Netherlands, and she could hope to circumvent him only by appealing directly to her brother. She was especially fearful of what might happen to Egmont and William of Orange, and the effects of Alva's harsh rule on the people.

Meanwhile, in her humble house, Clärchen was happily singing; that night Egmont would come to her. Brackenburg watched her anxiously, for he loved her and he was certain that no good would come of that love affair between a count and a commoner. When Clärchen, looking from her windows, saw a mob in the street, she asked Brackenburg to learn the cause of the disturbance. During his absence her mother reproached Clärchen bitterly for rejecting Brackenburg's suit. Even now, the mother declared, the burgher would be glad to marry Clärchen. Brackenburg returned to tell them the people had heard of the outbreaks in Flanders, and were heartened by that uprising against their oppressors.

A group of commoners argued about their rights as citizens. One, who could read, told them of their rights under the constitution and of their forefathers' vigilance in protecting their privileges. Egmont, arriving on the scene, advised them to be moderate in their talk but to preserve their ancient liberties. After he left, a keen observer remarked that Egmont's head would make a dainty morsel for the headsman.

In his residence Egmont attended to duties of state. One of his letters came from Count Oliva, his old preceptor, who counseled him to be more circumspect in his behavior and less free in his talk. Egmont threw the letter aside, remarking that every one was different; he himself believed in doing what was right without fear or favor. Let others play the part of fawning courtier.

William of Orange arrived to talk over the coming of Alva. William was in favor of caution; they would do nothing until they knew what Alva had been sent to accomplish. Egmont reminded him that they were both Knights of the Golden Fleece. As members of that order they could not be punished except through a trial by their peers. Prince William was inclined to place little trust in their rights, however, for Philip was a determined and ruthless ruler. William declared that he himself would remain on his own estate and refuse to meet the Duke of Alva. Egmont, on the other hand, decided to speak his mind freely. If he had to be a rebel, he would openly do his best to advance the welfare of The Netherlands.

Margaret, in the meantime, had received a dispatch from Philip. The letter was gentle and considerate in tone, a fact ominous in itself. The king informed her officially of Alva's mission and told in detail of the formidable army the duke was bringing to garrison the recalcitrant towns. Margaret knew that her authority as regent had been superseded.

In the evening Clärchen received Egmont with joy. For a time Egmont was remote in his conduct, even keeping on his mantle. Then he showed her that he was wearing his full uniform, decorated with the emblem of the Golden Fleece, and said that he had come thus attired because she had asked him to do so as a favor. Clärchen, particularly impressed by the decoration of the Golden Fleece, was touched by that evidence of his regard.

The inhabitants of the town grew fearful. Alva's soldiers had been stationed at every strategic point and his spies were everywhere, so that the citizens dared not congregate to discuss their new woes. The ordinary people were afraid for Egmont; it was rumored that he would be killed.

In his palace Alva had made his plans, with his trusted guards forming so tight a cordon around the residence that no one could get in or out. To his natural son Ferdinand he announced his intentions. He was expecting Egmont and William of Orange. At the end of the audience, Alva would detain Egmont on a pretext. Prince William would be arrested outside. As soon as he was safely in custody, Ferdinand, acting as the duke's messenger, was to return to the reception chamber. His arrival would be the signal to arrest Egmont. Ferdinand, uneasy over the success of the plot, was nevertheless flattered by the part he was to play.

William of Orange was too cautious to fall into the duke's trap, however, and he stayed away from the audience. Egmont, who knew no fear, went without hesitation and discussed at great length the troubled situation in The Netherlands. He was a skillful debater. At every point he upheld the dignity of the burghers and wisely counseled patience and tact in dealing with them. At last Alva became impatient and abruptly ordered his arrest. He read a document in which Philip decreed Egmont had been tried and found guilty of treason. Because the King of Spain did not acknowledge the authority of the Knight of the Golden Fleece, Egmont failed in his demand for immunity.

Clärchen was distraught when she heard of Egmont's arrest. Accompanied by faithful Brackenburg, she wandered about the town in an attempt to incite the citizens to rescue Egmont. But Alva had done his work well; the burghers were all afraid even to discuss the matter. Returning to the house, Clärchen thought of the vial of poison that Brackenburg had once shown her when he was discorsolate. Thinking to quiet her temporarily, he gave her the vial. Clärchen immediately drank the poison and left the room to die.

Meanwhile, in the palace prison, Egmont had been wakeful. When he finally dozed off he was wakened by Ferdinand and Silva. The latter read Egmont's sentence; he was to be executed publicly in the market place as a warning to the people. Silva left, but Ferdinand remained behind to condole with the count. Although he had had a part in the plot, he really sympathized with Egmont.

When Egmont slept again, a vision appeared. Freedom was reclining on a cloud. Her features were those of Clärchen. She held above his head a wreath of victory. Egmont awoke at dawn to strains of martial music. The guards were at his door.

THE EGOIST

Type of work: Novel
Author: George Meredith (1828-1909)
Type of plot: Social satire
Time of plot: Nineteenth century
Locale: England
First published: 1879

Principal characters:
SIR WILLOUGHBY PATTERNE, the egoist
VERNON WHITFORD, his cousin
COLONEL DE CRAYE, his relative
LAETITIA DALE, a neighbor
CLARA MIDDLETON, Sir Willoughby's betrothed
DOCTOR MIDDLETON, her father
CROSSJAY PATTERNE, Sir Willoughby's distant kinsman

Critique:

The Egoist creates a fantastic world where, in scenes of subtle comedy, the characters are treated realistically. The effect is one of drollery. Each character is a symbol of some virtue or vice rather than a living individual. All the characters speak alike, and they speak the language of Meredith. This novel stands apart from Meredith's other novels, 'distinguished as it is by its originality of technique and purpose. It is, to use Meredith's own term, "a comedy in narrative."

The Story:

On the day of his majority Sir Willoughby Patterne announced his engagement to Miss Constantia Durham. Laetitia Dale, who lived with her old father in a cottage on Willoughby's estate, bore her love for him—she thought—secretly, but everyone, including Willoughby himself, knew about it. Ten days before the wedding day Constantia astonished her betrothed by eloping with Harry Oxford, a military man. For a few weeks after that, the proud Willoughby courted Laetitia while the neighborhood gossiped about the poor girl's chances to become his wife. There was great disappointment when he suddenly decided to go abroad for three years. On his return to his estate he brought with him his cousin, Vernon Whitford, as an adviser in the management of his properties, and a young distant kinsman named Crossjay Patterne.

At first Laetitia, the faithful, was overjoyed at Willoughby's return, but soon she saw that again she was to lose him, for he became engaged to Clara Middleton, the daughter of a learned doctor. Middleton and his daughter came to Willoughby's estate to visit for a few weeks. It might have been the controversy over Crossjay or even the existence of Laetitia that caused Clara to see Willoughby for what he really was. In spite of Willoughby's objections, Vernon wanted Crossjay to enter the Marines and the young man was sent to Laetitia to be tutored for his examination. Vernon, a literary man, wanted to go to London, but Willoughby overruled him. Noting Willoughby's self-centered attitude toward Crossjay, his complete and selfish concern with matters affecting himself and his attempt to dominate her own mind, Clara began to feel trapped by her betrothal. She reflected that Constantia had escaped by finding a gallant Harry Oxford to take her away, but she sorrowfully realized that she had no one to rescue her.

When Clara attempted to break her engagement, she found Willoughby intractable and her father too engrossed in his studies to be disturbed. Meanwhile, Willoughby had picked Laetitia Dale as Vernon's wife. This was Willoughby's

1042

plan to keep near him both his cousin and the woman who fed his ego with her devotion. Vernon could retire to one of the cottages on the estate and write and study. Asked by Willoughby to aid him in his plan, Clara took the opportunity to ask Vernon's advice on her own problem. He assured her that she must move subtly and slowly.

In desperation, she persuaded Doctor Middleton to agree to take a trip to France with her for a few weeks. From such a trip she hoped never to return to Willoughby. But this wary lover introduced Dr. Middleton to his favorite brand of claret. Two bottles of the wine put the doctor in such an amiable mood that when Clara asked him if he were ready to go to London with her, he told her that the thought was preposterous. Willoughby had won the first round.

Colonel De Craye arrived to be best man at the wedding. Little by little he sensed that Clara was not happy at the prospect of her approaching marriage. In desperation Clara resorted to other means of escape. She wrote to her friend Lucy Darleton in town and received from that young lady an invitation to visit her in London.

Clara gave Crossjay the privilege of accompanying her to the train station. A hue and cry was raised at her absence from the estate, and Vernon, accidentally discovering her destination, followed her to the station and urged her to come back. Only because she believed that her behavior might cause an injury to Crossjay's future did Clara return to her prison. If she were to leave now, Willoughby would have full control of the young boy, for Vernon was soon to go to London to follow his writing career.

Complications resulted from Clara's attempted escape. At the station Vernon had had her drink some brandy to overcome the effects of the rainy weather. The neighborhood began to gossip. Willoughby confronted Crossjay, who told him the truth about Clara's escape. Clara hoped that Willoughby would release her because of the gossip, but he refused. Doctor Middleton seemed ignorant of what was happening. He was determined that his daughter should fulfill her pledge to marry Sir Willoughby. Furthermore, he liked Willoughby's vintage wines and Willoughby's estate.

By this time the Egoist knew that his marriage to Clara would not take place. He decided upon the one move that would soothe his wounded vanity—he asked Laetitia to become his wife. She refused, declaring she no longer loved him.

Colonel De Craye shrewdly surmised what had happened. He told Clara the hopeful news. Clara felt that her only remaining obstacle was her father's insistence that she must not break her promise to Willoughby. Now she could show that Willoughby had broken his promise first by proposing to Laetitia while he was still pledged to Clara.

Willoughby's world blew up in his face. Dr. Middleton announced firmly that Clara need not marry Willoughby. He had decided that he admired Vernon's scholarship more than he liked Willoughby's wines. But the twice-jilted lover had other plans for his own protection. He must even the score. If he could get Clara to consent to marry Vernon, he felt there would be some measure of recompense for himself, for such a marriage would have the ironic touch to satisfy Willoughby. But Clara told him it was already her intention to wed Vernon as soon as her engagement to Willoughby could be broken. The Egoist's selfishness and arrogance had brought them together.

The Egoist was defeated. He went straight to Laetitia, offering her his hand without love. He was willing for her to marry him only for money. Laetitia accepted on the condition that Crossjay be permitted to enter the Marines. Clara and the doctor planned to leave for Europe. Vernon arranged to meet them in the Swiss Alps, where he and Clara would marry.

ELECTIVE AFFINITIES

Type of work: Novel
Author: Johann Wolfgang von Goethe (1749-1832)
Type of plot: Philosophical romance
Time of plot: Eighteenth century
Locale: Germany
First published: 1808

> Principal characters:
> EDWARD, a wealthy nobleman
> CHARLOTTE, his wife
> OTTILIE, Charlotte's protégée
> THE CAPTAIN, Edward's friend
> LUCIANA, Charlotte's daughter by a previous marriage
> NANNY, a youngster, Ottilie's protégée
> HERR MITTLER, a self-appointed marriage counselor

Critique:

Although written late in the author's career, *Elective Affinities (Die Wahlverwandtschaften)* illustrates some of the romantic tendencies usually found in Goethe's earlier works. The emotionalism of Edward, the quasi-scientific theme, and the poetically fitting (if unrealistic) deaths are examples of the romantic elements. At the same time, it is only fair to classify the novel as a philosophical piece of fiction. The human relationships (both the actual and the symbolic), the passages discussing education and pedagogical techniques, and the comments found in the passages taken from Ottilie's fictional diary all contribute to the philosophical effect. *Elective Affinities* is a novel in which psychological actions and reactions are important, while of physical action there is so little that one can almost say there is none, just as there is almost no plot as ordinarily defined.

The Story:

Edward, a wealthy nobleman, had long been in love with Charlotte, but each had been forced to wed someone else. Both their first spouses died before many years elapsed, and soon afterward Edward and Charlotte were married. With Charlotte's daughter Luciana placed in a good school, the pair, happily married at last, settled down to an idyllic existence at Edward's rural castle. They spent their time working at pleasant tasks about the castle and its park, leading together the kind of life they had long dreamed about and hoped for.

But one day a letter came to threaten the happy couple. The Captain, long a friend of Edward, was out of a position. Edward immediately suggested that his friend be invited to the castle, where he could help in improving the grounds and buildings. At first Charlotte withheld her consent, but finally she agreed to her husband's earnest desire. She revealed that she, too, had thought of inviting someone to the castle, the daughter of a dead friend. Charlotte had taken the girl, Ottilie, as her protégée because of her friendship for the girl's mother. Ottilie, who was at school with Luciana, was not immediately invited for the visit Charlotte planned.

When the Captain arrived, as he did shortly, his presence soon made marked differences in the household. In order that he and Edward might work together undisturbed and with greater convenience, Edward moved from the wing in which Charlotte's rooms were located to the wing in which the Captain had been placed; and Charlotte saw less and less of her husband. One evening the three read about the elective affinities of chemical elements and fell to speculating on how people were also attracted to one another in different combinations and in varying degrees. The invitation to Ottilie

1044

was again discussed. Since the girl was not doing well in school, and because Charlotte obviously needed additional companionship, Ottilie was immediately sent for.

When Edward had seen the girl and been in her company on previous occasions, Ottilie had made no impression on him. Seeing her in the same household, however, he soon became aware of her attractiveness. It became obvious, too, that Ottilie found Edward attractive. The two fitted together strangely well. When they played duets, Ottilie's very mistakes coincided with Edward's. Gradually, as the two spent more and more time together, Charlotte and the Captain often found themselves together, too, much to their delight. After some weeks had passed, Edward realized the extent of his passion and his influence on Ottilie, all of which made him rejoice. Recognizing the force of his passion, he made efforts to cause it to grow, as it did steadily and swiftly. Although Charlotte noticed the attentions he paid the girl, she refused to become upset by them; since she had discovered her own regard for the Captain, she could more easily overlook her husband's behavior.

One day, while Charlotte and the Captain were out boating, their passion for each other could no longer be concealed. Being mature people, however, they immediately controlled their emotions and resolved, after a few kisses, to adhere strictly to the moral path in their conduct. Also, during one of their periods together, Ottilie and Edward discovered their love for each other. Being more easily swayed and emotionally immature, they welcomed the passion and did not try to curb their emotions.

While the relationships among the four were developing, more guests came to the castle. They were a countess and a baron who were spending a vacation as lover and mistress while away from their respective spouses. On the night of their arrival, Edward showed the baron the way to the countess' rooms, that the lovers might be together. While wishing he could enter Ottilie's room with· the same freedom as the baron had entered that of his mistress, Edward found himself at his wife's door. He knocked and was admitted. He remained the night with Charlotte, but when he and his wife embraced they did not think of each other, but of Ottilie and the Captain.

The four people had all been working on plans for improving the grounds of the castle, with the hope, especially on Edward's part, that everything might be finished in time for Ottilie's birthday. On the day of the birthday celebration Edward made a public spectacle of himself, proving almost a fool in his ardor for Ottilie. Finally, Charlotte suggested that Ottilie be returned to school or sent to live with other friends. Edward, angry and frustrated in his love, left the castle. When he left he vowed he would have nothing more to do with Ottilie, as Charlotte wished, so long as the girl remained. On the same day the Captain, who had received a position which promoted him to the rank of major, also left the castle.

Shortly after Edward's departure, Charlotte, discovering that she was pregnant as the result of the night her husband had spent in her apartments, called on the services of Herr Mittler, a volunteer marriage counselor. But Herr Mittler was unable even to begin a reconciliation with Edward, whose passion for Ottilie had conquered him completely. Having been accustomed all his life to doing as he pleased, Edward could not see why he should not have his way in this matter. When war broke out, he entered the king's service. He served gallantly and won many honors. He believed that if he lived through the war he was fated to have Ottilie.

Charlotte, meanwhile, endured her pregnancy, but she and Ottilie were no longer so close to each other, for the younger woman had become suspicious of Charlotte. For a time life at the castle was enlivened when Luciana arrived for

1045

a visit with a large party of her friends. During the entertainment of the visit, Luciana pointedly left Ottilie out of the activities arranged for the guests.

Ottilie's friend during the trying weeks after Edward had gone was a young architect hired to supervise the building of a summerhouse. His work completed, Charlotte had kept him on to redecorate the local church. The young man admired Ottilie very much. A young schoolmaster who had taught Ottilie also expressed interest in marrying the girl, but Ottilie could think only of Edward.

At last a son was born to Charlotte. At the christening Ottilie and Herr Mittler, who stood as sponsors for the baby, were surprised to note how much the infant resembled both Ottilie and the Captain, a resemblance soon noted by others. Charlotte, remembering how she had dreamed of the Captain while embracing her husband, guessed that Edward had been dreaming at the same time of Ottilie. In a sense the child, named Otto, was a symbol of the parents' double adultery.

Edward returned to a nearby farm when the war ended. Meeting the Captain, he made a proposal to solve everyone's problems. He suggested that he and Charlotte be divorced, so that he could marry Ottilie and Charlotte could marry the Captain. Although the ethics of the plan did not appeal to him, the Captain agreed to take the suggestion to Charlotte. When the Captain set out for the castle, Edward also visited the grounds in hopes of seeing Ottilie. They met, and Ottilie was much upset, so much so that while returning to the castle alone in a small boat she dropped Charlotte's baby overboard. The child was drowned. When the Captain arrived at the castle, Charlotte showed him the little corpse that was a miniature of himself.

Ottilie decided to go away. Edward, meeting her at an inn, persuaded her to return to the castle with him. There the four—Edward, Charlotte, Ottilie, and the Captain—tried to resume the happy life they had known before. But Ottilie seldom spoke and ate her meals in her rooms. One day she died suddenly, having starved herself to death. It came out that Nanny, her little protégée, had been persuaded to eat the food intended for Ottilie. Edward also began a fast. When he died a short time later, although not as the result of his fasting, he was laid in a tomb beside the girl he had loved. In death for one, in life for the other, the two couples were finally united.

ELECTRA

Type of work: Drama
Author: Euripides (480-406 B.C.)
Type of plot: Classical tragedy
Time of plot: After the fall of Troy
Locale: Argos
First presented: c. 413 B.C.

Principal characters:
ELECTRA, daughter of Agamemnon
ORESTES, her brother
CLYTEMNESTRA, her mother
AEGISTHUS, lover of Clytemnestra

Critique:

The Electra of Euripides is a psychological study of a woman's all-consuming hatred for her mother and stepfather on the one hand, and love for her murdered father and exiled brother on the other. The character of Electra clearly dominates the action, for it is she who spurs her brother on to kill those whom she hates. In Electra, her brother, and her mother, Euripides created three characters who are as alive today as they were on the Athenian stage.

The Story:

After Agamemnon, King of Argos, had returned home from the Trojan War, his wife, Clytemnestra, and her lover, Aegisthus, murdered him in cold blood during the home-coming banquet. Afterward Aegisthus and Clytemnestra were married, and Aegisthus became king. Orestes, young son of Agamemnon, was sent by a relative to Phocis before Aegisthus could destroy him. Electra, the daughter, remained, but was given in marriage to an old peasant, lest she marry a warrior powerful enough to avenge her father's death.

One day, after Electra and the peasant had gone out to do the day's work, Orestes came in disguise with his best friend, Pylades, to the farm to seek Electra. They heard her singing a lament for her lot and for the death of her father. A messenger interrupted her lament with word that a festival would be held in honor of the Goddess Hera and that all Argive maidens were to attend. Electra

said she preferred to remain on the farm away from the pitying eyes of the people of Argos. The messenger advised her to pay honor to the gods and to ask their help.

Electra mistook Orestes and Pylades for friends of her brother and told them the story of her grief. She urged that Orestes avenge the death of Agamemnon and the ill treatment of himself and Electra. Aegisthus, meanwhile, had offered a reward for the death of Orestes.

The peasant returned from his work and asked Orestes and Pylades to remain as his guests. Electra sent her husband to bring the relative who had taken Orestes away from Argos. On his way to the peasant's cottage, the old foster father noticed that a sacrifice had been made at the tomb of Agamemnon and that there were some red hairs on the grave. He suggested to Electra that Orestes might be in the vicinity, but Electra answered that there was no chance of his being in Argos. When Orestes came out of the cottage, the old man recognized a scar on his forehead; thus brother and sister were made known to each other.

At the advice of the old peasant, Orestes planned to attend a sacrificial feast over which Aegisthus would preside. Electra sent her husband to tell Clytemnestra that she had given birth to a baby. Electra and Orestes invoked the aid of the gods in their venture to avenge the death of their father.

Orestes and Pylades were hailed by

1047

Aegisthus as they passed him in his garden. The pair told Aegisthus that they were from Thessaly and were on their way to sacrifice to Zeus. Aegisthus informed them that he was preparing to sacrifice to the nymphs and invited them to tarry. At the sacrifice of a calf, Orestes plunged a cleaver into Aegisthus' back while Aegisthus was examining the entrails of the beast. Orestes then revealed his identity to the servants, who cheered the son of their former master. Orestes carried the corpse of Aegisthus back to the cottage where it was hidden after Electra had reviled it.

At the sight of Clytemnestra approaching the peasant's hut, Orestes had misgivings about the plan to murder her. He felt that matricide would bring the wrath of the gods upon his head. But Electra, determined to complete the revenge, reminded Orestes that an oracle had told him to destroy Aegisthus and Clytemnestra.

Clytemnestra defended herself before Electra with the argument that Agamemnon had sacrificed Iphegenia, their child, as an offering before the Trojan venture and that he had returned to Argos with Cassandra, princess of Troy, as his concubine. Electra indicted her mother on several counts and said that it was only just that she and Orestes murder Clytemnestra. The queen entered the hut to prepare a sacrifice for Electra's supposed first-born; within, she was killed by Orestes, who moaned in distress at the violence and bloodshed and matricide in which the gods had involved him.

The Dioscuri, twin sons of Zeus and brothers of the half-divine Clytemnestra, appeared to the brother and sister, who were overcome with mixed feelings of hate and love and pride and shame at what they had done. The twin gods questioned the wisdom of Apollo, whose oracle had advised this violent action; they decreed that Orestes should give Electra to Pylades in marriage and that Orestes himself should be pursued by the Furies until he could face a trial in Athens, from which trial he would emerge a free man.

THE EMIGRANTS

Type of work: Novel
Author: Johan Bojer (1872-1959)
Type of plot: Regional romance
Time of plot: Late nineteenth century
Locale: Norway and the American West
First published: 1925

Principal characters:
ERIK FOSS, an emigrant leader
OLA VATNE, a laborer
ELSE, his wife
MORTEN KVIDAL, a joiner
KAL SKARET, a crofter
KAREN, his wife
PER FÖLL, a young workman
ANNE, his wife
BERGITTA, Morten's wife; Anne's sister

Critique:

The Emigrants is a saga of the Norwegians who settled the wheat lands of the Dakotas. Bojer is well qualified for his subject. A Norwegian, he knows the stock from which our prairie pioneers came, and his visits to America have made him familiar with the American scene. The result is a lasting novel, an American story written in Norwegian. It is a vital part of our cultural heritage.

The Story:

Erik Foss came back to Norway after some time spent working in America, and to the cramped, class-conscious farmers and laborers of his Norwegian countryside he held out hope for a more free and generous life in the new country. Many resolved to join his party of emigrants to America.

There was Ola, the colonel's hired boy. Ola had a way with people, especially with girls, and Else, the colonel's daughter, looked on him with eager eyes. But Ola was poor and the stories about him did not please the colonel. After his dismissal from the farm, Ola set fire to the barn. He spent a year in prison and came out in time to join the emigrants. Else came too, as Ola's wife. There was Per Föll, a big, hulking

man and his new wife, Anne, the most attractive girl in the parish, already carrying a baby who was to be born too soon after her marriage. There were Kal Skaret and Karen, a kindly and slow-moving couple. The tax collector took their only cow when they could not pay even the previous year's taxes. There was Morten Kvidal, a skilled joiner.

When the steamer left, the little band sorrowed to leave Norway. But Erik was strong and he knew the way and he had enough money to help them.

That first summer the emigrants reached Wisconsin. They stayed there during the bleak winter, the men working in the sawmills to add to their meager funds. Early the next spring, they started out across the prairie. Erik had been to the Red River Valley before; he had tested the soil and knew it was good. The settlers had wagons and oxen, now, and all their supplies.

Erik said they had arrived when they came to a vast level land covered with a six-foot stand of grass.

Kal took the quarter farthest to the west. There he swung his scythe in sweeping strokes. The children and Karen piled the fodder, enough to feed a cow all winter! Now he would plow. Mor-

THE EMIGRANTS by Johan Bojer. Translated by A. G. Jayne. By permission of Curtis Brown, Ltd. Published by The Century Co. Copyright, 1925, by Johan Bojer.

ten took no heed of the buffalo grass; he set his great breaking plow and turned it under. They built their homes from the grass, too, piling squares of turf for their sod houses.

That summer there was drought and the wheat crop was poor. Ola went into town with one of the loads, and gambled and drank up all his money. Without the help of the others, Ola and Else would never have survived the winter. During a blizzard Erik's feet were frostbitten while he hunted his strayed stock. When gangrene set in, Morten made the long trip to town on skis; but he returned too late with medicine for the sick man.

After Erik's death, the leadership of the small band fell to Morten. Good times and bad followed.

Per thought long and bitterly about Anne, for he could never forget that his first-born boy had come into the world too soon after his marriage. When Morten's young brother visited his house too frequently, Per began to roam the prairie. They had to tie him finally and take him to the madhouse, leaving Anne with her children and a sense of sin.

Although well established, Morten felt compelled to go back to Norway. When he returned to Dakota, he brought with him a wife, Bergitta, Anne's sister. He became an agent for the new railroad. He said that the people should have their own bank and grain elevators so that they would not be at the mercy of speculators. The Norwegians became Americans. At a party they put up an American flag beside the Norwegian banner.

Kal and Karen built outbuildings of wood, and each son took up another quarter. Before long Kal's fields stretched to the horizon, and he had to ride from one wheat planting to the other. When the steam thresher came, an army of laborers piled up the mounds of grain; it poured too fast to cart away. In his machine shed, in a tiny strong room, Kal stored wheat, so that his family would never be hungry. Under his bed, in his emigrant chest, he kept his money. He and Karen were proud on the day their son came back from school in St. Louis and preached in their own church.

Morten grew old. He still acted for the railroad; he ran the bank; he was elder of the church; he put up buildings for the growing town. Bergitta died. A lamp exploded in Morten's face, blinding him. Now his grandson read to him. The old man thought of Norway often. He went back, blind and old, to his home. His people were dead; only the old land remained. It must be like that, he realized. The old settlers are a part Norwegian always, but their children belong to the new world.

THE EMIGRANTS OF AHADARRA

Type of work: Novel
Author: William Carleton (1794-1869)
Type of plot: Local color romance
Time of plot: 1840's
Locale: Ireland
First published: 1848

Principal characters:
BRYAN M'MAHON, an honest young farmer
KATHLEEN CAVANAGH, in love with Bryan M'Mahon
HYCY (HYACINTH) BURKE, a well-to-do libertine and rascal
JEMMY BURKE, Hycy's father
NANNY PEETY, a beggar girl
KATE HOGAN, Nanny's aunt, a tinker's wife
PATRICK O'FINIGAN, master of a hedge-school

Critique:

William Carleton's fiction is best known for his realistic pictures of Irish peasant life during the nineteenth century, and *The Emigrants of Ahadarra* is one of his best novels in this respect. The most noteworthy sections are the chapters describing such things as a "kemp" (a spinning contest among the peasant women), a country funeral, an election, and illegal distillation of whiskey. While his treatment of these matters is outstanding, the entire novel is filled with specific and colorful details of peasant life. The speech of the people, the homes they live in, the farm routine, landlord-peasant relations, whiskey smuggling, the character of the people—all these are related with a view to giving the reader a true picture of rural Irish life a century ago. Although Carleton's fiction is now little read, it deserves attention from the student of the novel as an example of early realism well done.

The Story:

Hycy Burke was the son of a well-to-do and respected peasant who had allowed his wife, a woman with social pretensions of her own, to spoil the young man, and Hycy, with his mother's approval, had become a dissolute young man. Because his father, Jemmy Burke, tried to curb him, Hycy entered into partnership with whiskey smugglers to supplement the dimin-

ished allowance from his father.

When one of the prettiest girls in the area, Kathleen Cavanagh, caught Hycy's eye, he determined to seduce her. Unfortunately for his plans, he misdirected two letters: one, intended for Kathleen, went to Bryan M'Mahon, who truly loved the girl; another, intended for young M'Mahon, went to Kathleen. Later, publicly snubbed on more than one occasion, Hycy resolved to have revenge on the girl and her true admirer. Any additional villainy could scarcely put him in greater danger, for he had already been an accomplice to burglarizing his father's house, taking a large sum of money, as well as an active accomplice of smugglers. It was through his fellow smugglers that he planned to get his revenge. At the time there was a law in Ireland which required the inhabitants of a township to pay fines for illegal distillation and smuggling of whiskey if the actual culprits were not known. Bryan M'Mahon's farm at Ahadarra covered an entire township; if he were required to pay such a fine by himself he would be ruined. To carry out his plan, Hycy tried to get the help of the nephew of the local gauger. Hycy promised the exciseman's nephew the chance to lease a fine farm if the latter would press Hycy's suit for his sister's hand. The farm, of course, was Bryan M'Mahon's.

Bryan was not the only member of his

family facing tragedy. Both his and his father's farm leases had run out, and death had prevented the absentee landlord from renewing them. The new landlord, a well-meaning but weak and inexperienced young man, was ruled by his agent, who wished to see the M'Mahons lose their farms, leased by the family for generations.

Hycy carefully made his plans. What he failed to realize, however, was that he had made enemies while Bryan had made friends, so that some persons who knew of his villainy were prepared to take measures to thwart him. In his father's house was Nanny Peety, a pretty, virtuous beggar girl who resented Hycy's attempts to seduce her. She knew something of his plans and she had been a witness to the burglary Hycy and his accomplice had committed. Nanny Peety's aunt, Kate Hogan, loved her niece and thought highly of Kathleen Cavanagh. She was willing to help them and could because she was married to one of Hycy's smuggling associates. Also friendly to Kathleen and Bryan was Patrick O'Finigan, the drunken master of the local hedge-school.

The plot against Bryan was put into operation when Hycy's anonymous letter sent the gauger to discover the illicit still at Ahadarra, on Bryan's farm. Faced with financial ruin and his family's loss of their leases, the young peasant did not know what to do. Because his own honesty kept him from believing that Hycy was working against him in that manner, Bryan even took advice from the man who was bent on ruining him. Before long he found himself worse off by his taking that advice. A parliamentary election was about to take place, in which the M'Mahons' landlord was standing for a seat. The voting turned out to be a tie until Bryan, angry with his landlord and following Hycy's advice, voted for his landlord's opponent. By doing so he made himself appear false in everyone's eyes, for his landlord was a liberal who favored the Irish peasantry and religious freedom, while the opponent was a conservative who worked against the peasants and the Roman Catholic Church.

When Hycy sent another letter enclosing a fifty-pound note, it looked as if Bryan had accepted a bribe for his vote. The evidence was so damning that even Kathleen, who loved Bryan sincerely, was forced to believe him guilty. Faced with calamity and disfavor in his community, Bryan and his family planned, like so many unfortunate Irish at the time, to emigrate to America in order to start a new and more successful life.

But Bryan's friends began to work for him. Kate Hogan, displeased at Hycy's treatment of her niece and the troubles facing Kathleen when she lost her fiancé, began investigating Hycy's activities. She, Patrick O'Finigan, Nanny Peety's father, and others gathered additional information and presented it to the magistrates with demands for a hearing. At the hearing it was proved that Hycy had robbed his father, had been an accomplice of the whiskey smugglers, had placed the still at Ahadarra to incriminate Bryan, had plotted to make his victim appear to have taken a bribe, and had also become a counterfeiter. Confronted with these proofs, Jemmy Burke gave his son two hundred pounds to leave the country and stay away. Hycy's accomplices were arrested, convicted, and transported as criminals from Ireland, thus becoming the "emigrants" of Ahadarra. Cleared of all charges, Bryan resumed his rightful place in the community and in the affections of Kathleen.

ÉMILE

Type of work: Novel
Author: Jean Jacques Rousseau (1712-1778)
Time: Eighteenth century
Locale: France
First published: 1762

Principal characters:
JEAN JACQUES ROUSSEAU, in the role of tutor
ÉMILE, a French orphan, healthy and intelligent
SOPHIE, a wellborn, warm-hearted young woman

Rousseau's treatise on education—a novel in name only—is addressed to mothers in the hope that, as a result of learning Rousseau's ideas on education, they will permit their children to develop naturally without letting them be crushed by social conditions. Children cannot be left to themselves from birth because the world as it is would turn them into beasts. The problem is to educate a child in the midst of society in such a manner that society does not spoil him.

Rousseau argues that education comes from nature, from men, and from things. The education from men and from things must be controlled so that habits conformable to nature will develop. Children have natural tendencies which should be encouraged, for nature intends children to be adults; the aim of education, according to Rousseau, is to make a boy a man. Yet by swaddling children, by turning them over to wet nurses, and by punishing them for not doing what is said to be their duty, parents turn children from natural ways of acting and spoil them for life.

Rousseau insists that the proper way to bring up a child is to begin by having the mother nurse the child and the father train him. But if substitutes must be found, a wet nurse of good disposition who was lately a mother should be selected; and a young tutor should be chosen, preferably one with the qualities of Rousseau.

In order to explain his theory of education, Rousseau refers to an imaginary pupil, Émile. The child should come from France, since inhabitants of temperate zones are more adaptable and more intelligent than those from other climates. He should be from a wealthy family, since the poor are educated by life itself, and he should be an orphan in order to allow Rousseau free range as tutor. Finally, he should be healthy in body and mind.

Rousseau recommends a predominantly vegetable diet, particularly for the nurse, since the milk would be better if meat were not eaten. The tutor should see to it that the child is taken out to breathe the fresh air of the country, and, if possible, the family should live in the country: "Men are devoured by our towns." The child should become accustomed to frequent baths, but he should not be softened by warm water or by other pampering which destroys his natural vigor.

The child should not be allowed to fall into habits other than that of having no habits. He should not have regular meal times or bedtimes, and as far as possible he should be free to act as he chooses. He may injure himself or become ill, but it is better for him to learn how to live naturally than to become a weak and artificial adult.

"The natural man is interested in all new things," wrote Rousseau, and he urged that the child be introduced to new things in such a way that he would not be encouraged to fear whatever is not naturally fearful. He offers, as an example of the proper kind of education in this respect, an account of what he would do to keep Émile from becoming afraid of masks. He would begin with a pleasant mask and then proceed to less pleasing and, finally, to hideous ones, all the while laughing at each mask and trying it on different persons. Similarly, to accustom Émile to the sound of a gun, Rousseau would start with a small charge, so that Émile would be fascinated by the sudden flash, then proceed to greater charges until Émile could tolerate even large explosions.

Rousseau maintained that cries and tears are the child's natural expression of his needs. The child should not be thwarted, for he has no other way of learning to live in the world, and education begins with birth. On the other hand, he should not become the master of the house, demanding obedience from his parents.

It was Rousseau's conviction that children must be given more liberty to do things for themselves so that they will demand less of others. A natural advantage of the child's limited strength is that he cannot do much damage even when he uses his power freely. A child will learn to speak correctly, to read and write, if it is to his advantage to do so; threats and coercion only hinder him.

Speaking of a mode of education which burdens a child with restrictions and is, at the same time, overprotective, Rousseau wrote, "Even if I considered that education was wise in its aims, how could I view without indignation those poor wretches subjected to an intolerable slavery and condemned like galley-slaves to endless toil . . . ? The age of harmless mirth is spent in tears, punishments, threats, and slavery. You torment the poor thing for his good; you fail to see that you are calling Death to snatch him from these gloomy surroundings." Instead of torturing children with excessive care, one should love them, laugh with them, send them out into the meadows, and play with them.

"When our natural tendencies have not been interfered with by human prejudice and human institutions, the happiness alike of children and men consists in the enjoyment of their liberty." Here the principle behind Rousseau's theory of education becomes clear. The effort of the tutor or the parent is so to educate the child in such fashion that he will learn through his own efforts to be as free as possible within society. If he is educated by rules and threats he becomes a slave, and once free he seeks to enslave others. The most satisfactory general rule of education, Rousseau argued, is to do exactly the opposite of what is usually done.

Since the child is supposed to learn through his own experience, misdeeds should be punished only by arranging matters so that the child comes to experience the natural consequences of what he has done. If there is any rule which can be used as a moral injunction, it would be, "Never hurt anybody"; only trouble comes from urging children or men to do good to others.

Rousseau rejected the use of tales and fables for children. An amusing analysis illustrates his conviction that even the simplest fable, such as "The Fox and the Crow," strikes the child as ridiculous and puzzling and encourages him to use language carelessly and to behave foolishly.

After the child has reached adolescence, the education of his intellect should begin. Prior to this time the concern of the tutor was to give Émile the freedom to learn the natural limits of his powers. Now he teaches Émile by showing him the natural advantages of the use of the intellect. The tutor answers questions, but just enough to make the child curious. His explanations are always in language the child can understand, and he encourages the child to solve his own problems and to make his own investigations. Interest should lead the child to increase his experience and knowledge; it is a mistake to demand that he learn. Jean Jacques, as the tutor, shows Émile the value of astronomy by gently encouraging him to use the knowledge that he has in order to find his way out of the woods.

Rousseau's accounts of his efforts to

teach Émile owe some of their charm to the author's willingness to show himself unsuccessful in some of his efforts. Nevertheless, the pupil Émile never becomes a distinctive character; Émile is merely a child-symbol, just as later in the book Sophie is, even as the author indicates, a woman-symbol devised to enable Rousseau to discuss marriage problems.

By the time Émile is fifteen he has gained a considerable amount of practical and scientific knowledge; he can handle tools of all sorts, and he knows he will have to find some trade as his life's work. In Book IV of *Émile*, Rousseau discusses the most difficult kind of education: moral education, the study of the self in relation to other men.

Rousseau presents three maxims which sum up his ideas concerning human sympathy, the foundation of moral virtue:

> *First Maxim.*—It is not in human nature to put ourselves in the place of those who are happier than ourselves, but only in the place of those who can claim our pity.
> *Second Maxim.*—We never pity another's woes unless we know we may suffer in like manner ourselves.
> *Third Maxim.*—The pity we feel for others is proportionate, not to the amount of the evil, but to the feelings we attribute to the sufferers.

These maxims fortify the tutor, but they are not imparted to Émile. The youth is gradually made aware of the suffering of individuals; his experience is broadened; and he comes to know through personal experience the consequences of various kinds of acts. The important thing is to turn his affections to others.

Émile is given insight concerning religious matters by hearing a long discourse by "a Savoyard priest" who tells of the difficult passage from doubt to faith. He affirms man's natural goodness and the reliability of conscience when uncontaminated by philosophers or by mere convention.

Sophie, "or Woman," is introduced in Book V, since Émile must have a helpmate. Rousseau begins curiously by saying, "But for her sex, a woman is a man"; but when he considers her education it is apparent that sex makes quite a difference. Woman need not be given as many reasons as man, and she can get along with less intellect; but she must have courage and virtue. Rousseau offers a great deal of advice, even concerning Sophie's refusal of Émile's first attempt to share her bed. The book closes, after a charming digression on travel, with Émile's announcement that he is about to become a father and that he will undertake the education of his child, following the example of his beloved tutor.

Émile is as full of good humor as it is of good advice. Rousseau pursued an educational philosophy which is, on the whole, humane and sensible. He desired to make the child neither a noble savage nor a cultivated gentleman, but a man, living fearlessly and forthrightly according to impulses and abilities which were naturally his. Although Rousseau's psychology is sometimes naïve, it is seldom far from the modern view; and that, if anything, is a compliment to the modern view.

EMILIA GALOTTI

Type of work: Drama
Author: Gotthold Ephraim Lessing (1729-1781)
Type of plot: Romantic tragedy
Time of plot: Early eighteenth century
Locale: Guastalla and Sabionetta, two mythical principalities in Italy
First presented: 1771

Principal characters:
EMILIA GALOTTI, a beautiful, middle-class young woman
ODOARDO GALOTTI, her father
CLAUDIA GALOTTI, her mother
HETTORE GONZAGA, Prince of Sabionetta and Guastalla
COUNT APPIANI, betrothed to Emilia
THE MARQUIS MARINELLI, chamberlain to the prince
THE COUNTESS ORSINA, a mistress spurned by the prince

Critique:

This play, romantic though it now seems, was one of the first tragedies which broke from strict adherence to the French neo-classic unities. The best tragedy of Lessing's small group of plays, *Emilia Galotti* takes its theme from classical antiquity, the story of the innocent maiden who dies at the hand of her father in order to prevent the loss of her chastity. A drama of middle-class life, the work is also a problem play, with revolt from the tyranny of the aristocracy presenting in interesting development an underlying social theme.

The Story:

Prince Hettore Gonzaga, once happily in love with and loved in return by Countess Orsina, had unhappily fallen in love with Emilia Galotti. She, the daughter of a soldier who resisted the conquest of Sabionetta by the prince, was to be married to Count Appiani, of the neighboring principality of Piedmont. This desirable union of a nobleman and a beautiful, middle-class woman was the result of her mother's studied plan.

The treacherous Marquis Marinelli proposed that the prince retire to his palace at Dosalo after sending Count Appiani on a mission to the Princess of Massa, soon to be the prince's bride. The absence of her betrothed would leave Emilia open to the designs of the prince.

Motivated by lechery, the ruler eagerly agreed to this plan.

Odoardo Galotti, having readied his villa at Sabionetta in preparation for the wedding, returned to his wife in Guastalla in order to accompany the bridal party. A young assassin garnered from a family servant all these facts so that he could plan the abduction of Emilia, who, pursued by the prince, had just returned from church. This action of Prince Hettore's the honest patriot father or the independent husband-to-be would have avenged, but the unsophisticated Emilia did not know how to treat the prince's lustful behavior.

Count Appiani, disturbed by presentiments of evil, rejected the prince's proposal to send him off on his wedding day, and he was killed for his temerity when the bridal party was attacked.

Closely guarded, Emilia was taken to the palace under pretense of a rescue from brigands. There the prince, playing the gallant, allayed the fears of Emilia by apologizing for his former behavior and promising to escort her to her mother. Claudia, in the meantime, had been made frantic by separation from her daughter, and, hysterical over the death of Count Appiani, she accused Marinelli of plotting this deed of treachery and violence. The prince, now beset by a hysterical mother and a swooning young woman whom he desperately desired, had not reckoned with the wrath of a rejected mistress as well. The Countess Orsina, whose spies had uncovered all the prince's guilty secrets, arrived at the palace in Dosalo and, failing in an attempt at blackmail, revealed Prince Hettore's guilt to Odoardo Galotti when he came in haste and unarmed to the aid of his daughter and wife. The countess, determined to have revenge on her former lover, gave Galotti the dagger she had intended to use on the prince. Galotti insisted on his rights as a father to take his daughter to her home, but his petition was denied by the crafty Marinelli. Meanwhile, the prince, unaware of Galotti's knowledge and purpose, tried to appear as a benefactor who would see justice done in the courts. Until that time, however, he would keep Emilia apart for security's sake. To this arrangement Galotti seemed to agree, ironically commenting on each provision of treachery as it was proposed.

When the anxious father was finally allowed to see his daughter, she told her fears that her virtue might yield where force could never prevail, the arts of seduction being so brilliantly practiced in Prince Hettore's court. To protect her innocence, Galotti stabbed Emilia, presented her body to the lustful prince, threw the dagger at his feet, and went off to give himself up to the authorities.

EMINENT VICTORIANS

Type of work: Biography
Author: Lytton Strachey (1880-1932)
Time: Nineteenth century
Locale: England, Scutari, the Sudan
First published: 1918

Principal personages:
HENRY EDWARD MANNING, a Cardinal of the Roman Catholic Church
FLORENCE NIGHTINGALE, a nineteenth-century career woman
DR. THOMAS ARNOLD, an English educator
CHARLES GEORGE GORDON, a British general

Though possibly controversial, the biographical writings of Lytton Strachey are never dull; and when they address themselves to the Victorian Period they possess a special interest. For the biographer himself was a product of that period, and his feelings about it, while mixed, were far from being vague or uncertain. The Age of Victoria both fascinated and repelled him; he loved it while he hated it. Even though its pretentiousness exasperated the artist in Strachey, he could not help acknowledging its solidity and force, as manifested in many outstanding scientists and men of action.

Four such people, including one woman, are his subjects in Eminent Victorians. Not the greatest of their time, these four yet belong among the most appropriate of its decorations. Superficially diverse in their activities, they include an ecclesiastic, a woman of action, an educational authority, and a man of adventure. As drawn by their biographer, they provide a striking illustration of the many-faceted era in which they lived and worked.

This quartet of portraits proved to be a critical and financial success. It became the cornerstone in an increasingly solid career, and after it appeared, Strachey was no longer in need of assistance from family or friends. Yet his treatment of Cardinal Manning, Florence Nightingale, Arnold of Rugby, and General Gordon did not go unchallenged. The author was accused of undue severity with his subjects, of handling facts with carelessness, and of superficiality in his judgments.

Such indictments derived, in general, from people friendly to one or more of the individuals pictured in Eminent Victorians; but not infrequently they were joined by critics of influence and standing.

Some of these critics overlooked the point that Strachey's biographical method aimed at verisimilitude instead of photographic realism. It is true that his determination to rise above mere facts sometimes carried him too far—as far as outright and sometimes outrageous caricature —but the writing remained brilliant and stimulating. The intelligent reader is more likely to be diverted than deceived by his prejudices, for his dislike for such targets as Florence Nightingale and Thomas Arnold is hardly disguised. Whatever charges may be brought against Strachey today, his services to biographical writing are generally admitted: he brought to it good proportion, good style, and colorful realism.

For such talents, the life of Cardinal Manning provides ideal material. But Manning, despite his distinction as a churchman, does not escape a touch of the Strachey lash. He is revealed, this representative of ancient tradition and uncompromising faith, as a survival from the Middle Ages who forced the nineteenth century to accept him for what he was. Practical ability, rather than saintliness or learning, was the key to his onward march. In the Middle Ages, says Strachey, he would have been neither a Francis nor an Aquinas, but he might have been an Innocent.

Very early in his life, Manning's hopes became fixed on a position of power and influence in the world. Upon leaving college he aspired to a political career, but its doors were abruptly closed to him by his father's bankruptcy. Next he tried the Church of England as another, perhaps less promising, avenue to fulfillment. By 1851, already over forty, he had become an archdeacon, but such rank was not enough. For some time his glance had been straying to other pastures; finally, he made the break and became a convert to Roman Catholicism. In the process he lost a friend—a rather important one—named Gladstone.

Thereafter his ecclesiastical career was an almost unbroken series of triumphs and advances. One important asset was the ability to make friends in the right places, especially if one of those places was the Vatican. Brooking no rivals, Manning became the supreme commander of the Roman Church in England, then a cardinal. His magnetism and vigor spread his influence beyond Church boundaries; and at his death crowds of working people thronged the route of his funeral procession. At the end of a long and twisted road, his egoism, fierce ambition, and gift for intrigue accomplished some unexpected rewards; not least among them the regard of the poor.

The second of Strachey's eminent Victorians is Florence Nightingale. Here, in his treatment of one of the most remarkable women of any age, the biographer is conspicuously successful in resisting any urge to be gallant. What her friends called calm persuasiveness, he characterized as demoniac fury; it is clear that to him the "Lady with a Lamp" might be extremely capable but she was also tiresomely demanding and disagreeable. Nevertheless, his account does disclose the almost miraculous energy and endurance which carried Miss Nightingale past obstacle after obstacle.

For the sake of convenience, Strachey divides the accomplishments of Florence Nightingale into two phases. The first is her dramatic contribution to the welfare of British wounded during the course of the Crimean campaign; the second deals with her unflagging efforts, after the war, to transform the Army Medical Department, revolutionize hospital services, and even to work much needed reform in the War Office itself. These aims dominated her completely; in the prosecution of them she drove her friends ruthlessly, but she used herself with even less mercy. Enduring to the age of ninety, she became a legend; but, ironically and cruelly, her last years brought senility and softness upon her. They also brought, after consciousness had dulled almost into insensibility, the Order of Merit.

Dr. Thomas Arnold is generally considered the father, not only of Matthew Arnold, poet and critic, but of the British public school system as well. Neither of these products inspires Strachey with much respect, and his bias against the doctor is obvious in *Eminent Victorians*. Dr. Arnold, for instance, was determined to make good Christians, as well as good Englishmen, out of his public school boys, whereas Strachey had little patience for either Christianity or Christian institutions. This fact, incidentally, seems to color his attitude toward all his subjects in *Eminent Victorians*, since the latter are, without exception, religiously employed or inclined to a very strong degree.

Dr. Arnold's prefectorial system, as he instituted it at Rugby, also meets with strong disapproval. Strachey credits it with two dubious, if unexpected, effects on later English education, the worship of athletics and the worship of good form. To some Victorians, Dr. Arnold may have seemed one of their most influential teachers; to Strachey, he is the apostle of ideas obviously harmful and absurd.

With apparent alacrity, the biographer turns to his fourth and final portrait. It is a long step from the educator to the general, involving as it does the distance between the single-mindedness of Arnold and the maddening inconsistencies of Gordon. For Charles George Gordon is unveiled as a mass of contradictions whom no biographer could ever hope completely to unravel. A mischievous, unpredictable boy, he developed into an undisciplined, unpredictable man. A romantic legend wove itself about his early, swashbuckling exploits in China and Africa. His deeds were genuinely heroic—no one has ever questioned Gordon's bravery—but they combined oddly with his passion for religion. He was influenced strongly, and to an approximately equal degree, by brandy and the Bible. Inclined, on the whole, to be unsociable, he maintained an icy reserve, except for fits of ungovernable temper vented upon unlucky servants or trembling subordinates.

This is the man who, in his fifties, was chosen by the English government for a delicate African mission. Strangely, considering the qualifications of the man selected, it was not military in its nature, but diplomatic, requiring the utmost in self-control, tact, and skill of a negotiator. For General Gordon was to arrange for inglorious evacuation of the Sudan by British forces, a project for which he was disqualified by his opinions, his character, and everything in his life. What followed, not surprisingly, was the tragedy at Khartoum, an episode seldom matched in military annals for the mystery and horror with which it enveloped the fate of the principal actor.

Thus, on a dramatic note, ends the biographer's searching glance at four eminent Victorians. Widely differing in background, vocation, and personality, they illustrate different phases of existence in England of the later nineteenth century. Each is bound to the others, however, by the possession of a restless, questing vitality, and each has left a mark upon his age.

1060

EMMA

Type of work: Novel
Author: Jane Austen (1775-1817)
Type of plot: Social comedy
Time of plot: Early nineteenth century
Locale: Surrey, England
First published: 1816

Principal characters:
EMMA WOODHOUSE, heiress of Hartfield
MR. WOODHOUSE, her father
HARRIET SMITH, Emma's protégée
MISS BATES, the village gossip
JANE FAIRFAX, Miss Bates' niece
MR. GEORGE KNIGHTLEY, Emma's brother-in-law
MRS. WESTON, Emma's former governess
FRANK CHURCHILL, stepson of Emma's former governess
MR. ELTON, a rector
ROBERT MARTIN, a yeoman

Critique:

The major problem in the world of Jane Austen's novels is that of getting the characters properly married, and *Emma* is no exception. Its plot is concerned with the complications taking place before the couples are paired off correctly, and with Emma's sometimes unwise attempts to help things along. She is perhaps a less generally appealing heroine than Elizabeth Bennet in *Pride and Prejudice,* but she is excellently done, as are her father and the rest of the Highbury circle. Miss Bates and Mrs. Elton remain unsurpassed in English satire.

The Story:

Emma Woodhouse, rich, clever, beautiful, and no more spoiled and self-satisfied than one would expect under such circumstances, had just seen her friend, companion, and ex-governess, Miss Taylor, married to a neighboring widower, Mr. Weston. While the match was suitable in every way, Emma could not help sighing over her loss, for now only she and her father were left at Hartfield and Mr. Woodhouse was too old and too fond of worrying about trivialities to be a companion for his daughter.

The Woodhouses were the great family in the village of Highbury. In their small circle of friends there were enough middle-aged ladies to make up card tables for Mr. Woodhouse but no young lady to be friend and confidante to Emma. Lonely for her beloved Miss Taylor, now Mrs. Weston, Emma took under her wing Harriet Smith, the parlor boarder at a nearby boarding-school. Harriet was an extremely pretty girl of seventeen, not in the least brilliant, but with pleasing, unassuming manners, and a gratifying habit of looking up to Emma as a paragon.

Harriet was the natural daughter of some mysterious person, and Emma, believing that the girl might be of noble family, persuaded her that the society in which she had moved was not good enough for her. She encouraged her to give up her acquaintance with the Martin family, respectable farmers of some substance though of no fashion. Instead of thinking of Robert Martin as a husband for Harriet, Emma influenced the girl to aspire to Mr. Elton, the young rector.

Emma believed from Mr. Elton's manner that he was beginning to fall in love with Harriet, and she flattered herself upon her matchmaking schemes. Mr. Knightley, brother of a London lawyer married to Emma's older sister and one of the few people who could see Emma's faults, was concerned about her intimacy with Harriet. He warned her that no good could come of it for either Harriet or herself, and he was particularly upset when he learned that Emma had influenced Harriet to turn down Robert Martin's proposal of marriage. Emma herself suffered from no such qualms, for she was certain that Mr. Elton was as much in love with Harriet as Harriet—through Emma's instigation—was with him.

Emma suffered a rude awakening when Mr. Elton, finding her alone, asked her to marry him. She suddenly realized that what she had taken for gallantries to Harriet had been meant for herself, and what she had intended as encouragement to his suit of her friend, he had taken as encouragement to aspire for Emma's hand. His presumption was bad enough, but the task of breaking the news to Harriet was much worse.

Another disappointment now occurred in Emma's circle. Frank Churchill, who had promised for months to come to see his father and new stepmother, again put off his visit. Churchill, Mr. Weston's son by a first marriage, had taken the name of his mother's family. Mr. Knightley believed that the young man now felt himself above his father. Emma argued with Mr. Knightley, but she found herself secretly agreeing with him.

Although the Hartfield circle was denied Churchill's company, it did acquire an addition in the person of Jane Fairfax, niece of the garrulous Miss Bates. Jane rivaled Emma in beauty and accomplishment, one reason why, as Mr. Knightley hinted, Emma had never been friendly with Jane. Emma herself blamed Jane's reserve for their somewhat cool relationship.

Soon after Jane's arrival, the Westons received a letter from Churchill setting another date for his visit. This time he actually appeared, and Emma found him a handsome, well-bred young man. He called frequently upon the Woodhouses, and also upon the Bates family, because of prior acquaintance with Jane Fairfax.

Emma rather than Jane was the recipient of his gallantries, however, and Emma could see that Mr. and Mrs. Weston were hoping that the romance would prosper.

About this time Jane Fairfax received the handsome gift of a pianoforte, anonymously given. It was presumed to·have come from some rich friends with whom Jane, an orphan, had lived, but Jane herself seemed embarrassed with the present and refused to discuss it. Emma wondered if it had come from Mr. Knightley, after Mrs. Weston pointed out to her his seeming preference and concern for Jane. Emma could not bear to think of Mr. Knightley's marrying Jane Fairfax, and after observing them together, she concluded to her own satisfaction that he was motivated by friendship, not love.

It was now time for Frank Churchill to end his visit, and he departed with seeming reluctance. During his last call at Hartfield, he appeared desirous of telling Emma something of a serious nature; but she, believing him to be on the verge of a declaration of love, did not encourage him because in her daydreams she always saw herself refusing him and their love ending in quiet friendship.

Mr. Elton returned to the village with a hastily wooed and wedded bride, a lady of small fortune, extremely bad manners, and great pretensions to elegance. Harriet, who had been talked into love by Emma, could not be so easily talked out of it; but what Emma had failed to accomplish, Mr. Elton's marriage had, and Harriet at last began to recover. Her recovery was aided by Mr. Elton's rudeness to her at a ball. When he refused to dance with her, Mr. Knightley, who rarely danced, offered himself as a partner, and Harriet, without Emma's knowledge, began to think of him instead of Mr. Elton.

Emma herself began to think of Churchill as a husband for Harriet, but she resolved to do nothing to promote the match. Through a series of misinterpretations, Emma thought Harriet was praising Churchill when she was really referring to Mr. Knightley.

The matrimonial entanglement was further complicated because Mrs. Weston continued to believe that Mr. Knightley was becoming attached to Jane Fairfax. Mr. Knightley, in his turn, saw signs of some secret agreement between Jane Fairfax and Frank Churchill. His suspicions were finally justified when Churchill confessed to Mr. and Mrs. Weston that he and Jane had been secretly engaged since October. The Westons' first thought was for Emma, for they feared that Churchill's attentions to her might have had their effect. Emma assured Mrs. Weston that she had at one time felt some slight attachment to Churchill, but that that time was now safely past. Her chief concerns now were that she had said things about Jane to Churchill which she would not have said had she known of their engagement, and also that she had, as she believed, encouraged Harriet in another fruitless attachment.

When she went to break the news gently to Harriet, however, Emma found her quite unperturbed by it, and after a few minutes of talking at cross purposes Emma learned that it was not Churchill but Mr. Knightley upon whom Harriet had now bestowed her affections. When she told Emma that she had rea-sons to believe that Mr. Knightley returned her sentiments, Emma suddenly realized the state of her own heart; she herself loved Mr. Knightley. She now wished she had never seen Harriet Smith. Aside from the fact that she wanted to marry Mr. Knightley herself, she knew a match between him and Harriet would be an unequal one, hardly likely to bring happiness.

Emma's worry over this state of affairs was soon ended when Mr. Knightley asked her to marry him. Her complete happiness was marred only by the fact that she knew her marriage would upset her father, who disliked change of any kind, and that she had unknowingly prepared Harriet for another disappointment. The first problem was solved when Emma and Mr. Knightley decided to reside at Hartfield with Mr. Woodhouse as long as he lived. As for Harriet, when Mr. Knightley was paying attention to her, he was really trying to determine the real state of her affections for his young farm tenant. Consequently Mr. Knightley was able to announce one morning that Robert Martin had again offered himself to Harriet and had been accepted. Emma was overjoyed that Harriet's future was now assured. She could always reflect that all parties concerned had married according to their stations, a prerequisite for their true happiness.

THE EMPEROR JONES

Type of work: Drama
Author: Eugene O'Neill (1888-1953)
Type of plot: Expressionistic melodrama
Time of plot: Early twentieth century
Locale: West Indies
First presented: 1920

Principal characters:
BRUTUS JONES, Emperor
SMITHERS, a Cockney trader
LEM, a native

Critique:

Eugene O'Neill departed from traditional dramatic writing when he created this play, which concerns itself expressionistically with the forces that make a man what he is. *The Emperor Jones* goes forward and backward simultaneously: Brutus Jones is carried, in the realm of the stage-actual, from his position as emperor to his death from fear; while, in the short, interrelated, and dynamic episodes which symbolize Jones' and his race's history, the action regresses in point of time from the present to several hundred years ago in the Congo jungle. *The Emperor Jones* was first produced by the Provincetown Players, in 1920.

The Story:

Henry Smithers, a Cockney adventurer, learned from a Negro woman that the followers of Brutus Jones, self-styled emperor of a West Indian island, were about to desert their ruler. With Smithers' help, Jones, a former Pullman porter and jail-breaker, had duped the natives into believing he was a magician. The superstitious natives made him emperor of the island. Smithers disclosed to the emperor the disaffection of his subjects, who had been taxed and cheated by the pair beyond human endurance. Jones had judged that he had six more months of power before the natives caught on to his skullduggery. He had had a silver bullet cast for a good luck charm; besides, the

bullet might be useful if he were ever caught by his subjects.

At Smithers' suggestion, Jones rang a bell for his attendants; no one appeared. Jones resigned his position as emperor on the spot and made immediate plans to escape through the jungle to the coast. Drums began to beat in the hills. The ex-emperor gave the palace to Smithers, took up his white Panama hat, and walked boldly out the front door.

At the edge of the jungle Brutus Jones searched unsuccessfully for tinned food he had cached for such an emergency. The drums continued to beat, louder and more insistent. Night fell, and formless fears came out of the jungle to beset Jones. The moon rose. Jones came into a clearing and there in the moonlight he saw Jeff, a Pullman porter he thought he had killed in a razor duel. Jeff was throwing dice. When the kneeling figure refused to answer him, Jones shot at him. The phantom disappeared. Drums still thudded in the distance. Jones, now sick with fright, plunged into the inky jungle.

After a while he came upon a road and paused to rest. A chain gang came out of the forest. The guard of the gang motioned to Jones to take his place in the gang and get to work. When the guard whipped him, Jones lifted his shovel to strike him, but he discovered that he actually had no shovel. In his rage of fear and frustration, he fired his revolver at the guard. The road, the guard, and the chain gang disappeared; the jungle closed in. The louder beat of the tom-toms drove Jones on in frantic circles.

Now in tatters, the terrified Jones repented the murders he had committed and the way he had cheated the islanders. He came next upon a slave auction attended by whites dressed in the costumes of the 1850's. An auctioneer put Jones on the auction block. Frightened, Jones shattered this apparition by firing one shot at the auctioneer and another at a planter. He dashed into the forest, mad with fear. The drums continued to beat.

At three o'clock Jones came to a part of the jungle which strangely resembled the hold of a slave ship. He found himself one of a cargo of slaves who were swaying slowly with the motion of the ship. Jones and the other slaves moaned with sorrow at being taken away from their homeland. Having only the silver bullet left in his revolver, Jones saved it and dashed on again into the black of the night.

Next he came upon an altar-like arrangement of boulders near a great river. He sank to his knees as if to worship. A Congo witch doctor appeared from be-hind a large tree and began a primitive dance. Jones was hypnotized by the ritual. The witch doctor indicated to Jones in pantomime that the ex-emperor must offer himself as a sacrifice in order to overcome the forces of evil. A great green-eyed crocodile emerged from the river; Jones fired the silver bullet at the monster and the witch doctor disappeared behind a tree, leaving Jones lying on the ground completely overcome by fear.

At dawn Lem, the leader of the rebels, came with Smithers and a group of natives to the edge of the jungle where Jones had entered the night before. Lem had been delayed in pursuing Jones because of the necessity of manufacturing silver bullets, which, Lem believed, were the only means of taking Jones' life. Several of Lem's men entered the jungle. They soon found the prostrate Jones, who had run in circles all the night. One shot him through the chest with a silver bullet. Jones' body was brought back to Lem, who thought that the silver bullet was what had really killed Jones. But Smithers, looking at Brutus Jones' fear-contorted face, knew differently.

ENDYMION

Type of work: Drama
Author: John Lyly (c. 1554-1606)
Type of plot: Romantic comedy
Time of plot: Remote antiquity
Locale: Ancient Greece
First presented: 1588

Principal characters:
ENDYMION, a courtier
CYNTHIA, the queen, loved by Endymion
TELLUS, in love with Endymion
EUMENIDES, Endymion's friend
SEMELE, loved by Eumenides
CORSITES, in love with Tellus
DIPSAS, an enchantress
GERON, her long-lost husband
SIR TOPHAS, a fop
FLOSCULA, Tellus' friend

Critique:

Endymion; or, The Man in the Moon, is undeniably an effete, even trivial play: the plot is singularly inconsequential and artificial; the characters are unreal; the dialogue is pedantic. But Endymion was important historically for these very reasons, in that Lyly was trying to make the drama an art. Writing for the court rather than the populace, Lyly replaced the earthiness and crudity of earlier English plays with refinement and polish, thereby setting new standards which later dramatists, including Shakespeare, were to emulate.

The Story:

To his friend Eumenides, Endymion declared his love for Cynthia, goddess of the moon. Eumenides chided Endymion, reminding him of the moon's inconstancy, whereupon Endymion extolled inconstancy and change as virtues, attributes of everything beautiful. Convinced that Endymion was bewitched, Eumenides prescribed sleep and rest for the love-sick swain, but Endymion rejected the advice and berated his friend.

In hopes of misleading his friends, Endymion had also professed love for Tellus, a goddess of the earth. Enraged by his apparent perfidy, Tellus swore to take revenge. Since she still loved En-

dymion, Tellus was unwilling for him to die; therefore she resolved to resort to magic and witchcraft in order to awaken his love for her. Her friend Floscula warned that love inspired by witchcraft would be bitter, but Tellus ignored the warning and left to consult Dipsas, an enchantress.

In contrast to Endymion and Tellus, Sir Tophas habitually scoffed at love and dedicated his life to war—against blackbirds, mallards, and wrens. When mocked by Endymion's and Eumenides' pages, Dares and Samias, Sir Tophas swore to kill them, but pardoned them when they explained that they had been speaking in Latin.

Meanwhile, Tellus had found Dipsas, whom she consulted about the possibility of killing Endymion's love for Cynthia and supplanting it by magic with love for the earth goddess herself. Dipsas declared that since she was not a deity, she could only weaken love, never kill it. At Tellus' request Dipsas agreed to enchant Endymion in such a way that his protestations of love for Cynthia would be doubted. Accompanied by Floscula and Dipsas, Tellus confronted Endymion in a garden and tried to make him confess his love for Cynthia. Though he admitted that he honored Cynthia above all other women,

1066

he insisted that he loved Tellus.

Later, the two pages, Dares and Samias, strolled in the gardens with their own lady loves, whom they had shown Endymion and Eumenides in the act of mooning over their loves. As a jest, Dares and Samias asked the two girls to feign love for Sir Tophas, who, as usual, was playing at warfare in the gardens. The girls complied, but Sir Tophas, ignoring them, reiterated his contempt for love and his passion for war.

Still later, Dipsas came upon Endymion asleep in a grove. Assisted by Bagoa, her servant, Dipsas spelled Endymion into a sleep from which he would not awake until he was old and gray. In a dream, three women appeared to Endymion, and one of them started to stab him. She desisted at the importuning of the third, peered into a looking glass, and threw down her knife. At this moment an old man appeared carrying a book which contained only three pages. Endymion refused to read the book until the man had torn up two of the pages.

When informed of Endymion's mysterious slumber, Cynthia agreed with Eumenides that the sages of the world should be consulted about a remedy. Also, angered by the impertinence of Tellus, Cynthia made her a prisoner in Corsites' palace, where she was to weave tapestries depicting stories of people who had been punished for their long tongues.

On the way to Thessaly, where Cynthia was sending him to seek a cure for Endymion, Eumenides met Geron, an old hermit. Geron said that Eumenides, if he were a faithful lover, could learn the cure from a magic fountain nearby. Since Eumenides had always been true to Semele, the fountain promised to grant any single wish he might make. Although tempted to wish that his love for Semele might be requited, dutifully he asked for a cure for his friend. The fountain answered that the cure was a kiss from Cynthia.

In the meantime Tellus, slowly pining away in prison, promised Corsites, her jailer and suitor, that she would marry if he could perform the impossible task of bringing Endymion to a cave, where she might see him once more. Corsites undertook 'his task but was himself pinched into a slumber by fairies guarding Endymion's body.

And so Cynthia found two sleeping men when she came to the grove accompanied by wise men who she hoped would wake Endymion. But the sages succeeded in waking only Corsites, who freely confessed his love for Tellus and what he had dared to do, inspired by that love.

At last Eumenides returned and persuaded Cynthia to attempt the cure. And so, upon her kiss, Endymion awoke. But his forty-year slumber had withered him: he was so senile that he could not stand. At Cynthia's request, however, he related his strange dream, explaining that in the book which the old man had given him to read, he saw Cynthia being attacked by beasts of ingratitude, treachery, and envy. Cynthia promised to listen later to a fuller account of this vision.

A short time later Bagoa disclosed that Tellus and Dipsas had been responsible for enchanting Endymion. For her pains Bagoa was transformed into an aspen tree by Dipsas.

Cynthia, however, was more lenient than Dipsas. Learning that Tellus had been motivated by unrequited love, Cynthia forgave her and gave her to Corsites as his wife. Dipsas, too, was pardoned on condition that she would be reunited with Geron, her husband, whom she had sent away many years ago. This reunion displeased Sir Tophas, who had discarded his armor out of love for Dipsas; he was content, however, when Cynthia disenchanted Bagoa and gave her to Tophas as his wife. To Eumenides she promised Semele, but Semele objected on the grounds that Eumenides had not asked for her at the magic fountain. She was placated, however, when Geron explained that Eumenides would not have learned the fountain's secret had he not been

1067

faithful. Most important, Cynthia restored the youth of Endymion and bade him persevere in his love.

AN ENEMY OF THE PEOPLE

Type of work: Drama
Author: Henrik Ibsen (1828-1906)
Type of plot: Social criticism
Time of plot: Late nineteenth century
Locale: Southern Norway
First presented: 1883

Principal characters:
DOCTOR THOMAS STOCKMANN, a medical officer
MRS. STOCKMANN, his wife
PETRA, his daughter
EILIF, and
MORTEN, his sons
PETER STOCKMANN, his brother, the mayor
MORTEN KIIL, Mrs. Stockmann's father
HOVSTAD, an editor
BILLING, a sub-editor
ASLAKSEN, a printer
CAPTAIN HORSTER, Dr. Stockmann's friend

Critique:

Known as the foremost dramatist of the nineteenth century, Ibsen was in constant conflict with the society of his time. He believed that it was the *majority* who caused people to stagnate. In *An Enemy of the People,* Doctor Stockmann stood alone, far in advance of the majority of the people. He was persecuted and ridiculed by those he tried to serve only because he was in conflict with established institutions of society. Ibsen saw himself as a Doctor Stockmann, and through the doctor gave the world ideas of universal significance.

The Story:

All the citizens of the small Norwegian coastal town were very proud of the Baths, for the healing waters were making the town famous and prosperous. Doctor Stockmann, the medical officer of the Baths, and his brother Peter, the mayor and chairman of the Baths committee, did not agree on many things, but they did agree that the Baths were the source of the town's good fortune. Hovstad, the editor of the *People's Messenger,* and Billing, his sub-editor, were also loud in praise of the Baths. Business was good and the people were beginning to enjoy prosperity.

Then Doctor Stockmann received from the University a report stating that the waters of the Baths were contaminated. Becoming suspicious when several visitors became ill after taking the Baths, he had felt it his duty to investigate. Refuse from tanneries above the town was oozing into the pipes leading to the reservoir and infecting the waters. This meant that the big pipes would have to be relaid, at a tremendous cost to the owners or to the town. When Hovstad and Billing heard this news, they asked the doctor to write an article for their paper about the terrible conditions. They even spoke of having the town give Doctor Stockmann some kind of testimonial in honor of his great discovery.

Doctor Stockmann wrote up his findings and sent the manuscript to his brother so that his report could be acted upon officially. Hovstad called on the doctor again, urging him to write some articles for the *People's Messenger.* It was Hovstad's opinion that the town had fallen into the hands of a few officials who did not care for the people's rights, and it was his intention to attack these men in his paper and urge the citizens to get rid of them in the next election.

Aslaksen, a printer who claimed to

have the compact majority under his control, also wanted to join in the fight to get the Baths purified and the corrupt officials defeated. Doctor Stockmann could not believe that his brother would refuse to accept the report, but he soon learned that he was wrong. Peter went to the doctor and insisted that he keep his knowledge to himself because the income of the town would be lost if the report were made public. He said that the repairs would be too costly, that the owners of the Baths could not stand the cost, and that the townspeople would never allow an increase in taxes to clean up the waters. He even insisted that Doctor Stockmann write another report, stating that he had been mistaken in his earlier judgment. He felt this action necessary when he learned that Hovstad and Billing knew of the first report. When the doctor refused either to change his report or withhold it, Peter threatened him with the loss of his position. Even his wife pleaded with him not to cross his powerful brother; he was sustained in his determination to do right only by his daughter Petra.

Hovstad, Billing, and Aslaksen were anxious to print the doctor's article so that the town could know of the falseness of the mayor and his officials. They thought his words so clear and intelligible that all responsible citizens would revolt against the corrupt regime. Aslaksen did plead for moderation, but promised to fight for what was right.

Peter Stockmann appeared at the office of the *People's Messenger* and cleverly told Aslaksen, Hovstad, and Billing that the tradespeople of the town would suffer if the doctor's report were made public. He said that they would have to stand the expense and that the Baths would be closed for two years while repairs were being made. The two editors and the printer then turned against Doctor Stockmann and supported Peter, since they felt that the majority would act in this way.

The doctor pleaded with them to stand by the promises they had given him, but they were the slaves of the majority opinion which they claimed to mold. When they refused to print his article, the doctor called a public meeting in the home of his friend, Captain Horster. Most of the citizens who attended were already unfriendly to him because the mayor and the newspaper editors had spread the news that he wanted to close the Baths and ruin the town. Aslaksen, nominated as chairman by the mayor, so controlled the meeting that a discussion of the Baths was ruled out of order.

Doctor Stockmann took the floor, however, and in ringing tones told the citizens that it was the unbelievable stupidity of the authorities and the great multitude of the compact majority that caused all the evil and corruption in the world. He said that the majority destroyed freedom and truth everywhere because the majority was ignorant and stupid. The majority was really in slavery to ideas which had long outlived their truth and usefulness. He contended that ideas become outdated in eighteen or twenty years at the most, but the foolish majority continued to cling to them and deny new truths brought to them by the intelligent minority. He challenged the citizens to deny that all great ideas and truths were first raised by the persecuted minority, those few men who dared to stand out against the prevailing opinions of the many. He said that the real intellectuals could be distinguished as easily as could a thoroughbred animal from a cross breed. Economic and social position had no bearing on the distinction. It was a man's soul and mind that separated him from the ignorant masses.

His challenge fell on deaf ears. As he knew from the beginning, the majority could not understand the meaning of his words. By vote they named him an enemy of the people. The next day they stoned his house and sent him threatening letters. His landlord ordered him to move. He lost his position as medical director of the Baths, and his daughter Petra was dismissed from her teaching position. In each case the person responsible for the move against him stated that it was only public opinion that forced the move. No one had anything against him or his family, but no one would fight the opinion of the majority. Even Captain Horster, a friend who had promised to take the Stockmanns to America on his next voyage, lost his ship because the owner was afraid to give a ship to the man, the only man, who had stood by the radical Dr. Stockmann.

Then the doctor learned that his father-in-law had bought up most of the now undesirable Bath stock with the money which would have gone to Mrs. Stock-mann and the children. The townspeople accused the doctor of attacking the Baths so that his family could buy the stock and make a profit, and his father-in-law accused him of ruining his wife's inheritance if he persisted in his stories about the uncleanliness of the Baths. Reviled and ridiculed on all sides, Doctor Stockmann determined to fight back. He could open a school. Starting only with any urchins he could find on the streets, he would teach the town and the world that he was stronger than the majority, that he was strong because he had the courage to stand alone.

ENOCH ARDEN

Type of work: Poem
Author: Alfred, Lord Tennyson (1809-1892)
Type of plot: Sentimental romance
Time of plot: Late eighteenth century
Locale: England
First published: 1864

Principal characters:
ENOCH ARDEN, a shipwrecked sailor
ANNIE LEE, his wife
PHILIP RAY, his friend
MIRIAM LANE, a tavern keeper

Critique:

To some modern readers the language of Enoch Arden may seem stilted and the story of his unselfish love mawkishly romantic, but we must remember that it was written during a period when unrequited love and unselfish devotion to one's family were favorite subjects of the reading public of England and America. Tennyson has one virtue not shared by all of his contemporaries; his poems are easily read and understood. He expressed better than any other poet of his time the essential character of the English people of the nineteenth century.

The Story:

Annie Lee, Philip Ray, and Enoch Arden played together as children. Sometimes Philip was the husband, sometimes Enoch, but Annie was always the mistress. If the boys quarreled over her, Annie would weep and beg them not to quarrel and say she would be a wife to both of them.

As they grew older and ceased their childish games, Enoch and Philip grew to love Annie. Enoch told her of his love, but Philip kept silent. Philip was the miller's son and a rich boy; Enoch was a poor orphan. He bought a small boat and became a fisherman. He sailed aboard a merchant ship for a full year before he had enough money to make a home for Annie. When he reached his twenty-first year he asked her to be his wife. While the two lovers talked together, Philip looked down on them as they sat at the edge of the wood. He went away quietly, locking his love for Annie deep in his heart.

For seven years Enoch and Annie lived in health and prosperity. They had two children, a girl and a boy. Then misfortune came. Enoch slipped and fell and lay months recovering. While he was ill, a sickly child was born, his favorite. There was no money and the children were hungry, and Enoch's heart almost broke to see his family in want.

The chance came for him to sail again on a merchantman bound for China. He sold his fishing boat that he might get a small store of goods and set Annie up as a trader while he was gone, so that she and the children might not be in want before his return. Annie begged him for their children's sake not to take this dangerous voyage. But Enoch laughed at her fears and told her to give all her cares to God, for the sea was His as well as the land, and He would take care of Enoch and bring him safely home. Annie cut a lock of hair from the sickly child and gave it to Enoch when he sailed.

For many months Annie waited for word from Enoch. Her business did not prosper; she did not know how to bargain. In the third year the sickly child died and Annie was crushed by grief.

After the funeral Philip broke his silence. He begged to send the children to school and care for them for the sake of his friendship with her and Enoch. Enoch had been gone for ten long years before Philip asked Annie to be his wife. He had not spoken before because he

1072

knew that she still waited for Enoch's return. Annie asked him to wait one year more. Six months beyond the year passed before she and Philip were wed. But still she feared to enter her own house and thought that one day she would see Enoch waiting for her. It was not until after she bore Philip a child that she was at peace with herself.

Enoch had been shipwrecked and cast upon a desert island. Although he did not lack for food and shelter, his heart was heavy with loneliness and worry about his wife and children. One day a ship came to the island and took him aboard. When he returned to England he was old and stooped and no one knew him. Finding his old house empty, he took lodging in a tavern kept by a widow, Miriam Lane. Not knowing who he was, Mrs. Lane told him of Annie and Philip and their new baby. Enoch could only murmur that he was lost. Watching from a high wall behind Philip's house, he saw Annie and the children in their happiness. He knew he could never shatter that new life.

He lived quietly and did what work he could and told no one his name or from where he came. At last, sick and dying, he called Mrs. Lane to his bedside and told her his story. He asked her to tell Annie and Philip and the children that he died blessing them, and he sent the lock of hair to Annie so she would know he spoke the truth. His was a great unselfish love until the end.

THE ENORMOUS ROOM

Type of work: Novel
Author: E. E. Cummings (1894-1962)
Type of plot: Autobiographical fiction
Time of plot: 1917
Locale: France
First published: 1922

Principal characters:
E. E. CUMMINGS, an American ambulance driver
W. S. B., his American friend
APOLLYON, head of the French prison
ROCKYFELLER,
THE WANDERER,
ZOO-LOO,
SURPLICE, and
JEAN LE NÈGRE, fellow prisoners

Critique:

The Enormous Room tells of more than three uncomfortable months in prison; it tells of the outrage and terror and hope and fear of men caught in the mesh of wartime government. E. E. Cummings did not want the book to stand merely as an indictment of the French government; he wanted it to tell of the strange and amazing things he had learned about people while in prison. In reading the book, one gets to know not only the author and his friend B., but all the inmates of the enormous room. Each is a study of some human quality. Abounding with sharply drawn scenes and portraits, the novel is compelling in its vivid detail. The book is not so much a study of the stupidity and brutality of war as it is a quietly passionate vindiction of the animal Man.

The Story:

E. E. Cummings and his friend, B., were unhappy as members of the Norton-Harjes Ambulance Service, a unit sent by Americans to aid the French during World War I. One day they were arrested by French military police. From hints dropped during an investigation Cummings gathered that B. had written some letters suspected by the censor. Because they were good friends, both men were held for questioning. Exactly what they were suspected of doing they never found out. On one occasion Cummings was asked whether he hated the Germans. He replied that he did not, that he simply loved the French very much. The investigating official could not understand how one could love the French and not hate Germans. Finally Cummings and B. were separated and sent to different prisons. As time went by, Cummings was questioned again and again and moved from one spot to another, always under strict guard.

Late one night he was taken to a prison in the little provincial town of Macé. There he was thrown into a huge darkened room, given a straw mattress, and told to go to sleep. In the darkness he counted at least thirty voices speaking eleven different languages. Early the next morning he was told that B., his friend, was in the same room. The two men were happy to see each other again. B. told him that the prisoners in the room were all suspected of being spies, some only because they spoke no French.

That morning he learned the routine of the prison. The enormous room was lined with mattresses down each side, with a few windows to let in light at one end. It smelled of stale tobacco and sweat. Some of the men in the room were mad; most of them were afraid they might become so. To all of them life consisted of following dull prison routine. At five-thirty in the morning someone went down to the kitchen under guard and brought back a bucket of sour, cold coffee. After coffee, the prisoners drew lots to see who would clear the room, sweep the floors, and collect the trash. At seven-thirty they were allowed to walk for two hours in a small, walled-in courtyard. Then came the first meal of the day, followed by another walk in the garden. At four they had supper. At eight they were locked in the enormous room for the night.

There was little entertainment except fighting and conversation. Some of the men spent their time trying to catch sight of women kept in another part of the prison. Cummings began to accustom himself to the enormous room and to make friends among the various inmates. One of the first of these was Count Bragard, a Belgian painter who specialized in portraits of horses. The count was a perfect gentleman, even in prison, and always looked neat and suave. He and Cummings discussed painting and the arts as if they were at some polite party. Before Cummings left, the count began to act strangely. He withdrew from his old friends. He was losing his mind.

One day Cummings was taken to see the head of the prison, a gross man he called Apollyon, after the devil in *Pilgrim's Progress*. Apollyon had no interest in the prisoners as long as they made as little trouble as possible for him. He questioned Cummings for a considerable time in an effort to learn why the American was there, a circumstance over which the American himself often wondered.

When new inmates arrived in the room, everyone looked them over hopefully, some to find a man with money he would lend, some to find a fellow-countryman, and some to find a friend. One day a very fat, rosy-cheeked man joined the group. He had been a successful manager of a disreputable house. Because he had a large sum of money with him, he was nicknamed Rockyfeller. He hired a strong man to act as his bodyguard. Nobody liked him, for he bought special privileges from the guards.

During his stay in the room, Cummings met three men, very different from each other, whose personal qualities were such that they made life seem meaningful to him. He called them the Delectable Mountains, after the mountains Christian found in *Pilgrim's Progress*. The first was the Wanderer, whose wife and three little children were in the women's ward of the prison. He was a strong man, simple in his emotions and feelings. Cummings liked to talk with him about his problems. One of the Wanderer's children, a little boy, sometimes came to the enormous room to visit his father. His pranks and games both bothered and amused the men. The Wanderer treated his son with love and the deepest kind of understanding. Until he was sent away he remained Cummings' best friend.

The second Delectable Mountain was called Zoo-loo, a Polish farmer who could speak neither French nor English, but who could communicate by signs. In a short time he and Cummings knew all about each other. Zoo-loo had a knack for hiding money, and despite the fact that the head of the prison had him searched from head to toe, and all his belongings searched, he seemed always able to produce a twenty franc note from his left ear or the back of his neck. His kindnesses to Cummings and B. were innumerable.

The third Delectable Mountain was an amazing little man named Surplice. Everything astonished him. When Cummings had some candy or cheese, Surplice was sure to come over to his cot and ask questions about it in a shy manner. His curiosity and friendly conversation made everything seem more important and interesting than it really was.

One morning Jean le Nègre was brought to the enormous room, a gigantic, simple-minded Negro whom Cummings was to remember as the finest of his fellow prisoners. Jean was given to practical jokes and tall tales; he had been arrested for impersonating an English officer and had been sent to the prison for psychopathic observation. Because of his powerful body, the women prisoners called their approval and admiration when he walked in the courtyard. His favorite was Lulu, who smuggled money and a lace handkerchief to him. When she was sent to another prison, Jean was disconsolate. When one of the prisoners pulled at Lulu's handkerchief, Jean handled him roughly. A scuffle followed. The guards came and Jean was taken away for punishment. Calls from the women prisoners aroused him so that he attacked the guards and sent them flying until he was quieted and bound by a fellow prisoner whom he trusted. After that experience Jean grew quiet and shy.

Just before Cummings himself was released, B. was sent away. Jean le Nègre tried to cheer Cummings with his funny stories and exaggerated lies, but without much success. Cummings was afraid B. might never get free from the prisons of France, a groundless fear as he learned later. He himself left the enormous room knowing that in it he had learned the degradation and nobility and endurance of human nature.

AN ENQUIRY CONCERNING HUMAN UNDERSTANDING

Type of work: Philosophical treatise
Author: David Hume (1711-1776)
First published: 1748

"Philosophical decisions," says Hume toward the end of his *Enquiry,* "are nothing but the reflections of common life, methodised and corrected." This simple, homely epigram conceals a great deal. For one thing, the *Enquiry* is actually a sort of popularized revision of ideas that were systematically developed in Book I of his precocious *Treatise of Human Nature* (1739-1740), which, although it was completed before the author was twenty-five, has been characterized as one of the most profound, thoroughly reasoned, and purely scientific works in the history of philosophy. Secondly, Hume's method for correcting the reflections of common life actually involves a thorough attack on the obscurities of metaphysical idealists.

Born in an age of reason, Hume at first shared the optimism of those who were certain that pure reason could unlock the secrets of nature, and as he read Bacon, Newton, Hobbes, and Locke, he longed for fame equal to theirs. But, as he reported in a letter to Sir Gilbert Elliot, though he "began with an anxious search after arguments, to confirm the common opinion; doubts stole in, dissipated, returned; were again dissipated, returned again; and it was a perpetual struggle of restless imagination against inclination, perhaps against reason." That last, "perhaps against reason," is the crucial phrase, for no philosopher before Hume used reason so brilliantly in an attack against the certainties of reason. The twelve essays of the *Enquiry* reflect his three principal attacks: (1) against rationalism, the doctrine of innate ideas, faith in ontological reasoning and an ordered universe; (2) against empiricism, both the kind that led to Lockian dualism and Berkeleyan idealism, on the ground that neither the physical nor the spiritual can be proved; and (3) against deism, based on universal axioms and the law of causality. It is not surprising that since Hume religions have largely made their appeals to faith rather than to reason.

Considering what remains when such thoroughgoing skepticism rejects so much of the beliefs of rational men, Hume himself readily admitted (in the fourth essay, "Sceptical Doubts Concerning the Operations of the Understanding") that as a man he was quite satisfied with ordinary reasoning processes, but that as a philosopher he had to be skeptical. For reasoning was not based on immediate sense experience. "The most lively thought is still inferior to the dullest sensation," he asserted in his second essay, "The Origin of Ideas." Unless the mind is "disordered by disease or madness," actual perceptions have the greatest "force and vivacity," and it is only on such matters of basic mental fact rather than on the abstract relations of ideas, as in mathematics, that we must depend for certainties about life. For example, no amount of reasoning could have led Adam in the Garden of Eden to believe that fluid, transparent water would drown him or that bright, warm fire would burn him to ashes. "No object ever discovers [reveals], by the qualities which appear to the senses, either the causes which produced it, or the effects which arise from it." In dealing with this idea, Hume is quite dogged and persistent; he backs every argument into a corner, into some "dangerous dilemma." What is more he enjoys himself immensely while doing it—"philosophers that gave themselves airs of superior wisdom and sufficiency, have a hard task when they encounter persons of inquisitive dispositions," he says. Concerning cause and effect, he argues that we expect similar effects from causes that appear similar; yet this relationship does not always exist and, though it is observed, it is not reasoned. Furthermore, it is merely an arbitrary assumption, an act of faith, that events which we remember as having occurred sequentially in the past will continue to do so in the future. Causation thus was merely a belief, and belief he had defined as a "lively idea related to or associated with a present impression."

This seemed to Hume not merely an impractical philosophical idea, but a momentous discovery of great consequence. Since causation was an *a priori* principle of both natural and moral philosophy, and since causation could not be reasonably demonstrated to be true, a tremendous revolution in human thought was in preparation. Only in the pure realm of ideas, logic, and mathematics, not contingent upon the direct sense awareness of reality, could causation safely (because arbitrarily) be applied—all other sciences are reduced to probability. The concluding essay, "Of the Academical or Sceptical Philosophy," reaches grand heights of eloquence, when Hume argues that *a priori* reasoning can make anything appear to produce anything: "the falling of a pebble may, for aught we know, extinguish the sun; or the wish of a man control the planets in their orbits. . . ."

> When we run over libraries, persuaded of these principles, what havoc must we make? If we take in hand any volume; of divinity or school metaphysics, for instance; let us ask, Does it contain any abstract reasoning concerning quantity or number? No. Does it contain any experimental reasoning concerning matter of fact and existence? No. Commit it then to the flames: for it can contain nothing but sophistry and illusion.

The polemic vigor of the essays stems in large part from the bitter experiences Hume had in the years immediately preceding the publication of the *Enquiry*. In 1744 he had sought to fill a vacancy in the chair of Ethics and Pneumatical Philosophy at Edinburgh University, but to his astonishment his *Treatise* was invoked to prevent the appointment: "such a popular clamor has been raised against me in Edinburgh, on account of Scepticism, Heterodoxy, and other hard names . . . that my Friends find some Difficulty in working out the Point of my Professorship." Then he was dismissed without full salary as tutor to the mad son of the Marquis of Annandale. These experiences helped sharpen the hard cutting edge of his thought and prose style.

After refining his conception of reason and its modes of function, Hume applies it to four crucial problems: "Liberty and Necessity," "Reason of Animals," "Miracles," and "Particular Providence and a Future State."

Concerning liberty and necessity, Hume argues that since the subject relates to common life and experience (unlike topics such as the origin of worlds or the region of spirits), only ambiguity of language keeps the dispute alive. For a clear definition, he suggests that it be consistent with plain matters of fact and with itself. Difficulty arises when philosophers approach the problem by examining the faculties of the soul rather than the operations of body and brute matter. In the latter, men assume that they perceive cause and effect, but in the functioning of their minds they feel no connection between motive and action. However, we cannot invoke the doctrine of cause and effect without, ultimately, tracing all actions—including evil ones—to the Deity whom men refuse to accept as the author of guilt and moral turpitude in all his creatures. As a matter of fact, freedom and necessity are matters of momentary emotional feeling "not to be controuled or altered by any philosophical theory or speculation whatsoever."

The "Reason of Animals" consists—as it does in children, philosophers, and mankind in general—not so much in logical inferences as in experience of analogies and sequential actions. Observation and experience alone teach a horse the proper height which he can leap or a greyhound how to meet the hare in her tracks with the least expenditure of energy. Hume's learning theory here seems to be based on the pleasure-pain principle and forms the background for some theories of twentieth-century psychology. However, Hume ends this essay with a long qualification in which he cites the Instincts, unlearned knowledge derived from the original hand of nature, and then adds this curious final comment: "The experimental reasoning itself, which we possess in common with beasts, and on which the whole conduct of life depends, is nothing but a species of instinct or mechanical power, that acts in us unknown to ourselves."

The essay on miracles is perhaps the most spirited of the entire collection and it is the one which Hume expected, correctly, would stir the greatest opposition. Nevertheless, he was certain that his argument would be, for the wise and the learned, "an everlasting check to all kinds of superstitious delusion, and consequently . . . useful as long as the world endures." Events can be believed to happen only when they are observed, and all reports of events not directly observed must be believed only to the degree that they conform with probability, experimentally or experientially derived. A miracle is a violation of the laws of nature; therefore it violates all probability; therefore it is impossible. History gives no instance of any miracle personally attended to by a sufficient number of unquestionably honest, educated, intelligent men. Despite the surprise, wonder, and other pleasant sensations attendant upon reports of novel experiences, all new dis-

coveries that achieve credibility among men have always resembled in fundamentals those objects and events of which we already have experience. The most widespread belief in miracles exists among primitive barbarians. Finally, since there is no objective way of confirming miracles, believers have no just basis for rejecting those claimed by all religions. "So that, on the whole, we may conclude, that the *Christian Religion* not only was at first attended with miracles, but even at this day cannot be believed by any reasonable person without one. Mere reason is insufficient to convince us . . . to believe what is most contrary to custom and experience."

In the 1777 posthumous edition of the *Enquiry* appeared the announcement that these unsystematic essays be *alone* regarded as containing Hume's philosophical sentiments and principles. Despite the fact that professional philosophers, especially the logical positivists, still prefer the earlier *Treatise of Human Nature*, it is well that the *Enquiry* with its livelier style and popular appeal stands as his personal testament. In it he said that he would be "happy if . . . we can undermine the foundations of an abstruse philosophy, which seems to have hitherto served only as a shelter to superstition, and a cover to absurdity and error." The irony is that he succeeded so well in undermining reason that he opened the door to the romanticism of the late eighteenth and early nineteenth centuries. But his voice has outlasted that babel and his humanistic skepticism survives. "Be a philosopher," he cautioned himself, "but amidst all your philosophy, be still a man."

THE EPIC OF GILGAMESH

Type of work: Poem
Author: Unknown
Type of plot: Heroic adventure
Time of plot: Remote antiquity
Locale: The ancient world
First transcribed: c. 2,000 B.C.

Principal characters:
GILGAMESH, ruler of Uruk
ENGIDU, his companion
ANU, the chief god
ISHTAR, divinity of fertility
UTNAPISHTIM, a man who found the secret of life
UR-SHANABI, boatman on the waters of death
NINSUN, a goddess
SIDURI, the divine cup-bearer
KHUMBABA, a dragon

Critique:

The idea of the superman is not a new one. Demigods who overcame great obstacles enjoy a long and honored literary tradition. Achilles, Odysseus, Hercules, Samson, Beowulf, Roland and King Arthur all have epic stature. Earlier than any of these, however, is Gilgamesh, the valiant hero of a Babylonian epic written about four thousand years ago. A figure of heroic proportions, Gilgamesh knew love and conflict, friendship and loyalty, joy and sorrow, courage and fear, and ultimately the horror and mystery of death. Thus the Gilgamesh epic embraces the enduring themes of literature, and its hero remains an enduring affirmation of life in all its transience and mystery.

The Story:

Gilgamesh was the wisest, strongest and most handsome of mortals, for he was two-thirds god and one-third man. As king of the city-state of Uruk he built a monumental wall around the city, but in doing so he overworked the city's inhabitants unmercifully, to the point where they prayed to the gods for relief.

The god Anu listened to their plea and called the goddess Aruru to fashion another demigod like Gilgamesh in order that the two heroes might fight, and thus give Uruk peace. Aruru created the warrior Engidu out of clay and sent him to live among the animals of the hills.

A hunter of Uruk found Engidu and in terror reported his existence to Gilgamesh. Gilgamesh advised the hunter to take a priestess to Engidu's watering place to lure Engidu to the joys of civilization and away from his animal life. The priestess initiated Engidu into civilization with her body, her bread, and her wine. Having forsaken his animal existence, Engidu and the priestess started for Uruk. On their arrival she told him of the strength and wisdom of Gilgamesh and of how Gilgamesh had told the goddess Ninsun about his dreams of meeting Engidu, his equal, in combat.

Engidu challenged Gilgamesh by barring his way to the temple. An earth-shaking fight ensued in which Gilgamesh stopped Engidu's onslaught. Engidu praised Gilgamesh's strength and the two enemies became inseparable friends.

Gilgamesh informed Engidu of his wish to conquer the terrible monster, Khumbaba, and challenged him to go along. Engidu replied that the undertaking was full of peril for both. Gilgamesh answered that Engidu's fear of death deprived him of his might. At last Engidu

THE EPIC OF GILGAMESH by William Ellery Leonard. By permission of the publishers, The Viking Press, Inc. Copyright, 1934, by William Ellery Leonard.

agreed to go with his friend. Gilgamesh then went to the elders and they, like Engidu, warned him of the perils he would encounter. Seeing his determination, the elders gave him their blessing. Gilgamesh then went to Ninsun and she also warned him of the great dangers, but to no avail. Then she took Engidu aside and told him to give Gilgamesh special protection.

Upon climbing the cedar mountain to reach Khumbaba, Gilgamesh related three terrible dreams to Engidu, who shored up Gilgamesh's spirit by placing a favorable interpretation on them. On reaching the gate to the cedar wood where Khumbaba resided, the pair were stopped by the watchman, who possessed seven magic mantles. The two heroes succeeded in overcoming him. Accidentally, Engidu touched the magic portal of the gate; immediately he felt faint and weak, as if afraid of death. The champions entered the cedar wood and with the aid of the sun god slew Khumbaba.

Upon their return to Uruk after their victory, the goddess Ishtar fell in love with Gilgamesh and asked him to be her consort. But Gilgamesh, being wiser than her previous consorts, recalled all of the evil things she had done to her earlier lovers. Ishtar then angrily ascended to heaven and reported his scornful refusal to Anu. Threatening to destroy mankind, she forced Anu to create a monster bull that would kill Gilgamesh.

Anu formed the bull and sent it to Uruk. After it had slain five hundred warriors in two snorts, Engidu jumped on its back while Gilgamesh drove his sword into its neck. Engidu then threw the bull's thighbone in Ishtar's face, and Gilgamesh held a feast of victory in his palace.

Engidu, still ailing from touching the portal to the cedar wood, cursed those who had showed him civilization. He related his nightmares to Gilgamesh, grew faint-hearted, and feared death. Since he had been cursed by touching

the gate, he died. Gilgamesh mourned his friend six days and nights; on the seventh he left Uruk to cross the steppes in search of Utnapishtim, the mortal who had discovered the secret of life.

Upon reaching the mountain named Mashu, he found scorpion men guarding the entrance to the underground passage. They received him cordially when they learned he was seeking Utnapishtim, but they warned him that no one had ever found a way through the mountain.

Gilgamesh traveled the twelve miles through the mountain in pitch darkness, and at last he entered a garden. There he found Siduri, the cup-bearing goddess, who remarked on his haggard condition. Gilgamesh explained that his woeful appearance had been caused by the loss of Engidu, and that he sought Utnapishtim. The goddess advised him to live in pleasure at home and warned him of the dangers ahead.

Gilgamesh went on his way, seeking the boatman Ur-Shanabi, who might possibly take him across the waters of death. On finding Ur-Shanabi's stone coffers, Gilgamesh broke them in anger, but he made up for them by presenting the boatman with huge poles. Ur-Shanabi then ferried Gilgamesh across the waters of death.

Utnapishtim, meeting Gilgamesh on the shore, also spoke of his haggard condition. Gilgamesh told him about the loss of Engidu and his own search for the secret of life. Utnapishtim replied that nothing was made to last forever, that life was transient, and that death was part of the inevitable process.

Gilgamesh then asked how Utnapishtim had found the secret of eternal life, and Utnapishtim told him the story of the Great Flood.

Utnapishtim had been told in a dream of the gods' plans to flood the land. So he built an ark and put his family and all kinds of animals on it. When the flood came, he and those on the ark survived, and when the flood subsided he found himself on Mount Nisser. After the waters had returned to their normal level, he gave thanks to the gods, and in return the god Ea blessed him and his wife with the secret of life everlasting.

After finishing his story Utnapishtim advised Gilgamesh to return home, but before going he had Ur-Shanabi bathe and clothe Gilgamesh in a robe that remained clean as long as he lived. As Gilgamesh was leaving Utnapishtim gave him the secret of life, a magic plant which grew at the bottom of the waters of death. However, as Gilgamesh bathed in a pool on his way home, an evil serpent ate the plant.

On arriving home Gilgamesh went to Ninsun to inquire how he could reach Engidu in the land of the dead. Although Ninsun directed him, he failed in his attempt because he broke some of the taboos that she had laid out for him. Deeply disappointed, he made one final appeal to the god Ea, the lord of the depths of the waters, and Engidu was brought forth. Gilgamesh asked Engidu what happened to one after death, and Engidu laid bare the full terrors of the afterworld. Worms, neglect, and disrespect were the lot of the dead.

EPIGRAMS OF MARTIAL

Type of work: Verse epigrams
Author: Martial (Marcus Valerius Martialis, c. 40-c. 104)
First transcribed: 80-104

The fourteen books of epigrams which were written by Martial during a pivotal period in the history of Rome display a rare form of literary accomplishment, the adoption and complete individual mastery of a literary form by one man. From the time of his arrival at Rome, about the age of twenty-three, until his return to his birthplace in Spain, Martial wrote verse epigrams on a wide variety of subjects and in many different styles.

Almost all that we know of Martial we learn from his epigrams, and a great deal of our present knowledge of Rome from the death of Nero, in A.D. 68, until the end of the first century comes from the same source. What Martial tells us is the sort of information that could not, perhaps, be gained in any other way. One of the most common subject areas of Martial's verse is the everyday life of ancient Rome. He took an active part in that life, and it is realistically mirrored in his writings.

There are roughly five other kinds of epigrams that Martial produced. The first of these, probably the most important to him personally, is the epigram written in praise of the emperor or some other man of wealth and power. This type was written largely as a means of subsistence, patronage being the primary system by which poets lived. The contemplative epigrams, usually addressed to friends, show that Martial was realistic almost to the point of cynicism. He reached no great heights of philosophy, wishing only to be comfortable and peaceful. His desire for peace and solitude is expressed in another type of epigram in which he praises life in the country. In these Martial sees the country with the enthusiasm often found in the city dweller, but he did not write pastoral verse; he saw the Italian countryside as it really existed. The epigrammatic epitaphs, often written on children, or an-

imals, are among his best work, revealing sentiments that are rare in Martial, feeling often leavened by humor. In the epigrams on friendship he comes the closest to real emotion. Romantic love is usually treated satirically, and his discussions of that passion in himself seem devoid of sincere feeling.

Perhaps the chief fault that has been found with his work is found in Martial's personal situation, his toadying to men of position. When he begged the Emperor Domitian, whose name has become synonymous with cruel despotism and wicked licentiousness, for a special position (pleading as the father of three children), for example, his epigram has a self-abasement that may disgust the modern reader:

> Welfare and glory of the earth, while thee
> We safe behold, we gods believe to be;
> If my slight books did e'er thee entertain,
> And oft to read them thou didst not disdain,
> What nature does deny, do thou bestow:
> For *father of three children* make me go.
> When my verse takes not, this will be an ease;
> A high reward, in case it thee do please.

It is important, however, to understand the position poets held in Rome at that time. Only through patronage, from the emperor if possible, could a poet lead a comfortable life. Everyone who hoped to be looked upon as a gentleman wrote verses, and those who wrote to live were compelled to praise and praise highly in order to be heard. Martial was certainly not alone in this respect. Completely a product of his time, he accepted the necessity to praise great men as a part of the literary milieu in which he lived.

Criticism that may carry more weight today is Martial's lack of poetic vision. He is never profound, seldom lyrically imaginative. His subjects are the people and things around him, and he depicts them as they are. It is this accuracy of portrayal that makes his verse so valuable in understanding his era. Counterbalancing this absence of elevated vision, however, is Martial's technical grasp of the form in which he wrote. Although he did not create the epigram, he is usually considered the first epigrammatist. He adopted the form, wrote exclusively in it, and did with it all that could be done.

The verse epigram customarily has two major parts, the exposition and the conclusion. The parts may vary in length —Martial's epigrams are from two to over thirty verses long—but usually the exposition takes up most of the poem, with the conclusion being short, often containing a sharp twist of meaning. Within this general framework Martial used direct address, questions, brief transition from exposition to conclusion, satire, irony, and sarcasm. Striking exaggerations and sudden surprises are common, as are plays on words and brief aphorisms. Rhetorical devices abound. His epigram "On a Pretender," for example, shows the quick turn of meaning at the close:

He whom you see to walk in so much state,
Waving and slow, with a majestic gait,
In purple clad, passing the nobles' seat,
My Publius not in garments more complete;—
Whose new rich coach, with gilt and studded reins,
Fair boys and grown-men follow in great trains,
Lately his very ring in pawn did lay
For four poor crowns, his supper to defray.

Along with his technical skill goes an animation and a lively perception that make his epigrams often sound like casual conversation. With all the conciseness so necessary for the successful epigram, Martial has an ease that removes from his verses the tenseness that very often causes epigrams to be painful reading.

Although he himself was poor, Martial was the associate of rich men, and so had full opportunity to see Roman life in all its aspects. Slaves as well as emperors are the subjects of his epigrams. Dinner parties are described along with great monuments. Everywhere he shows a sharp eye and a penetrating wit. Hating pretension, he pricks many a pompous bubble. Few elements of physical or human nature escape his attention.

Apart from Martial's clear pictures of Rome at the end of the first century, probably his greatest importance lies in his influence upon later writers of the epigram. Certainly it would be difficult to find any seventeenth- or eighteenth-century writer of this form in England who did not turn to Martial as his inspiration and guide. That there are at least seven French translations of the epigrams testifies to his popularity on the Continent.

Shortly after the accession of the Emperor Trajan, whom Martial flattered in verse with little effect, the poet returned, in 94, to his birthplace, Bilbilis, a Roman colony in Spain, where he lived on a comfortable estate given to him by a woman whom he probably later married. Characteristically, he was given money for the trip by a friend, Pliny, because of some verses written to him. It is equally characteristic that Martial continued his writing in Spain, sending his epigrams to Rome promptly, but now with frequent expressions of longing for the excitements and pleasures of the city that was to be for only a short time longer the capital of the world.

THE EPINICIA

Type of work: Poetry
Author: Pindar (c. 522-c. 443 B.C.)
First transcribed: 502-452 B.C.

Pindar, by general consent the supreme lyric poet of Greece, is one of the least read of the world's great writers. A number of reasons have been given by various Greek scholars for the neglect of Pindar by modern readers. His language, based upon the Dorian dialect, poses problems for readers of his poems in the original Greek. Because all his *epinicia* or victory odes (his only complete poems extant) were written for special occasions and for special audiences, today's readers must depend upon scholarly notes for explanations of his many allusions and his abrupt transitions. The nature of the victory odes, too, makes them seem monotonous and even somewhat repetitious if a number of them are read at one time.

Edith Hamilton has said that Pindar is the most resistant of all poets to translation; the intricate form of his poems has never been more than faintly approximated in most of the attempts that have been made. In these odes Pindar achieved a masterly blend of carefully balanced structure and apparent emotional freedom, so that while he seems carried away by his feelings, he is at the same time in full control of his art. Such a fusion is difficult enough, one would suppose, for a poet himself to attain. It is even more so for a scholar or another poet to imitate successfully in translating Pindar's Greek. Ernest Myers and Sir John Sandys simply turned the Greek poems into English prose.

One reason for the tenuous appeal of Pindar was mentioned a half-century ago by Robert Tyrrell. "It is hard," says Tyrrell,

for us to figure to the imagination a form of art which partakes in nearly equal parts of the nature of a collect,

a ballad, and an oratorio; or to enter into the mind of a poet who is partly also a priest, a librettist, and a ballet master; who, while celebrating the victory of (perhaps) a boy in a wrestling match, yet feels that he is not only doing an act of divine service and worship, but preaching the sacred truth of the unity of the Hellenes and their common descent from gods and heroes.

Yet the reader who does make the attempt to imagine the ancient occasions when these odes were first performed and to understand their effect upon the Greeks who watched and listened, even if he reads them only in translation, will be richly rewarded as he becomes familiar with their form and purpose and with the artistry of the poet who wrote them.

The *epinicia* were written on contract to celebrate the winning of such events as chariot races, foot races, boxing and wrestling contests, and the combination pentathlon in four regularly held great "games" or athletic meets. (The Pythian games included competition in singing to the flute and playing on the flute and lyre, as well as the usual athletic events and horse races.) These games were religious as well as secular, and they honored particular gods: the Olympian and Nemean games were in honor of Zeus, the Pythian of Apollo, and the Isthmian of Poseidon. The events were Panhellenic, open only to contestants from Greece or from such Greek island colonies as Rhodes and Sicily. Any soldier bearing arms to the games, which were held during periods of truce, was liable to arrest and could be freed only by ransom.

The odes were not written at the time of the victories which they celebrated but

THE ODES OF PINDAR. Translated by Richard Lattimore. Excerpts reprinted by permission of the publishers, The University of Chicago Press. Copyright, 1947, by The University of Chicago.

were composed for presentation at a later time. Exact details are not known but it is believed that the odes, commissioned by the family or patron of the victor, were presented by trained singers at some private entertainment.

Though a close study of all forty-five of the *Epinicia* reveals many individual differences (several, in fact, are not really victory odes), most of them follow a general pattern. Composed in groups of three stanzas—strophe, antistrophe, and epode—they contain an introduction which invokes divine aid to the poet, praises the victor, and may include some reference to the contest itself (which is never actually described); a myth about gods or heroes; and eulogy of the victor, his family, and his city, along with social, moral, or even semi-philosophical commentary on life. Though the moral observations and exhortations are usually reserved for the concluding section of an ode, they often appear in other sections. The odes vary considerably in length: Olympia 12, for example, contains only nineteen lines, whereas Pythia 4 runs to 299. The present order of the odes does not follow the chronology of their composition. They are grouped according to the games in which the victories were won; and even within the four groups chronology is not followed.

Pindar belonged to the aristocracy and in the odes he celebrates the virtues and accomplishments of aristocratic families for whom the poems were composed. This praise is to be expected since he had been paid to write the poems, but one gathers that Pindar had scant interest in the less fortunate classes, whom he rarely mentions. When he says, in Pythia 2, that "wealth, with wisdom allotted thereto, is the best gift of Fortune," he seems to be expressing his own belief. A similar sentiment is found in Nemea 9: "For if with much possession a man win conspicuous honor,/there lies beyond no mark for a mortal to overtake with his feet."

The many lines in which Pindar states his faith in the gods or praises them for their gifts to men suggest the earnest sincerity of his religion. In Pythia 2 he reminds Hieron, tyrant of Syracuse, that

It is God that accomplishes all term to hopes,
God, who overtakes the flying eagle, outpasses the dolphin in the sea; who bends under his strength the man with thoughts too high,
while to others he gives honor that ages not.

In Isthmia 3 he says: "Great prowess descends upon mortals,/Zeus, from you." He often invokes the Graces or indicates his great debt to them. One of the most beautiful of the briefer *Epinicia* is Olympia 14, which is less a victory ode than a hymn in praise of the Graces who bless mankind. It begins:

You who have your dwelling
in the place of splendid horses, founded beside the waters of Kephisos:
O queens of song and queens of shining
Orchomenos: Graces: guardians of the primeval Minyai,
hear! My prayer is to you. By your means all delight,
all that is sweet, is given to mankind.

The poet refers to the Olympian victory itself only at the very end, when he asks that Echo tell Kleodamos that his son has "crowned his youthful locks with garlands won from the ennobling games."

Though there is an air of joyousness in the *Epinicia*, with many references to drinking and feasting and to processional singing to the music of flute or lyre, they are dignified by relating mortal victories of strength and skill to the glorious deeds of the gods or great heroes of the past. The myths either alluded to or told in detail include stories about Zeus, Herakles, Belerophon, Tantalus, Jason, Orestes, Peleus, and Hippolyta. The poems are also elevated by the beauty of Pindar's style, his frequent adjurations to right living, and his reminders that man's life is filled with both lights and shadows. In Pythia 8 he praises the sweetness of

1086

life when God's brightness shines on men. Yet he reminds us in Pythia 12:

> Success for men, if it comes ever, comes not unattended with difficulty. A god can end it, even today. That which is fated you cannot escape.

Though the fame of Pindar rests almost entirely upon his *Epinicia*, he is known to have written several other types of lyrics, among them hymns, paeans, dithyrambs, eulogies, and dirges. Of these, more than three hundred fragments have survived, enough to show Pindar's considerable versatility both in form and in style. Among the more beautiful of the fragments are those from the dirges, as in this picture of the dead in Elysium:

> For them the sun shineth in his strength, in the world below, while here 'tis night; and, in meadows red with roses, the space before their city is shaded by the incense-tree, and is laden with golden fruits. . . .

EPITAPH OF A SMALL WINNER

Type of work: Novel
Author: Joaquim Maria Machado de Assis (1839-1908)
Type of plot: Philosophical realism
Time of plot: 1805-1869
Locale: Rio de Janeiro, Brazil
First published: 1880

Principal characters:
BRAZ CUBAS, a wealthy, cultured Brazilian
MARCELLA, his first mistress
VIRGILIA, his fiancée, later his mistress
LOBO NEVES, Virgilia's husband
QUINCAS BORBA, a philosopher and pickpocket

Critique:

This novel, written by one of Brazil's leading men of letters, was not made available in English translation until 1952, even though it had long been a favorite with readers in the original Portuguese and in Spanish translations. Machado de Assis himself was president of the Brazilian Academy of Letters from its foundation in 1897 until his death in 1908. *Epitaph of a Small Winner* is the story of an ordinary man who sums up the profit of living as nothing, except that he had left no children to whom he could pass on the misery of human existence. Because he left no children to endure life, he was, says the author, a small winner in the game of life. Obviously Machado de Assis' attitude is one of complete and ironic pessimism. As the English translator points out, the book combines the twin themes of nature's indifference to man and man's own egoism. Readers familiar with eighteenth-century fiction will recognize many stylistic peculiarities similar to those in Sterne's *Tristram Shandy.*

The Story:

Braz Cubas, a wealthy Brazilian, died of pneumonia in his sixty-fifth year. After his death he decided to write his autobiography, to while away a part of eternity and to give mankind some record of his life.

Braz was born in 1805. His childhood was an easy one, for his father was extremely wealthy and indulgent, only pretending to be severe with his child for the sake of appearances. One of the earliest experiences the boy remembered was the elation of the Brazilians over the defeat of Napoleon, an occasion marked in his memory by the gift of a small sword. The sword was the most important aspect of the occasion, and Braz remarked that each person has his own "sword" which makes occasions important.

As a child, Braz Cubas did not like school. In his seventeenth year he had his first love affair with a courtesan named Marcella. Trying to please his mistress, Braz spent all the money he could borrow from his mother, and then gave promissory notes to fall due on the day he inherited his father's estate. His father, learning of the affair, paid off his son's debts and shipped him off to a university in Spain. At first Braz hoped to take Marcella with him. She refused to go.

Graduated from the university and awarded a degree, Braz admitted that he knew very little. He then took advantage of his father's liberality and wealth and spent several years traveling about Europe. Called back to Rio de Janeiro by news that his mother was dying of cancer, he arrived home in time to see her before she died. After her death he went into retirement, remaining in seclusion until his father came to him with plans for a marriage and a seat in the Brazilian legislative body. After some vacillation Braz decided to obey his father's wishes. The reason for his hesitation was a love affair with a rather beautiful girl. His discovery that she was lame, however, turned him away from her. On his return to social life he learned that the young woman his father had picked out for him, a girl named Virgilia, had position, wealth, and beauty. It was through her father's influence that the elder Cubas expected his son to get ahead politically. Unfortunately for the schemes of both father and son, Virgilia met Lobo Neves, a young man with more ambition and greater prospects. She decided to marry him, a decision which ended, at least temporarily, prospects of a political career for Braz.

Disappointed and disgruntled with life, he accidentally met Marcella, his former mistress. He found her greatly changed, for smallpox had destroyed her beauty. After losing her looks, she had left her earlier profession to become the keeper of a small jewelry shop.

Disappointment over his son's failure to win Virgilia was too much for his father, who died shortly afterward. There was a great to-do after the father's death, for Braz' brother-in-law turned out to be an avaricious man who wanted his wife, Braz' sister, to have as much of the estate as possible. Braz accepted calmly the selfish and unfortunate aspect of human nature thus revealed and agreed, for his sister's sake, to be reconciled with his greedy brother-in-law.

Not very long after his father's death, Braz learned from Virgilia's brother that Virgilia and her husband were returning to Rio de Janeiro. Braz was pleased; he was still in love with her. A few days after the return of Virgilia and her husband, he met them at a ball. Virgilia and Braz danced several waltzes together and fell more deeply in love than they had ever been while Braz was courting her. They continued to meet and before long Virgilia became his mistress.

One day Braz found a package in which were several bundles of banknotes. He kept the money and later used it to establish a trust fund for Doña Placida, a former servant of Virgilia's family, who maintained the house in which Virgilia and Braz kept their assignations. They managed for several years to keep their affair a secret, so that Braz could be a guest in Virgilia's home as well. In fact, he and Lobo Neves were good friends.

One day Braz met Quincas Borba, an old schoolmate who had been reduced to begging. The man took some money from Braz and, as he discovered later, also stole his watch. That night Braz suggested to Virgilia that they run away. She refused to do so. They had a lovers' quarrel, followed by a tender scene of repentance.

A short time later Lobo Neves was offered the governorship of a province, and he suggested that Braz accompany him as his secretary. The situation was inviting to the two lovers, but they knew that in the smaller provincial capital their secret could not long be hidden. Their problems were unexpectedly solved when superstitious Neves refused the government post because the document appointing him was dated on the thirteenth of the month.

The love affair continued until Virgilia became pregnant. Neither of the lovers doubted that Braz was the father of the child, and he acted very much like a husband who expected to be presented with his first-born. The child, not carried the full time, died at birth, much to the sorrow of Virgilia and Braz, and of the husband as well, who thought the child was his.

One day Braz received a letter from Quincas Borba, the begging schoolmate who had stolen his watch. Having improved his finances, the beggar had become a philosopher, a self-styled humanist. Borba's ideas fascinated Braz, who had always fancied himself an intellectual and a literary man. He was also pleased when Borba sent him a watch as good as the one he had stolen. Braz spent a great deal of time with Borba, for Neves had become suspicious of the relationship between his wife and her lover, and the two were discreet enough to stay away from each other for a time.

At last Virgilia and her husband left Rio de Janeiro after Neves received another political appointment. For a time Braz felt like a widower. Lonely, he himself turned to public life. Defeated for office, he then became the publisher of an opposition newspaper, but his venture was not successful. He also fell in love and finally decided to get married. Once more he was disappointed, for his fiancée died during an epidemic.

The years passed rather uneventfully. Braz grew older, and so did his friends. Not many weeks after the death of Quincas Borba, who had become a close companion, Braz himself fell ill of pneumonia. One visitor during his last illness was Virgilia, whose husband had died, but even her presence was not enough to keep Braz from slipping into delirium. In his dying moments he cast up the accounts of his life and decided that in the game of life he was the winner by only a small margin, in that he had brought no one else into the world to suffer the misery of life.

EREC AND ENIDE

Type of work: Poem
Author: Chrétien de Troyes (c.1140-c.1190)
Type of plot: Chivalric romance
Time of plot: Sixth century
Locale: Arthurian England
First transcribed: Before 1164

Principal characters:

KING ARTHUR
QUEEN GUINEVERE
EREC, a knight of the Round Table and son of King Lac
ENIDE, his bride
GUIVRET THE LITTLE, Erec's friend and benefactor

Critique:

Erec and Enide is chronologically the first of a group of metrical romances by a master tale teller of the medieval period about whom very little is known. More important, it is the oldest romance on Arthurian materials extant in any language. In it the more primitive Celtic elements of the writer's sources have been lost or are almost completely obscured; King Arthur and his knights are now models of the highly sophisticated and intricately detailed chivalric code growing out of the courts of love which flourished in France during the Middle Ages. Written in eight-syllable rhyming couplets, and sometimes called the first novel because of its consistent plot, this story is one of four which give us the most idealized expression of the code of chivalry by a single writer of medieval times.

The Story:

One Easter season, while King Arthur held his court in the royal town of Cardigan, he summoned all his knights to a hunt for the White Stag. Sir Gawain, hearing of the king's wish, was displeased and said that no good would come of that ancient custom, for the law of the hunt decreed that the successful hunter must also kiss the lady whom he considered the most beautiful damsel of the court. As Sir Gawain noted, there was likely to be dissension among the assembled knights; each was prepared to defend his own true love as the loveliest and gentlest lady in the land, and he would be angered by the slight put upon her if she were not so chosen.

At daybreak the hunters set out. After them rode Queen Guinevere, attended by Erec, a fair and brave knight, and one of the queen's damsels, a king's daughter. While they waited by the wayside to hear the baying of the hounds or the call of a bugle, they saw coming toward them a strange knight, his lady, and a dwarf who carried a knotted scourge. First the queen sent her damsel to ask who the knight and his fair companion might be, but the dwarf, barring her way, struck the damsel across the hand with his whip. Then Erec rode forward and the dwarf lashed him across the face and neck. Being unarmed, Erec made no attempt to chastise the dwarf or his haughty master, but he vowed that he would follow the strange knight until he could find arms to hire or borrow that he might avenge the insult to the queen.

In the fair town to which the strange knight and his companions presently led him, Erec found lodgings with a vavasor who told him the reason for all the stir and bustle that Erec had seen as he rode through the gates. On the next day a fine sparrow hawk would be given to the knight who could defend against all comers the beauty and goodness of his lady. The haughty knight, who had won the

EREC AND ENIDE by Chrétien de Troyes, from ARTHURIAN ROMANCES by Chrétien de Troyes. Translated in prose with introduction, notes and bibliography, by W. W. Comfort. From EVERYMAN'S LIBRARY. By permission of the publishers, E. P. Dutton & Co., Inc. All rights reserved.

bird in two successive years, would be allowed to keep it if his challenge went unanswered on the morrow. At the home of the vavasor Erec met his host's daughter Enide, who in spite of her tattered garments was the most radiantly beautiful damsel in Christendom. With her as his lady and with arms borrowed from his host, Erec challenged and defeated in single combat the arrogant knight who was defending the hawk. Then Erec dispatched the vanquished knight, whose name was Yder, to Queen Guinevere to do with at her pleasure, along with his lady and his dwarf. With them he sent word that he would return with his beautiful bride, the damsel Enide.

Erec promised Enide's father great riches and two towns to rule in his own land, but he refused all offers to have Enide dressed in robes suitable to her new station: he wished all in King Arthur's court to see that in spite of her humble garments she was the most beautiful lady who ever lived. So great was her beauty that King Arthur, who himself had killed the White Stag, kissed her without a demur from the assembled knights and ladies. The king also granted Eric the boon of a speedy marriage, so eager was the young knight for the love of his promised bride. The ceremony was performed by the Archbishop of Canterbury at the time of the Pentecost before an assemblage of knights and ladies from every corner of the kingdom, and the celebration continued for a fortnight.

A month after Pentecost a great tournament was held near Tenebroc and in the lists there Erec showed himself the most valiant of all the knights assembled. On his return he received from the king permission to visit his own land, and he and Enide set out with an escort of sixty knights. On the fifth day they arrived in Carnant, where King Lac welcomed his son and his bride with much honor. Meanwhile, Erec found so much pleasure in his wife's company that he had no thought for other pastimes. When tournaments were held in the region around, he sent his knights to the forays but he himself remained behind in dalliance with the fair Enide. At last people began to gossip and say that he had turned a craven in arms. These reports so distressed Enide that one morning while they were still abed she began to lament the way in which the brave and hardy knight had changed because of his love for her. Overhearing her words, Erec was moved to anger, and he told her to rise and prepare herself at once to take the road with him on a journey of knight-errantry in search of whatever perils he might encounter by chance. At the beginning of the journey he gave orders that she was never to tell him of anything she might see, nor to speak to him unless he addressed her first.

As Enide rode ahead, forbidden to speak, she lamented her disclosure and their sudden departure from the life she had enjoyed with her loving husband. She disobeyed him, however, when they were about to be attacked by three robber knights, and again when they were assailed by five recreants. Erec, having overcome all who opposed him, felt no gratitude for her wifely warnings and fears for his safety, but spoke harshly to her because she had disobeyed his command that she was under any circumstance to remain silent until he gave her leave to speak.

That night, since they knew of no town or shelter nearby, they slept in an open field. There the squire of Count Galoin came upon them the next day and conducted them to lodgings in the town where the count was master. That nobleman, going to pay his respects to the strange knight and his lovely lady, was much smitten with Enide's beauty, so much so that, going to the place where she sat apart, he expressed his pity for her obvious distress and offered to make her mistress of all his lands. When Enide refused, he declared that he would take her by force. Fearful for her husband's life, Enide pretended to do his pleasure. It was arranged that on the next day the

1092

count's knights were to overtake the travelers and seize Enide by force. Erec, coming to her rescue, would be killed, and she would be free to take the count as her lord. Once more Enide disobeyed her husband and told him of Count Galoin's plan. Forewarned, Erec overcame his assailants and knocked the false count senseless from his steed. When Galoin's followers would have pursued Erec and Enide, the count restrained them, praising Enide's prudence and virtue and the bravery of her knight.

Departing from Count Galoin's lands, the travelers came to a castle from which the lord came riding on a great steed to offer Erec combat at arms. Enide saw him coming but did not dare tell her husband for fear of his wrath. At last she did speak, however, and Erec realized her love for him that made her disobedient to his commands. The knight who challenged Erec was of small stature but stout heart and both were wounded in the fight. Though the doughty little knight lost, he put up such a good fight that he and Erec became friends. Guivret the Little invited Erec to have his wounds dressed and to rest at his castle, but Erec thanked him courteously and rode with Enide on his way.

At length they arrived at a wood where King Arthur had come with a large hunting party. By then Erec was so begrimed and bloodied that Sir Kay the seneschal did not recognize him. When he would have taken the wounded knight to the king's camp, Erec refused and they fought until Sir Kay was unhorsed. Sir Gawain then rode out to encounter the strange knight, and he was able to bring Erec to the place where the king had ordered tents set up in anticipation of their coming. There was great joy in that meeting for the king and Queen Guinevere, but distress at Erec's wounds. Although the king pleaded with Erec to rest there until his hurts were healed, the knight refused to be turned aside or delayed on his journey, and early the next morning he and Enide set out once more.

In a strange forest they heard the cries of a lady in distress. Leaving Enide to await his return, Erec rode in the direction of the sound and found a damsel weeping because two giants had carried away her knight. Riding in pursuit, Erec killed the giants and rescued the knight, whose name was Cadoc of Tabriol. Later he sent Cadoc and the damsel to King Arthur's camp, to tell the story of how he fared. Meanwhile, Erec's wounds had reopened and he lost so much blood that he fell from his horse in a swoon.

While Enide was weeping over his prostrate body, a count with his suite came riding through the forest. The nobleman gave orders that the body was to be taken to Limors and prepared for burial. On their arrival at the count's palace he declared his intention of espousing Enide at once. Although she refused to give her consent, the ceremony was performed in great haste and guests were summoned to a wedding banquet that night.

Erec, recovering from his deep swoon, awoke in time to see the wretched count strike Enide across the face because her grief was so great that she could neither eat nor drink at her new husband's bidding. Springing from the funeral bier, he drew his sword and struck the count on the head with such force that blood and brains flowed out. While the other knights and squires retreated in fear of the ghostly presence that had so suddenly returned to life, the two made their escape, Erec meanwhile assuring his wife that he was now convinced of her devotion and love.

Meanwhile, Guivret the Little had received word that a mortally wounded knight had been found in the forest and that the lord of Limors had carried off the dead man's wife. Coming to see that the fallen knight received proper burial and to aid his lady if she were in distress the doughty little knight came upon Erec, whom he failed to recognize in the murky moonlight, and struck a blow which knocked Erec unconscious. Enide and

Guivret remained by the stricken man all that night, and in the morning they proceeded to Guivret's castle. There, attended by Enide and Guivret's sisters, Erec was nursed back to health. After his recovery, escorted by Guivret and burdened with gifts, the couple prepared to return to King Arthur's court.

Toward nightfall the travelers saw in the distance the towers of a great fortress. Guivret said that the town was named Brandigant, in which there was a perilous passage called the "Joy of the Court." King Evrain welcomed the travelers with great courtesy, but that night, while they feasted, he also warned Erec against attempting the mysterious feat which no knight had thus far survived. Despite the disapproval of his friend and his host Erec swore to attempt the passage.

The next morning he was conducted into a magic garden filled with all manner of fruits and flowers, past the heads and helmets of unfortunate though brave knights who had also braved danger in order to blow the magic horn whose blast would signify joy to King Evrain's land. At the end of a path he found a beautiful damsel seated on a couch. While he stood looking at her, a knight appeared to engage him in combat. They fought until the hour of noon had passed; then the knight fell exhausted. He revealed that he had been held in thrall in the garden by an oath given to his mistress, whose one wish had been his eternal presence by her side. Erec then blew the horn and all the people rejoiced to find him safe. There was great joy also when the knight of the garden was released from his bondage and the beautiful damsel identified herself as the cousin of Enide.

Erec and Enide, with Guivret, continued their journey to the court of King Arthur, where they were received with gladness and honor. When his father died, Erec returned to reign in his own land. There he and Enide were crowned in a ceremony of royal splendor in the presence of King Arthur and all the nobles of his realm.

EREWHON

Type of work: Novel
Author: Samuel Butler (1835-1902)
Type of plot: Utopian satire
Time of plot: 1870's
Locale: Erewhon and England
First published: 1872

Principal characters:
STRONG, a traveler in Erewhon
CHOWBOK, a native
NOSNIBOR, a citizen of Erewhon
AROWHENA, his daughter

Critique:

Erewhon is an anagram of nowhere, but the institutions satirized·in this story of an imaginary land are unmistakably British. Beginning as an adventure story, the book becomes an elaborate allegory. Some of Butler's satire grows out of the ideas of Darwin and Huxley. In the main the book is original and often prophetic, The "straighteners" of Erewhon are the psychologists of today, and the treatment of Erewhonian criminals is somewhat like that advocated by our own liberal thinkers. The novel is humorous, but it is also serious.

The Story:

Strong, a young man of twenty-two, worked on a sheep farm. From the plains he looked often at the seemingly impassable mountain range that formed the edge of the sheep country and wondered about the land beyond those towering peaks. From one old native named Chowbok he learned that the country was forbidden. Chowbok assumed a strange pose when questioned further and uttered unearthly cries. Curious, Strong persuaded Chowbok to go on a trip with him into the mountains. They were unable to find a pass through the mountains. One day Strong came upon a small valley and went up it alone. He found that it led through the mountains. When he went back to get Chowbok, he saw the old native fleeing toward the plains. He went on alone. After climbing down treacherous cliffs and crossing a river on a reed raft,

he finally came to beautiful rolling plains. He passed by some strange manlike statues which made terrifying noises as the wind circled about them. He recognized in them the reason for Chowbok's performance.

Strong awoke next morning to see a flock of goats about him, two girls herding them. When the girls saw him they ran and brought some men to look at him. All of them were physically handsome. Convinced at last that Strong was a human being, they took him to a small town close by. There his clothing was searched and a watch he had with him was confiscated. The men seemed to be especially interested in his health, and he was allowed to leave only after a strict medical examination. He wondered why there had been such confusion over his watch until he was shown a museum in which was kept old pieces of machinery. Finally he was put in jail.

In jail he learned the language and something of the strange customs of the country, which was called Erewhon. The oddest custom was to consider disease a crime; anyone who was sick was tried and put in jail. On the other hand, people who committed robbery or murder were treated sympathetically and given hospital care. Shortly afterward the jailor informed Strong that he had been summoned to appear before the king and queen, and that he was to be the guest of a man named Nosnibor. Nosnibor had embezzled a large sum of money from a poor widow, but he was now recovering from his illness. The widow, Strong learned, would be tried and sentenced for allowing herself to be imposed upon.

In the capital Strong stayed with Nosnibor and his family and paid several visits to the court. He was well received because he had blond hair, a rarity among the Erewhonians. He learned a great deal about the past history of the country. Twenty-five hundred years before a prophet had preached that it was unlawful to eat meat, as man should not kill his fellow creatures. For several hundred years the Erewhonians were vegetarians. Then another sage showed that animals were no more the fellow creatures of man than plants were, and that if man could not kill and eat animals he should not kill and eat plants. The logic of his arguments overthrew the old philosophy. Two hundred years before a great scientist had presented the idea that machines had minds and feelings and that if man were not careful the machine would finally become the ruling creature on earth. Consequently all machines had been scrapped.

The economy of the country was unusual. There were two monetary systems, one worthless except for spiritual meaning, one used in trade. The more respected system was the valueless one, and its work was carried on in Musical Banks where people exchanged coins for music. The state religion was a worship of various qualities of godhead, such as love, fear, and wisdom, and the main goddess, Ydgrun, was at the same time an abstract concept and a silly, cruel woman. Strong learned much of the religion from Arowhena, one of Nosnibor's daughters. She was a beautiful girl, and the two fell in love.

Because Nosnibor insisted that his older daughter, Zulora, be married first, Strong and his host had an argument, and Strong found lodgings elsewhere. Arowhena met him often at the Musical Banks. Strong visited the University of Unreason, where the young Erewhonian boys were taught to do anything except that which was practical. They studied obsolete languages and hypothetical sciences. He saw a relationship between these schools and the mass-mind which the educational system in England was producing. Strong also learned that money was considered a symbol of duty, and that the more money a man had the better man he was.

Nosnibor learned that Strong was meeting Arowhena secretly. Then the king began to worry over the fact that Strong had entered the country with a watch, and he feared that Strong might try to bring machinery back into use. Planning an escape, Strong proposed to the queen that he make a balloon trip to talk with the god of the air. The queen was delighted with the idea. The king hoped that Strong would fall and kill himself.

Strong smuggled Arowhena aboard the balloon with him. The couple soon found themselves high in the air and moving over the mountain range. When the balloon settled on the sea, Strong and Arowhena were picked up by a passing ship. In England, where they were married, Strong tried to get up an expedition to go back to Erewhon. Only the missionaries listened to his story. Then Chowbok, Strong's faithless native friend, showed up in England teaching religion, and his appearance convinced people that Erewhon actually did exist. Strong hoped to return to the country soon to teach it Christianity.

ESSAIS

Type of work: Essays
Author: Michel Eyquem de Montaigne (1533-1592)
First published: Books I-II, 1580; I-II, revised, 1582; I-III, 1588; I-III, revised, 1595

Montaigne began his essays as a stoical humanist, continued them as a skeptic, and concluded them as a human being concerned with man. Substantially, this evolution is the one upon which Montaigne scholars are agreed. Surely these three phases of his thought are apparent in his Essais, for one may find, in these volumes, essays in which Montaigne considers how a man should face pain and die, such as "To Philosophize Is to Learn to Die"; essays in which the skeptical attack on dogmatism in philosophy and religion is most evident, such as the famous "Apology for Raimond Sebond"; and essays in which the writer makes a constructive effort to encourage men to know themselves and to act naturally for the good of all men, as in "The Education of Children."

Montaigne retired to his manor when he was thirty-eight. Public life had not satisfied him, and he was wealthy enough to live apart from the active life of his times and to give himself to contemplation and the writing of essays. He did spend some time in travel a few years later, and he was made mayor of Bordeaux, but most of his effort went into the writing and revision of his Essais, the attempt to essay, to test, the ideas which came to him.

An important essay in the first volume is "That the Taste for Good and Evil Depends in Good Part upon the Opinion We Have of Them." The essay begins with a paraphrase of a quotation from Epictetus to the effect that men are bothered more by opinions than by things. The belief that all human judgment is, after all, more a function of the human being than of the things judged suggested to Montaigne that by a change of attitude human beings could alter the values of things. Even death can be valued, provided the man who is about to die is of the proper disposition. Poverty and pain can also be good provided a person of courageous temperament develops a taste for them. Montaigne concludes that "things are not so painful and difficult of themselves, but our weakness or cowardice makes them so. To judge of great and high matters requires a suitable soul. . . ."

This stoical relativity is further endorsed in the essay "To Study Philosophy Is to Learn to Die." Montaigne's preoccupation with the problem of facing pain and death was caused by the death of his best friend, Étienne de la Boétie, who died in 1563 at the age of thirty-three, and then the deaths of his father, his brother, and several of his children. In addition, Montaigne was deeply disturbed by the Saint Bartholomew Day massacres. As a humanist, he was well educated in the literature and philosophy of the ancients, and from them he drew support of the stoical philosophy suggested to him by the courageous death of his friend La Boétie.

The title of the essay is a paraphrase of Cicero's remark "that to study philosophy is nothing but to prepare one's self to die." For some reason, perhaps because it did not suit his philosophic temperament at the time, perhaps because he had forgotten it, Montaigne did not allude to a similar expression attributed by Plato to Socrates, the point then being that the philosopher is interested in the eternal, the unchanging, and that life is a preoccupation with the temporal and the variable. For Montaigne, however, the remark means either that the soul in contemplation removes itself from the body, so to speak; or else that philosophy is concerned to teach us how to face death. It is the latter interpretation that interested him.

Asserting that we all aim at pleasure,

even in virtue, Montaigne argued that the thought of death is naturally disturbing. He refers to the death of his brother, Captain St. Martin, who was killed when he was twenty-three by being struck behind the ear by a tennis ball. Other instances enforce his claim that death often comes unexpectedly to the young; for this reason the problem is urgent. With these examples before us, he writes, how can we "avoid fancying that death has us, every moment, by the throat?" The solution is to face death and fight it by becoming so familiar with the idea of death that we are no longer fearful. "The utility of living," he writes, "consists not in the length of days, but in the use of time. . . ." Death is natural, and what is important is not to waste life with the apprehension of death.

In the essay "Of Judging the Death of Another," Montaigne argues that a man reveals his true character when he shows how he faces a death which he knows is coming. A "studied and digested" death may bring a kind of delight to a man of the proper spirit. Montaigne cites Socrates and Cato as examples of men who knew how to die.

Montaigne's most famous essay is his "Apology for Raimond Sebond," generally considered to be the most complete and effective of his skeptical essays. Yet what Montaigne is skeptical of is not religion, as many critics have asserted, but of the pretensions of reason and of dogmatic philosophers and theologians. When Montaigne asks "Que sais-je?" the expression becomes the motto of his skepticism, "What do I know?"—not because he thinks that man should give up the use of the intellect and imagination, but because he thinks it wise to recognize the limits of these powers.

The essay is ostensibly in defense of the book titled *Theologia naturalis: sive Liber creaturarum magistri Raimondi de Sebonde,* the work of a philosopher and theologian of Toulouse, who wrote the book about 1430.

Montaigne considers two principal objections to the book: the first, that Sebond is mistaken in the effort to support Christian belief upon human reasons; the second, that Sebond's arguments in support of Christian belief are so weak that they may easily be confuted. In commenting upon the first objection, Montaigne agrees that the truth of God can be known only through faith and God's assistance, yet Montaigne argues that Sebond is to be commended for his noble effort to use reason in the service of God. If one considers Sebond's arguments as an aid to faith, they may be viewed as useful guides.

Montaigne's response to the second objection takes up most of the essay, and since the work is, in some editions, over two hundred pages long, we may feel justified in concluding from length alone the intensity of Montaigne's conviction. Montaigne uses the bulk of his essay to argue against those philosophers who suppose that by reason alone man can find truth and happiness. The rationalists who attack Sebond do not so much damage the theologian as show their own false faith in the value of reason. Montaigne considers "a man alone, without foreign assistance, armed only with his own proper arms, and unfurnished of the divine grace and wisdom . . ." and he sets forth to show that such a man is not only miserable and ridiculous but grievously mistaken in his presumption. Philosophers who attempt to reason without divine assistance gain nothing from their efforts except knowledge of their own weakness. Yet that knowledge has some value; ignorance is then not absolute ignorance. Nor is it any solution for the philosopher to adopt the stoical attitude and try to rise above humanity, as Seneca suggests; the only way to rise is by abandoning human means and by suffering, cause oneself to be elevated by Christian faith.

In the essay "Of the Education of Children," Montaigne writes that the only objective he had in writing the essays was to discover himself. In giving his opinions concerning the education of children Montaigne shows how the study of himself took him from the idea of philosophy as a study of what is "grim and formidable" to the idea of philosophy as a way to the health and cheerfulness of mind and body. He claims that "The most manifest sign of wisdom is a continual cheerfulness," and that "the height and value of true virtue consists in the facility, utility, and pleasure of its exercise. . . ." Philosophy is "that which instructs us to live." The aim of education is so to lead the child that he will come to love nothing but the good, and the way to this objective is an education that takes advantage of the youth's appetites and affections. Though his love of books led Montaigne to live in such a manner that he was accused of slothfulness and "want of mettle," he justifies his education by pointing out that this is the worst men can say of him.

Not all of Montaigne's essays reflect the major stages of his transformation from stoic and skeptic to a man of good will. Like Bacon, he found satisfaction in working out his ideas concerning the basic experiences of life. Thus he wrote of sadness, of constancy, of fear, of friendship (with particular reference to La Boétie), of moderation, of solitude, of sleep, of names, of books. These essays are lively, imaginative, and informed with the knowledge of a gentleman well trained in the classics. Yet it is when he writes of pain and death, referring to his own long struggle with kidney stones and to the deaths of those he loved, and when he writes of his need for faith and of man's need for self-knowledge, that we are most moved. In such essays the great stylist, the educated thinker, and the struggling human being are one. It was in the essaying of himself that Montaigne became a great essayist.

AN ESSAY CONCERNING HUMAN UNDERSTANDING

Type of work: Philosophical treatise
Author: John Locke (1632-1704)
First published: 1690

Locke's purpose in *An Essay Concerning Human Understanding* was to inquire into the origin and extent of human knowledge, and his answer—that all knowledge is derived from sense experience—became the principal tenet of the new empiricism which has dominated Western philosophy ever since. Even George Berkeley (1685-1753), who rejected Locke's distinction between sense qualities independent of the mind and sense qualities dependent on the mind, produced his idealism in response to Locke's provocative philosophy and gave it an empirical cast which reflected Western man's rejection of innate or transcendental knowledge.

An Essay Concerning Human Understanding is divided into four books: Book I, "Of Innate Notions"; Book II, "Of Ideas"; Book III, "Of Words"; and Book IV, "Of Knowledge, Certain and Probable."

In preparation for his radical claim that all ideas are derived from experience, Locke began his *Essay* with a careful consideration of the thesis that there are innate ideas, that is, ideas which are a necessary part of man's convictions and are, therefore, common to all men. Locke's attack on this claim is from two directions. He argues that many of the ideas which are supposed to be innate can be and have been derived naturally from sense experience, that not all men assent to those ideas which are supposed to be innate. He maintained that even if reason enables men to discover the truth of certain ideas, those ideas cannot be said to be innate; for reason is needed to discover their truth.

In Book II, "Of Ideas," Locke considers the origin of such ideas as those expressed by the words "whiteness," "hardness," "sweetness," "thinking," "motion," "man," and the like. The second section states his answer:

Let us then suppose the mind to be, as we say, white paper void of all characters, without any ideas. How comes it to be furnished? . . . Whence has it all the *materials* of reason and knowledge? To this I answer, in one word, from *experience.* . . . Our observation, employed either about *external sensible objects,* or about the *internal operations of our minds perceived and reflected on by ourselves, is that which supplies our understandings with all the materials of knowledge.*

The two sources of our ideas, according to Locke, are *sensation* and *reflection.* By the senses we come to have perceptions of things, thereby acquiring the ideas of yellow, white, cold, for example. Then, by reflection, by consideration of the mind in operation, we acquire the ideas of thinking, doubting, believing, knowing, willing, and so on.

By sensation we acquire knowledge of external objects; by reflection we acquire knowledge of our own minds.

Ideas which are derived from sensation are simple; that is, they present "one uniform appearance," even though a number of simple ideas may come together in the perception of an external object. The mind dwells on the simple ideas, comparing them to each other, combining them, but never inventing them. By a "simple idea" Locke meant what some modern and contemporary philosophers have called a "sense-datum," a distinctive, entirely differentiated item of sense experience, such as the odor of some particular glue, or the taste of coffee in a cup. He called attention to the fact that we use our sense experience to imagine what we have never perceived, but no operation of the mind can yield novel simple ideas.

By the "quality" of something Locke meant its power to produce an idea in someone sensing the thing. The word "quality" is used in the *Essay* in much the same way the word "characteristic" or "property" has been used by other, more recent, writers. For Locke distinguished between primary and secondary qualities. Primary qualities are those which matter has constantly, whatever its state. As primary qualities Locke names solidity, extension, figure, motion or rest, and number. By secondary qualities Locke meant the power to produce various sensations which have nothing in common with the primary qualities of the external objects. Thus, the power to produce the taste experience of sweetness is a secondary quality of sugar, but there is no reason to suppose that the sugar itself possesses the distinctive quality of the sensation. Colors, tastes, sounds, and odors are secondary qualities of objects.

Locke also referred to a third kind of quality or power, called simply "power," by which he meant the capacity to affect or to be affected by other objects. Thus, fire can melt clay; the capacity to melt clay is one of fire's powers, and such a power is neither a primary nor a secondary quality.

Locke concluded that primary ideas resemble external objects, but secondary ideas do not. It is this particular claim which has excited other professional philosophers, with Berkeley arguing that primary qualities can be understood only in terms of our own sensations, so that whatever generalization can be made about secondary qualities would have to cover primary qualities as well, and other philosophers arguing that Locke had no ground for maintaining that primary ideas "resemble" primary qualities, even if the distinction between primary and secondary qualities is allowed.

Complex ideas result from acts of the mind, and they fall into three classes: ideas of modes, of substances, and of relations. *Modes* are ideas which are considered to be incapable of independent existence since they are affections of substance, such as the ideas of triangle, gratitude, and murder. To think of *substances* is to think of "particular things subsisting by themselves," and to think in that manner involves supposing that there is a support, which cannot be understood, and that there are various qualities in combination which give various substances their distinguishing traits. Ideas of *relations* are the result of comparing ideas with each other.

After a consideration of the complex ideas of space, duration, number, the infinite, pleasure and pain, substance, relation, cause and effect, and of the distinctions between clear and obscure ideas and between true and false ideas, Locke proceeded to a discussion, in Book III, of words and essences. Words are signs of ideas by "arbitrary imposition," depending upon observed similarities which are taken as the basis for considering things in classes. Words are related to "nominal essences," that is, to· obvious similarities found through observation, and not to "real essences," the actual qualities of things. Locke then discussed the imperfections and abuses of words.

In Book IV Locke defined knowledge as "the perception of the connection of and agreement, or disagreement and repugnancy, of any of our ideas." An example cited is our knowledge that white is not black, Locke arguing that to know that white is not black is simply to perceive that the idea of white is not the idea of black.

Locke insisted that knowledge cannot extend beyond the ideas we have, and that we determine whether ideas agree or disagree with each other either directly, by intuition, or indirectly, by reason or sensation. Truth is defined as "the joining or separating of signs, as the things signified by them do agree or disagree one with another." For example, the proposition "White is not black" involves the separation by "is not" of the signs "white" and "black," signifying the disagreement between the ideas of white and black; since the ideas are different, the proposition is true. Actually to have compared the ideas and to have noted their disagreement is to know the fact which the true proposition signifies.

Locke devoted the remaining chapters of Book IV to arguing that we have knowledge of our existence by intuition, of the existence of God by demonstration, and of other things by sensation. Here the influence of Descartes is clearly evident. But it is the empiricism of the earlier parts of the book which won for Locke the admiration of philosophers.

ESSAYS

Type of work: Essays
Author: Sir Francis Bacon (1561-1626)
First published: 1597; added to and revised, 1612, 1625

Sir Francis Bacon was a man of many accomplishments—scientist, philosopher, and politician; he was adept, too, at taking bribes and for that was imprisoned. Yet it is as a literary man that he is perhaps best remembered, a writer so competent with the pen that for decades there have been persons willing to argue that Bacon wrote the plays attributed to Shakespeare.

The essay form is rare in our age, although there are some faint signs of its revival. As Bacon used it, the essay is a carefully fashioned statement, both informative and expressive, by which a man comments on life and manners, on nature and its puzzles. The essay is not designed to win men to a particular cause or to communicate factual matter better put in scientific treatises. Perhaps that is one reason why it is not so popular in an age in which it is always pertinent to ask whether a claim can be proved and whether knowing it makes a practical difference.

The *Essays* first appeared, ten in number, in 1597. They were immediately popular because they were brief, lively, humane, and well written. Perhaps they were effective in contrast to the rambling, florid prose written by most writers of the time. A considerable part of their charm lay in what keeps them charming, their civilized tone. In these essays Bacon revealed himself as an inquisitive but also an appreciative man with wit enough to interest others.

The first edition contained the following essays: "Of Studies," "Of Discourse," "Of Ceremonies and Respects," "Of Followers and Friends," "Of Suitors," "Of Expense," "Of Regiment of Health," "Of Honour and Reputation," "Of Faction," and "Of Negociating."

By 1612 the number of essays had been increased to thirty-eight, the earlier ones having been revised or rewritten. By the last edition, in 1625, the number was fifty-eight. Comparison of the earlier essays with those written later shows not only a critical mind at work but also a man made sadder and wiser, or at least different, by changes in fortune.

The essays concern themselves with such universal concepts as truth, death, love, goodness, friendship, fortune, and praise; with such controversial matters as religion, atheism, "the True Greatness of Kingdoms and Estates," custom and education, and usury; and with such intriguing matters as envy, cunning, innovations, suspicion, ambition, praise, vainglory, and the vicissitudes of things.

The *Essays or Counsels, Civil and Moral,* as they are called in the heading of the first essay, begins with an essay on truth and entitled directly, "Of Truth." The title formula is always the same, simply a naming of the matter to be discussed, as, for example, "Of Death," "Of Unity in Religion," "Of Adversity."

"*What is Truth?* said jesting Pilate; and would not stay for an answer." One expects a sermon—and is pleasantly surprised. Bacon uses his theme as a point of departure for a discussion of the charms of lying, trying to fathom the love of lying for its own sake. "A mixture of a lie doth ever add pleasure," he writes. But this pleasure is ill-founded; it rests on error resulting from depraved judgment. Bacon reverses himself grandly: ". . . truth, which only doth judge itself, teacheth that the inquiry of truth, which is the love-making or wooing of it, the knowledge of truth, which is the presence of it, and the belief of truth, which is the enjoying of it, is the sovereign good of human nature."

What of death? Bacon begins by admitting that tales of death increase man's natural fear of it, but he reminds the reader that death is not always painful. By references to Augustus Caesar, Tiberius, Vespasian, and others Bacon showed that even in their last moments great men maintained their characters and composure. Death is natural, he concludes, and it has certain advantages: it opens the gate to good fame and puts an end to envy. The good man is in no fear of death because he has better things to do and think about, and when he dies he knows he has obtained "worthy ends and expectations."

The essay "Of Adversity" is particularly interesting since it reflects Bacon's own experience after imprisonment, the loss of friends and position, and enforced retirement. He writes, "Prosperity is the blessing of the Old Testament; Adversity is the blessing of the New; which carrieth the greater benediction, and the clearer revelation of God's favour." Adversity puts life's brighter moments into effective contrast, and it allows a man the chance to show his virtues.

Bacon is no casual essayist. We do not need the report of history to tell us that the essays as we find them are the product of numerous revisions. Sentences do not achieve a careful balance and rhythm accidentally, nor does a moment's reflection provide apt allusions, pertinent Latin phrases, and witty turns of thought.

The essay "Of Beauty" begins with a well-fashioned, complex statement: "Virtue is like a rich stone, best plain set; and surely virtue is best in a body that is comely, though not of delicate features; and that hath rather dignity of presence, than beauty of aspect." The essay continues by commenting on the sad fact that beauty and virtue are not always conjoined, but then Bacon remembers some noble spirits who were "the most beautiful men of their times"—Augustus Caesar, Titus Vespasianus, Philip le Bel of France, Edward the Fourth of England, Alcibiades of Athens, and Ismael the Sophy of Persia. Then he comes to a striking thought in a simple line: "There is no excellent beauty that hath not some strangeness in the proportion."

Although appreciative of beauty, Bacon was modern in his appreciation of use. "Houses are built to live in," he writes in the essay "Of Building"—"therefore let use be preferred before uniformity, except where both may be had." He is aware of the importance of location; he warns the reader to beware of an "ill seat" for his house, and mentions in particular the discomfort that results from building a house in a hollow of ground surrounded by high hills. So much aware is he of the mistakes that a builder can make that Bacon follows a catalogue of dangers and difficulties with a charming and involved description of an ideal dwelling: a place for entertaining, a place for dwelling, and the whole a beautiful construction of rooms for various uses, courts, playing fountains—all of large, but proper dimensions, and built to take account of summer sun and winter cold.

Although there is a prevailing moral character to the essays so that, in retrospect, they seem to be a series of beautiful commands to erring spirits, there is enough of wisdom, education, humor, and common sense in them to save the author from the charge of moral arrogance. For example, Bacon does not begin his essay on anger by declaring how shameful anger is; he says instead, "To seek to extinguish Anger utterly is but a bravery of the Stoics." He then gives practical advice: To calm anger there is no other way but to consider the effects of anger, to remember what it has done in the past; and to repress particular angry acts, Bacon advises the reader to let time pass in the belief that the opportunity for revenge will come later; and he particularly warns against the bitterness of words and the doing of any irrevocable act.

In writing of atheism Bacon combined philosophical argument with moral persuasion and intensity of expression. If it seems strange that a scientist, the father of induction, should take so seriously the ordinary arguments of the Church, it is only because we tend to think of men as playing single roles and as living apart from their times. In any .case, Bacon's philosophic skill was most at evidence in scientific matters, and there is no more reason to expect that he would be adept at philosophizing about religion than to expect that he should have anticipated Einstein in his reflections about science: as an Elizabethan he did as well as we have a right to ask. The essay contains the famous line: "It is true, that a little philosophy inclineth man's mind to atheism; but depth in philosophy bringeth men's mind about to religion."

Although the essays naturally reflect a lifetime of experience, they do so in general, not in particular. One looks in vain for reports of adventures and misadventures at court—and Bacon had many of both. He sounds like the better side of Machiavelli in his essay on simulation and dissimulation, but there are no personal references to events in which he was involved and from which he acquired the knowledge imparted here. Nor would we suspect that Bacon was one of the leading scientific minds of his age; he discourses on friendship, parents and children, gardens, study, and the rest, as a gentle, humane scholar. We realize that in the *Essays* Bacon gave up the roles which ambition made him play. In his contemplative moments he sought to satisfy a two-fold goal: to present the wisdom of his living, the wisdom that comes from experience and reflection on it, and to make this presentation by means of a style designed to be economical and ornamental at the same time.

ESSAYS: FIRST AND SECOND SERIES

Type of work: Philosophical essays
Author: Ralph Waldo Emerson (1803-1882)
First published: First Series, 1841; Second Series, 1844

Emerson's *Essays* proclaim the self-reliance of a man who believed himself representative of all men since he felt himself intuitively aware of God's universal truths. He spoke to a nineteenth century that was ready for an emphasis on individualism and responsive to a new optimism that linked God, nature, and man into a magnificent cosmos.

Emerson himself spoke as one who had found in Transcendentalism a positive answer to the static Unitarianism of his day. He had been a Unitarian minister for three years at the Old North Church in Boston (1829-1832), but he had resigned because in his view the observance of the Lord's Supper could not be justified in the Unitarian Church.

Transcendentalism combined Neoplatonism, a mystical faith in the universality and permanence of value in the universe, with a pervasive moral seriousness akin to the Calvinist conviction and with a romantic optimism that found evidence of God's love throughout all nature. Derivative from these influences was the faith in man's creative power, the belief that the individual, by utilizing God's influence, could continue to improve his understanding and his moral nature. Knowledge could come to man directly, without the need of argument, if only he had the courage to make himself receptive to God's truth, manifest everywhere.

Through his essays and addresses Emerson became not only the leading Transcendentalist in America, but also one of the greatest if least formal of American philosophers. The latter accomplishment may be attributed more to the spirit of his philosophy than to its technical excellence, for Emerson had little respect for logic, empiricism, and linguistic analysis—features common to the work of other great American philosophers such as Charles Sanders Peirce, William James, and John Dewey. Nor can Emerson be compared in his method to such a philosopher as Alfred North Whitehead, for Emerson disdained speculative adventures; he believed himself to be affirming what nature told him, and nature spoke directly of God and of God's laws.

Emerson's *Nature* (1836) was the first definitive statement of his philosophical perspective, and within this work may be found most of the characteristic elements of Emerson's thought. The basic idea is that nature is God's idea made apparent to men. Thus, "the whole of nature is a metaphor of the human mind," "The axioms of physics translate the laws of ethics," and "This relation between the mind and matter is not fancied by some poet, but stands in the will of God, and so is free to be known by all men." Emerson asserted emphatically that "day and night, river and storm, beast and bird, acid and alkali, preexist in necessary Ideas in the mind of God"; hence he agreed with those who supposed that nature reveals spiritual and moral truths. Not only does nature reveal truths: it also disciplines men, rewarding them when nature is used properly, punishing them when it is abused.

One secret of Emerson's charm was his ability to translate metaphysical convictions into vivid images. Having argued that nature is the expression of God's idea, and having concluded that "The moral law lies at the center of nature and radiates to the circumference," he illustrated the moral influence of nature by asking, "Who can guess how much firmness the sea-beaten rock has taught the fishermen?" The danger in Emerson's method, however, was that readers tended to forget that his idealism was philosophically, not merely poetically, intended; he believed literally that only spirit and its ideas are real. He admitted the possibility that nature "outwardly exists," that is, that physical objects corresponding to his sensations exist, but he pointed out that since he was not able to test the authenticity of his senses, it made no difference whether such outlying objects existed. All that he could be sure of were his ideas, and that, whether directly or indirectly, the ideas came from God. For Emerson, then, idealism was not only a credible philosophy, but also the only morally significant one.

If nature is God's idea made apparent to men, it follows that the way to God's truth is not by reason or argument but by simple and reverent attention to the facts of nature, to what man perceives when his eye is innocent. Emerson criticized science not because it was useless, but because more important matters, those having a moral bearing, confronted man at every moment in the world of nature; the individual needed only to intuit nature, to see it as it was without twisting it to fit his philosophy or his science, in order to know God's thoughts. Thus, in the essay "Nature" Emerson wrote that "Nature is the incarnation of a thought, and turns to a thought again. . . . The world is mind precipitated. . . ." He added, with assurance, "Every moment instructs, and every object; for wisdom is infused into every form."

The ideas which Emerson had endorsed in *Nature* found explicit moral application in the address titled "The American Scholar," delivered before the Phi Beta Kappa Society at Cambridge in 1837. Emerson defined the scholar as "Man Thinking," and he declared that the main influences of the scholar's education are nature, books, and action. The duties of a scholar all involve self-trust; he must be both free and brave. The rewards of such freedom and bravery are inspiring: the mind is altered by the truths uncovered, and the whole world will come to honor the independent scholar. It was in this address that Emerson said that "the ancient precept, 'Know thyself,' and the modern precept, 'Study nature,' become at last one maxim."

The essay "Self-Reliance," included in the First Series, emphasizes the importance of that self trust to which Emerson referred in his Phi Beta Kappa address. It is understandable that this emphasis seemed necessary to Emerson. If nature reveals the moral truths which God intends for man's use, then three elements are involved in the critical human situation: nature, man, and man's attitude toward nature. It is possible to be blind to the truths about us; only the man who is courageous enough to be willing to be different in his search and convictions is likely to discover what is before every man's eyes. Emerson emphasized self-reliance not because he regarded the self, considered as a separate entity, important, but because he believed that the self is part of the reality of God's being and that in finding truth for oneself, provided one faces nature intuitively, one finds what is true for all men. "To believe your own thought, to believe that what is true for you in your private heart is true for all men—that is genius," Emerson wrote in "Self-Reliance"; he added that it is a kind of genius that is possible for anyone who is willing to acquire it.

Believing that each man's mind is capable of yielding important truth, Emerson distinguished between goodness and the name of goodness. He urged each man to work and act without being concerned about the mere opinions of others. "Whoso would be a man, must be a nonconformist," and whoever would advance in the truth should be willing to contradict himself, to be inconsistent: "A foolish consistency is the hobgoblin of little minds, adored by little statesmen and philosophers and divines."

That Emerson's philosophy was not an endorsement of selfish behavior is clear from his emphasis upon the use of the mind as an instrument for the intuitive understanding of universal truths and laws, but it is possible to misinterpret "Self-Reliance" as a joyous celebration of individuality. A sobering balance is achieved by the essay "The Over-Soul" in which Emerson subordinates the individual to the whole: "Meantime within man is the soul of the whole . . . the eternal One." Using language reminiscent of Platonism, Emerson wrote that the soul "gives itself, alone, original and pure, to the Lonely, Original and Pure, who, on that condition, gladly inhabits, leads and speaks through it."

Emerson valued the poet because the poet uses his imagination to discern the meanings of sensuous facts. The poet sees and expresses the beauty in nature because he recognizes the spiritual meaning of events; he takes old symbols and gives them new uses, thereby making nature the sign of God. In the essay "The Poet" Emerson wrote that the poet's insight is "a very high sort of seeing," a way of transcending conventional modes of thought in order to attend directly to the forms of things.

It is a misunderstanding of Emerson to regard him as a sentimental mystic, as one who lay on his back and saw divinity in every cloud. Emerson's transcendental insight is more akin to the intelligence of the Platonic philosopher who, having recognized his own ignorance, suddenly finds himself able to see the universal in the jumble of particular facts. Emerson may be criticized for never satisfactorily relating the life of contemplation to the life of practical affairs, but he cannot be dismissed as an iconoclastic mystic. For him the inquiring soul and the heroic soul were one, and the justification of self-reliance and meditation was in terms of the result, in the individual soul, of the effort to recognize the unity of all men. In "Experience," Emerson chooses knowing in preference to doing, but it is clear that he was rejecting a thoughtless interest in action and results. In "Character" and again in "Politics" he emphasized the importance of coming to have the character of transcending genius, of spirit which has found moral law in nature and has adapted it for use in the world of men. The transforming power of spirit properly educated and employed was something Emerson counted on, and he was concerned to argue that such power is not easily achieved.

Emerson defended democracy as the form of government best fitted for Americans whose religion and tradition reflect a desire to allow the judgments of citizens to be expressed in the laws of the state. But he cautioned that "Every actual State is corrupt," and added, "Good men must not obey the laws too well." Here the independent spirit, concerned with the laws of God, demands heroism and possibly, like Thoreau, civil disobedience.

Scholars have written innumerable articles and books attempting to account for Emerson's influence—which continues to be profound—on American thought. If agreement is ever reached, it seems likely that it will involve acceptance of the claim that Emerson, whatever his value as a philosopher, gave stirring expression to the American faith in the creative capacity of the individual soul.